# Remediating Sound

New Approaches to Sound, Music and Media

Series Editors: Carol Vernallis, Holly Rogers and Lisa Perrott

Forthcoming Titles:
*Musical New Media* by Nicola Dibben
*David Bowie and the Art of Music Video* by Lisa Perrott
*David Bowie and the Expansion of Music Video* by Lisa Perrott
*Popular Music, Race and Media since 9/11* by Nabeel Zuberi
*Haunted Soundtracks: Audiovisual Cultures of Memory, Landscape and Sound* edited by K.J. Donnelly and Aimee Mollaghan
*Bellini on Stage and Screen* edited by Emilio Sala, Graziella Seminara and Emanuele Senici
*Traveling Music Videos* edited by Tomáš Jirsa and Mathias Bonde Korsgaard
*Kahlil Joseph's Transmedia Works: The Audiovisual Atlantic* by Joe Jackson

Published Titles:
*Transmedia Directors* by Carol Vernallis, Holly Rogers and Lisa Perrott
*Dangerous Mediations* by Áine Mangaoang
*Resonant Matter* by Lutz Koepnick
*Cybermedia: Science, Sound and Vision* edited by Carol Vernallis, Holly Rogers, Jonathan Leal, Selmin Kara
*The Rhythm Image: Music Videos in Time* by Steven Shaviro
*YouTube and Music: Cyberculture and Everyday Life* edited by Holly Rogers, Joana Freitas and João Francisco Porfírio
*More Than Illustrated Music: Aesthetics of Hybrid Media Between Pop, Art and Video* edited by Elfi Vomberg and Kathrin Dreckmann
*Remediating Sound: Repeatable Culture, YouTube and Music* edited by Holly Rogers, Joana Freitas and João Francisco Porfírio

# Remediating Sound

## *Repeatable Culture, YouTube and Music*

Edited by Holly Rogers, Joana Freitas and
João Francisco Porfírio

BLOOMSBURY ACADEMIC
NEW YORK • LONDON • OXFORD • NEW DELHI • SYDNEY

BLOOMSBURY ACADEMIC
Bloomsbury Publishing Inc, 1385 Broadway, New York, NY 10018, USA
Bloomsbury Publishing Plc, 50 Bedford Square, London, WC1B 3DP, UK
Bloomsbury Publishing Ireland, 29 Earlsfort Terrace, Dublin 2, D02 AY28, Ireland

BLOOMSBURY, BLOOMSBURY ACADEMIC and the Diana logo
are trademarks of Bloomsbury Publishing Plc

First published in the United States of America 2023
This paperback edition published 2025

Copyright © Holly Rogers, Joana Freitas and João Francisco Porfírio, 2023
Each chapter copyright © by the contributor, 2023

For legal purposes the Acknowledgements on p. x constitute
an extension of this copyright page.

Cover image: Lil Nas X performs onstage at YouTube Theater on October 19, 2022 in
Inglewood, California. (Photo by Emma McIntyre/Getty Images for Lil Nas X)

All rights reserved. No part of this publication may be: i) reproduced or
transmitted in any form, electronic or mechanical, including photocopying,
recording or by means of any information storage or retrieval system without prior
permission in writing from the publishers; or ii) used or reproduced in any way
for the training, development or operation of artificial intelligence (AI) technologies,
including generative AI technologies. The rights holders expressly reserve this
publication from the text and data mining exception as per Article 4(3) of the
Digital Single Market Directive (EU) 2019/790.

Bloomsbury Publishing Inc does not have any control over, or responsibility for,
any third-party websites referred to or in this book. All internet addresses given
in this book were correct at the time of going to press. The author and publisher
regret any inconvenience caused if addresses have changed or sites have
ceased to exist, but can accept no responsibility for any such changes.

Library of Congress Cataloging-in-Publication Data
Names: Rogers, Holly, editor. | Freitas, Joana, editor. | Porfírio, João Francisco, editor.
Title: Remediating sound : repeatable culture, YouTube and music / edited by Holly Rogers,
Joana Freitas, and João Francisco Porfírio.
Description: [1st.] | New York : Bloomsbury Academic, 2023. | Series: New approaches
to sound, music, and media | Includes bibliographical references and index. | Summary:
"An exploration of YouTube as a platform for remix, reuse, and sampling"– Provided by publisher.
Identifiers: LCCN 2023007982 (print) | LCCN 2023007983 (ebook) | ISBN 9781501387326
(hardback) | ISBN 9781501387364 (paperback) | ISBN 9781501387333 (ebook) |
ISBN 9781501387340 (pdf) | ISBN 9781501387357 (ebook other)
Subjects: LCSH: Music and the Internet. | YouTube (Electronic resource) |
Music–Philosophy and aesthetics. | Mashups (Music)–History and criticism. |
Remixes–History and criticism. | Music videos–History and criticism. |
Composition (Music)–Collaboration. | Social media. | Sampling (Sound)
Classification: LCC ML3877 .R49 2023 (print) | LCC ML3877 (ebook) |
DDC 781.1/7—dc23/eng/20230331
LC record available at https://lccn.loc.gov/2023007982
LC ebook record available at https://lccn.loc.gov/2023007983

ISBN: HB: 978-1-5013-8732-6
PB: 978-1-5013-8736-4
ePDF: 978-1-5013-8734-0
eBook: 978-1-5013-8733-3
XML: 978-1-5013-8735-7

Series: New Approaches to Sound, Music and Media

Typeset by RefineCatch Limited, Bungay, Suffolk

For product safety related questions contact productsafety@bloomsbury.com.

To find out more about our authors and books visit www.bloomsbury.com
and sign up for our newsletters.

**Joana**  *For the two and four-legged loved ones of my life.*

**João**  *For the three furry creatures who live with me.*

**Holly**  *For John, Polly, Jigs and Daisy. And in memory of my besties, Monty and Tico.*

# Contents

How to Use This Book's YouTube Channel — ix
Acknowledgements — x
Foreword *by Jay Bolter* — xi

Introduction: 'I feel like I've heard it before': The Audiovisual Echoes of YouTube   *Holly Rogers, Joana Freitas, João Francisco Porfírio* — 1

1  'Technology Allows More People to do Things': Artificial Intelligence, Mashups and Online Musical Creativity  *Christine Boone and Brian Drawert* — 35

2  From Contagion to Imitation: On Bass Drop Memes, Trolling Repertoires and the Legacy of Gabriel Tarde  *Edward Katrak Spencer* — 51

3  Sincere, Authentic, Remediated: The Affective Labour and Cross-Cultural Remediations of Music Video Reaction Videos on YouTube  *Michael Goddard* — 73

4  Internet Archiving: The Many Lives of Songs in the YouTube Age  *Henrik Smith Sivertsen* — 93

5  Listening Through Social Media: Soundscape Composition, Collaboration and Networked Sonic Elongation  *Holly Rogers* — 113

6  'Only People with Good Imaginations Usually Listen to this Kind of Music': On the Convergence of Musical Tags, Video Games and YouTube in the Epic Genre  *Joana Freitas* — 145

7  Of Clouds and Vapours: Transcending Ironic Distance in Networked Composition  *Jonas Wolf* — 165

8  Performing Beyond the Platform: Experiencing Musicking on and Through YouTube, TikTok and Instagram  *Juan Bermúdez* — 187

9  Library Music as the Soundtrack of YouTube  *Júlia Durand* — 203

10 Meme and Variations: How Video Mashups of John
   Coltrane's 'Giant Steps' Became a Thing  *Scott B. Spencer*      223

11 'Spinning Straw Into Gold': Nacho Video and the Exquisite
   Corpse of Fan-editing  *Lisa Perrott*                             243

12 Music Videos as Protest Communication: The Gezi Park
   Protest on YouTube  *Olu Jenzen, Itir Erhart, Hande Eslen-Ziya,
   Derya Güçdemir, Umut Korkut and Aidan McGarry*                    267

List of Contributors                                                 289
Index                                                                295

# How to Use This Book's YouTube Channel

*Remediating Sound* is a book about music, sound and remediation in online culture and on YouTube. It comes with its own YouTube channel, and most chapters have their own playlist.

You can access the main channel here:

The QR code and link for each chapter provides direct access to each specific playlist. These codes can be found at the top of each chapter.

You can access the main channel here:
rebrand.ly/54607a

Introduction rebrand.ly/1d539e
Chapter 1 rebrand.ly/qc5ti1z
Chapter 2 rebrand.ly/4m2vzwx
Chapter 3 rebrand.ly/ee0f0jt
Chapter 4 rebrand.ly/iy06gb6
Chapter 5 rebrand.ly/2ruzn3w
Chapter 6 rebrand.ly/oowxvc3
Chapter 7 rebrand.ly/e28d7d
Chapter 8 rebrand.ly/8755db
Chapter 9 rebrand.ly/r49r7th
Chapter 10 rebrand.ly/ddgtqhh
Chapter 11 rebrand.ly/omh5k4b
Chapter 12 rebrand.ly/d1yu8wh

# Acknowledgements

This book, and its sister volume *YouTube and Music*, have only been possible thanks to all the marvellous scholars and researchers who, in October 2020, joined us either online or in Lisbon, for the *Like, Share and Subscribe: YouTube, Music and Cyberculture Before and After the New Decade* international conference. We would like to express our most sincere gratitude to all the participants, many of whom have contributed to this book. Without their innovative, challenging and insightful work, neither of these volumes would have been possible. It has been an unquestionable joy to work with you all.

João and Joana would also like to thank, from the bottom of their hearts, Holly (and her alien-like energy!) for allowing this project to take form and for bringing it up to the highest level of quality and novelty. These last two years have made us into a team – a trio – and our collective desire to keep on working on music and online culture has made us realise that, now, more than ever, our research is meaningful and valid.

Holly would like to acknowledge that this project on YouTube and Music – the conference and both volumes – was the brainchild of João and Joana. Their networking powers are responsible for gathering together this amazing gang of researchers who are making a real difference to the interdisciplinary study of music. It has been wonderful to get to know so many different scholars in so many different countries through this process: I have learnt so much from you all. João and Joana have paved the way for refreshed approaches to the study of music and online culture, and it's been a complete and humbling pleasure to work with two such inspiring and energizing people. Thank you for asking me to join you.

We would all like to thank Jay Bolter for writing our foreword. We are delighted to have one of the pioneering scholars of YouTube framing this project. We'd also like to thank Regan Bowering for her editing and indexing prowess. And, of course, great appreciation goes to the hard work of our open-minded, approachable and super-efficient team at Bloomsbury: Leah Babb-Rosenfeld and Rachel Moore. We owe you a big drink!

# Foreword

Jay Bolter

YouTube both invites and frustrates simple characterization. Since its inception in 2005, it has become the site of interlocking media forms and practices, as the contributions to both this volume and its companion demonstrate. As a mass medium for distributing audiovisual content, the salient comparison is to traditional broadcast and cable television. Like television, YouTube is now a major media ecosystem with technological, aesthetic, sociocultural and economic dimensions. The cultural practices implied in YouTube's early motto 'Broadcast yourself' (the creation and distribution of an individual's televisual persona) still constitute a part of this ecosystem. But the amateur and casual uses implied by that motto now coexist with a variety of other uses, because so much of YouTube's content comes from commercial sources, such as entertainment corporations. The tremendous volume of YouTube's content is made possible by the ubiquity of the Internet; its variety by the practices of user-generation and sharing that characterize Web 2.0.

Although Richard Grusin and I developed the concept of remediation in the 1990s in the context of Web 1.0, the concept still provides one appropriate theoretical framework for many current media developments, including YouTube.[1] In fact, YouTube illustrates a key direction that remediation has taken since 2000 – a development that Grusin described with his term *premediation*.[2] In the *YouTube Reader*, he argued that the platform is a cardinal example of premediation with its 'intensification and multiplication of media networks'.[3] Where Grusin sees these processes as different in kind (hence the term premediation), I see them as variations on the dichotomy of immediacy and hypermediacy that we identified in our original work. In the media economy of the 1990s, remediation had already manifested itself in conflicting tendencies

---

[1] Jay Bolter and Richard Grusin, *Remediation: Understanding New Media* (Cambridge Mass.: MIT Press, 1999).
[2] Richard Grusin, *Premediation: Affect and Mediality After 9/11* (New York: Palgrave Macmillan, 2010).
[3] Richard Grusin, 'YouTube at the End of New Media,' in *The YouTube Reader*, ed. Pelle Snickars and Patrick Vonderau (London: Wallflower Press, 2010), 63.

toward convergence and divergence of earlier media forms. For example, news websites, such as CNN, were a convergence of the qualities of printed newspapers and television broadcast news, while on the other hand, websites, in general, were diverging into a number of genres, each remediating particular configurations from newspapers, magazines, books, television, film, etc. In the 2000s, the trends of convergence and divergence both continued. YouTube is characteristic in the way that it both combined earlier forms and blossomed into a number of subgenres.

## Algorithmic Hypermediacy

Remediation in YouTube proceeds on two levels. YouTube remediates the television or radio network as a platform for distributing media content, although instead of a single programming channel, it presents a collection of many millions of small channels. YouTube's interface, like that of many social media platforms, offers its user the impression of order and control, but it only barely conceals the chaos underneath. Searching or browsing, the user encounters a plenitude of individual units of media content, videos and audios, set in pages that include user comments and links to other recommended videos and audios. The media units may each embody their own remediations, referring to previously independent forms of film, television and music. At this granular level, the whole range of remediating possibilities are available.

For example, YouTube's media units may consist of short film or television excerpts, as well as whole films and programmes. These types of videos do not purport to be new forms at all, but simply reflect the aesthetic transparency of most Hollywood films and long-form television dramas. Many other YouTube genres, however, are hybrids of earlier forms: e.g. video game playthroughs, reaction videos, influencer videos on a variety of subjects, etc. What is novel about YouTube is the context in which individual videos are imbedded: the web page, the comments and the linking and recommending that accrues around these videos. The YouTube page is designed to facilitate a hypermediated viewing practice in which the viewers are encouraged to hop from video to video following links of affinity. The links themselves are the product of an automated recommendation system that customizes YouTube for each user and each user session. Its recommendation system transforms YouTube from a database into a 'database narrative', an aesthetic form that Lev Manovich predicted would become characteristic of the era of 'new media' in general.[4] This new form could also be called algorithmic hypermediacy. The dangers of the recommendation algorithms are now a focus of academic research, including by Shoshana Zuboff in her definitive monograph, *The Age of Surveillance Capitalism*.[5] Whatever the economic and political dangers of recommendation systems, their algorithmic hypermediacy also constitutes a new aesthetic in today's media culture – an aesthetic that YouTube both facilitates and reflects. This is certainly true of the music on YouTube.

As Holly Rogers notes in her introductory essay in this book's companion volume, *YouTube and Music*, YouTube operates as a 'cultural lens' into our music culture, and, as both of these volumes illustrate, YouTube refashions the relationship between the artists, entertainment companies, distribution channels and audiences.[6] YouTube remediates earlier recording eras and the economic and cultural impact of recording on vinyl and CD. It has also defined its own particular era of musical practice, especially for amateur music production. In and through YouTube, a plenitude of earlier and contemporary musical products and practices are available, but algorithmic hypermediacy means that each individual listener will generally encounter only those elements of this plenitude that fit into their own musical profile. The songs recommended and the links they follow constitute a customized narrative of what music was and is. In this respect, YouTube, and especially YouTube Music, are analogous to other music streaming services, such as Apple Music and Spotify.

## Music and Remix

Long before YouTube Music and the other major streaming services, YouTube was home to the music video, itself a notable remediating form that arose in the age of cable TV. The music video was a surprising combination of art form and promotional advertisement, remediating pop music with avant-garde filmic practices. Music videos were an early form of remix. The videos are consumed as

---

[4] Lev Manovich, *The Language of New Media* (Cambridge, MA: MIT Press, 2001).
[5] Shoshana Zuboff, *The Age of Surveillance Capitalism: The Fight for a Human Future at the New Frontier of Power* (New York: PublicAffairs, 2019).
[6] Holly Rogers, 'Introduction – "Welcome to your world": YouTube and the Reconfiguration of Music's Gatekeepers,' in *YouTube and Music: Online Culture and Everyday Life*, ed. Holly Rogers, Joana Freitas and João Porfírio (New York: Bloomsbury, 2023), 1–38.

a visual realization or elaboration of a popular song. However original and compelling the combination of music and moving image might be, the viewer is aware that in most cases the song can be appreciated (and usually purchased) without the video. The song comes first.

Even beyond music videos, YouTube has both reflected and contributed to the growing importance of remix. As a musical practice and cultural phenomenon, remix long predated YouTube. The combination of samples from a variety of sources had become characteristic of hip-hop in the 1980s and 1990s, and reached a high degree of technical and musical sophistication, but within a relatively limited community of artists and sound engineers. The 2000s was the decade in which sound and video-editing software and more capable computer hardware became inexpensive and relatively easy to use, this meant a larger number of young amateurs could create their own remixes, consisting of audio alone, as well as audio tracks synchronized to video. It became apparent that YouTube and remix, especially amateur remix, were made for each other. The advent of YouTube gave amateur remixers a platform for publishing their efforts to a potential audience of hundreds of millions. Lawrence Lessig, the editors of *The Routledge Companion to Remix Studies and Digital Humanities* and many other media scholars have realized that we can now speak of a *remix culture,* in which the practice is widely used for personal and aesthetic expression, and for social and political critique.[7]

Remix as remediation has always elided the distinction between creator and consumer, just as YouTube does. A remix is defined by a sharing of creative production among various sources and the remixer, and so, by definition, it employs a strategy of hypermediacy. Musical remixes combine two and often many more disparate music samples, and the listener or viewer is always aware of the process of combination, even if they cannot always identify the sources. Remixes in which musical soundtracks underlay videos also clearly foreground their hypermediacy. Remixes of both types often impress us with the craft that they display in merging different elements into a finished whole, but we can only be impressed if we recognize the remix process itself.

---

[7] Lawrence Lessig, *Remix: Making Art and Commerce Thrive in the Hybrid Economy* (London: Bloomsbury, 2008); Eduardo Navas, Owen Gallagher and xtine burrough, *The Routledge Companion to Remix Studies and Digital Humanities* (New York: Routledge, 2015).

I have suggested two ways in which YouTube remediates: through remix practices that characterize much of its music content, and through the algorithmic hypermediacy that presents that content to users. The theory of remediation certainly cannot fully explain YouTube's contribution to contemporary music culture. The chapters to this volume apply several other and equally productive analytic frameworks. Nevertheless, I believe that the theory can still contribute in significant ways to a full account of YouTube and music.

# Introduction

## 'I feel like I've heard it before': The Audiovisual Echoes of YouTube

Holly Rogers, Joana Freitas, João Francisco Porfírio

### Part 1: Holly Rogers

'I'm going to say that's the wildest video I've ever seen.'[1] When YouTuber Jucee uttered these words with a mixture of horror, intrigue and excitement, in a reaction video to Lil Nas X's 2021 'MONTERO (Call Me By Your Name)' video (directed by Tanu Muino and Lil Nas X), she contributed to a swirl of attention, comment, spinoff and discussion that had taken the Internet by storm (Figure 0.1a). The MONTERO project was made up of numerous paratexts. Prequel and sequel videos extended the project's world in multiple directions, and the musician extensively remediated his own music and images, sending versions, interpretations and his own reaction videos (Figure 0.1b) across YouTube, TikTok, Instagram and Twitter.[2] In October 2022, this transmedial spread moved out into the real world for the live MONTERO gig at California's YouTube Theatre (see the cover of this book), which used large screens, live dancers and lavish costumes to realize the project's audiovisual aesthetics in multiple

---

[1] Nicole, Jucee & Rex, 'WHEEWWW! | Lil Nas X – MONTERO (Call Me By Your Name) (Official Video)    REACTION', *YouTube video*, 00:10:36, 26 March 2021, https://www.youtube.com/watch?v=xY6cde00TGg.

[2] Emily Thomas traces this transmedial spread in 'Quare(-in) the Mainstream: YouTube, Social Media and Augmented Realities in Lil Nas X's *MONTERO*,' in *YouTube and Music: Online Culture and Everyday Life*, ed. Holly Rogers, Joana Freitas and João Francisco Porfírio (New York: Bloomsbury Academic, 2023), 65–89. Zach Campbell, 'Lil Nas X "MONTERO (Call Me By Your Name)" REACTION WITH LIL NAS X!!,' *YouTube video*, 00:12:45, 26 March 2021, https://www.youtube.com/watch?v=h2OAuf4G6CI.

dimensions. Footage from numerous mobile phones (seen at the bottom of the cover image) instantly relayed the performance back onto YouTube, where the multiple perspectives joined the rapid spread of fan noise from reaction videos, mashups, cover versions, vids, supercuts, samples and lyric videos. MONTERO's universe was also generating controversy from artist and director Andrew Thomas Huang, who meticulously pointed out the music video's marked similarities with his earlier video for FKA Twigs' 'Cellophane' (2019).[3] As the song, its video, its multiple reimagined paratexts and its criticisms ricocheted through social media, Sidemen's reaction video voiced confusion over the music video's origins: 'It's not a bad song either man, I'll give him that.' 'I feel like I've heard it before.' 'You might have heard it on TikTok already?' 'Maybe' (Figure 0.1c).[4] Where does 'MONTERO (Call Me By Your Name)' start, and where does it end? And whose work is it?

When a piece of music moves through what Carol Vernallis calls the great 'media swirl' of the twenty-first century, it can quickly gain cultural traction by transforming from a discreet, authored text to a participatory hub of creative activity.[5] '[V]alue is primarily generated via "spreadability"', writes Henry Jenkins; 'Through reuse, reworking and redistribution, spreadable media content "gains greater resonance in the culture, taking on new meanings, finding new

**Figure 0.1a** Nicole, Jucee & Rex, "WHEEWWW! | Lil Nas X – MONTERO (Call Me By Your Name) (Official Video) | REACTION" (26 March 2021).

**Figure 0.1b** Zach Campbell, 'Lil Nas X 'MONTERO (Call Me By Your Name)' REACTION WITH LIL NAS X!!' (26 March 2021).

**Figure 0.1c** SidemanReacts, 'Sideman React to Lil Nas X – MONTERO (Call Me By Your Name)' (28 March 2021).

---

[3] Jackson Langford, 'Director of FKA twigs' "Cellophane" video responds to similarities in Lil Nas X's "Montero" video', *NME*, 29 March 2021, at https://www.nme.com/news/music/director-of-fka-twigs-cellophane-video-responds-to-similarities-in-lil-nas-xs-montero-video-2909922.
[4] SidemanReacts, 'Sideman React to Lil Nas X – MONTERO (Call Me By Your Name)', *YouTube video*, 00:08:45, 28 March 2021, https://www.youtube.com/watch?v=0Yb0EJdJSww.
[5] Carol Vernallis, *Unruly Media: YouTube, Music Video and the New Digital Cinema* (Oxford: Oxford University Press, 2013), 3.

audiences, attracting new markets, and generating new values".[6] But the specificity of such spreadability is reliant on the evolving affordances of different online platforms. Although musicians and industry personnel work the generative qualities of new media for their marketing and distribution potential, it is fans who engender the greatest traction for music by developing and sharing cover versions, supercuts, mashups, remakes, fanvids, lyric, literal and reaction videos, parodies, memes and other chain or iterative collaborations. This simultaneity of commerce and fandom, and professional and amateur creativity, has had a profound influence on contemporary music cultures and practices.

Since its launch in 2005, YouTube has been a key driver in the regeneration of music through and across online spaces. With easy-to-use software and slogans such as 'Broadcast Yourself', the platform has encouraged its users to participate by adding their own videos, or by liking, sharing, commenting on, manipulating and appropriating previously uploaded material.[7] In this book's companion text, *YouTube and Music: Online Culture and Everyday Life*, our authors show how YouTube's participatory nature has determined how we produce, consume, circulate and analyse networked musical creativity. Here, we narrow our gaze to focus on the sonic repeatability that floods the platform through the appropriations, adaptations, intertextualities, samples, quotations, re-combinations, reworkings and even cannibalisms of various music practices. Following Michael Mandiberg's observation that YouTube has helped to 'destabiliz[e] the one-directional broadcast from a reporter to an audience into a multivoiced conversation among participants', and with a focus on the technologies and aesthetics of remediation, our authors explore what YouTube can reveal about music culture, social media users and the contemporary music industry.[8]

## 'The people formally known as the audience'

YouTube's potential for interaction rests within the wider affordances of new media. When the term Web 2.0 was first coined by Darcy DiNucci in 1999, the

---

[6] Henry Jenkins, 'Confronting the Challenges of Participatory Culture: Media Education for the 21st Century (Part One),' *Nordic Journal of Digital Literacy* 2, no. 1 (24 May 2007): 20.
[7] For an in-depth discussion of this process of professionalisation, see Holly Rogers, '"Welcome to your world": YouTube and the Reconfiguration of Music's Gatekeepers,' in *YouTube and Music*, 1–32.
[8] Michael Mandiberg, 'Introduction,' in *The Social Media Reader*, ed. Michael Mandiberg (New York and London: New York University Press, 2012), 3.

ways in which Internet users could contribute to and drive the aesthetics of online culture were only just beginning to be realized.[9] Tim O'Reilly, when he brought the term into popular parlance during a conference speech five years later, demonstrated how the capacity for what he referred to as 'hackability' and 'remixability' was being built into new platforms. The products of '"born digital" industries and media, such as software, computer games, websites and social networks', writes Lev Manovich, 'are explicitly designed to be customized by the users'.[10] A few months after O'Reilly's speech, the principles of 'hackability' and 'remixability' became the cornerstone of YouTube, the platform that was about to move music production, marketing and creativity into (what seemed to be) a more democratic space.

Initially, and despite YouTube's early call to 'Broadcast Yourself', professionally made content dominated the platform. This could be new footage uploaded by commercial enterprises – music videos, adverts, film trailers, concert footage – or fan-uploaded clips of pre-existent work – film, television shows and other broadcast material. Although the platform's content rapidly diversified, its signature as a video-sharing site remained strong. In her 2013 research into YouTube's content, José van Dijck found that more than two-thirds of user-uploaded clips were taken from professional sources: 'over 63 per cent of the most popular uploaders do not contribute user-*generated* content (UGC) but user-*copied* content (UCC) to the site – user-copied meaning that the videos are not created by uploaders themselves. These research outcomes certainly warrant the conclusion that YouTube has gradually shifted towards being a site for recycling professionally generated content (PGC).'[11] More recently, the notion of recycling PGC has become complicated. Although pre-existing videos can be shared or recycled without intervention, there has been an increasing tendency to disrupt, to recall Mandiberg, 'the one-directional broadcast from a reporter to an audience' by also remodelling and recrafting them. Other users may then copy and recycle the transformed music or video rather than the original version, reworking it further and muddling the distinctions between professional work and UGC.

---

[9] Darcy DiNucci, 'Fragmented Future,' *Print Magazine* 53, no. 4, (April 1999): 32.
[10] Lev Manovich, 'The Practice of Everyday (Media) Life,' in *Video Vortex Reader: Responses to YouTube*, ed. Geert Lovink and Sabine Niederer (Amsterdam: Institute of Network Cultures, 2008), 37.
[11] José van Dijck, *The Culture of Connectivity: A Critical History of Social Media* (Oxford: Oxford University Press, 2013), 119.

On the one hand, the combination of free and easy-to-use editing software, combined with YouTube's educational opportunities, such as Next Up and the Partnership Programme, meant that amateur uploaders were able to create more professional-looking videos, a process clearly seen in the emergence of the proficient YouTuber able to monetize the platform's stylish and current aesthetics. On the other hand, the process of what Vernallis has called 'YouTubification' saw the platform's audiovisual vernacular bleed beyond its boundaries.[12] Commercial music video directors and filmmakers increasingly draw on the aesthetics of online Do-It-Yourself (DIY) and amateur culture in their professional work, leading to a reciprocal flow of influence between contemporary media forms. On YouTube, this entangled reciprocity taps into and enlivens the contemporary mania for remediation. In his work on new media, Axel Bruns forwards the portmanteau '*produsage* – **the collaborative and continuous building and extending of existing content in pursuit of further improvement**'.[13] This term, which embodies both an activation of what Jay Rosen calls 'the people formally known as the audience' and the process of collaborative, iterative creation, is significant for YouTube.[14] When users edit and reupload moving image clips (whether the original material is professionally created or produced by another amateur user), distinctions between the creator of the material and its consumer are diminished. Other users can work on already manipulated versions; simultaneous interpretations can take affect and meaning in different directions; edits and reworkings can fractal out to other genres; and revoiced clips can reach between echo chambers and communities. This movement of material through online culture allows it to accumulate perspectives, styles, meanings and gestures. Although there is a distinction to be made, then, between videos uploaded by professional musicians as part of a commercial venture, and UGC that, although it may become commercial, is often motivated by different aesthetics, YouTubification and produsage can significantly confound these boundaries. When commercially created high-budget primary material is reconfigured through amateur processes, or when DIY uploads enter the Internet's swirl of repetition, a new hybrid type of absorptive moving-image media emerges that is alive and responsive to the fleeting resonances of popular culture.

---

[12] Vernallis, *Unruly Media*.
[13] Axel Bruns, 'Produsage: A Working Definition,' *Produsage.org* (December 2009), at https://produsage.org/node/9 (bold in the original).
[14] Jay Rosen, 'The People Formerly Known as the Audience,' in *The Social Media Reader*, 15.

## 'I feel like I've heard it before': Musical Retromania

The revoicing of creative material is of course no new thing, and visual and moving image histories have been reconfigured across their many styles, articulations and mediums. The multiple histories of music have also been driven by repetitions and remediations. Internal musical repetition is an integral part of compositional practice, directing the theme and variation, sonata form's recapitulations, da capo arias, folk music's versification, leitmotivic transformation, African drum patterns, the rondo form, the dub beat, minimalism's insistent reiterations, the song chorus, trance music and the circularities of the Javanese Gamelan. Intertextual references and echoes also cascade through the centuries, passing through many different styles, from the reuse of specific structures in the sixteenth-century imitation mass based on existing *cantus firmus* (or melody), the jazz contrafact where new melodies are woven above an existing chord pattern, and the folk song that transformed as it was passed orally through communities and centuries. But with the unfolding twentieth century and the loosening of Modernism's drive for innovation and originality, came an emerging sensibility for explicit creative borrowing. Moving through the wider, cultural, mid-century postmodern aesthetic and its 'incredulity toward metanarratives' identified by Jean-François Lyotard, an explosion of musical intertextuality, borrowing, appropriation, quotation and multiplicity began to dissolve linear time and coherent space in a way that was quite different from what had gone before.[15] The emergence of affordable recording technologies – tape from the 1940s, video from the 1960s, sampling equipment and Digital Audio Workstations from the 1970s and 1980s – enabled an even clearer connection to the sonic past, by allowing the reuse of actual recorded music artefacts, an opportunity that unleashed what Simon Reynolds has called a turn towards 'retromania'.[16] Hastened by the affordances of these new technologies, the invigorated zeal for reusing sonic material moved through tape music, dub versions, hip-hop sampling, turntablism, plunderphonics, electronica, Afrofuturism and, as the new millennia got underway, the eclectic

---

[15] Jean-François Lyotard, *The Postmodern Condition: A Report on Knowledge* (Manchester: Manchester University Press, 1979), xxiv.
[16] Holly Rogers, *Sounding the Gallery: Video and the Rise of Art-Music* (Oxford: Oxford University Press, 2013); Holly Rogers, 'Instruments,' in Tom Perchard, Stephen Graham, Tim Rutherford-Johnson and Holly Rogers, *Twentieth-Century Music in the West: An Introduction* (Cambridge: Cambridge University Press, 2022), 202–26; Simon Reynolds, *Retromania: Pop Culture's Addiction to its Own Past* (London, Faber & Faber: 2012).

mix of 1980s and 1990s audiovisual samples that drove Internet genres such as vaporwave.

Fundamental to all these cultures of sonic remixability is the loosening hold of traditional music education over musical creativity. Technology enabled wider access to the tools of music composition and performance. This activated different groups of musicians and fuelled the surge of bedroom music culture and an increased presence of women in music technology environments and practices.[17] In his work on contemporary music processes, for example, Ellis Jones notes how today it is 'hard to maintain' the idea of 'separate worlds' for DIY and mainstream music practice. Where once DIY signified 'cultural resistance' (an aesthetic that drove punk for example), new technologies – and social media in particular— have repositioned it as an active and productive process of doing.[18]

In his work on postmodern music, Jonathan D. Kramer notes the emerging sensibility for quotation-embraced contractions between 'highbrow' and 'lowbrow' styles, between the past and the present, traditions and cultures, and between meanings and temporalities.[19] With its tendrils in multiple histories and diverse styles, quotation-heavy music holds a double life as both a newly constructed piece and as one that comments on the original material, as David Metzer writes:

> It is the ways in which quotation handles the 'what' and the 'how' that make it such an effective cultural agent. The gesture latches on to a specific work, often a familiar one, and places that work squarely in front of us. The borrowed material is tightly gripped and prominently featured rather than being merely alluded to or buried in the background. This directness calls attention to the cultural associations of the original, for the more discernible and intact the borrowing, the more apparent those associations.[20]

When music is visualized, these resonances can become even more palpable by drawing on, and combining, both visual and sonic histories. Sometimes, as we shall see below, when moving image fragments are combined, the 'cultural associations of the original' texts form comedic or parodic configurations, or, in the case of music video, can draw attention to the intertextuality of the form, as

---

[17] Mary Celeste Kearney, *Girls Make Media* (London: Routledge, 2006).
[18] Ellis Jones, *DIY Music and the Politics of Social Media* (London: Bloomsbury Publishing, 2020), 8, 38.
[19] Jonathan D. Kramer, 'Postmodern Concepts of Musical Time,' *Indiana Theory Review* 17, no. 2 (2012): 21–60.
[20] David Metzer, *Quotation and Cultural Meaning in Twentieth-Century Music* (Cambridge: Cambridge University Press, 2003), 6.

Mathias Korsgaard has shown in his work on polyphonic videos.[21] At other times, these associations take on powerful political resonances. Hip-hop artists have long used quotation as an articulation of political critique and cultural lineage, for example, allowing musicians to link back to earlier African-American pop music traditions and jazz, but also to the 'multimedia borrowings' from 1970s blaxploitation film soundtracks and other expressions of black womanhood and representation.[22]

The participatory spaces of Web 2.0, the enmeshing of professional and amateur or DIY sensibilities, and the opportunities for 'remixability' afforded by YouTube moved these professional practices of audiovisual remediation into the public, amateur sphere. At the same time, they reinvigorated the familiar historiographic narratives of musical retromania. On YouTube, these convergences now manifest in two ways. First, with more than 720,000 hours of new material uploaded every day, the platform supplies a significant repository of audiovisual content for appropriation.[23] This includes uploads from the record industry but also footage uploaded and organized by fans as part of crowd-sourced cataloguing and preservation to form what's become known as YouTube's 'long tail', as Chris Anderson writes:

> You can find everything out there on the Long Tail. There's the back catalogue, older albums still fondly remembered by long-time fans or rediscovered by new ones. There are live tracks, B-sides, remixes even (gasp) covers. There are niches by the thousands, genre within genre within genre: imagine an entire Tower Records devoted to '80s hair bands or ambient dub. There are foreign bands, once priced out of reach in the Import aisle, and obscure bands on even more obscure labels, many of which don't have the distribution clout to get into Tower at all.[24]

Internet music, such as vaporwave, chillwave and hypnagogic pop explicitly ransacks YouTube's archives for creative material, remediating existing sounds and images to perform what Reynolds refers to as 'echo-jams' through

---

[21] Mathias Korsgaard, *Music Video After MTV: Audiovisual Studies, New Media and Popular Music* (London: Routledge, 2017).
[22] Joanna Demers, 'Sampling the 1970s in Hip-Hop,' *Popular Music* 22, no. 1 (2003): 42. Gwendolyn D. Pough, *Check It While I Wreck It: Black Womanhood, Hip-Hop Culture and the Public Sphere* (Boston: Northeastern University Press, 2004).
[23] Jason Wise, 'How Many Videos are Uploaded to YouTube in 2022?,' *Earthweb* (15 October 2022), at https://earthweb.com/how-many-videos-are-uploaded-to-youtube-a-day/.
[24] Chris Anderson, 'The Long Tail,' *Wired* 12 (2004), at https://www.wired.com/2004/10/tail/.

online culture.²⁵ Second, the platform provides the tools and know-how to sample and revoice the copious clips within these deposits.

Remediation (and the 'echo-jams' it initiates) is key to YouTube's process of audiovisual regeneration, leading to the common feeling, as Sidemen suggest in their reaction video, that we've 'heard it before'. Proposed in 1999 by Jay Bolter and Richard Grusin, as an update of Marshall McLuhan's 1964 assertion that 'the "content" of any medium is always another medium' for the digital age, remediation can be understood as 'the representation of one medium in another'.²⁶ For Bolter and Grusin, media history is not a series of displacements in which new media (for example, the Internet) make old media (such as the radio) obsolete. Instead, new media transform older media, retaining some of their features while discarding others. In their own words, remediation is 'the way in which one medium is seen by our culture as reforming or improving upon another'; it is 'the formal logic by which new media refashion prior media forms'.²⁷ This refashioning arises through a two-way process of integration and evolution, by which new media both intervenes into and alters older media, while the specificities and affordances of new media then prompts changes in the aesthetics of older technologies. Key to this duality are the differences, but also the interrelations, between the processes of immediacy – looking through – and hypermediacy – looking at. Immediacy, present in computer-generated imagery (CGI), 3D technologies and immersive sound, write the authors, 'dictates that the medium itself should disappear and leave us in the presence of the thing represented.' By contrast, hypermediacy 'calls attention to the medium', foregrounding its specificities and technological applications.²⁸ Remediation, then, can come from a collision of media (when one technology makes direct use of another to enhance its own processes, for example the use of digital technologies for special effects to enhance a film's immersion) or through mimicry (when one form of media uses its own specificities to take on the vocabularies of another).

YouTube constantly performs both kinds of remediation: as Grusin later said in his work on new media, 'YouTube sets out to remediate TV not merely as a

---

[25] Reynolds, *Retromania*, 80.
[26] Marshall McLuhan, *Understanding Media: The Extensions of Man* (New York: McGraw-Hill, 1964), 8; Jay David Bolter and Richard Grusin, *Remediation: Understanding New Media* (Boston: MIT Press, 2000).
[27] Ibid., 59, 273.
[28] Ibid., 6.

neutral intermediary but as an active mediator.'[29] Videos can promote immediacy through traditional filmmaking techniques, such as perspective, point of view and audition, framing, audiovisual synchronicity and smooth editing. And yet, when placed within the patchwork of YouTube, they jostle against thumbnails and recommendations, comments and adverts, which draws attention to the surface of the screen and the opacity of the medium. In other videos, stylized and first-person addresses – technologies notable in the recent ways that musicians market themselves through behind-the-scenes footage and vlogs – play with hypermediacy from the outset. This can be seen in the direct-to-camera address, abrupt editing, shaky camera work and the use of text, collage, split screen and other techniques that highlight the materiality of YouTube as a medium. As Bolter writes in the foreword to this volume, then, YouTube remediates in two ways: 'through remix practices that characterize much of its music content and through the algorithmic hypermediacy that presents that content to users.'

## Audiovisual Remediation on YouTube

Bolter's and Grusin's theory is located in the remediation of the image and the aesthetics of looking. But it can be productively applied to music and the act of listening to and beyond the materiality of sound. The appropriation of orchestral sounds through digital media and the jagged tapestry of sampling, hip-hop, polystylism and vaporwave all force the hypermediacy of the remediation process into the foreground; and yet, if the revoicing is seamlessly woven into the new sonic textures, reducing the rupture of juxtaposition, music can generate a more transparent sense of immediacy. Mashups of pre-existing music are a good example of this. These are extremely popular on YouTube and can either be produced from a compilation of similar tracks, or by modifying two songs into a new and coherent structure. Sir Mashalot's 'Mindblowing SIX song country mashups', for example, reveals the identical chord structure beneath six of country music's biggest hits,[30] while Dj Pyromania and Yabanci Müzikler's audiovisual mashup of around twenty-three of 2016's most famous pop hits, uses Wordplay and Harmonic Mixing to blend together the different sonorities

---

[29] Richard Grusin, 'YouTube at the End of New Media,' in *The YouTube Reader*, ed. Pelle Snickars and Patrick Vonderau (New York: Columbia University Press, 2010), 99.

[30] Sir Mashalot, 'Sir Mashalot: Mind-Blowing SIX Song Country Mashup,' *YouTube video*, 00:03:55, 4 November 2014, https://www.youtube.com/watch?v=FY8SwIvxj8o&t=3s.

and textures.³¹ Sonic mashups can also draw attention to extra musical resonances, such as Atlasito's heady mix of Lil Nas X's 'Industry Baby' and Michael Jackson's 'Beat It'.³² Although this mix plays on the differences between the songs' lyrics – Jackson warns his protagonist away from violence and confrontation; Lil Nas confronts his problems head on and shows inmates escaping from a burning prison – other mashups work to smooth over potential disjunctions. DJ Earworm, for instance, uses wordplay to create a new track where singers complete the lyric or phrase started by another to create a different, yet harmonically and tonally consistent, track.³³ Here, although the fragments remain recognizable, they coalesce into a new, tuneful and plausible song. In her work on Internet music, Georgina Born argues that the affordances of new media have expanded the aesthetic and communicative possibilities of contemporary musicking.³⁴ Here, we can see how refreshed creative possibilities emerge by colliding digital music and social media practices.

When combined with the moving image, music can generate both states of remediation simultaneously. Existing music can be re-visualized with different material; the moving image can be re-sounded. In our first collection of essays on YouTube and Music, Vernallis et al. show how lyric videos enact a process of redactive revisualization by adding a double, subversive or fresh reading of the original material.³⁵ A literal video, such as 'Total Eclipse of the Heart Literal Video Version' (2013), for instance, throws the music video form into the foreground, highlighting its tropes and cliches, and drawing our attention to the weirdness of our learnt behaviours.³⁶

Mashups, rather than literal videos or visualizers, destabilize expectation in slightly different ways because both sound and image are pre-existent, as Korsgaard points out:

---

[31] Yabancı Müzikler, 'Pop Songs World 2016 – Mega Mashup (Dj Pyromania),' *YouTube video*, 00:07:02, 15 September 2016, https://www.youtube.com/watch?v=yyJ3GmDGrPE&t=1s.

[32] Atlasito, 'Lil Nas X ft. Michael Jackson – Industry Baby X Beat It (Atlas Mashup),' *YouTube video*, 00:03:37, 28 August 2021, https://www.youtube.com/watch?v=xt_seNeuDrs.

[33] DJ Earworm, 'DJ Earworm – United State of Pop 2009 (Blame It on the Pop),' *YouTube video*, 00:04:45, 27 December 2009, https://www.youtube.com/watch?v=iNzrwh2Z2hQ&t=2s.

[34] Georgina Born and Christopher Haworth, 'Music and Intermediality After the Internet: Aesthetics, Materialities and Social Forms,' in *Music and Digital Media: Towards a Planetary Anthropology*, ed. Georgia Born (London: UCL Press, 2022), 378–438.

[35] Carol Vernallis, Laura McLaren, Virginia Kuhn and Martin Rossouw, 'm ☺ Re tH@n WorD\$: Aspects and Appeals of the Lyric Video,' in *YouTube and Music*, 149–68.

[36] Artistwithouttalent, 'Total Eclipse of the Heart Literal Video Version,' *YouTube video*, 00:05:33, 1 September 2013, https://www.youtube.com/watch?v=fsgWUq0fdKk.

> Fanvids often display the potent pairings of image and music sources; in these cases the videos offer a double reading of both the musical and the visual source material, in which one sheds new light on the other … The 'shreds', literal versions, and autotune forms instead disrupt their sources' meaning by substituting or transforming elements, thereby creating new associations.[37]

The combination of material from one or more sources can reveal a 'double reading' through insightful or witty commentary that emerges through the hypermediacy of irregularities or similarities. Often highly satirical, political mashups tend to be infused with quotation, appropriation and intertextuality to produce folk cultural responses to dominant and official narratives. These abrupt visual cut-ups are usually collaged to accord with musical rhythms and structures. JOE's June 2022 satire 'Boris Johnson's Mashup Years – No Confidence Vote Remix', for instance, tunes speech snippets from the former UK prime minister and Michael Gove into an assortment of popular tunes, including Andrew Lloyd Webber's 'Any Dream Will Do' (*Joseph and The Amazing Technicolour Dreamcoat*, 1991) and Shakin' Stevens' 1985 hit 'Snow is Falling'.[38] Although this video reorganizes the politician's speech as a form of satire, Sam Dubs' 2018 'Donald Trump Singing Baby Shark' mashup simply highlights what the YouTuber understands as the former president's empty and repetitive rhetoric (Figure 0.2).[39]

Much can be learned about the popular cultural role of a particular type of music from its spread through YouTube. As part of his work on opera and its resonances in contemporary society, for example, Carlo Cenciarelli collected together YouTube versions of users faux operatic singing along to a recording of Verdi's aria 'Brindisi' from *La Traviata* (1853) to produce 'Twilight Brindisi: A YouTube Mashup'.[40] At the time of posting, the aria had recently found fame in *Twilight* (2008). As his mashup moves through various versions of over-the-top, sing-a-longs to Verdi's aria, the 'emphasis on performance rather than on storytelling, open[s] up the music's field of cultural connotations', writes Cenciarelli.[41] And yet, the continual parodic nature of the singing and farcical

---

[37] Korsgaard, *Music After MTV*, 209.
[38] JOE, 'Boris Johnson's Mashup Years – No Confidence Vote Remix,' *YouTube video*, 00:04:09, 6 June 2022, https://www.youtube.com/watch?v=tTD3Yo6DbOE.
[39] Sam Dubs, 'Donald Trump Singing Baby Shark,' *YouTube video*, 00:01:42, 27 November 2018, https://www.youtube.com/watch?v=cXNWGjK74Lo.
[40] Carlo Cenciarelli, 'Twilight Brindisi – A YouTube Mashup,' *YouTube video*, 00:03:28, 24 June 2014, https://www.youtube.com/watch?v=JyiEUGykkRI.
[41] Carlo Cenciarelli, '"Warped Singing": Opera From Cinema to YouTube,' in *Verdi on Screen*, ed. Delphine Vincent (Lausanne: L'Age d'Homme, 2015), 266.

**Figure 0.2** Sam Dubs, 'Donald Trump Singing Baby Shark' (27 November 27 2018).

gestures tells us a lot about the ways in which opera is imagined within today's popular culture. It is also an example of how material can be reappropriated in ways inappropriate to or unimaginable for the original artist, becoming twice displaced as it moves through a blockbuster movie and social media's iterative processes. Such iterative remediation can have negative effects, such as the harmful whitewashing of black culture behind the Harlem Shake meme's progression across social media. In her work on YouTube, Kyra D. Gaunt explores the aftermath of Miley Cyrus's appropriation of twerking, which went viral after she posted a video to Facebook in March 2013. The video kickstarted a twerking craze which spread rapidly across the internet. Gaunt notes how this initiated a 'subversion of the history, complexity and meaningfulness of the black social dance and the role black females play/played in it began'.[42] As Cyrus's video garnered massive social media views, it quickly eclipsed its previous expressions on YouTube, often performed by black girls who 'do not make the cover of magazines or even the most-watched videos, despite the fact that black girls' performances definitely help generate, define, and trigger the viral trend of twerking...'.[43] This appropriation ricochets negative cultural connotations through YouTube and destabilises what Gaunt describes as 'the translocal and

---

[42] Kyra D. Gaunt, 'YouTube, Twerking & You: Context Collapse and the Handheld Co-Presence of Black Girls and Miley Cyrus', *Journal of Popular Music Studies* 27, no. 3 (2015), 244.
[43] Ibid., 245–6.

ethnic sense of belonging that the imagined community of African American girls attribute to participating in twerking'.[44]

Even when the original artist, song or dance remains at the heart of a viral spread, it is not always a positive attribution. A powerful example of this is bait-and-switch trolling, where a link, placed in a variety of contexts, takes users repeatedly to the same place rather than the promised content. The most notable instance of this is the art of Rickrolling, where users are taken to Rick Ashley's 1987 hit video for 'Never Gonna Give You Up', a bait-and-switch so embedded in popular culture that the White House's official Twitter handle made use of it in 2011. Although 'Twilight Brindisi' relishes its audiovisual disjunctions and self-consciously low-fi quality, other YouTube mashups enjoy a more unified, cinematic quality. In these cases, music can be employed filmicly to cover edits and jumps in time and space. SUPERCUT's 2012 video, '50 Heartbreaking Movie Moments / SUPERCUT', for instance, draws the visual tapestry together via the continuous strains of John Murphy's *Sunshine (Adagio in D Minor)* (2008).[45] Here, the music acts like conventional film music, providing a sonic wash that stitches together images, unites narrative threads and helps to reinforce particular positions and understandings.

Vidding also starts with music. This practice involves collaging television and film clips to pre-existent music, usually songs. Rather than generate a new music video from scratch, explains Francesca Coppa, this form of media fandom collates images from one or more audiovisual texts (known as a garbage can vid) to construct an analytical rereading of the original that follows the rhythmic or aesthetic contours of the chosen music, which can be completely extraneous to the original source material: it 'is a visual essay that stages an argument, and thus it is more akin to arts criticism than to traditional music video'.[46] The focus can lie on one character, or the relationship between several (often rethinking a heterosexual relationship into a same-sex one, known as slash or femslash collage, for example); it can subvert the original meaning, or reveal its perceived issues; it can draw out connections that have remained hidden; or it can tell another story entirely. To do so, though, requires the 'directness' noted by Metzer

---

[44] Ibid., 245.
[45] SUPERCUT, '50 Heartbreaking Movie Movements | SUPERCUT', *YouTube video*, 00:08:15, 7 December 2012, https://www.youtube.com/watch?v=58VQ7_Hugbg.
[46] Francesca Coppa, 'Women, *StarTrek*, and the Early Development of Fannish Vidding,' *Transformative Works and Cultures* 1 (2008): at https://journal.transformativeworks.org/index.php/twc/article/view/44/64; See also Tisha Turk, 'Transformation in a New Key: Music in Vids and Vidding,' *Music, Sound, and the Moving Image* 9, no. 2 (2015): 174.

above, which 'calls attention to', but also subverts, 'the cultural associations of the original'.

Fannish vids (which are also known as fanvids or songvids, or anime music video if the source footage is anime) interpret performatively, using the same technologies and aesthetics as the media they critique. With dedicated fan conventions and a large following, these forms play a significant role in YouTube's critical remediations and potential for 'hackability'. They also embrace the platform's capacity to link transmediality to other media sites. Fannish vids critique their source material using the tropes, styles and in-jokes that populate online viddish forums. When revoiced and repositioned on YouTube, these references demonstrate the platform's powerful capacity for building community and affinity spaces, as Jenkins explains: vids 'articulate [...] what the fans have in common: their shared understandings, their mutual interests, their collective fantasies' and 'focus on those aspects of the narrative that the community wants to explore'.[47] With found-footage images cut to existing music, fannish vids perform an important part in YouTube's sonic remediations. Here, music is used to analyse the cut-up and re-sequenced visual material. In her work on the genre, Tisha Turk explains that 'Vidders' use of music is critical to this collaborative construction of meaning: the song and its lyrics provide narrative and emotional information that the audience must decode ... music is a vid's most obvious and essential discursive feature'.[48] Her analysis rests on the narrative positioning of the chosen songs and, although noting that songs sung from the first person are most common, as they allow the lyrics to draw out a character's emotions, other modes of narration allow for larger cultural resonances to accumulate. In sisabet's 2010 vid edited from Quentin Tarantino's *Kill Bill* Vols. 1 and 2 (2003 to 2004), for example, Bob Dylan's 1989 song 'Ring Them Bells', infused with Biblical and spiritual imagery sung from an unknown narrator, is used to draw attention away from the film's ultra-violence towards what Turk describes as the films' 'causes and consequences of violence' and 'cultural narratives about gender and sexuality'.[49] This 'double reading' (Korsgaard) relies on the hypermediacy of the original visual and sonic material, and the knowing,

---

[47] Henry Jenkins, *Textual Poachers: Television Fans and Participatory Culture* (New York: Routledge, 1992), 249.
[48] Tisha Turk, '"Your Own Imagination": Vidding and Vidwatching as Collaborative Interpretation,' *Film and Film Culture* 5 (2020): 99.
[49] Ibid., 90. sisabet, 'Kill Bill – Ring Them Bells,' *YouTube video*, 00:03:05, 23 October 2010, https://www.youtube.com/watch?v=Xc9Jqc53DQA.

shared cultural knowledge of the viddish forums for its success. The tapestries of all these forms of repetition, then, involve playing with fragments, reassigning meaning and deconstructing (or revealing) intention through the affordances of online culture.

Although vidding remediates both sound and image, no-budget user-made cover songs transform music but usually offer completely new, rather than remediated, visual material. The cover song is so popular that it has become, argues Costas Constandinides, a 'YouTube genre in its own right'.[50] Covers of popular songs – often acoustic and recorded as live versions – can achieve viral success irrespective of the musical life and fan culture of the original, base version. Erato's acapella, cup version of Robyn's 2011 electropop hit, 'Call Your Girlfriend' (music video directed by Max Vitali, Figure 0.3a), performed with hand claps and empty butter dishes, gained significant traction as soon as it was uploaded to YouTube in January of the following year, for example (Figure 0.3b).[51] This version received its own cover, this time by the young sisters Lennon and Maisy, who echoed Erato's hand-cup rhythms and acapella style rather than Robyn's original electropop groove. This cover of a cover became an instant viral hit, propelling the young sisters into the public consciousness and into leading roles in ABC's *Nashville* (2012 to 2018; Figure 0.3c).[52] The popularity of Lennon and Maisy's version initiated a torrent of other 'Call Your Girlfriend' covers, and it soon became increasingly unclear whether musicians had come to the song via Robyn, Erato, Lennon and Maisy or another version entirely: 'the base song,' writes Constandinides, 'entails the possibility that at a certain moment in the history of a song, which holds the status of the base song, a paradigmatic cover may take the original song's position as a base

---

[50] Costas Constandinides, '"You Just Got Covered": YouTube Cover Song Videos as Examples of Para-Adaptation,' in *Adaptation in the Age of Media Convergence*, ed. Johannes Fehrle and Werner Schäfke-Zell (Amsterdam: Amsterdam University Press, 2019), 113. In his case study of teenage Wade Johnston, Christopher Cayari shows how the musician uses YouTube to enlarge the genre of the cover version by including material from his recording sessions, direct to camera videos that explain his process, vlogs, collaborative versions and live footage: Christopher Cayari, 'The YouTube Effect: How YouTube has Provided New Ways to Consume, Create and Share Music,' *International Journal of Education & the Arts* 12, no. 6 (2011): 1–30.
[51] Erato, 'Erato – Call Your Girlfriend,' *YouTube video*, 00:02:24, 7 December 2011, https://www.youtube.com/watch?v=fQoCEvVL57E.
[52] lennonandmaisy, 'Lennon & Maisy // "Call Your Girlfriend" // Robyn Erato,' *YouTube video*, 00:01:53, 30 May 2012, https://www.youtube.com/watch?v=7_aJHJdCHAo. Suraj Saifullah drew my attention to this particular chain of versions in a wonderful conference presentation: starting at 06:16:24, watch Suraj Saifullah's talk at the *Like, Share and Subscribe YouTube, Music and Cyberculture Before and After the New Decade* international conference, CysMus-CESEM, 'Day 3,' *YouTube video*, 10:29:52, 25 January 2021, https://www.youtube.com/watch?v=1XHyrP3jsbc&t=22586s.

**Figure 0.3a** Robyn, 'Call Your Girlfriend' (directed by Max Vitali, 2011).
**Figure 0.3b** Erato, 'Erato – Call Your Girlfriend' (7 December 2011).
**Figure 0.3c** Lennonandmaisy, 'Lennon & Maisy // "Call Your Girlfriend" // Robyn and Erato' (30 May 2012).

song or base song performance due to its popularity or charismatic performance of the covering artist.'[53] He describes this chain process of abstraction as 'para-adaptation ... that creatively "disturbs" commercial source products, and may eventually achieve a status that surpasses the "ordinary" expectations of its creator(s)'.[54] A strong example of this is David Guetta's double-platinum 2011 collaboration with Sia, 'Titanium,' which spawned versions by other celebrity musicians, such as Rick Ashley in 2020 (Figure 0.4a), but also launched the careers of several YouTubers, including SUNN ST. CLAIRE and Madilyn Bailey.[55] These last two versions use YouTube's common vernacular to reconfigure the original song into audiovisual forms with a uniquely social media vibe. SUNN ST. CLAIRE's acoustic guitar and voice version (which has received almost 3.5 million views), uses many of the platform's common vlogging tropes, including a direct address introduction to the camera, a messy domestic background and an amateur camera angle that cuts off the top of her head and half her guitar (Figure 0.4b). Bailey's version, although sharing many of the same traits, offers a more professional aesthetic. Established YouTube presence Bailey had already received great acclaim for her cover versions while still at school, but it was her 2015 cover of 'Titanium' (Figure 0.4c), which currently has more than 119 million views, that gained her a contract with a French Warner Music Group label that saw her version chart in France and Belgium, and led to a successful 2016 album of covers (*Muse Box*). The spreadability of media, then, doesn't always lead to greater exposure for the original; sometimes, the original

---

[53] Constandinides, '"You Just Got Covered",' 116.
[54] Ibid., 111.
[55] Rick Astley, 'Rick Astley – Titanium (Cover),' *YouTube video*, 00:04:06, 13 August, 2020, https://www.youtube.com/watch?v=L_vnEHDjfZ8; SUNN ST. CLAIRE, 'Titanium David Guetta ft. Sia Cover Singing by SUNN,' *YouTube video*, 00:03:15, 14 September 2011, https://www.youtube.com/watch?v=KrQb8JIDCxM; Madilyn Bailey, 'Titanium – David Guetta ft. Sia – Official Acoustic Music Video – Madilyn Bailey – on iTunes,' *YouTube video*, 00:03:46, 2 June 2012, https://www.youtube.com/watch?v=PGoCtJzPHkU.

**Figure 0.4a** Rick Astley, 'Rick Astley – Titanium (Cover)' (13 August, 2020).

**Figure 0.4b** SUNN ST. CLAIRE, 'Titanium David Guetta ft. Sia Cover Singing by SUNN' (14 September 2011).

**Figure 0.4c** Madilyn Bailey, 'Titanium – David Guetta ft. Sia – Official Acoustic Music Video – Madilyn Bailey – on iTunes' (2 June 2012).

**Figure 0.4d** Madilyn Bailey, 'Titanium (Official Video)' (Warner Music France, 16 June 2015).

can be eclipsed by subsequent covers and versions by becoming a reference original, as Henrik Smith Sivertsen and Edward Katrak Spencer show later in this book.

Other musicians have found fame through their highly individual interpretations of pre-existent music, such as Walk off the Earth's 2012 version of Gotye's 'Someone that I used to Know' performed with five musicians playing, hitting and strumming various parts of a single guitar (Figure 0.5a).[56] 'YouTube performers may reference the source song (wrongly or otherwise), but they don't always wish to communicate the (hi)story of this song or express a sense of devotion to the "owner" of the song . . .; rather, they wish to promote their talents through a deliberate performance of the song,' suggests Cayari.[57] This sort of virtuosic covering of well-known material has also entered the art music world with videos, such as 'Salut Salong "Wettstreit zu viert" / Competitive Foursome'

---

[56] Songs of the Underground, 'Somebody That I Used to Know – Walk off the Earth (Gotye – Cover),' *YouTube video*, 00:04:24, 10 March 2012, https://www.youtube.com/watch?v=P9mybTArlsk.

[57] Constandinides, '"You Just Got Covered,"' 128.

**Figure 0.5a** Songs of the Underground, 'Somebody That I Used to Know – Walk off the Earth (Gotye – Cover)' (10 March 2012).

**Figure 0.5b** Salut Salon, 'Salut Salon "Wettstreit zu viert" | "Competative Foursome"' (4 February 2014).

**Figure 0.5c** 2CELLOS, '2CELLOS – The Trooper Overture [OFFICAL VIDEO]' (21 October 2014).

showing the all-female piano quartet playing their instruments upside down and in various other fiendish positions for a performance of Vivaldi's Summer from the Four Seasons (1718–1720: Figure 0.5b).[58] Covers can also work through unexpected instrumentation, such as 2Cellos' take on Iron Maiden (with their permission) in 'The Trooper Overture' (Figure 0.5c).[59]

YouTube's cover versions come in many forms, then, but usually take advantage of the platform's audiovisual capabilities. Although Lennon and Maisy's cover feels relatively DIY – they sit at a table with their names scrawled on the wall behind them, the microphones are clearly in view and the fixed camera angle remains unchanged – Bailey's original 2012 version of 'Titanium' feels more professional: multiple closeups from a variety of angles, a roaming camera and various visual effects position the video's gestures somewhere between amateur and professional. Although situated more firmly within the music industry's arena, her following official video for 'Titanium' – which has received more than 25 million views – retains the simplicity of many YouTube cover versions.[60] Although the roaming camera and high definition gives a slick feel, there are no effects, complex rhythmic editing, scene changes, props, narrative or symbolism: using her earlier version as a reference original, Bailey simply stands atop a cliff and sings her heart out (Warner Music France, Figure 0.4d).

---

[58] Salut Salon, 'Salut Salon "Wettstreit zu viert" | "Competative Foursome"', *YouTube video*, 00:03:24, 4 February 2014, https://www.youtube.com/watch?v=BKezUd_xw20&t=65s.

[59] 2CELLOS, '2CELLOS – The Trooper Overture [OFFICIAL VIDEO]', *YouTube video*, 00:05:30, 21 October 2014, https://www.youtube.com/watch?v=eVH1Y15omgE&t=154s.

[60] Warner Music France, 'Madilyn Bailey – Titanium (Official Video),' *YouTube video*, 00:03:51, 16 June 2015, https://www.youtube.com/watch?v=yUKdufSG4tQ.

The para-adaption of songs, such as 'Call Your Girlfriend' and 'Titanium' allow particular pieces of music to form a large and roaming conversation. In cases like these, the idea of remediation and remixability plays with social media's aesthetics of virality, sharing and growth. If something is endlessly replicated through shares, adaptation and reference, it suggests that it has entered the popular psyche to such an extent that it can be manipulated and parodied, while still being instantly recognizable. It allows people to personalize things within a universal framework of signs, references and allusions. In the next section, my co-editors Joana Freitas and João Francisco Porfírio introduce the main themes of this book as they continue to explore how sonic remediation and memory have not only led to new forms of exposure for musicians and YouTubers, but have also generated complex legal issues unique to online culture.

## Part 2: Joana Freitas and João Francisco Porfírio

### What is not Being Remediated: The Musical Upside Down of Online Culture

Above, Holly explores how musical versioning, mashups, vidding and remixing can fragment and reconfigure pre-existent music through the processes of para-adaptation and audiovisual mashup. But a piece of music doesn't have to be fragmented or visually revoiced to gather new meaning and reach new audiences. Here, while introducing the chapters that make up this collection, we (Joana and João) consider how YouTube's processes of fandom and nostalgia can determine the afterlife of musical multimedia, and how legal issues can propel or hamper the processes of online sonic remediation.

Each summer has its own soundtrack. Pop hits, disco beats and other top-of-the-charts songs make their way to radio stations, Spotify playlists and, for those that are still 'old school', annual CD compilations.[61] Although physical compilations of summer hits usually feature recently-released commercial pop and R&B chart hits, the processes of selection that occur online are more complex. Unlike chart music and record sales, online musical virality cannot be quantified (at least not solely) through financial success. Musical memes, remixes, TikToks, cover versions, vids and mashups reach millions of users in a wide

---

[61] The most famous compilation CDs are edited by Sony Music from the Universal Music group. In 2021, their CD was titled *So Fresh: The Hits of Summer 2021 + The Best of 2020*.

variety of contexts, propelling sonic fragments, forgotten songs and unknown bedroom artists into the Internet's most listened to material. Although this can be at the expense of the original artist whose work may not be acknowledged, it can also lead to a significant revival of attention and corresponding financial gain.

Although the Internet's summer soundtrack of 2022 featured the expected range of newly-composed material and stock Instagram reel tracks, it also saw a resurgence of 1980s music, thanks to the resounding popularity of series 4 of *Stranger Things* (Netflix, 2022). During the first episode, Kate Bush's 1985 hit 'Running Up That Hill (A Deal With God)' is played by Max, one of the protagonists, through her Walkman's headphones, providing a moment of sonic introspection that is shared by the audience (Figure 0.6a). Since its 1985 release, the song has enjoyed several resurgences thanks to various cover versions and remixes, the most notable being Placebo's 2003 cover, which charted thanks to its use in the fourth season of *The O.C.* (2007). But the 2022 resurgence was different. Not only was it the original version that regained popularity, almost instantly, the show's worldwide audience thrust the song into a swirl of online remediation.[62] By June, and almost forty years after its release, it had become the second most-played song on the main global streaming platforms and a US Top 10 hit.[63] Soon after, and fuelled by a barrage of musical memes, remixes and mashups of the PGC, a raft of contemporary events tapped into the nostalgic turn. Arriving before the second set of episodes dropped, Netflix teamed up with Doritos to produce 'Live From the Upside Down – The Doritos Music Fest '86', a 'concert from another dimension' that streamed live on 23 June 2022 to millions of users eager to see a variety of 1980s hits performed by contemporary music artists, such as Charli XCX and Corey Hart.[64] In less than a month, *Stranger Things* had positioned Kate Bush's hit – and her music video in particular – at the centre of a vibrant 1980s nostalgia that was remediated via multiple online voices into a distributed and contemporary existence. If we return to Bolter and Grusin's quote above, we can see how online culture reformed and refashioned the 'prior media form' of music video.

[62] In the show, listening to their favourite song is the only way the characters have to avoid Vecna, a monster villain who wants to kill them and take their souls to the 'Upside Down', a dark and hostile parallel universe (see Figure 0.6b).
[63] Ben Beaumont-Thomas, 'Kate Bush Earns First Ever US Top 10 Hit with Running Up That Hill,' *The Guardian*, 7 June 2022, at, https://www.theguardian.com/music/2022/jun/07/kate-bush-earns-first-us-top-10-hit-running-up-that-hill-stranger-things.
[64] The concert is available on YouTube here: Andy Gibbons, 'Live From The Upside Down,' *YouTube video*, 00:31:34, 27 June 2022, https://youtu.be/prjx7VuqFrA.

**Figures 0.6a and b** Max listens to "Running Up That Hill (A Deal With God)" (Kate Bush, 1985), in *Stranger Things* (The Duffer Brothers / Netflix, Series 4 2022).

*Stranger Things*, then, reinvigorated the 'spreadability' of 'Running Up That Hill', bringing new listeners to Kate Bush's work and garnering her a whole new generation of fans.[65] At the same time, although the song re-entered the airwaves, making Apple Music and Spotify playlists (where it is now possible to build a playlist that will save you from the show's evil monster Vecna) and moving through participatory social media platforms, the Netflix series saw its marketing and distribution possibilities skyrocket.[66] Although *Stranger Things* is only available on Netflix, the 'Doritos Music Fest '86 concert' was streamed live on YouTube, where it is now also possible to see several clips and trailers from the series and, of course, listen to and watch the original music video of 'Running Up That Hill'. Taken together, these events helped to *reviralize* Bush's original sonic material. This process, though, is not always positive. Elsewhere in the series, Eddie, one of the central characters, plays Metallica's 1984 metal hit 'Master of Puppets' on his electric guitar as a diversion so that the remaining characters can reach Vecna (Figures 0.7a and 0.7b). Thrust into the spotlight of a younger generation, Metallica welcomed their new listeners on their social media pages despite the gatekeeping efforts of their older fans, many of whom were uncomfortable with the band's move into mainstream popular culture. However, they were soon to be targeted by what Liz Scarlett called TikTok's 'cancel culture-hungry' communities, as users investigated the band's past and highlighted

---

[65] Jenkins, 'Confronting the Challenges of Participatory Culture,' 20.
[66] Gabriela Vatu, 'Spotify Tells You Which Song Would Save You From Vecna in Stranger Things,' *MUO*, 1 July 2022, at https://www.makeuseof.com/which-spotify-song-save-you-from-stranger-things-vecna/; Tara Bitran, 'These Are The Songs That Would Save You from Vecna,' *Netflix Tudum*, 29 June 2022, at https://www.netflix.com/tudum/articles/stranger-things-vecna-spotify-personalized-playlist; Evelyn Lau, 'Upside Down Spotify Playlist: The Songs To Save You From "Stranger Things" Villain Vecna,' *The National*, 1 July 2022, at https://www.thenationalnews.com/arts-culture/music/2022/07/01/upside-down-spotify-playlist-the-songs-to-save-you-from-stranger-things-villain-vecna/.

**Figure 0.7a and b** Eddie plays Metallica's "Master of Puppets" (1984) in *Stranger Things* (The Duffer Brothers / Netflix, Series 4 2022).

several problematic incidents.[67] One highly visible user, Serena Trueblood, produced a video alleging several racist incidents in their past and kickstarted a negative response to their representation of a heterosexual and white *status quo*. And yet, despite this backlash, the band's social capital, combined with their appearance in a highly popular TV series, allowed them to weather the storm in ways that are unusual today.

Later in this book, several of our authors dig into the online afterlife of artists and songs to explore how fandom can rejuvenate, but also reimagine creative work and artistic personae by confounding the boundaries between PGC and UGC. In her pioneering work on YouTube, Jean Burgess explains that 'any particular video produces cultural value to the extent that it acts as a hub for further creative activity by a wide range of participants in this social network – that is, the extent to which it contributes to what Jonathan Zittrain might call YouTube's "generative qualities"'.[68] In her chapter here, Lisa Perrott, as a self-confessed 'aca-fan', shares her research into YouTube's generative content dedicated to the life and work of David Bowie.[69] Her analysis of the 'deep-fan' work of YouTube user Nacho reveals how the fan labour of recovering, restoring and editing lost footage of Bowie since his death in 2016 negotiates a complicated and collaborative interaction between nostalgia and reality, and immediacy and hypermediacy, which makes use of YouTube's potential for 'hackability' and 'remixability'.

In his chapter on para-adaptation, Henrik Smith Sivertsen takes a different approach to the musical afterlife of songs. Although Perrott focuses on the

---

[67] Liz Scarlett, with contributions from Merlin Alderslade, 'Why Are Some Stranger Things Fans Now Trying To "Cancel" Metallica?', *Metal Hammer*, 9 August 2022, at https://www.loudersound.com/news/why-are-some-stranger-things-fans-now-trying-to-cancel-metallica.
[68] Jonathan Zittrain, *The Future of the Internet and How to Stop It* (New Haven: Yale University Press, 2008).
[69] Jenkins, *Textual Poachers*.

creation of new work from pre-existent footage, Smith Sivertsen employs Internet archiving techniques to investigate how 'musical versioning practices' can generate virality. His research traces one particular song – Lukas Graham's '7 Years' (2019) – through its YouTube reiterations as fan footage, rewrite covers, cover versions, lyric videos, translations and parodies. His work shows how the platform has become a significant portal for both the creative remediation and archiving of all kinds of contemporary musicking. This double existence calls for a rethink of the concept of the reference original – a cover version that becomes the launchpad for subsequent versions, as we saw happening to the song 'Call Your Girlfriend' above. And yet, the 'generative qualities' of YouTube also create archiving issues for contemporary sonic remediation.

YouTube's multifaceted remediation of sonic nostalgia can also be seen in its reaction videos, which, whether produced by major magazines, music labels or enthusiastic fans, return millions of search results and generate their own subcommunities based on their style or genre. The 'kids react' category, for instance, exposes children to iconic musicians who were active decades before their birth, such as Nirvana or Queen, and offers a unique take on how YouTube can recycle PGC. In terms of *reviralization*, reaction videos work in one of two ways: the reaction to a popular video causes the music used to go viral, causing a renewed surge of interest in a song, band or musician; or a specific reaction to a song can itself become viral, becoming the reference original for memes and other audiovisual content. Here, Michael Goddard examines reaction channels managed by African-American creators, which includes rock genres previously coded as white by both musicians and audiences. In his chapter, Goddard shows how the digital remediation of music, where audiences can interact and re-live previous experiences with familiar musical material, reveals the affective labour of the YouTubers in renegotiating and translating music across cultural contexts. The reaction videos he analyses are examples of the boundary destabilization between YouTube's 'UGC and UCC' (Dijck) discussed by Holly above.

YouTube, then, is more than an audiovisual repository: it is a (musical) social network that can help to destabilize cultural barriers. Community creation takes place through shared *affective* experiences of interacting with and listening to musical content. While writing this Introduction, we received an email from YouTube stating that soon all of us would be able to choose our own nickname or handle. This new form of identification, it promised, will allow users to find and interact with channels in a more social way: 'For many creators, YouTube isn't just a place to upload and comment on videos, it's a community and home base. That's why today we're introducing handles, a new way for people to easily find and engage with creators and each other on YouTube. Every channel will have a unique handle, making it easier for fans to discover content and interact with creators they love.'[70] These elements of interactivity – similar to those found on other social media platforms, such as Instagram or Twitter – are designed to strengthen the community *feel* of YouTube and encourage users to converge on specific videos, shorts or channels. And yet, as Emily Thomas points out in her chapter in our companion book, YouTube does not operate in isolation but is part of the interconnected universe of social media, something demonstrated in the multiplatform world of MONTERO, in which Lil Nas X tapped into the spreadability of meme culture by using YouTube to remediate and parody his own official work, while simultaneously engaging with the specificities of TikTok, Instagram and Twitter as the iterative material moved across platforms.[71] Here, Edward Katrak Spencer focuses on similar forms of sonic virality, contagion and replication in his chapter on the social potential of YouTube's sonic remediations, using bass drop memes, such as the Harlem Shake and trolling repertoires to show how the movement of small musical fragments across the Internet can 'imitate and reconfigure' the social and cultural aesthetics of certain communities.

## (Re)mediating, (Re)valuating, (Re)appropriating, (Re)musicking

> [...] new digital media oscillate between immediacy and hypermediacy, between transparency and opacity. This oscillation is the key to understanding how a medium fashions its predecessors and other contemporary media. Although each medium promises to reform its predecessors by offering a more immediate or authentic experience, the promise of reform inevitably leads us to become aware of the new medium as a medium. Thus, immediacy leads to hypermediacy. The process of remediation makes us aware that all media are at one level a 'play of signs', [...] this process insists on the real, effective presence of media in our culture. Media have the same claim to reality as more tangible cultural artifacts; photographs, films, and computer applications are as real as airplanes and buildings.[72]

---

[70] YouTube, 'Introducing: YouTube Handles,' Email sent to the authors, 20 October 2022.
[71] Thomas, 'Quare(-in) the Mainstream.'
[72] Bolter and Grusin, *Remediation*, 17.

Today, the Internet is not only as 'real' as the airplanes that Bolter and Grusin refer to in their 1999 quote above, but is, for many of us, an omnipresent and indispensable part of our daily life and culture. YouTube, as a 'tangible cultural artifact' that fosters a sense of community, is an integral part of the (hyper)real and (hyper)immediate fabric of online and offline culture. And yet, although the platform is marketed as a universal resource, to navigate through its search engines, playlists and billions of hours of content requires a degree of media literacy, a reliable Internet connection, access to technology, an able body and a location that doesn't perform censorship. In our last book, we noted the global structural and economic inequalities that the Internet poses, and how the 'participation gap' observed by Jenkins challenges YouTube's claims that it affords a democratized creative space.[73] In her work on the signed-song videos of Beyoncé's music, Áine Mangaoang draws attention to the 'participation gap' experienced by global deaf, hearing-loss communities. Noting the 'importance of embodied expression', she calls for a more inclusive, democratic and egalitarian networked space.[74] Later in this book, Joana Freitas' work on the spaces of YouTube's echo chambers, exposes a different reading of online community building. Her chapter shows how YouTube communities form around the idea of a musical genre – in this case the 'epic' genre – and how this reflects the convergent culture associated with today's audiovisual content. In certain cases, user-generated epic music videos can reflect outdated views on gender in a way that ultimately reinforces the mechanisms of power and patriarchal domination related to musical discourse.

While engaging with the darker side of YouTube's affordances, it is nevertheless possible to find rich possibilities for creativity across the platform. Here, Christine Boone and Brian Drawert discuss how new technologies, such as Artificial Intelligence (AI), have enabled refreshed forms of audiovisual mashup, which, although not directly tackling issues of inequality and in-accessibility, nonetheless offer users the tools to remediate and recombine sonic content in creative, and sometimes political, ways: 'the role of YouTube in this is the same as that of the mashup artist: user-created content, and a platform that is accessible to almost everyone, democratizes the role of the artist and gives everyone the potential to create – with or without AI.' While Boone and Drawert focus on the positives of

---

[73] Jenkins, 'Confronting the Challenges of Participatory Culture'; Rogers, 'Welcome to your world.'
[74] The almost-complete oral presentation by Mangaoang can be accessed here: CysMus – CESEM, 'Day 1 • Part 1 (Morning),' *YouTube video*, 01:44:21, 1 October 2020, https://youtu.be/nd75h4c2Twc.

new media and its ability to include voices from different contexts and backgrounds in the current flow of creative production, the multinational research team, Olu Jenzen, Itir Erhart, Hande Eslen-Ziya, Derya Güçdemir, Umut Korkut and Aidan McGarry investigate the role of YouTube in drawing together protest-oriented communities, which use music as a political tool. In their chapter on the Gezi Park protests, which took place in Turkey in 2013, the authors analyse how YouTube was used 'as a platform for protest communication' in the form of online music videos that became sites of digital activism.

Investigating YouTube's place within social media platforms, Holly Rogers approaches these potentialities from a more DIY perspective in her chapter on networked soundscape composition. With a focus on compositional practice that lies beyond the realms of traditional music education, she traces chains of sonic manipulation to show how creativity often moves between platforms while incorporating the specificities of each:

> The platform now sits within a tightly connected nexus of post-media potentialities, its content spreading across social media sites and out into everyday life [...] it continues to provide ample raw material for composers to play with; and with well-established algorithms, search engines and communities, material can easily be passed between users. When uploaded, tags and comments provide a useful way to link between remixed works. Yet significantly, YouTube also acts as a vital conduit between various existing and bespoke online platforms.

Like the transmedial spread of Lil Nas X's MONTERO, the collaborative chains of interpretation embedded in online soundscape practices discussed by Rogers remediate both the real world and subsequent creative interpretations of it. This consistent repetition, recycling and circulation of content, points out Jonas Wolf in his chapter on ironic distance and networked composition, '(...) constituents of the productive conditions of possibility regarding discursive formations of musical vernaculars, which serve to integrate socio-aesthetics and ethe into subcultural everyday communication and creativity.' From mainstream styles to the niche genres that Wolf delves into – including SoundCloud rap, vaporwave and mumble rap – YouTube and its reach towards other media platforms also promotes a creative interchangeability between different aural aesthetics, cultural influences and dialogues, and juxtaposes mixed, mashed up, original and remixed content. These processes of social media remediation alter definitions of originality, with the spectrum ranging from 'new' or 'created from scratch' to 'yet another copied copy', which in turn raises issues of authorship and copyright.

What material can be remixed or collaged on YouTube and how? Who retains authorship in mashups and fanvids, and how does the diversification of voice trouble clear processes of monetization and control?

Digital technology has always posed a significant threat to the record industry, as Jim Rogers explains: 'The unauthorized use of copyrighted material is undermining the record industry's ability to make money and has produced a "crisis" for a sector that had grown exponentially on the back of the CD-boom.'[75] As a result, strict permission laws developed around the sharing, dissemination and reuse of music. In his work on remix culture, Lawrence Lessig shows how textual quotation and adaptation are permitted, within certain parameters of fair use and citation, in academic work and literature, and yet the sampling of music, without authorization, violates strict copyright laws.[76] With the emergence of MP3 files and tools to replicate CDs at home, the fight against copying and piracy has become a major concern for musicians and labels. The easy circulation of music online has amplified the music industry's 'crisis' of regulation, as Siva Vaidhyanathan explains: within the legal field of intellectual property, copyright law 'encourages the dissemination of creative and informative work' while aiming to protect its creators and authors; ultimately copyright laws become a '(…) common and unavoidable practice that affect daily life and commerce around the world'.[77]

In the audiovisual arena of YouTube, with its constant and viral sonic remediations, the rules of music and moving image permissions can be difficult to navigate. Juan Bermudez tackles these issues in his ethnographic research into cross-platform musicking. With a focus on flashmob dances that move across YouTube, TikTok and Instagram, his chapter reveals how the nexus of interconnected practices shared by platforms, artists and labels complicates the virality and spreadibility of sonic imitation. When social media users use viral song fragments as a backdrop for their videos, they rarely credit the original source, and this can throw up legal issues. In 2009, the murky terrain of music copyright was thrown into relief when Calvin Harris's new music video, 'Ready for the Weekend', which he had uploaded to his YouTube channel, was removed after a copyright claim was launched against it. 'IT'S MY F**KING SONG YOU ABSOLUTE BASTARDS. This

---

[75] Jim Rogers, *The Death and Life of the Music Industry in the Digital Age* (New York: Bloomsbury, 2013), 4.
[76] Lawrence Lessig, *Remix: Making Art and Commerce Thrive in the Hybrid Economy* (London: Penguin Books, 2009).
[77] Siva Vaidhyanathan, *Intellectual Property: A Very Short Introduction* (Oxford, New York: Oxford University Press, 2017), 11–12.

is enough to tip me over the edge, I'm not joking. There are videos up there that other people have uploaded of the same song, and they haven't been removed!? But mine does!', he raged on his Twitter account.[78] Although this error shows how confusing YouTube's copyright laws can be for whole songs, the remediation of fragments can also incur copyright, even if the material undergoes significant transformation. What material can be remixed or collaged on YouTube and how? Who retains authorship in mashups and fanvids, and how does the diversification of voice trouble clear processes of monetization and control?

After it was bought by Google in 2006, YouTube introduced strict regulation and control mechanisms. Video ID was brought in, enabling rights holders – mainly companies and media agents – to either block, promote, or, through a partnership, monetize particular content. In 2010, the technological developments that allowed more refined identification and filtering led to the current iteration of Content ID, which includes both audio and video, and maintains the same options for the 'original' rights holders. Given that one of the dominant categories of YouTube is music, and that its main activity revolves around music videos, the company has taken responsibility for implementing copyright mechanisms in order, above all else, to protect major music companies and record labels. Before YouTube was purchased by Google, the free use of copyrighted songs on the platform wasn't an issue for companies; however, as Jin Kim explains, by 2011, five years after Google bought YouTube, '72 out of the top 100 all-time popular YouTube clips are music videos, which are mostly copyrighted and provided by major music labels.'[79] Within YouTube's mediascape of UGC, these companies also want to claim the copyright 'even for amateur users' singing their songs or the use of portions of their songs in home videos'.[80] We experienced the regulation process ourselves when editing footage of a conference attended by many of our contributors.[81] Most participants used YouTube clips during their presentations and, when we tried to upload the talks to YouTube, almost every segment was flagged as copyright infringement. After being given the option to replace the sound with a free-to-use track from YouTube's own library or to simply remove the sound, we had to heavily re-edit the videos to get through the platform's stringent filters.

---

[78] Calvin Harris, Twitter Post, 23 July 2009.
[79] Jin Kim, 'The Institutionalization of YouTube: From User-Generated Content To Professionally Generated Content,' *Media, Culture & Society* 34, no. 1 (1 January 2012): 55.
[80] Ibid.
[81] International Conference *Like, Share and Subscribe: Youtube, Music and Cyber-Culture Before and After The New Decade*, Lisbon, 1–3 October 2022.

But there are ways around this. In her chapter, Júlia Durand draws our attention to royalty-free music, or library music, which she calls the 'soundtrack of YouTube'. Vast databases of ready-to-use music are available in commercial catalogues, which are either accessible through affordable licenses or for free under Creative Commons licenses. Durand's analysis of the ways in which composers and videographers use these catalogues reveals how well-established musical stereotypes can be reused or reappropriated to gather specific vocabularies for YouTubers.

When one of the Sidemen YouTubers cried out, 'I feel like I've heard it before,' then, he captured one of the fundamental aesthetics of YouTube. The platform's emphasis on 'remixability' and its blurring of 'UGC and UCC' has opened up new possibilities for the remediation of sound that sends sonic echoes and fragments ricocheting through its many long tails. The following chapters in this book develop the research presented in our companion text to explore what it means to have heard something before. Our authors consider the spreadibility and remediation of sound through a variety of YouTube's most popular forms, including memes, fanvids, cover songs, protest videos, mashups, reaction videos and flashmobs. YouTube's extraordinary range of users, tools and (co)creative possibilities not only provides an incessant flow of resources, but also reinforces the idea that cybercommunities perform vital and energizing interventions into the ways in which music and sound are created, disseminated and engaged with in the twenty-first century.

## Bibliography

Anderson, Chris. 'The Long Tail,' *Wired* 12 (2004), at https://www.wired.com/2004/10/tail/.

Beaumont-Thomas, Ben. 'Kate Bush Earns First Ever US Top 10 Hit with Running Up That Hill,' *The Guardian*, 7 June 2022, at https://www.theguardian.com/music/2022/jun/07/kate-bush-earns-first-us-top-10-hit-running-up-that-hill-stranger-things.

Bitran, Tara. 'These Are The Songs That Would Save You from Vecna,' *Netflix Tudum*, 29 June 2022, at https://www.netflix.com/tudum/articles/stranger-things-vecna-spotify-personalized-playlist.

Bolter, Jay David and Richard Grusin. *Remediation: Understanding New Media*. Boston: MIT Press, 2000.

Born, Georgia and Christopher Haworth. 'Music and Intermediality After the Internet: Aesthetics, Materialities and Social Forms.' In *Music and Digital Media: Towards a Planetary Anthropology*, edited by Georgia Born, 378–438. London: UCL Press, 2022.

Bruns, Axel. *Blogs, Wikipedia, Second Life and Beyond: From Production to Produsage.* New York: Peter Lang Publishing, 2008.

Bruns, Axel. 'Produsage: A Working Definition.' *Produsage.org*, December 2009, at https://produsage.org/node/9.

Burgess, Jean. '"All Your Chocolate Rain Are Belonging to Us?": Viral Video, YouTube and the Dynamics of Participatory Culture.' In *Art in the Global Present*, edited by Nikos Papastergiadis and Victoria Lynn, 86–96. Broadway: UTS ePRESS, 2014.

Cayari, Christopher. 'The YouTube Effect: How YouTube has Provided New Ways to Consume, Create, and Share Music.' *International Journal of Education & the Arts* 12, no. 6 (2011): 1–30.

Cenciarelli, Carlo. 'Warped Singing': Opera From Cinema to YouTube.' In *Verdi on Screen*, edited by Delphine Vincent, 251–67. Lausanne: L'Age d'Homme, 2015.

Constandinides, Costas. '"You Just Got Covered": YouTube Cover Song Videos as Examples of Para-Adaptation.' In *Adaptation in the Age of Media Convergence*, edited by Johannes Fehrle and Werner Schäfke-Zell, 111–32. Amsterdam: Amsterdam University Press, 2019.

Coppa, Francesca. 'Women, *Star Trek* and the Early Development of Fannish Vidding.' *Transformative Works and Cultures* 1 (2008): at https://journal.transformativeworks.org/index.php/twc/article/view/44/64.

Demers, Joanna. 'Sampling the 1970s in Hip-Hop.' *Popular Music* 22, no. 1 (2003): 41–56.

Dijck, José van. *The Culture of Connectivity: A Critical History of Social Media.* Oxford: Oxford University Press, 2013.

DiNucci, Darcy. 'Fragmented Future.' *Print Magazine* 53, no. 4 (April 1999): 221–2.

Gaunt, Kyra D. 'YouTube, Twerking & You: Context Collapse and the Handheld Co-Presence of Black Girls and Miley Cyrus.' *Journal of Popular Music Studies* 27, no. 3 (2015): 244–73.

Grusin, Richard. 'YouTube at the End of New Media.' In *The YouTube Reader*, edited by Pelle Snickars and Patrick Vonderau, 98–105. New York: Columbia University Press, 2010.

Jenkins, Henry, Sam Ford and Joshua Green. *Spreadable Media: Creating Value and Meaning in a Networked Culture.* New York; London: New York University Press, 2013.

Jenkins, Henry. 'Confronting the Challenges of Participatory Culture: Media Education for the 21st Century (Part One).' *Nordic Journal of Digital Literacy* 2, no. 1 (2007): 23–33.

Jenkins, Henry. *Confronting the Challenges of Participatory Culture: Media Education for the 21st Century.* Cambridge, MA: The MIT Press, 2009.

Jenkins, Henry. *Textual Poachers: Television Fans and Participatory Culture.* New York: Routledge, 1992.

Jones, Ellis. *DIY Music and the Politics of Social Media.* London: Bloomsbury Publishing, 2020.

Kearney, Mary Celeste. *Girls Make Media*. London: Routledge, 2006.

Kim, Jin. 'The Institutionalization of YouTube: From User-Generated Content to Professionally Generated Content.' *Media, Culture & Society* 34, no. 1 (2012): 53–67.

Korsgaard, Mathias. *Music Video After MTV: Audiovisual Studies, New Media, and Popular Music*. London: Routledge, 2017.

Kramer, Jonathan D. 'Postmodern Concepts of Musical Time.' *Indiana Theory Review* 17, no. 2 (2012): 21–60.

Langford, Jackson. 'Director of FKA twigs' "Cellophane" Video Responds to Similarities in Lil Nas X's "Montero" Video.' *NME*, 29 March 2021, at https://www.nme.com/news/music/director-of-fka-twigs-cellophane-video-responds-to-similarities-in-lil-nas-xs-montero-video-2909922.

Lau, Evelyn. 'Upside Down Spotify Playlist: The Songs to Save You from "Stranger Things" Villain Vecna'. *The National*, 1 July 2022, at https://www.thenationalnews.com/arts-culture/music/2022/07/01/upside-down-spotify-playlist-the-songs-to-save-you-from-stranger-things-villain-vecna/.

Lessig, Lawrence. *Remix: Making Art and Commerce Thrive in the Hybrid Economy*. London: Penguin Books, 2009.

Lyotard, Jean-François. *The Postmodern Condition: A Report on Knowledge*. Manchester: Manchester University Press, 1979.

Mandiberg, Michael (ed.). *The Social Media Reader*. New York and London: New York University Press, 2012.

Manovich, Lev. 'The Practice of Everyday (Media) Life: From Mass Consumption to Mass Cultural Production?' In *Video Vortex Reader: Responses to YouTube*, edited by Geert Lovink and Sabine Niederer, 33–44. Amsterdam: Institute of Network Cultures, 2008.

McLuhan, Marshall. *Understanding Media: The Extensions of Man*. New York: McGraw-Hill, 1964.

Metzer, David. *Quotation and Cultural Meaning in Twentieth-Century Music*. Cambridge: Cambridge University Press, 2003.

Pough, Gwendolyn D. *Check it While I Wreck It: Black Womanhood, Hip-Hop Culture and the Public Sphere*. Boston: Northeastern University Press, 2004.

Reynolds, Simon. *Retromania: Pop Culture's Addiction to its Own Past*. London, Faber & Faber: 2012.

Rogers, Holly. '"Welcome to your world": YouTube and the Reconfiguration of Music's Gatekeepers.' In *YouTube and Music: Online Culture and Everyday Life*, edited by Holly Rogers, Joana Freitas and João Francisco Porfírio, 1–32. New York: Bloomsbury Academic, 2023.

Rogers, Holly. 'Instruments.' In Tom Perchard, Stephen Graham, Tim Rutherford-Johnson and Holly Rogers, *Twentieth Century Music in the West: An Introduction*, 202–26. Cambridge: Cambridge University Press, 2022.

Rogers, Holly. *Sounding the Gallery: Video and the Rise of Art-Music*. Oxford: Oxford University Press, 2013.

Rogers, Jim. *The Death and Life of the Music Industry in the Digital Age*. New York: Bloomsbury, 2013.

Rosen, Jay. 'The People Formerly Known as the Audience.' In *The Social Media Reader*, edited by Michael Mandiberg, 13–16. New York and London: New York University Press, 2012.

Scarlett, Liz. 'Why Are Some Stranger Things Fans Now Trying to "cancel" Metallica?' *Metal Hammer*, 9 August 2022, at https://www.loudersound.com/news/why-are-some-stranger-things-fans-now-trying-to-cancel-metallica.

Thomas, Emily. 'Quare(-in) the Mainstream: YouTube, Social Media and Augmented Realities in Lil Nas X's *MONTERO*.' In *YouTube and Music: Online Culture and Everyday Life*, edited by Holly Rogers, Joana Freitas and João Francisco Porfírio, 65–89. New York: Bloomsbury Academic, 2023.

Turk, Tisha. '"Your Own Imagination": Vidding and Vidwatching as Collaborative Interpretation.' *Film and Film Culture* 5 (2020): 95–6.

Turk, Tisha. 'Transformation in a New Key: Music in Vids and Vidding.' *Music, Sound, and the Moving Image* 9, no. 2 (2015): 163–76.

Vaidhyanathan, Siva. *Intellectual Property: A Very Short Introduction*. Oxford, New York: Oxford University Press, 2017.

Vatu, Gabriela. 'Spotify Tells You Which Song Would Save You From Vecna in Stranger Things.' *MUO*, 1 July 2022, at https://www.makeuseof.com/which-spotify-song-save-you-from-stranger-things-vecna/.

Vernallis, Carol, Laura McLaren, Virginia Kuhn and Martin P. Rossouw. 'm ☺ Re tH@n WorD$: Aspects and Appeals of the Lyric Video.' In *YouTube and Music: Online Culture and Everyday Life*, edited by Holly Rogers, Joana Freitas and João Francisco Porfírio, 149–68. New York: Bloomsbury Academic, 2023.

Vernallis, Carol. *Unruly Media: YouTube, Music Video and the New Digital Cinema*. Oxford: Oxford University Press, 2013.

Wise, Jason. 'How Many Videos are Uploaded to YouTube in 2022?' *Earthweb*, 15 October 2022, at https://earthweb.com/how-many-videos-are-uploaded-to-youtube-a-day/.

# 1

# 'Technology Allows More People to do Things': Artificial Intelligence, Mashups and Online Musical Creativity

Christine Boone and Brian Drawert

The recent rise in popularity and sophistication of AI has many musicians wondering how long until these computer algorithms replace humans in the creation of new music? Will tomorrow's musicians be competing with robots for the top of the Billboard charts? Although AI tools to create entirely original music currently exist (and have existed for more than half a century), the general rise in popularity of AI has recently brought this concept to the forefront of the public mind.[1] In this chapter we explore the concept of AI-created art with regard to a single genre of music: mashups. A mashup is a new song created by blending two or more pre-recorded songs. The most common type of mashup (an A+B mashup) is made by layering the vocal track of one song over the instrumental track of another, and changing the tempo and key of one or both songs as necessary. Most mashups are made from popular songs and depend upon the listener being able to recognize the songs used in their construction.[2] The most acclaimed mashups (by both music critics and fans) are those that contain a 'genre clash'; this means mixing two artists who perform very different types of music and would never be found on an actual stage together. A mashup

---

[1] Prafulla Dhariwal, Heewoo Jun, Christine Payne, Jong Wook Kim, Alec Radford and Ilya Sutskever, 'Jukebox: A Generative Model for Music,' *ArXiv:2005.00341* (2020), at https://arxiv.org/abs/2005.00341; Lejaren A. Hiller, Jr. and Leonard M. Isaacson, 'Musical Composition with a High-Speed Digital Computer,' *Journal of the Audio Engineering Society* 6, no. 3 (July 1958): 154–60.

[2] Christine Boone, 'Mashing: Toward a Typology of Recycled Music,' *Music Theory Online* 19, no. 3 (2013): 1–14.

that contains a genre clash often reveals hidden similarities between two disparate artists, and is also often humorous to the listener.

YouTube is a particularly interesting platform to investigate mashups, for three reasons. Firstly, mashups became popular in the twenty-first century because of the democratization of digital music editing technology. The earliest versions of mashups were made a decade earlier, but only professional musicians had access to the kind of technology that was necessary to make them. Cheap (or free), easily accessible software is what allows the vast majority of people to make mashups on their personal computers. This is also the main purpose of YouTube: anyone can be a creator, and anyone's creation can go viral. Secondly, YouTube seems to be supporting some mashup creators by not taking down their work. DJ Cummerbund, for example, has more than 227,000 subscribers to his YouTube channel, where he has posted hundreds of mashups, all of which are technically illegal.[3] Finally, YouTube is so easily sharable between users; links can be embedded on social media sites or sent directly in text messages. Since mashups aren't played on the radio or on streaming music services (and the mashup websites of the early 2000s are mostly defunct now), sharing direct links to tracks is the most common way that they are shared between listeners in the early 2020s.

There are many different computer algorithms and methods that are currently known as AI, however we are going to focus on a specific algorithm that has been successfully used to make creative artwork: the Generative Adversarial Network (GAN). One application of GANs that has made news recently in the creation of new (potentially artistic) content, is its ability to create realistic faces of people that do not exist in real life. By using data (photos) from actual human faces, the website Stylebreeder uses a GAN to create new, mashed up images of fictional faces.[4] Stylebreeder, whose URL is *thispersondoesnotexist.com*, generates a new face with each page refresh. This type of technology has become newsworthy during a time when deepfakes have the potential to sway public opinion by creating alternate realities.[5] Although this class of AI methods is relatively good

---

[3] DJ Cummerbund's YouTube Channel is here: https://www.youtube.com/channel/UC-_SoG6x0XvcQRgQEh7Ce9Q/videos.

[4] Rachel Metz, 'These People Do Not Exist. Why Websites Are Churning Out Fake Images of People (and Cats),' *CNN Business* (28 February 2019), at https://www.cnn.com/2019/02/28/tech/ai-fake-faces/index.html.

[5] It is worth noting that counter to many predictions, only a few deepfake videos were produced to influence the 2020 US presidential election. Unfortunately, 'simple deceptions like selective editing or outright lies have worked just fine.' Tim Mak and Dina Temple-Raston, 'Where Are The Deepfakes In This Presidential Election?,' *Morning Edition* (NPR, 1 October 2020), at https://www.npr.org/2020/10/01/918223033/where-are-the-deepfakes-in-this-presidential-election.)

at creating composited human faces, it is not foolproof. This same GAN was used to generate images of cats by compositing images of other cats on the website *thiscatdoesnotexist.com*. Although many artificially created cats appear realistic, there are a number of 'fails' (creations that do not look like a cat) and many of them look very disturbing.[6] The most likely reason for these 'fails' is that most of the stock human faces that the GAN is using as inputs are taken from a relatively straight-ahead perspective, while the stock photos of cats include cats in many poses and positions, making it harder to generate composite images without unsettling errors. In other words, although GANs *model* human thought processes, they are not actual humans – they need a specific kind of input data and training. Computers are still not able to independently extrapolate and analyse new data when it is presented in an unfamiliar format. One of the ways that less tech-savvy people became aware of GAN websites was through YouTube videos. YouTube creators have gone to these websites and compiled their results into explanatory videos, videos of people looking for fails and even videos of people finding a fictional person that looks exactly like them!

Machine learning algorithms generally operate by feeding in training data, which the algorithm uses to learn what is a good result. This process is supervised and managed by the operator until the algorithm is able to work correctly according to the specifications it was built for. Once that is done, testing data is fed to the algorithm to validate that it is working correctly. A GAN is a specific type of machine learning algorithm with two parts: a Generator and a Discriminator. The Generator creates 'random data' that is similar to the training data (i.e. image or audio data); the data created is a series of combinations and transformations applied to the original training set. For images, this could be random combinations of images from a large image archive with random effects (such as colour transformations) applied to them. For audio, the 'random data' could be arbitrary clips from a database of songs with random effects (for example, pitch/tempo changes) applied. The Discriminator part of the GAN takes that 'random data' and tries to determine if the data is 'real' or 'fake', based on what it has seen before in the training phase. Since GANs use two neural networks, they must be trained alternately. First, the operator holds the Generator constant and trains the Discriminator to recognize the difference between a database of real images and

---

[6] haunted_admin, '"This Cat Does Not Exist" Is Creating Horrifying AI-Generated Nightmare Fuel,' *Cheezburger Memebase* (blog), at https://cheezburger.com/7799813/this-cat-does-not-exist-is-creating-horrifying-ai-generated-nightmare-fuel.

a database of images created by the Generator. Then the operator holds the Discriminator constant and trains the Generator to create 'better' images until it can successfully fool the Discriminator into thinking its images are real. The process is then repeated, each time first training the Discriminator to recognize fake images from the new Generator, and then training the Generator to fool the new Discriminator, until the images the Generator produces are of sufficient quality, as determined by the human operator.

If AI can be used fairly reliably to create convincing images of nonexistent humans using pre-existing data, it follows that AI should also be able to produce musical mashups using pre-existing songs. The most scathing critiques of mashups tend to reference Theodor Adorno, pointing out that the modular nature of popular music makes it both simple and lazy to create a mashup.[7] Connoisseurs of the genre know that the process is usually more nuanced than critics claim, and that the best mashup creators are true artists, crafting genuinely original works using finished songs as raw material. Despite the clear artistry that goes into the production of high-quality mashups, for those who may still wonder if Adorno's argument holds water, one question still remains: can mashup construction be automated? Multiple teams are working to do just that. This chapter investigates three web-based platforms that claim to automatically generate mashups: the Magic iPod, YouTube DJ and Rave DJ. Additionally, we look into how YouTube plays a part in each of these platforms.

## The Magic iPod

The first website we came across that looked like it might be creating automated mashups was the Magic iPod. The 'iPod' in the title makes a reference to the fact that the heyday of the mashup has perhaps passed. Although the genre has not disappeared – in fact, it is now fully entrenched in our culture – it was *au courant* in the early 2000s, the age of the iPod. The website is also marked with the telling phrase, '2007 forever', on its tab (see Figure 1.1).[8]

There are twenty tracks on the left and a user can drag and drop any of them onto any one of the twenty-three tracks on the right, and an on-the-spot mashup

---

[7] For instance, Kembrew McLeod, 'Confessions of an Intellectual (Property): Danger Mouse, Mickey Mouse, Sonny Bono, and My Long and Winding Path as a Copyright Activist-Academic,' *Popular Music and Society* 28, no. 1 (2005): 86.
[8] Race Archibold, 'The Magic iPod,' at http://themagicipod.com/.

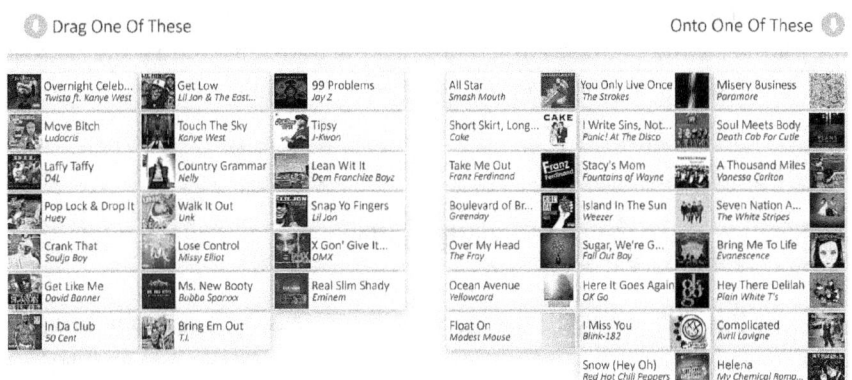

Figure 1.1 Screenshot of The Magic iPod. Used with permission by Race Archibold.

is made. The total number of combinations between twenty and twenty-three songs (assuming only two songs are being layered at one time) is 460, however, once a user begins to experiment, it becomes clear that things are a bit more limited than they first appear to be. When a user clicks on 'Move Bitch' (2000) by Ludacris, for example, only eight tracks on the other side of the screen become highlighted – it can't be combined with *any* of the twenty-three other songs. 'Move Bitch' can be mashed with 'All Star' (1999) by Smash Mouth, but not with 'Stacy's Mom' (2010) by Fountains of Wayne, for example. When one counts the actual mashing possibilities, as revealed by the highlighted tracks, there are only 151 potential matches that could result from the site. Still impressive, but not anywhere near the apparent 460. When a user drags 'Move Bitch' onto 'All Star', a track begins playing. Steve Harwell's familiar vocals begin, 'Somebody once told me the world is gonna roll me; I ain't the sharpest tool in the shed.' After the very next line, Harwell's voice is replaced by Ludacris: 'Move, bitch, get out the way!' This is a basic mashup that uses Smash Mouth's instrumentals, and vocals from both Smash Mouth and Ludacris. It is incredibly well-made, and it sounds great.

However, it turns out that this is not actually AI. The interactive format makes the user think that it might be, but an online magazine did an interview with Race Archibold, the creator of the Magic iPod, who reveals that, indeed, all 151 mashups were manually created in advance.[9] No beat matching or key adjustments are being made in real time. Regardless, this information should not

---

[9] Victor Luckerson, 'Meet the Man Behind the Magic iPod,' *The Ringer* (20 February 2017), at https://www.theringer.com/2017/2/20/16042438/meet-the-man-behind-the-magic-ipod-a79465631fb0.

diminish the site in any way. This website went viral in 2017, and the drag-and-drop format was doubtless a big part of its appeal. If Archibold had simply posted individual links to 151 of his mashups, it probably would not have been shared by nearly as many people.

## YouTube DJ

Next, we found the website YouTube DJ, which makes the connection between user-created content and YouTube explicit in its title. The site uses an interface that looks like an actual DJ setup: two turntables, a fader between them and individual volume controls for each turntable (see Figure 1.2).[10]

There is a search box over each turntable that is connected to YouTube, and when a user types into the search box, two options pop up for them to potentially check: 'Acapella' or 'Instrumental.' This makes it very clear that the software is mimicking what an actual DJ would do in a live situation. DJs often use special versions of songs (sometimes released by record companies and sometimes produced illegally) with isolated vocal tracks, called acapellas, and tracks where the vocals have been deleted, called instrumentals. Checking one or both of these boxes returns a YouTube search specifically for these types of tracks. It also

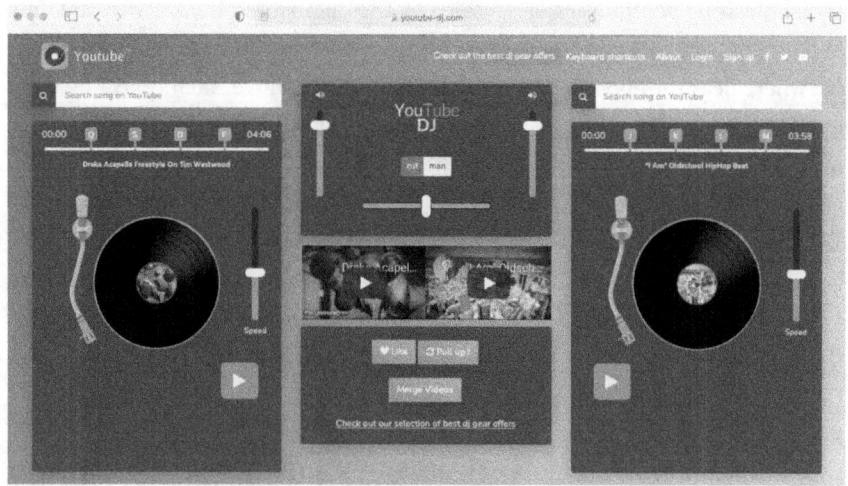

**Figure 1.2** Screenshot of YouTube DJ.

[10] Romain Malnoult, 'Youtube DJ,' at https://youtube-dj.com/.

reveals YouTube as a popular site where actual DJs search for tracks to work with for their sets; YouTubeDJ wouldn't be able to integrate with YouTube if there wasn't a wealth of search results to choose from. The site comes preloaded with an acapella of Drake doing a freestyle rap on a radio show (2010) on the left turntable and an instrumental called '"I Am" Oldschool HipHop Beat' (Blunted Beatz, 2014) on the right turntable. As would be expected from a demo track, these two mix together quite well, with no alterations necessary from the user. In order to make a mashup that fits together well, a user needs to consider two main aspects: beat matching and pitch matching. Two songs being mashed together need to either be at the same tempo, or in tempos with a 2:1 ratio. With regard to pitch and key, the simplest explanation is that two songs being mashed together should share as many pitches as possible. This often, but not always, means that they should be in the same key. There are other musical factors involved in making a good mashup, such as song form and phrasing, but these aren't involved in YouTube DJ.

Using the search feature, we found an acapella of Aretha Franklin singing '(You Make Me Feel like a) Natural Woman' (1968) and a recording of the breakbeat section of 'Funky Drummer' (1970) by James Brown that had been looped so that it lasted for ten hours. Early hip-hop DJs would loop drum break sections like this one from funk and soul records so that MCs could rap over these extended 'breakbeats'. Now digital recordings of these loops can be found on YouTube for current DJs to use. When these two tracks are played simultaneously, it becomes immediately apparent that they are not at the same tempo. Indeed, 'Funky Drummer' is at 100 beats per minute (BPM) and 'Natural Woman' is at 114 BPM. YouTubeDJ accounts for this incongruence by adding sliders to adjust for speed beside each turntable. However, the limitation here is that although the function is presented graphically as a slider, it does not actually adjust tempo in analogue.[11] There are discrete speeds at which you can play each record: 0.5, 0.75, 1 (normal speed), 1.25, 1.5 and 2. This means that the tempos for these two songs can never match; the options are not fine-tuned enough. For beats to line up for a mashup, the tempos can either be at 1:1 or 2:1 ratio.[12]

---

[11] The volume control and the fader between the two tracks are also presented as sliders and DO adjust in analogue. The speed playback feature is linked to YouTube's own playback features, which allows a user to adjust playback tempo at these same discrete speeds.

[12] Other ratios (4:1, 8:1, etc.) are mathematically possible, but mashup artists generally don't use these ratios when matching tempos, because it would mean that one or both of the songs used were at an unusually fast or slow tempo and wouldn't sound good to a listener.

100 and 114 won't be in either of those ratios with each other if only allowed to adjust to these certain discrete speeds. In order to make them match, a user would need to be able to adjust the tempo of 'Natural Woman' to 0.877 or 'Funky Drummer' to 1.14 speed, for instance, to make a 1:1 ratio.

As it turns out, YouTubeDJ is not powered by AI either. The website is not producing instrumental and acapella tracks; it is simply searching for them on YouTube. It is not choosing what songs it thinks will mash well together; a user decides that themselves. It is not doing any beat matching; the tempo 'slider' must be adjusted by the user to match beats and even then, the discrete intervals between speeds is quite limiting. Finally, this website does not adjust for pitch, either automatically or as controlled by the user. This means that it would be feasible to combine an acapella with a singer (singing a melody) with a breakbeat, but not an instrumental track with a bassline and chords (unless the vocal melody and the instrumental track happened to already fit together well without pitch alteration, which is possible, but very rare). If a user wanted an instrumental track with harmonies, they would do best to combine it with unpitched, rapped vocals, such as the acapella Drake track that the website uses as a demo. Like the Magic iPod, YouTubeDJ is still a great website, and the interface is fun and easy to use; it is just not an example of AI. It does, however, make use of YouTube's extensive music content and its specific search features. Embedding a platform that is made up of user-uploaded content into a website for user-created content makes the connection between these two websites, and the democratization of technology, explicit.

## Rave DJ

The final website we found that promised to create mashups automatically was Rave DJ. This website allows a user to input any number of songs from YouTube (or Spotify) and the site promises to mash them together using AI. A screenshot of its interface is presented as Figure 1.3.[13]

We randomly selected 'Caroline No' (1966) by the Beach Boys and 'Ride of the Valkyries' (1856) by Richard Wagner. The website selects words from each title to give the track a new mashed-up name; in this case, 'Beach of the Boys.' There are

---

[13] Rave, 'Rave DJ,' n.d., https://rave.dj/mix.

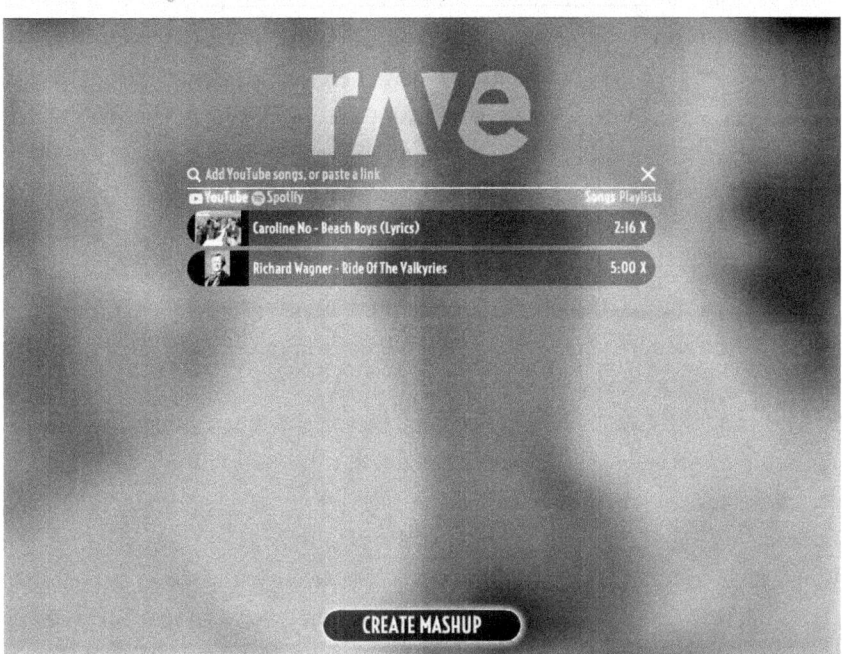

**Figure 1.3** Screenshot of Rave DJ.

significant differences between Rave DJ and the other two websites mentioned in this chapter. First, there is not a limited repertoire to choose from. A user can literally pick anything that exists on YouTube. This means that the resulting tracks cannot be premixed like with the Magic iPod; it is just not possible. Additionally, the user is not able to make any alterations for tempo, as with YouTube DJ. To be clear: tempo alterations *are* being made, but they are not in the control of the user; Rave DJ is actually AI and the AI does all of the work. 'Caroline No' is originally around 79 BPM; there are many recordings of 'Ride of the Valkyries', but the one we used is around 104 BPM. Rave DJ sped up the tempo of the Beach Boys' song for this mashup to match it to Wagner's. Rave DJ also adjusts for pitch automatically. 'Ride of the Valkyries' is originally in B minor and it has been transposed up a whole step, to C-sharp minor, for its inclusion in the mashup. Software can easily identify pitches that are present in songs, and we hypothesize that the goal of the software is to try and make the two songs share as many pitches as they can. 'Caroline No' is originally in F-sharp minor and is not adjusted for the mashup. It is not clear why the software chose to transpose

'Ride of the Valkyries' instead of 'Caroline No'. It could have transposed the second song down a whole step, which would have resulted in the same intervals when the songs were combined. The same question remains with the tempo adjustment as well. Why did it speed up 'Caroline No' instead of slow down 'Ride of the Valkyries'? We did an experiment where we inputted the same two songs in the opposite order and the result was exactly the same as the first mashup. So, the AI made a choice; but it is not clear what that choice was based on. In a personal interview, the CEO of Rave said that although he could not tell us precisely what factors the AI uses to make these decisions because of proprietary issues, he did confirm that it will make the same decision every time given the same input, regardless of the order of that input.[14]

The problem, though, is that the track that resulted from 'Caroline No' and 'Ride of the Valkyries' is not exactly definable as a mashup. It sounds very chaotic and does not hit many of the factors that listeners value when evaluating mashups.[15] One of the main reasons for this is that the tracks we chose to input were not an acapella and an instrumental – they were entire songs in their own right. The way that Rave DJ works is that the tracks that a user inputs are simply laid on top of one another and faded in and out. The website does not automatically isolate vocals from instrumentals; although it is possible to do this, it is very difficult to do consistently, which makes it almost impossible to automate (at least at this point in time). So, we did our second experiment using the same acapella and instrumental tracks that YouTube DJ used as its example tracks (preloaded on the interface): 'Drake Acapella Freestyle On Tim Westwood' and '"I Am" Oldschool HipHop Beat'. Drake's acapella is slightly inconsistent with regard to tempo, since it is completely acapella, but it settles in at around 77 BPM; the instrumental is around 91 BPM. Both YouTube DJ and Rave DJ sped up Drake's tempo to match the instrumental track, but Rave DJ (AI) adjusted the pitch of both tracks; while with YouTube DJ, even if the human who input these tracks had wanted to make pitch adjustments, they are not possible. Rave DJ's neural network decided to lower the pitch of the acapella track by a whole step – from A minor to G minor – and it also changed the pitch of Drake's voice (made it higher) as it sped up his track. It is easy for a human to hear that Drake is rapping, not singing, and that neither of these pitch adjustments were necessary. However, we do speak and rap on pitch! It may be more difficult for AI to detect

---

[14] Michael Pazaratz, Personal Interview (13 October 2021), 5.
[15] Boone, 'Mashing'.

the difference between singing and rapping than it is for humans, which might be why both tracks were transposed for the resulting track. It does indeed sound like a mashup, although not a great one. When Drake's voice is sped up *and* raised in pitch, he sounds a little bit like a chipmunk, and most mashup enthusiasts prefer a more natural sounding vocal, one that has not been audibly messed with.[16]

Next, we still wanted to try to help Rave DJ create something that sounds more like a traditional mashup using complete songs. To do this, we tried two songs that we know mash well together with very little adjustment. 'California Gurls' (2010) by Katy Perry and 'Tik Tok' (2009) by Ke$ha are already in the same key and the same tempo, and have essentially the same chord progression, instrumentation and texture. Because of these similarities, DJ Place Boing created a mashup in 2010 called 'Tik Tok and California Gurls are the same song?' An unusual aspect of this mashup is that DJ Place Boing lets both Katy Perry and Ke$ha sing lead, cutting quickly between their two voices. This results in mixed up sentences and incomplete words. DJ Place Boing may have chosen to jump between the two singers' voices like this in order to draw attention to the extreme similarity between the two songs.[17] He did not have to do much from a technical standpoint to get these songs to mash together well, so it seems like he overdid the jump-cutting on purpose to prove a particular point. Because of the pre-existing similarity between 'Tik Tok' and 'California Gurls', we put these two songs into Rave DJ, expecting a pleasing result. Indeed, the result passes a sort of auditory Turing test – it sounds like a mashup. In fact, it sounds more like a traditional mashup than DJ Place Boing's version, which was created by an actual human; it fits more of the characteristics that listeners value when assessing mashups.[18] These characteristics include beat matching, key/pitch matching, having recognizable source songs and maintaining a popular song form. Most importantly, the vocal interaction is incredibly different from putting in two random songs; there are even moments where Ke$ha is singing lead and Katy Perry is contributing backup vocals. This proves to be a successful mashup created by AI, although it took human knowledge to input two songs that allowed the AI to create something that sounded like a mashup.

---

[16] Jordan 'DJ Earworm' Roseman, *Audio Mashup Construction Kit* (Indianapolis: Wiley Publishing, Inc., 2007), 97.
[17] Christine Boone, 'Popular Song Remixed: Mashups, Aesthetic Transformation, and Resistance,' in *The Routledge Handbook of Remix Studies and the Digital Humanities*, ed. Eduardo Navas, Owen Gallagher and xtine burrough (New York: Routledge, 2021), 419–20.
[18] Boone, 'Mashing.'

Our final experiment with Rave DJ was to input two songs that work well when mashed together, but (unlike the previous example) require fine-tuning. We chose 'Jump' (1984) by Van Halen and 'Imagine' (1971) by John Lennon. These are the source songs for the existing mashup entitled 'Imagine a Jump' by DJ Mighty Mike. To make these two songs mash together effectively, DJ Mighty Mike sped up the tempo of 'Jump' to make the beats match with those of 'Imagine', but did not have to do any transposing as both source songs are already in the same key – C major. We put these two songs into Rave DJ and let the AI do its work. The outcome is not random; it is clear that AI has done some work here. First of all, the beats are matched, just as they were in the human-created version. But there is often too much happening at once. Since we are not using isolated vocals and instrumentals, the software fades between the two tracks, letting each take the lead occasionally. The problem is that there are still times when both John Lennon and David Lee Roth are singing lead vocals simultaneously; one is just louder than the other. The same thing happens with competing keyboard and piano riffs. And, despite the fact that both songs are in the same key, there are still moments when specific chords and pitches clash with each other. This example proves the point that DJ Earworm makes in his instructional manual. He basically implies that mashups need a human touch, or more specifically, a human ear, to judge what works and what does not.[19]

## Implications for Human Creativity

We were able to interview several members of the Rave DJ team: Mike Pazaratz (CEO), Matt Kirchhof (Developer) and Stefan Schneider (Developer), who shared that they have an in-house DJ that they use to help develop the neural networks that make Rave DJ work. However, they reported that the times that the software works best is when it does not work the way a human DJ would: 'I think that we are getting to a level whereby AI can make things that . . . are artistically valid, but no human being would ever consider them. [W]e've heard so many mashups that really no sane person would make and yet somehow they do work. . . . [I]t just took the bits, saw the opportunities and put it all together.'[20] Pazaratz continues, 'Sometimes it makes decisions that are rational and sometimes it makes brilliantly

---

[19] Roseman, *Audio Mashup Construction Kit*, 97.
[20] Pazaratz, Personal Interview, 2.

irrational decisions... And that's why even though we do have an in-house DJ, we learned pretty early on that just doggedly trying to do step by step what he does to get the same results is not only probably impossible, but maybe not even desirable.'[21] This result is because the GAN does not learn music and mashups like a person, rather, the Generator and Discriminator work against each other using a database of known good songs as examples. There are several reasons why this system will come up with songs that would be strange. Any database of songs must be inherently limited and thus the qualities or features of the 'real' songs would only be similar to those of the songs in the database. The Discriminator learns to make its own internal deciding factors on what is a 'real' song versus a 'fake' song, based on the limited database of known songs. The Generator takes random input, which could be very far from a normal input and thus as a result can search out creations that would be very far (intellectually) from what might be considered normal. Since the Discriminator is using its learned, artificial metrics on what is 'real' and 'fake', it can decide these strange creations are real, since they do have qualities that match those in the known song database, just not the qualities that are traditionally considered normal.

However, these AI-created works can teach us something about creativity. The randomness of these compositions could be thought of as akin to an avant-garde artist whose works are far from the norm. The works match all of our requirements of the genre (assuming we added them into the Discriminator), however no matter how well defined our criteria are, there will always be works that explicitly match our definition, but do not implicitly match. With random input, a Generator is able to sample the creative space far outside of what we could consider normal. We asked the Rave DJ team what they saw as the role of AI with regard to creativity and composition. They revealed that there are people out there who are currently DJing actual party gigs using Rave DJ. They know this because these people will get in contact with them in a panic when the website is down.[22] The developers say that Rave DJ and other types of AI can lower the barrier of entry for people who want to try to make mashups and DJ sets. The bottom line is that 'technology allows more people to do things'.[23] They note that even though it does not necessarily take a lot of money to create mashups anymore, the learning curve is steep. It takes a lot of practise to get good at mixing songs together: 'And so we

[21] Ibid., 10.
[22] Ibid.
[23] Ibid.

thought, what if we could just make a technology that allowed you to be creative?'[24] They also note that people who do make mashups on their own often use Rave DJ as a quick smoke test for whether or not two songs will sound good together, before putting in hours of work on their own. Some people fear that AI means the end of music composition, or the end of creativity. Mike Pazaratz disagrees: AI is not meant to usurp your creativity. It is meant to allow the other '99.9% of the population who can't do a given craft [to do it]'.[25] This draws a parallel with the democratization of technology that allowed mashups to become largely accessible during the early 2000s. Before this time, the technology needed to create mashups was prohibitively expensive and only people with a lot of resources could have experimented with this type of music (The Evolution Control Committee, for example, were pioneers of early digital mashups). With the advent of software with user-friendly interfaces and affordable prices, mashups became something that more people could try.[26] The decline of individual mashup-hosting websites and the advent of YouTube meant that there was a more centralized location for finding and uploading mashups. Adding AI to the mix has meant another step forward from the perspective of accessibility.

This chapter has shown that AI cannot, yet, produce convincing mashups with any sort of regularity. We have shown two examples of instances where it seemed like it could, but they were revealed to be either not AI, as in the case of the Magic iPod, or created with a very heavy human hand, as in the case of 'Tik Tok' and 'California Gurls'. Adorno's claims of a manufactured modular pop music also proved false, and it is for precisely this reason that good mashups are so pleasurable. It takes a clever composer to be able to put Van Halen and John Lennon together; someone who can imagine the possibility for combination and reveal hidden similarities between seemingly unrelated songs. But mashup-creating technology WILL get better. Automated isolation of vocal and instrumental tracks is not far out of reach. AI can already convincingly create newly-composed music that *does* pass an aural Turing test. Recently a new song was created based on the music of Nirvana, but perhaps the most convincing are computer-created chorales based on those of J.S. Bach.[27] However, Bach's chorales

---

[24] Ibid.
[25] Ibid., 13.
[26] Christine Emily Boone, 'Mashups: History, Legality, and Aesthetics' (Ph.D. Dissertation, University of Texas at Austin, 2011), 164.
[27] Kory Grow, 'In Computero: Hear How AI Software Wrote a "New" Nirvana Song,' *Rolling Stone* (2 April 2021), at https://www.rollingstone.com/music/music-features/nirvana-kurt-cobain-ai-song-1146444/.

form a finite set of information from a genre that is long dead and codified. Our own popular music is growing and changing; the hits of today do not sound like those of ten or twenty years ago. Our human hand keeps humanity in a genre, because once a genre becomes automatable, it could be considered dead. Within a few years, Rave DJ or something like it will be able to create convincing mashups using pop songs from a limited musical time period. This will not mean that popular music is dead, or that composers are out of a job. Rather, it remains the composer's job to create the work on the edges of genre as it continually grows and shifts. Perhaps composers of the future will be working with (not against) AI to produce works of art that would not be possible by humans or machines alone. The role of YouTube in this is the same as that of the mashup artist: user-created content, and a platform that is accessible to almost everyone, democratizes the role of the artist and gives everyone the potential to create – with or without AI.

## Bibliography

Boone, Christine. 'Mashing: Toward a Typology of Recycled Music.' *Music Theory Online* 19, no. 3 (2013): https://mtosmt.org/issues/mto.13.19.3/mto.13.19.3.boone.html.

———. 'Popular Song Remixed: Mashups, Aesthetic Transformation, and Resistance.' In *The Routledge Handbook of Remix Studies and the Digital Humanities*, edited by Eduardo Navas, Owen Gallagher and xtine burrough, 417–29. New York: Routledge, 2021.

Boone, Christine Emily. 'Mashups: History, Legality, and Aesthetics.' Ph.D. Dissertation, University of Texas at Austin, 2011.

Dhariwal, Prafulla, Heewoo Jun, Christine Payne, Jong Wook Kim, Alec Radford and Ilya Sutskever. 'Jukebox: A Generative Model for Music.' *ArXiv:2005.00341*, 30 April 2020.

Grow, Kory. 'In Computero: Hear How AI Software Wrote a "New" Nirvana Song.' *Rolling Stone*, 2 April 2021, at https://www.rollingstone.com/music/music-features/nirvana-kurt-cobain-ai-song-1146444/.

haunted_admin. '"This Cat Does Not Exist" Is Creating Horrifying AI-Generated Nightmare Fuel.' *Cheezburger Memebase* (blog), n.d. at https://cheezburger.com/7799813/this-cat-does-not-exist-is-creating-horrifying-ai-generated-nightmare-fuel.

Hiller, Jr., L. A., and L. M. Isaacson. 'Musical Composition with a High-Speed Digital Computer.' *Journal of Audio Engineering Society* 6, no 3 (1958): 154–60.

Luckerson, Victor. 'Meet the Man Behind the Magic IPod.' *The Ringer*, 20 February 2017, at https://www.theringer.com/2017/2/20/16042438/meet-the-man-behind-the-magic-ipod-a79465631fb0.

Mak, Tim and Dina Temple-Raston. 'Where Are The Deepfakes In This Presidential Election?' *Morning Edition*. NPR, 1 October 2020, at https://www.npr.org/2020/10/01/918223033/where-are-the-deepfakes-in-this-presidential-election.

McLeod, Kembrew. 'Confessions of an Intellectual (Property): Danger Mouse, Mickey Mouse, Sonny Bono, and My Long and Winding Path as a Copyright Activist-Academic.' *Popular Music and Society* 28, no. 1 (February 2005): 79–93.

Metz, Rachel. 'These People Do Not Exist. Why Websites Are Churning Out Fake Images of People (and Cats).' *CNN Business*, 28 February 2019, at https://www.cnn.com/2019/02/28/tech/ai-fake-faces/index.html.

Pazaratz, Michael, Stefan Schneider and Matthew Kirchhof. Personal Interview, 13 October 2021.

Roseman, Jordan. 'DJ Earworm.' *Audio Mashup Construction Kit*. Indianapolis: Wiley Publishing, Inc., 2007.

# 2

# From Contagion to Imitation: On Bass Drop Memes, Trolling Repertoires and the Legacy of Gabriel Tarde

Edward Katrak Spencer

**This Chapter Contains Offensive Language and Links to Obscene Web Content**

During the rise of Web 2.0, musical memes began to play a major role in reconfigurations of public consciousness via their online propagation and mediation.[1] From the early 'Hampster Dance' loop discussed by Paula Harper, to the John Coltrane 'Giant Steps' YouTube content discussed by Scott Spencer elsewhere in this book, to the recent iMarkkeyz Cardi B coronavirus remix, musical memes have powerful interpsychological functions and are attracting increasing scholarly attention.[2] In a basic sense, musical memes are catchy clips or soundbites

---

[1] The completion of this chapter was supported by the UKRI-funded project *Music and the Internet: Towards a Digital Sociology of Music* (AH/S00744X/1).
  As Georgina Born and Christopher Haworth explain, 'the shift from Web 1.0 to 2.0 is taken to signal a move from the web as a one-way information portal eliciting relatively passive uses to the web as a two-way participatory medium in which users actively supply content, exemplified by sites such as Wikipedia and YouTube.' Georgina Born and Christopher Haworth, 'From Microsound to Vaporwave: Internet-Mediated Musics, Online Methods, and Genre,' *Music and Letters* 98, no. 4 (2018): 644. Whereas Web 1.0 enabled physicists to share research papers, Web 2.0 has enabled users to share pictures of cute cats and to develop feline picture sites into billion-dollar franchises (in the case of *Lolcatz*). See Graham Meikle and Sherman Young, *Media Convergence: Networked Digital Media in Everyday Life* (Basingstoke: Palgrave Macmillan, 2011), 55.
[2] Paula Harper, 'Viral Musicking; Contagious Listening,' *84th Annual Meeting of the American Musicological Society* (San Antonio: Grand Hyatt Hotel, 2018); iMarkkeyz 2.0, 'iMarkkeyz – Cardi B Coronavirus Remix Video [FMOIG: @iMarkkeyz]', *YouTube video*, 00:01:01, 14 March 2020, https://www.youtube.com/watch?v=INaaafxb6EI. Scott Spencer, 'YouTube and the Making of a Musical Meme: How Video Mashups of John Coltrane's *Giant Steps* Became a Thing,' *Remediating Sound: Repeatable Culture, YouTube and Music*, ed. Holly Rogers, Joana Freitas and João Francisco Porfírio (New York: Routledge, 2023), 223–42.

that can be found in imitative and mostly audiovisual user-generated content (UGC), with YouTube being the most prominent 'breeding ground' for musical memes online. In some ways, music has always been a memetic medium, but its enmeshing with participatory culture on YouTube since 2005 necessitates careful reflection on issues of agency, sonification and sociality. Who are the web users responsible for the genesis and growth of musical memes on YouTube? What do these musical memes sound like and render audible? And how might we assemble a digital sociology of musical memes that intervenes in longstanding debates about the nature of memetics? Rather than relying on notions of virality, contagion and replication, I argue here that musical memes should be examined in terms of imitation practices and (anti)social trolling repertoires. Trolling is a key (sub) cultural logic that has come to define the lived experiences of many netizens during the first quarter of the twenty-first century, and musical memes are often the means through which various trolling practices take shape. These range from (relatively) harmless instances of joshing humour or banter ('kudos trolling'); to the sharing of absurd, inane, obscene or offensive memes for the sake of attention ('shitposting'); to strategies of deception and manipulation ('baiting', 'bait-and-switch'); to instances of deliberate antagonism, provocation and hate speech ('flaming', 'target trolling'). A paradigmatic example of bait-and-switch trolling is the practice known as 'Rickrolling', which involves the YouTube video for Rick Astley's song 'Never Gonna Give You Up' (1987)[3]; but musical memes have also been weaponized by the alt-right for the sake of political target trolling, while musical shitposting often foregrounds the sound of the digital age and its discontents.

In order to develop critical approaches to these various trolling repertoires, the chapter begins by considering the contested legacy of the French thinker Gabriel Tarde (1843–1904), a figure who has been hailed as the 'forefather' of memetics, notwithstanding the influence of Richard Dawkins (who coined the term 'meme' in his 1976 book *The Selfish Gene*).[4] The second half of the chapter develops a Tardean analysis of distinctive trolling repertoires by considering three bass drop memes. First, YouTube's sensational Harlem Shake meme from 2013 provides an example of competitive imitation by degree and an (anti)social trolling repertoire that I term *hooking*. Second, a 'mic drop' bass drop meme from the 'Great Meme War' of 2015 to 2016 can be understood in terms of imitation by sign and the

---

[3] Typically, users are enticed into clicking on a hyperlink that looks like it will lead them to what they are interested in, but instead the hyperlink directs them to the music video for 'Never Gonna Give You Up' on YouTube.
[4] Richard Dawkins, *The Selfish Gene* (Oxford: Oxford University Press 1976).

political trolling repertoire of *muting*. Third, a 2020 'bottle-flip' bass drop meme that caught attention during the global COVID-19 pandemic foregrounds imitation-as-invention and the nihilistic trolling repertoire of *shredding*. The closing remarks reflect on the wider significance of the research précised in this chapter in order to intervene in ongoing conversations about musical literacy and the future of music studies. Looking beyond score reading skills, memetic musical literacy is going to be vital to the survival of music disciplines, and it will foster a greater understanding of how YouTube music becomes used as a conspiratorial dog whistle by 'professional' (and highly dangerous) Internet trolls.

## From Imitation to Contagion and Back Again

First of all, it is worth considering the meme's traditional creation myth. Dawkins's 1976 neologism was presented as a cultural equivalent to the gene – a unit of transmission that possesses a tremendous capacity for replication. Interestingly, music and popular culture were an important part of Dawkins's memetic conception:

> Examples of memes are tunes, ideas, catchphrases, clothes, fashions, ways of making pots or of building arches. Just as genes propagate themselves in the gene pool by leaping from body to body via sperm or eggs, so memes propagate themselves in the meme pool by leaping from brain to brain via a process which, in the broad sense, can be called imitation.[5]

The emphasis on imitation here is deceptive, however. In the lines that follow, Dawkins turns his attention to beliefs in life after death, the 'God meme', and then to notions of natural selection that undermine conventional definitions of imitation. More broadly, Dawkins insists on the agency of religion itself (the 'God meme') in choreographing human behaviour over the centuries, though in explicitly neo-Darwinian terms that have been criticized by both biologists and philosophers.[6] Despite the contentiousness of Dawkins's idea, it was nevertheless

---

[5] Dawkins, *The Selfish Gene*, 249.
[6] Biologists include Patrick Bateson, 'Review of *The Selfish Gene*, by Richard Dawkins,' *Animal Behaviour* 26 (2006): 316–18; David Wilson and Elliott Sober, 'Reintroducing Group Selection to the Human Behavioral Sciences,' *Behavioural and Brain Sciences* 17, no. 4 (1994): 585–654. Philosophers include Simon Blackburn, 'Looking Out For Yourself' [Ch. 5], in *Ruling Passions: A Theory of Practical Reasoning* (Oxford: Clarendon Press, 1998); and Russell Gray, 'Selfish Genes or Developmental Systems?', in *Thinking About Evolution: Historical, Philosophical, and Political Perspectives*, ed. Rama Singh, Costas Krimbas, Diane Paul and John Beatty (Cambridge: Cambridge University Press, 2001), 184–207.

seductive – we might even say that his neo-Darwinian meme was quite contagious, and succeeded in influencing a great deal of scholarship in the humanities and social sciences, while Dawkins himself became a rather religious and mythologized figure in the nascent interdisciplinary field of 'memetics'. Often overlooked among musicologists interested in the social web is the work of Steven Jan, who champions the universal Darwinism proposed by Dawkins, and is principally concerned with the agency of musical memes at the poïetic level in the music of the First Viennese School (Mozart, Haydn, Beethoven).[7] As with Dawkins, a mentalist-driven conception of memes is privileged in Jan's memetics of music – they have an agential hold over the minds that carry them. But as Adam Ockelford has argued persuasively, Jan's memes are really just musical motifs, and the manner in which he relegates human agency (including that of composers, performers and listeners) is deeply problematic.[8]

Critically, in her perspicacious work on present-day Internet memes, Limor Shifman argues that this outdated mentalist-driven conception must be balanced by a behaviour-driven one, whereby memes are understood as constellations of human practice.[9] To put it necessarily bluntly: web users *do things* with musical memes, and some web users (ab)use others so that they become reified as musical memes themselves. The significance of Shifman's intervention cannot be overstated, since in this alternative conception, a meme has 'no existence outside the events, practices and texts in which it appears; that is, it is always experienced as encoded information'.[10] From this perspective, we might say that musical memes possess a synecdochic character as the sonification of (sub)cultural antagonism and (anti)social relations as well as sociocultural beliefs, values or mores writ large. But as encoded information, musical memes also necessitate particular kinds of literacy and afford (re)interpretation. It is through this very relationality and reciprocity that the idea of imitation in the proper sense of the term becomes more tenable.

---

[7] See, for instance, Steven Jan, *The Memetics of Music: A Neo-Darwinian View of Musical Structure and Culture* (Aldershot: Ashgate, 2007); and Steven Jan, 'From Holism to Compositionality: Memes and the Evolution of Segmentation, Syntax, and Signification in Music and Language,' *Language and Cognition* 8, no. 4 (2016): 463–500. Richard Dawkins, 'Universal Darwinism,' in *Evolution from Molecules to Men*, ed. Derek S. Bendall (Cambridge: Cambridge University Press, 1985), 403–25.

[8] Adam Ockelford, 'Review of *The Memetics of Music*, by Steven Jan,' *Psychology of Music* 37, no. 3 (2009): 379.

[9] Limor Shifman, 'Memes in a Digital World: Reconciling with a Conceptual Troublemaker,' *Journal of Computer-Mediated Communication* 18, no. 3 (2013): 362–77.

[10] Shifman, 'Memes in a Digital World,' 367.

Frustratingly, the legacy of Tarde is a point of contention in this regard, since his published work has been used as scaffolding for both mentalist-driven and behaviour-driven memetics. Tarde's many and varied ideas could well be cast as memes that have mutated over the past century or so, but it is perhaps better to approach them as 'facts' in the manner of Mary Morgan.[11] As 'facts', Tarde's *Laws of Imitation*,[12] his *Psychologie Économique*,[13] his flirtation with Darwin,[14] and – most obviously – his basic 'social fact' (the act of one consciousness upon another consciousness) have all been, to use Morgan's image, 'carried, rolled, squeezed, bounced, kicked, and thrown' over the course of their travels.[15] In two short papers published in the *Journal of Memetics* around the turn of the millennium, Paul Marsden casts Tarde as a 'forefather' of a nascent theoretical field and as a champion of social contagion in the proper (read neo-Darwinian) sense of the term.[16] Marsden's impatience with 'standard explanations' of social contagion (Emergent Norm Theory, Social Learning Theory, Convergence Theory) stems from his fervent faith in mentalist-driven memetics. He states that various attempts to 'explain away' social contagion are 'characterized by an almost desperate attempt to restore individual agency and rational action to the phenomenon'.[17] Revealingly, in Marsden's work, Tarde becomes aligned with a radical mentalist-driven conception of contagion rather than with imitation: he even posits that 'Tarde wished to stretch the already more inclusive meaning of the French word imitation' and thus 'has much in common with the [mentalist-driven] memetic project'.[18] In some respects, there is good reason for Marsden to cast Tarde as a sort of proto-Dawkins. Consider the following passage for instance, which might well have seemed prophetic to Dawkins's neo-Darwinian devotees a couple of decades ago:

---

[11] Mary Morgan, 'Travelling Facts,' in *How Well Do 'Facts' Travel? The Dissemination of Reliable Knowledge*, ed. Peter Howlett and Mary Morgan (Cambridge: Cambridge University Press, 2011), 3–39.
[12] Gabriel Tarde, *The Laws of Imitation*, trans. Elsie Parsons (Gloucester, MA: Peter Smith, [1890] 1962).
[13] Gabriel Tarde, 'Economic Psychology,' trans. Alberto Toscano, *Economy and Society* 36, no. 4 ([1902] 2007): 614–43.
[14] Gabriel Tarde, 'Darwinisme Naturel et Darwinisme Social,' *Revue Philosophique* 17 (1884): 607–37.
[15] Morgan, 'Travelling Facts,' 13.
[16] Paul Marsden, 'Memetics and Contagion: Two Sides of the Same Coin?,' *Journal of Memetics: Evolutionary Models of Information Transmission* 2 (1998): at http://cfpm.org/jom-emit/1998/vol2/marsden_p.html; Paul Marsden, 'Forefathers of Memetics: Gabriel Tarde and the Laws of Imitation,' *Journal of Memetics: Evolutionary Models of Information Transmission* 4 (2000): at http://cfpm.org/jom-emit/2000/vol4/marsden_p.html.
[17] Marsden, 'Memetics and Contagion'.
[18] Marsden, 'Forefathers of Memetics'.

> Any social production having some marked characteristics, be it an individual good, a verse, a formula, a political idea which has appeared somewhere in the corner of a brain, dreams like Alexander of conquering the world, tries to multiply itself by thousands and millions of copies in every place where there exist human beings and will never stop except if it is kept in check by some rival production as ambitious as itself.[19]

But as Matei Candea has stressed, such post-hoc contextualization is problematic, and although it is true that Tarde engaged with the work of Darwin, 'opinions vary on Tarde's closeness to Darwinian theory.'[20] Significantly, in attempting to lionize Tarde, Marsden makes the same move as Tarde's famous nemesis – Durkheim – in that he regards Tardean imitation as 'no more nor less than a form of contagion'.[21] This conflation, found at both the beginning and the end of the twentieth century, is a profound misreading. To put it in Bruno Karsenti's words (translated from the French by Candea):

> Imitation is not reducible to a subjective passivity. It is also the form of resistance, and thus of the activity, which we oppose to this flow: or better, of the activity within us which is opposed to this flow, activity which in turn is another form of passivity.[22]

Tardean imitation (in the strict sense of the term) is thus of great relevance to musical memes understood as creative practices. The strength of a Tardean approach lies in its close attention to imitation-as-opposition – to an inter-psychological and more-or-less-conscious creative act that does not merely replicate but rather recalibrates (or resists, or replies or reacts). How might we differentiate between different kinds of imitation-as-opposition, then? Following the basic yet helpful distinctions made by Georgina Born in her reading of Tarde, musical meme practices may be said to operate *by degree* (consider increasingly extreme and competitive versions of 'viral' dance fad uploads) or *by sign* (consider Fraxiom's recent queering of the brostep anthem 'Scary Monsters and Nice Sprites' (2010) by Skrillex through the use of a Bruno Powroznik meme: 'GAY SEX IS NORMAL').[23]

---

[19] Gabriel Tarde, *Monadologie et Sociologie* (Paris: Institut Synthelabo, [1893] 1999), 51.
[20] Matei Candea, 'Revisiting Tarde's House,' in *The Social After Gabriel Tarde: Debates and Assessments*, ed. Matei Candea (Abingdon: Routledge, 2010), 14, 3.
[21] Bruno Karsenti, 'Imitation: Returning to the Tarde-Durkheim Debate,' (trans. Matei Candea) in *The Social After Gabriel Tarde*, 47.
[22] Karsenti, 'the Tarde-Durkheim debate,' 49.
[23] Georgina Born, 'On Tardean Relations: Temporality and Ethnography,' in *The Social After Gabriel Tarde*, 235. For Fraxiom's track *Scawy Monstews and Nice Spwites :3* as well as the Bruno Powroznik soundbite used therein, see BroughtTheNoise, 'Fraxiom Scawy Monstews and Nice Spwites :3,' *WhoSampled*, https://www.whosampled.com/sample/778848/Fraxiom-Scawy-Monstews-and-Nice-Spwites-%3A3-Bruno-Powroznik-Gay-Sex-Is-Normal/.

Moreover, although Durkheim and his followers ensured that Tarde became typecast as an individualist for the best part of a century, this is perhaps a strength rather than a limitation for digital sociology when we consider our present social operating system of 'networked individualism'.[24] As David Toews argues, Tarde was able to get to the heart of humanity's *un*sociability, something that is of great relevance to the weaponization of musical memes on the (anti)social web.[25] This clarion call may well have been sounded more than ten years ago now, but it is certainly worth repeating:

> Sociology needs an understanding of unsociability – the unsociability of creative acts ... A promising way forward empirically, in my view, will be to examine areas such as the unsociability of practices of users of the Internet, particularly of Internet sites that are envisaged as so-called 'social media', which seem to non-practitioners to be unsociable in a random, unprincipled way, but which practitioners are nevertheless claiming as the future of the social. Internet practices are irreducible to the traditional, offline categories of individualism, thwart the Durkheimian forms of social analysis based on differences tied to functions, yet display continuities that in some way do mobilize forms of (un)sociability.[26]

Eight years on from Toews's call, he appears to have been answered by Adam Burgess, Vincent Miller and Sarah Moore in an important article that analyses challenge memes such as Neknomination and the Ice Bucket Challenge.[27] Contra Marsden and others, the authors stress that their work 'eschews the metaphors of virality and contagion that are often employed to understand digital culture, implying, as they do, a lack of agency and innovation on the part of individuals', and they fruitfully make use of Tarde's five categories of imitation in order to analyse their survey and focus group data (logical imitation, customary imitation, emotional imitation, prestige imitation, propinquity imitation).[28] But although there is much that is stimulating and instructive in this work – not least their argument that challenge memes do not constitute sheep-like acts of conformity

---

[24] Lee Rainie and Barry Wellman, *Networked: The New Social Operating System* (Cambridge, MA: MIT Press, 2012).
[25] David Toews, 'Tarde and Durkheim and the Non-Sociological Ground of Sociology,' in *The Social After Gabriel Tarde*, 80 ff.
[26] Toews, 'The Non-Sociological Ground of Sociology,' 91.
[27] Adam Burgess, Vincent Miller and Sarah Moore, 'Prestige, Performance and Social Pressure in Viral Challenge Memes: Neknomination, the Ice-Bucket Challenge and SmearForSmear as Imitative Encounters,' *Sociology* 52, no. 5 (2018): 1035–51.
[28] Ibid., 1041.

– it could also be said that the work of Burgess et al. is itself characterized by prestige imitation, such is their excessively close adherence to a Tardean analytics. Although Tarde has often been cast as an authoritative and visionary figure since the 'rediscovery' of his work, he is not the sole answer to all of our problems, and we cannot escape the shadow of his nemesis if we want to develop a truly critical digital sociology of musical memes.

In order to make sense of musical memes in the age of the (anti)social web, we need to return to that original flamewar – the epic debate between Tarde and Durkheim that took place at the École des hautes études sociales in 1903. Durkheim's structural holism (and its influence on mid-twentieth-century critical theory) is just as important a consideration as Tarde's inter-psychology (or 'micro-sociology', as it is sometimes characterized). Joel Robbins stresses this point eloquently in his work on Pentecostal rituals, when he suggests that the 'goal' of sociality among new converts 'is a Durkheimian basis for Tardean social dynamics'.[29] I make a similar claim in my analysis of 'the bass face' at online-offline electronic dance music (EDM) festivals.[30] Although the bass face may appear to be a natural, contagious and unlearned response, festivalgoers deliberately pull it (in Facebook groups and 'IRL') in order to get what they are after (hype, catharsis, social connection). Furthermore, their moves are partially choreographed by the festival's corporate infrastructure in collaboration with online platforms, through the process of what Peter Manning calls 'branding sociality': by embodying the bass face (or posting bass face memes) they are actually emulating bass music's brand.[31] In short, we cannot lose sight of the 'big picture' sociological perspectives introduced by Durkheim and developed by his disciples. For instance, a theoretical framework supporting the analysis of musical meme exchange might be obtained from the more anthropological work of Durkheim's nephew – Marcel Mauss – and from Anna Tsing's highly stimulating work on gifts and commodities in late capitalist societies.[32] In the

---

[29] Joel Robbins, 'If There is No Such Thing as Society, is Ritual Still Special? On Using *The Elementary Forms* after Tarde,' in *The Social After Gabriel Tarde*, 98.

[30] Edward Spencer, 'Music to Vomit To: The Dubstep Drop, the Bass Face, and the Sound of the Social Web,' in *Cultural Approaches to Disgust and the Visceral*, ed. Max Ryynänen, Susanne Ylönen and Heidi Kosonen (London: Routledge, 2022): 160–74.

[31] Paul Manning, 'The Semiotics of Brand,' *Annual Review of Anthropology* 39, no. 1 (2010): 44.

[32] Marcel Mauss, *The Gift: Forms and Functions of Exchange in Archaic Societies* (London: Cohen & West, 1954); Anna Tsing, 'Sorting Out Commodities: How Capitalist Value is Made Through Gifts,' *HAU: Journal of Ethnographic Theory* 3, no. 1 (2013): 21–43. For a case study of musical extractivism that develops a dialogue with Tsing, see Ofer Gazit and Elisa Bruttomesso, 'YouTube Logics and the Extraction of Musical Space in San Juan's La Perla and Kingston's Fleet Street,' in *YouTube and Music*, ed. Holly Rogers, Joana Freitas and João Francisco Porfírio (New York: Bloomsbury, 2023), 108–22.

**Figure 2.1** A screenshot of the initial Harlem Shake sequence featuring Pink Guy/ George Miller (right-hand side of image), 'FILTHY COMPILATION #6 – SMELL MY FINGERS' (30 January 2013).

digital age, attention is an especially valuable asset. Putting on a more Durkheimian hat would encourage us to continue ruminating on Pierre Bourdieu's forms of capital, as well as on the workings of the attention economy and musical manifestations of structural hegemony.[33] The so-called problem of the one and the many that Tarde and Durkheim wrestled with is still with us, and could even be imagined as the struggle that defines the (anti)social web. But to put it in less figurative terms, I want to suggest that a digital sociology of musical memes might involve a dialectical oscillation between Tarde on the one hand and more Durkheimian perspectives on the other.

## Three Bass Drop Memes – Three Trolling Repertoires

To imitate a delightful phrase used by Allan Moore, the time has come to offer some proof in the pudding.[34] Consider the case of the sensational Harlem Shake

---

[33] Pierre Bourdieu, 'The Forms of Capital,' in *Handbook of Theory and Research for the Sociology of Education*, ed. John Richardson (Westport, CT: Greenwood, 1986), 241–58; Michael Goldhaber, 'The Attention Economy and the Net,' *First Monday* 2, no. 4 (1997): at https://firstmonday.org/ojs/index.php/fm/article/view/519/440/.

[34] Allan Moore, 'Listening to the Sound Music Makes,' in *The Routledge Companion to Popular Music Analysis: Expanding Approaches*, ed. Ciro Scotto, Kenneth M. Smith and John Lowell Brackett (New York: Routledge, 2019), [legal deposit ebook edition].

meme from 2013. This dance routine was initially a short sequence in a deranged video uploaded by the notorious troll Filthy Frank / Pink Guy (George Miller, see Figure 2.1).[35] On initial impression, the meme is the very embodiment of 'cultural infection', both in terms of its audiovisual formula and its viral transmission. In the first version to replicate the Filthy Frank sequence, we watch a lone, masked figure perform pelvic thrusts in time with the build-up passage from the 2013 EDM trap track 'Harlem Shake' by Baauer, while others continue with what they are doing unawares.[36] The bass drop is synchronized with a jump-cut (0.16), upon which the scene suddenly changes from the ordinary to the orgiastic – the masked figure's debased dancing was highly contagious and has now spread to all of the others. One body has been stripped half-naked, all of the movements are unsynchronized and uncouth, and there is a short-lived slow-motion effect before a return to normal speed. The video ends at the thirty-second mark with the conclusion of a groaning-cum-snarling sound in Baauer's track, whereupon the half-naked body collapses onto a bed. The establishment of the Harlem Shake's format and formula was only the first stage of its lifespan, however. Its contagious spread was rapid and record-breaking, with more than 4,000 Harlem Shake videos uploaded to YouTube every day during the peak of the fad. Overall, it only took forty days for this UGC to reach a billion views on YouTube, half the time that it took for PSY's professionally produced 'Gangnam Style' music video to reach the same figure in 2012.[37]

Yet this sensational outward spread has overshadowed the imitative logics and trolling repertoires that define the phenomenon. Critically, the 'cancerous' spread of the Harlem Shake meme in the spring of 2013 was predicated on corporate choreography. On 7 February, a mere eight days after Filthy Frank's upload, the Harlem Shake came to the attention of Vernon Shaw, an employee at the Los Angeles company Maker Studios, a subsidiary of Time Warner. Having stumbled across the initial uploads via Reddit, Shaw 'thought the videos looked "pre-viral" and saw an opportunity to exploit them to promote Maker'.[38] A Harlem Shake video featuring Maker Studios employees dancing in the Maker

---

[35] DizastaMusic, 'FILTHY COMPILATION #6 - SMELL MY FINGERS,' *YouTube video*, 00:03:21, 30 January 2013, https://www.youtube.com/watch?v=GeO3yCpLt0Q.
[36] TheSunnyCoastSkate, 'The Harlem Shake v1 (TSCS original),' *YouTube video*, 00:00:30, 2 February 2013, https://www.youtube.com/watch?v=384IUU43bfQ.
[37] Michael Soha and Zachary J. McDowell, 'Monetizing a Meme: YouTube, Content ID, and the Harlem Shake,' *Social Media + Society* 2, no. 1 (2016): 1.
[38] Kevin Ashton, 'You Didn't Make the Harlem Shake go Viral – Corporations Did,' *Quartz* (2013): at https://qz.com/67991/you-didnt-make-the-harlem-shake-go-viral-corporations-did/.

Studios office was quickly created and uploaded. Although the original upload has since disappeared, the routine can still be viewed in a re-uploaded video.[39] The Maker Studios Harlem Shake was something of a *point de capiton*, since it initiated the 'memejacking' phase of the Harlem Shake's lifespan, a 'process by which marketers appropriate existing content for branding purposes'.[40] The Harlem Shake drop was now a highly prized asset in the attention economy, and brands from Maker Studios to Manchester City Football Club were using it to sell experiences and themselves.

At the risk of ventriloquizing Tarde and his *Psychologie Économique*, it could be argued that the Harlem Shake was defined by competitive imitation by degree, with each successive upload seeking to transgress the meme's inbuilt transgression and thus magnetize maximum attention. The 'virality' of the phenomenon was less a case of spreading out and more a case of buying in, such that it becomes possible to view its development in terms of strategic manoeuvres and processes of 'franchising'. Baauer's bass drop was a powerful asset as a form of musical clickbait, and from this perspective the bait-and-switch formula of the routine itself comes to seem like a lucrative trolling tactic that might be termed *hooking* (a word that captures both the musical devices and attention-stealing aspects of the phenomenon). Yet Tardean analysis can only take us so far. To riff with and against the gifted nephew of Tarde's nemesis, it must be stressed that the Harlem Shake also involved commodification, since elements of black vernacular culture were whitewashed and reified through their deracination. As Catherine Steele has put it, the routine seen in the Harlem Shake meme is 'in no way linked to the actual "Harlem Shake", a dance originating in Harlem in 1981 that became popular among African Americans in the 1990s and early 2000s'.[41] Rather than exemplifying the grassroots, liberalizing impetus of participatory culture as it was originally theorized by Henry Jenkins, or the idea of vernacular dance-as-a-gift articulated by Susan Foster, the Harlem Shake meme further marginalized a minority group through an act of cultural fetishization.[42] It is here that the

---

[39] HarlemShakeOriginal, 'The Harlem Shake Original Compilation (Part 3) – Maker Studios Edition,' *YouTube video*, 00:00:30, 12 February 2013, https://www.youtube.com/watch?v=ivMQZeYozA8.

[40] Whitney Phillips, *This Is Why We Can't Have Nice Things: Mapping the Relationship Between Online Trolling and Mainstream Culture* (Cambridge, MA: MIT Press, 2015), 139.

[41] Catherine Steele, 'Shaking off the "Other": Appropriation of Marginalized Cultures and the "Harlem Shake",' *AoIR Selected Papers of Internet Research*, 3 (2013): at https://journals.uic.edu/ojs/index.php/spir/article/view/8849.

[42] Henry Jenkins, *Fans, Bloggers, and Gamers: Exploring Participatory Culture* (New York: NYU Press, 2006); Susan Foster, *Valuing Dance: Commodities and Gifts in Motion* (New York: Oxford University Press, 2019).

insidious side of imitation becomes audible and visible. By listening to the voices of web users who authored comments on the first version to go viral, it became apparent that the routine was also seen to be plundering another black dance move: The Bernie. There are clear parallels with the disequilibrium of the more recent *Fortnite* dance phenomenon discussed by Wayne Marshall, a case study which also demonstrates that 'just because lots of people are doing the same dances, alas [it] doesn't mean we're dancing together'.[43] Harlem Shake participants were not entrained to a viral pulse that was fostering interpsychological oneness and turning the world upside down, but were actually labourers who were generating millions of dollars of revenue for YouTube because of the platform's algorithmic 'Content ID' mechanism. YouTube had a monopoly on the meme, and profited from its seemingly 'contagious' spread through the technocratic control of human creativity (using the irrational rationality of AI).

Other sobering imitation practices and trolling repertoires surface in adjacent research arenas. Consider the use of the dubstep track 'Centipede' by Knife Party in a series of YouTube videos titled *You Can't Stump The Trump*, which were uploaded during the 'Great Meme War' of 2015 to 2016 accompanying the US Presidential Race. Why *this* musical meme? Where had it come from? And how on earth did it become an anthem for the alt-right and less radical Trump supporters alike? Conventional diffusion analysis cannot provide answers to these questions, since Centipede's genesis as a musical meme occurred in an online environment that was far removed from r/The_Donald spatially and temporally. The story begins in r/montageparodies circa 2012, a subreddit in which members posted 'MLG montage parodies' for the sake of trolling first-person shooter (FPS) gaming montages and androcentric 'Major League Gaming' culture more broadly. During this initial phase of memetic development, 'Centipede' was involved in kudos trolling – it was being used as a sardonic synecdoche for the 'brostep' music favoured by 'skrubs' (pubescent male wannabes who uploaded montages of low-quality FPS gameplay overdubbed with tear-out bass drops in the hope of being signed by a professional gaming franchise). It was part of a canon of dubstep/brostep, drumstep and moombahcore tracks that were deemed to be most suitable for trolling the skrubs in this way.

---

[43] Wayne Marshall, 'Social Dance in the Age of (Anti-)Social Media,' *Journal of Popular Music Studies* 31, no. 4 (2019): 14.

In early January 2013, an r/montageparodies member posted a list of suitable MLG montage parody music that included 'Centipede'. An exchange between two users in the related comments thread is revealing, with the first user opining that most of the humour in MLG montage parodies comes from the centrality of awful dubstep music.'

Trawling through content in r/montageparodies becomes a disconcerting exercise once this material is cross-referenced with a Q&A thread featuring the creator of the 'You Can't Stump The Trump' videos in r/The_Donald. Interacting with fellow 'Trump fans' in the subreddit, the YouTuber was asked why he picked 'Centipede' as to which he replied:

> When I uploaded the first Trump video, I saw a comment saying that it resembled an MLG montage parody due to the title. That gave me the impetus to search for MLG dubstep tracks, and I stumbled upon a list that someone had shared [presumably the r/montageparodies music thread]. I recognized Knife Party from the use of one of their tracks in a popular TV series, so I decided to check out 'Centipede'. It was quite honestly the first dubstep track that I tried, and it worked so perfectly that I didn't even experiment with alternatives. Maybe it was fated to be the soundtrack for Trump's White House mission.[44]

The use of the track also gave rise to pro-Trump Twitter hashtags such as #Centipede and #NimbleNavigator, as well as the account @MAGApede. Artwork depicting Trump as a centipede and even pictures of pro-Trump centipede clothing began to circulate on Twitter. But, most revealingly, members of r/The_Donald were listed as 'centipedes' in the sidebar during the rest of The 'Great Meme War', a finding that suggests that this self-referential Reddit community was musically as well as politically imagined.

To return to Morgan's image, it was not only facts that were rolled, bounced, squeezed, kicked and thrown during the 'Great Meme War' – musical memes were manipulated and weaponized also. From a Tardean perspective, this case study of radical recalibration is enmeshed with the idea of imitation-as-opposition, an (anti)social process involved in what Born describes as 'the collective conflicts that occasion war'.[45] Fusing Tarde's imitation by sign with the more familiar Bourdieuian concept of symbolic violence, the trolling repertoire animated by 'Centipede' involved *muting* – in two senses of the term. First, this

---

[44] The text of this post has been slightly altered in order to follow the ethical recommendations set out in the Association of Internet Researchers 'Ethics 3.0' guidelines.
[45] Born, 'Tardean Relations', 235.

muting took the form of deformation and rerouting, since 'Centipede' was plucked from one memetic world and repurposed as musical propaganda in another having been weaponized by a 'Trump fan'. What proved to be significant was this behaviour-driven act of repurposing rather than the agency of 'Centipede' itself (to reprise the critique of Dawkins). Second, 'Centipede' delivered muting in the sense of shouting down and silencing Trump's adversaries. In 'Volume 4' of the upload series, the nimble navigator's first victim is the rival Republican candidate Rand Paul. During establishing shots of a Republican debate, Knife Party's track begins with a male voiceover from an American nature documentary and hissing rainforest ambiance. The build-up that follows comprises an oscillating semitone 'Jaws' rip-off coupled with a rising EQ sweep (0.18 to 0.31). We are then held in suspense when the music cuts out before the bass drop. Trump injects his paralyzing venom into Rand Paul through a one-line put-down ('I think you heard me, you're having a hard time tonight'), before the track's powerful drop at 0.34 casts this as an unanswerable 'mic drop'.

The muting delivered by 'Centipede' during the 'Great Meme War' renders audible the reactionary character of the (anti)social web, and serves as a reminder that musical memes have no existence outside the imitative trolling repertoires in which they are involved (to modify Shifman's contribution). But if the value of a Tardean approach lies in its close attention to contingency and microsociality, then how might one approach the fraught question of how musical memes relate to a much broader and more enduring zeitgeist? With this macrosocial vantage point in mind, consider the case of a musical shitpost shared on Facebook during the early stages of the global COVID-19 pandemic.[46] We are in some sort of library. A young black man walks in slow-motion and then enters a side office by kicking open a glass door with his foot. A textual annotation superimposed over the footage identifies this character as the 'Dude who ate a bat', and his movements are underscored by nauseating varispeed figures and sprinkler snares from the opening of the trap track 'Okay,ButThisIsTheLastTime' (2015) by BONES. In the side office, four members of an interview panel are waiting for him: they are 'US Economy'; 'Dow Jones'; 'Unemployment'; and 'S&P 500'. The music cuts out as 'US Economy' asks the interview candidate an initial question: 'Do you have any special talents?' With similar slow-motion swagger, the 'Dude who ate a bat' proceeds to lob a water bottle up into the air. It is labelled as '1 Corona Boi', along

---

[46] Thieves, '1 CORONA BOI 🦠 🍶', *Facebook* (24.3.20), https://www.facebook.com/watch/?ref=saved&v=238192734251382.

**Figure 2.2** Screenshot of '1 CORONA BOI 🦠 🦇'.

with the appropriate microscopic image of the COVID-19 virus. The candidate is already walking out of the room as the water bottle hovers in suspended animation during a vacuous pre-drop vocal sample ('frozen'). At the onset of a crushing 808 bass drop, which has been distorted through a memetic device known as 'ear rape', the '1 Corona Boi' lands on the desk – perfectly upright. The sheer force of this distorted '1 Corona Boi' bass drop is enough to topple 'US Economy' and 'Dow Jones' from their chairs, while 'Unemployment' drops his computer keyboard and 'S&P 500' spills his milky Frappuccino all over his face and suit. The 'Dude who ate a bat' then leaves this scene of chaos, still walking in slow-motion but now wearing a sleek pair of sunglasses (see Figure 2.2).

On initial impression, this piece of clickbait captures something of the alarm, frenzy and sardonicism that characterized the initial phases of the pandemic. But more broadly, it compels the web user to embrace a nihilistic kind of laughter that has come to define the networked world since the turn of the millennium. With reference to the 'Now Watch This Drive' meme (in which George Bush drives a golf ball into the Twin Towers), Whitney Phillips argues that the ever-increasing spread of perverse humour on the social web is a symptom of post-millennial anxiety writ large. In the wake of 9/11 and other crises, 'sometimes the only thing you could do to keep from crying was to laugh'.[47] The development of Web 2.0 and its nihilistic 'logic of lulz' occurred during a time of great unease,

---

[47] Phillips, *Online Trolling*, 121.

during which Westerners, continues Phillips, were liable 'to remain unmoored – from history, from war, from the suffering of others, from the suffering of fellow citizens'.[48] From this perspective, one might say that the '1 Corona Boi' bottle flip bass drop meme renders audible the ambivalent mixture of humour and hopelessness that defines the era of the (anti)social web within the age of late capitalism. The sound of the distorted 808 bass coupled with the milky oblivion is somehow a telling synecdoche of a world being torn apart, and we are forced to laugh despite ourselves. But there is something else at play too. We are not only watching the imitation of (literal) contagion, but are also being compelled to react to a reaction. The visceral response of 'US Economy' et al. is one that choreographs our own, such that the bass drop affords a kind of affective assimilation. In this manner, the shitpost causes a bleed between the viewer and the viewed, and this memetic content may appear to be collapsing any sense of aesthetic distance. However, this phenomenon is less a case of contagion or imitation, and much more a case of *interpellation* – we are called into a relationship with the shitpost through its societal specificity. We recognize this reaction, we live in an age of reactionism, and we are made to react as a result.

This first way of analysing the sociohistorical significance of the meme is partly unsatisfactory, however. The musical shitposting conjures a trolling repertoire that could be dubbed *shredding*, a term which captures both the delirious noisiness of the content itself, as well as the palimpsestic nature of its provenance and authorship. Significantly, by 2020 the bottle flip fad was very much a 'dead meme'. Its peak arrived in the summer of 2016, and the skit that we see in '1 Corona Boi' is in fact a YouTube video uploaded on 18 June of that year. This upload, created in collaboration with Matt Tavenner and others, was directed by the former Viner known as King Vader. The viral success of King Vader's bottle flip launched his YouTube career – but was no accident, as he has explained:

> Once I saw how viral this [bottle flipping] concept was, as just like a trend, I was like 'why don't I make this into a video?' ... So my whole group, we'll meet together at some location and we just take turns filming content ... and my boy Matt, he was in the room. He just came back from Starbucks, and I looked at his Starbucks cup and I was like 'when I record your shot, I need you to shake the coffee everywhere – I want the coffee to go flying, on you, on the desk, on everyone'. So he was like, 'you're asking for a lot', and I was like 'I know, but what if I can guarantee you that this video will get 100,000 views?' – that's all I said was

---

[48] Ibid., 122.

100,000 views. He was like, 'I'll do it for 200,000' – 'Ok, I mean I think I can make that promise'.[49]

The idea of the interview conceit together with the execution of the coffee spill upon the bass drop proved to be a winning formula (as King Vader predicted). Although the upload was imitating an established memetic trend, it delivered originality and uniqueness. Holistically, this case study provides a useful illustration of Tardean imitation-as-invention, but it also foregrounds the significance of transmediality (with content crossing from Vine to YouTube to Facebook) and intertextuality. There are many memes within this meme, as it were, including the 'deal with it' sunglasses reference, the earlier practice of 'milking' (a challenge meme whereby one pours a carton of milk over one's head) and the 'ear rape' audio distortion meme. In the '1 Corona Boi' version, the only new elements are the textual annotations, but this was enough to command attention. Of equal importance is the effacing of authorship. Neither Matt Tavenner nor King Vader are credited. The video was posted by a Facebook user called Thieves, and the upload is also overlaid with an incongruous Twitter handle (@bigdeckenergy_). This confusion compounds the sense in which the audiovisual allegory has an agency of its own accord, though it should be stressed that this rather esoteric conception of memes is more associated with the emic term 'cursed' in online contexts rather than with notions of contagion per se.

## From Contagion to Conspiracy

Notwithstanding the three case studies considered in the previous section, there is a lingering issue that haunts this entire chapter: the ontological status of music as a meme. What, exactly, is musical about musical memes? What do we or should we mean by this term? Are musical memes somehow different to other kinds of memes? There is a very real danger of musical exceptionalism in this regard, whereby sound is privileged over sight (or language for that matter) in a manner that resurrects the audiovisual litany.[50] But there is also an exciting opportunity to reconsider orthodox ideas about music when developing a digital

---

[49] King Vader, speaking in BETNetworks, 'King Vader, aka "Hood Naruto," Flipped His Fame From Vine To YouTube With A Bottle & Anime Parodies,' *YouTube video*, 00:07:02, 16 April 2020, https://www.youtube.com/watch?v=Z3xlPy--MSY, 1.41 ff., my transcription.

[50] For a discussion of the audiovisual litany (a concept introduced by Jonathan Sterne), see Will Schrimshaw, 'Exit Immersion,' *Sound Studies* 1, no. 1 (2015): 155–70.

sociology of musical memes. Conceptualized as a meme in Shifman's updated sense of the term, it could be argued that in the age of the (anti)social web, music's power lies not in its ineffability or even in its affectivity, but rather in its entanglements with explicit ideas, meanings and world views. From this perspective, musical memes are a means with which to imitate and reconfigure beliefs and desires (the substance of social life), and therefore necessitate media literacy. Since it is a pivotal site where musical memes are born, nurtured and reshaped (or weaponized), it will be especially important to listen to the workings of YouTube as a platform as well as to the voices of its users. At a time when some musicologists are lamenting declining levels of musical literacy (score reading skills), it could be argued that media literacy generally and memetic literacy in particular is actually going to be more important to the survival and future flourishing of music studies as an interdisciplinary field of enquiry. A valuable arena for future research concerns the toxic relationships between musical memes and conspiratorial communities online. Such work might well consider the musical memes known as 'Remove Kebab' and 'Gas, Gas, Gas' online, both of which were played by the Christchurch terrorist as he livestreamed mass murder on Facebook in March 2019. This sickening act of musical trolling combined all three of the trolling repertoires introduced in this chapter (*hooking, muting, shredding*) in order to further propagate dangerous far-right conspiracy theories. Through hooking, 'Gas, Gas, Gas' baited web users familiar with this musical meme from its use in gaming content on YouTube; through muting, 'Remove Kebab' was reopening and recalibrating a hermeneutic window from the 1990s Yugoslav Wars in order to silence those who did not belong to a white supremacist worldview; and both musical memes were posing as funny and senseless sonic shitposts through shredding in order to establish a smokescreen of plausible deniability. Soberingly, although dangerous conspiratorial sentiments tend to be associated with online 'cesspits' such as 4chan and 8chan, YouTube is a major breeding ground for the far-right's mutant musical memes. The relatively reputable and mainstream aura of YouTube as a platform could be said to have contributed to the sardonic smokescreen employed by the Christchurch terrorist, particularly in the case of 'Gas, Gas, Gas' (via the formula 'oh – I know this song from YouTube – this guy must be doing an IRL gaming montage – oh wait what is he doing . . .'). The music disciplines must therefore seek deeper knowledge of YouTube's musical memes in all their power and perversity.

# Bibliography

Ashton, Kevin. 'You Didn't Make the Harlem Shake go Viral – Corporations Did.' *Quartz* (2013): https://qz.com/67991/you-didnt-make-the-harlem-shake-go-viral-corporations-did/.

Bateson, Patrick. 'Review of *The Selfish Gene*, by Richard Dawkins.' *Animal Behaviour* 26 (1979): 316–18.

Blackburn, Simon. *Ruling Passions: A Theory of Practical Reasoning*. Oxford: Clarendon Press, 1998.

Born, Georgina and Christopher Haworth. 'From Microsound to Vaporwave: Internet-Mediated Musics, Online Methods, and Genre.' *Music and Letters* 98, no. 4 (2018): 601–47.

Born, Georgina. 'On Tardean Relations: Temporality and Ethnography.' In *The Social After Gabriel Tarde: Debates and Assessments*, edited by Matei Candea, 230–47. Abingdon: Routledge, 2010.

Bourdieu, Pierre. 'The Forms of Capital.' In *Handbook of Theory and Research for the Sociology of Education*, edited by John Richardson, 241–58. Westport, CT: Greenwood, 1986.

BroughtTheNoise. 'Fraxiom Scawy Monstews and Nice Spwites :3.' *WhoSampled* (2019–2020), at https://www.whosampled.com/sample/778848/Fraxiom-Scawy-Monstews-and-Nice-Spwites-%3A3-Bruno-Powroznik-Gay-Sex-Is-Normal/.

Burgess, Adam, Vincent Miller and Sarah Moore. 'Prestige, Performance and Social Pressure in Viral Challenge Memes: Neknomination, the Ice-Bucket Challenge and SmearForSmear as Imitative Encounters.' *Sociology* 52, no. 5 (2018): 1035–51.

Candea, Matei. 'Revisiting Tarde's House.' In *The Social After Gabriel Tarde: Debates and Assessments*, edited by Matei Candea, 1–23. Abingdon: Routledge, 2010.

Dawkins, Richard. 'Universal Darwinism.' In *Evolution from Molecules to Men*, edited by Derek S. Bendall, 403–25. Cambridge: Cambridge University Press, 1985.

Dawkins, Richard. *The Selfish Gene*. Oxford: Oxford University Press, 1976.

Foster, Susan. *Valuing Dance: Commodities and Gifts in Motion*. New York: Oxford University Press, 2019.

Gazit, Ofer and Elisa Bruttomesso. 'YouTube Logics and the Extraction of Musical Space in San Juan's La Perla and Kingston's Fleet Street.' *YouTube and Music: Online Culture and Everyday Life*, edited by Holly Rogers, Joana Freitas and João Francisco Porfírio, 108–22. New York: Bloomsbury, 2023.

Goldhaber, Michael. 'The Attention Economy and the Net.' *First Monday* 2, no. 4 (1997): https://firstmonday.org/ojs/index.php/fm/article/view/519/440/.

Gray, Russell. 'Selfish Genes or Developmental Systems?' In *Thinking About Evolution: Historical, Philosophical, and Political Perspectives*, edited by Rama Singh, Costas

Krimbas, Diane Paul and John Beatty, 184–207. Cambridge: Cambridge University Press, 2001.

Harper, Paula. 'Viral Musicking; Contagious Listening,' *84th Annual Meeting of the American Musicological Society*. San Antonio: Grand Hyatt Hotel, 2018.

Jan, Steven. 'From Holism to Compositionality: Memes and the Evolution of Segmentation, Syntax, and Signification in Music and Language.' *Language and Cognition* 8, no. 4 (2016): 463–500.

Jan, Steven. *The Memetics of Music: A Neo-Darwinian View of Musical Structure and Culture*. Aldershot: Ashgate, 2007.

Jenkins, Henry. *Fans, Bloggers, and Gamers: Exploring Participatory Culture*. New York: NYU Press, 2006.

Karsenti, Bruno. 'Imitation: Returning to the Tarde-Durkheim Debate.' Translated by Matei Candea. In *The Social After Gabriel Tarde: Debates and Assessments*, edited by Matei Candea, 44–61. Abingdon: Routledge, 2010.

Manning, Paul. 'The Semiotics of Brand.' *Annual Review of Anthropology* 39, no. 1 (2010): 33–49.

Marsden, Paul. 'Forefathers of Memetics: Gabriel Tarde and the Laws of Imitation.' *Journal of Memetics: Evolutionary Models of Information Transmission* 4 (2000): http://cfpm.org/jom-emit/2000/vol4/marsden_p.html.

Marsden, Paul. 'Memetics and Contagion: Two Sides of the Same Coin?' *Journal of Memetics: Evolutionary Models of Information Transmission* 2 (1998): http://cfpm.org/jom-emit/1998/vol2/marsden_p.html.

Marshall, Wayne. 'Social Dance in the Age of (Anti-)Social Media.' *Journal of Popular Music Studies* 31, no. 4 (2019): 3–15.

Mauss, Marcel. *The Gift: Forms and Functions of Exchange in Archaic Societies*. London: Cohen & West, 1954.

Meikle, Graham and Sherman Young. *Media Convergence: Networked Digital Media in Everyday Life*. Basingstoke: Palgrave Macmillan, 2011.

Moore, Allan. 'Listening to the Sound Music Makes.' In *The Routledge Companion to Popular Music Analysis: Expanding Approaches*, edited by Ciro Scotto, Kenneth M. Smith and John Lowell Brackett, [legal deposit ebook edition]. New York: Routledge, 2019.

Morgan, Mary. 'Travelling Facts.' In *How Well Do Facts Travel? The Dissemination of Reliable Knowledge*, edited by Peter Howlett and Mary Morgan, 3–39. Cambridge: Cambridge University Press, 2011.

Ockelford, Adam. 'Review of *The Memetics of Music*, by Steven Jan.' *Psychology of Music* 37, no. 3 (2009): 378–80.

Phillips, Whitney. *This Is Why We Can't Have Nice Things: Mapping the Relationship Between Online Trolling and Mainstream Culture*. Cambridge, MA: MIT Press, 2015.

Rainie, Lee and Barry Wellman. *Networked: The New Social Operating System*. Cambridge, MA: MIT Press, 2012.

Robbins, Joel. 'If There Is No Such Thing As Society, Is Ritual Still Special? On Using *The Elementary Forms* after Tarde.' In *The Social After Gabriel Tarde: Debates and Assessments*, edited by Matei Candea, 93–101. Abingdon: Routledge, 2010.

Schrimshaw, Will. 'Exit Immersion.' *Sound Studies* 1, no. 1 (2015): 155–70.

Shifman, Limor. 'Memes in a Digital World: Reconciling With a Conceptual Troublemaker.' *Journal of Computer-Mediated Communication* 18, no. 3 (2013): 362–77.

Soha, Michael and Zachary J. McDowell. 'Monetizing a Meme: YouTube, Content ID, and the Harlem Shake.' *Social Media + Society* 2, no. 1 (2016): 2056305115623801.

Spencer, Edward. 'Music to Vomit To: The Dubstep Drop, The Bass Face, and the Sound of the Social Web.' In *Cultural Approaches to Disgust and the Visceral*, edited by Max Ryynänen, Susanne Ylönen and Heidi Kosonen, 160–174. London: Routledge, 2022.

Spencer, Scott. 'YouTube and the Making of a Musical Meme: How Video Mashups of John Coltrane's 'Giant Steps' Became a Thing.' In *Remediating Sound: Repeatable Culture, YouTube and Music*, edited by Holly Rogers, Joana Freitas and João Francisco Porfírio, 233–42. New York: Bloomsbury, 2023.

Steele, Catherine. 'Shaking off the "Other": Appropriation of Marginalized Cultures and the 'Harlem Shake.' *Association of Internet Researchers Selected Papers of Internet Research* 3 (2013): https://journals.uic.edu/ojs/index.php/spir/article/view/8849.

Tarde, Gabriel. 'Darwinisme naturel et Darwinisme social.' *Revue Philosophique* 17 (1884): 607–37.

Tarde, Gabriel. 'Economic Psychology,' trans. Alberto Toscano. *Economy and Society* 36, no. 4 ([1902] 2007): 614–43.

Tarde, Gabriel. *Monadologie et sociologie*. Paris: Institut Synthelabo, [1893] 1999.

Tarde, Gabriel. *The Laws of Imitation*, trans. Elsie Parsons. Gloucester, MA: Peter Smith, [1890] 1962.

Toews, David. 'Tarde and Durkheim and the Non-Sociological Ground of Sociology.' In *The Social After Gabriel Tarde: Debates and Assessments*, edited by Matei Candea, 80–92. Abingdon: Routledge, 2010.

Tsing, Anna. 'Sorting out Commodities: How Capitalist Value is Made Through Gifts.' *HAU: Journal of Ethnographic Theory* 3, no. 1 (2013): 21–43.

Wilson, David and Elliott Sober. 'Reintroducing Group Selection to the Human Behavioral Sciences.' *Behavioural and Brain Sciences* 17, no. 4 (1994): 585–654.

3

# Sincere, Authentic, Remediated: The Affective Labour and Cross-Cultural Remediations of Music Video Reaction Videos on YouTube

Michael Goddard

'Like, comment and subscribe'– so begins almost every reaction video on YouTube that collectively constitute a strange ecology of affective labour and cultural translation that merits further attention. There have already been several studies of user generated content (UGC) and the 'free labour' of user activities on digital and social media platforms.[1] Reaction videos are different from these paradigms as, if successful, these channels are potentially a source of income through advertising, monetization, as well as, in most cases, Patreon or other subscription platforms that give subscribers extra 'rights' to request content. This economy and ecology of creator culture on social media platforms has only recently become the object of sustained academic research, and for a range of reasons. In part, this is because of a macro focus on the political economies of platforms as a whole, or a blanket critical rejection of the significance of the activities engaged with on such platforms, as Geert Lovink has argued: it is also because of outmoded approaches based on different entertainment industries, such as film and television that position users as similar to mass media audiences or fans who at most might produce UGC.[2] If attention has been paid to social media creators, it has been more in a promotional media context, which largely

---

[1] See Tiziana Terranova, 'Free Labour,' in *Network Culture: Politics for the Information Age* (London: Pluto Press, 2004), 73–97.
[2] Geert Lovink, *Networks without a Cause: A Critique of Social Media* (Cambridge: Polity, 2011).

sees such activities in terms of branding and marketing of both the self and other commodities. However, Stuart Cunningham and David Craig's work *Social Media Entertainment*, and their even more relevant edited collection *Creator Culture*, provides a valuable framework within which the cultural economy of music reaction videos can be usefully located.[3] Nevertheless, neither of these works discuss reaction videos of any kind explicitly.

The videos themselves involve intros followed by acts of listening to and viewing a range of music videos and other musical content. In some reaction videos, which can be called 'organized' reaction videos, specific age or other demographics are selected to listen to an already chosen music genre, band or performer. The 'React' channel, for example, has series of 'Kids React', 'Teens React' and 'Elders React' videos, confronting new audiences with older genres of popular music and vice versa. An extreme example of this is the 'Trybals' channel from Pakistan, in which 'Tribal' people are encouraged to react to everything from Opera to Rammstein. These kinds of reaction are not the focus of this chapter, however, since they involve some level of 'expert' curation rather than the direct, spontaneous forms of appropriation that can be found in 'spontaneous' reaction videos. In these reaction videos, creators react directly to music videos of their choosing, albeit influenced by subscriber requests and suggestions, without any expert mediation. Typically, this involves minimal context being given in advance, and is to genres and styles of music that are relatively unfamiliar to the creators, even if there are multiple exceptions to this tendency.

It is important to note that music video reaction videos are only a subset of reaction videos more generally, which have a complex transmedia history going back to transnational television reality and quiz formats, and arguably some forms of 1970s video art involving 'video loops', enabling participants to watch their own behaviour onscreen. An early example of this is the *Wipe Cycle* video installation (Frank Gillette and Ira Schneider, 1969), in which visitors to the exhibition space became visible on monitors in both real time and delay, and video artists such as Bruce Nauman explored such processes over multiple works. On television, reality formats from *Candid Camera* (1948 to 2014) to *Big Brother* (1999–) devised various different mechanisms for participants to see their own recorded behaviour, and in some instances for audiences to see these

---

[3] See Stuart Cunningham and David Craig, *Social Media Entertainment: The New Intersection of Hollywood and Silicon Valley* (New York: NYU Press, 2019) and Stuart Cunningham and David Craig (eds.), *Creator Culture: An Introduction to Global Social Media Entertainment* (New York: NYU Press, 2021).

acts of seeing. However, it was Japanese television quiz shows that pioneered the format of using an image within an image, known as a 'waipu' box, to display reactions, for example on *Naruhodu* (The World, 1981–), which featured celebrities and comedians reacting to short videos. This subsequently became a popular format globally, for example, on contemporary popular UK comedy panel shows. However, none of these televisual precursors are fully blown reaction videos, since they lack the DIY element made possible by digital platforms, such as YouTube, and were even rare in the early years of YouTube, since both the software infrastructures to support them and the associated technical skills required, were not immediately available to amateur users.

In fact, early YouTube reaction videos tended not to show what was being reacted to, but only usually terrified, disgusted or other extreme reactions to material that it would be impossible to share on the platform, such as the infamous so-called '2 Girls, 1 Cup' scatological fetish trailer (for *Hungry Bitches*, 2007), which gave rise to multiple of these types of reaction video.[4] The next era of reaction videos tended to be to film and television and related trailers, for example, to heightened moments of cult TV shows such as *Game of Thrones* (2011 to 2019), which already had multiple reaction videos by 2013. These reaction videos essentially developed the format that would be followed in music video reactions. Except in the case of full-length films or TV episodes, these would often be limited to trailers or edited highlights, so as not to infringe intellectual property and copyright rules that were increasingly being enforced on the platform with strong pressure from entertainment industries. Music video reactions were not immediately so common, partly because music videos were still circulating more on television than on YouTube early on, and partly because as a media form they lacked the status of high-profile and cult film and television. However, this all shifted in the 2010s, as YouTube became a primary location for disseminating music videos and popular music itself, while the music video form acquired a new status, both as an aesthetic and commercial product, and as a marker of specific popular music eras, scenes and histories.[5]

Although it is impossible to fully characterize the genres and eras of popular music involved in reaction videos, this is frequently historical material from the

---

[4] On the multiple responses to these reaction videos, see Heather Warren-Crow, 'Screaming Like a Girl: Viral Video and the Work of Reaction,' *Feminist Media Studies* 16, no. 6 [Online] (October 2016): 1,113–17. Although fascinating, these kind of reaction videos have little in common technically or textually with the reaction videos discussed here.

[5] See Gina Arnold, Daniel Cookney, Kirsty Fairclough and Michael Goddard (eds), *Music/Video: Histories, Aesthetics, Media* (London: Bloomsbury, 2017), 1–13 ff.

late-twentieth century; the material being processed largely coming from various forms of rock, punk, metal, indie, new wave and other forms of often 'white' music genres. Although there is also considerable diversity among reactors, in terms of ethnicity, gender, age and relations to popular music styles, there has been a recent tendency towards young African-American reactors, often but not necessarily coming more from backgrounds in hip-hop, reggae and pop music, but branching out well beyond this in their reactions. The affective labour of reactors therefore is not only in performing a 'sincere' reaction to the archival material, but also translating it in various ways to a new and often very different time period and cultural context. This cross-cultural mediation of popular music by reacting to music videos on YouTube, is an exponentially increasing form of YouTube content in recent years, and provides the basis for this chapter. These videos can range from the descriptive, to the extremely personal, from comments on the energy, beauty and power of performances, to the meanings or meaninglessness of the song lyrics. The framings of these responses in terms of everything from video intros to the *mise-en-scène* of the reactor space and use of costume and make-up, also play an essential role in the various styles of these responses.

This chapter will engage with several of these channels, including 'Sincerely KSO', 'Jayvee TV', 'The Jayy Show', 'India Reacts', 'Pink Metalhead', 'Kae and Livy' and 'Brad and Lex', to track how these reactors perform acts of media and cultural translation enabled but also constrained by the algorithmically determined affordances of the YouTube platform. These channels were selected based on the following criteria:

1. They are all popular channels that specialize in reactions to music videos with at least 70K subscribers.
2. They are all created by non-white creators, and are largely but not exclusively African-American creators.
3. They predominantly react to a range of rock-related music genres (classic rock, punk, pop punk, metal, emo), which are usually coded as being made by white performers for largely white audiences.

These criteria were used to emphasize cross-cultural acts of 'listening, viewing, interpretation and appropriation', alongside more subjective criteria, such as capturing a range of affective responses, or the quality of the interpretations provided. This chapter will interrogate how this work of listening, understanding and feeling operates as a kind of affective prosthesis for subscribers, by means of which they are able to re-experience familiar musical material with fresh ears and eyes, and look at a range of affective listening experiences enacted by the reactors. It will finally ask, especially given the context of Covid-19 social distancing, how the often-addictive experience of reaction videos constitutes a kind of substitute sociality, allowing for highly mediated performances of sincerity and authenticity, and constructing utopian relationships between subjects who might otherwise have little in common.

## Theoretical Approach

As indicated in the title, reaction videos are definitely instances of remediation, to use Jay Bolter and Richard Grusin's term, but ones that combine multiple layers of digital remediation.[6] After all, music videos are already remediations of recorded music, which attain further levels of remediation by being relocated to a social media platform, such as YouTube, and hence are already, in principle, subject to commentary, sharing and modification.[7] Reaction videos, however, add another layer to this, which doesn't correspond to conventional discussions of UGC, mashups or other social media phenomena. Reactors do not attempt to modify the content they react to, and instead tend to show it the utmost respect, treating the sometimes arbitrary combination of music and visuals as an integral whole to be felt and sometimes engaged with exegetically by intuitive interpretations or by reading out lyrics. The exception to this being the need to obscure, blur or otherwise disguise certain videos for copyright reasons. However, this incorporation necessarily takes place in a hypermediated form, in that reaction videos consist of two windows, a large one usually of the reactor and a smaller one of the material reacted to. This has several determinations both technical and economic, since 'owners' of the original content will often make claims against its remediation, especially if this might be profitable to reactors rather than to these proprietary companies; YouTube responds in various ways to these claims, from taking down videos, to eliminating the audio or video content, to even stopping reactors from uploading further material. Although some of these issues will be further engaged with, the focus of this paper will be on reaction videos as affective labour that requires further explanation.

---

[6] Jay David Bolter and Richard Grusin, *Remediation: Understanding New Media* (Cambridge, MA: MIT Press, 1999).
[7] Arnold, Cookney, Fairclough and Goddard, *Music/Video*, 12.

User activities online have often been seen in the context of 'free labour', as developed especially by Terranova. Terranova makes a complex argument that free labour encompasses both fully voluntary activities that played an essential role in developing the Internet, for example via free and open-source software development, as well as forms of exploitative unpaid labour, such as the unpaid production of content on online platforms that businesses then profit from, as she puts it:

> The new Web was made of the big players, but also of new ways to make the audience work. In the new Web, after the pioneering days, television and the Web converge is the one thing they have in common: their reliance on their audience/users as providers of the cultural labour which goes under the label 'real life stories'.[8]

This is incredibly prescient, since it predates the emergence of the major Web 2.0 platforms such as YouTube or Facebook, but already anticipates their digital economies based around the free labour of user activities, capitalized on immediately via various instruments from advertising to data commodification. But even before these developments, Terranova was able to pick up on a key distinction that informs this current research, namely that whereas earlier media, such as television mobilized the audience as both labour and spectacle, for example through reality and talk shows, this was always within a majoritarian and moralizing apparatus of power and knowledge, framed and remediated through the channel, the host and the format. In contrast, material circulates on the Web without these frameworks, allowing for a much greater heterogeneity and excess proliferation of 'unprofessional' or uncoded material, of which pornography would be an obvious example. In her words: 'the digital economy cares only tangentially about morality. What it really cares about is an abundance of production, an immediate interface with cultural and technical labour, whose result is a diffuse, non-dialectical antagonism and a crisis in the capitalist modes of valorization of labour as such'.[9] Although this might sound like an overly optimistic perspective based on the context of early 2000s web development before the new hegemonic platforms that would indeed take over some of the moralizing functions of television, what it points to is the emergence of new forms of organization of labour in online contexts that are highly relevant to the example of reaction videos, specifically in the ways that they mobilize the

[8] Terranova, 'Free Labour,' 96.
[9] Ibid.

collective intelligence and 'open potentiality of the many', while at the same time developing new forms of organization and constraints of this potential in order to extract surplus value via the ways in which platforms such as YouTube are constituted.[10]

The authors of a 2014 study of the creation of UGC around music videos on YouTube, identified a range of possible modes of remediation of music including covers, remixes, parodies, dancing and flash mobs, as well as reactions. Interestingly, it was the first four of these that was most prevalent, and the numbers of reaction videos across multiple genres was negligible.[11] Although these types of UGC remain popular, reaction videos have now taken a much more prominent place on YouTube, and some genres of UGC have migrated to other platforms, such as TikTok, which were developed precisely to facilitate this kind of content. However, discussion of the proliferation of this kind of UGC on TikTok as well as other platforms, such as Instagram or even YouTube shorts, is beyond the scope of this chapter. Whatever the case, there has certainly been a resurgence of reaction videos over the past few years, especially during the period of Covid lockdowns, as well as responses to these phenomena in mainstream media outlets.[12] Furthermore, I would question whether, in many cases, UGC is the most appropriate term to grasp the digital economies that are involved in the production and circulation of these materials.

So, if reaction videos are not yet another example of UGC as free labour, then what kind of labour are we talking about? My hypothesis is that this labour corresponds to free labour in the sense that it is freely chosen online activity that is determined for reasons beyond simply being a way of making money, but the economy behind these videos is more complex than simply being further free advertising for popular music industries. YouTube channels, if they have enough subscribers, can be monetized, and there are possibilities that their creators can make money through advertising. Furthermore, creators frequently also have Patreon or similar accounts, whereby subscribers can directly pay to receive 'benefits', like their requests going to the front of the queue, which is not

---

[10] Ibid., 97.
[11] Jaimie Y. Park, Jiyeon Jang, Alejandro Jaimes, Chin-wan Chung, Daejeon Korea and Sung-hyon Myaeng, 'Exploring the User-Generated Content (UGC) Uploading Behavior on YouTube', in *World Wide Web Conference 14 Proceedings* (2014), 529–34, 2014.
[12] See Jonathan Bernstein, 'How YouTube Reaction Videos Are Changing the Way We Listen: After a Viral Reaction to a Phil Collins Hit, Channel Creators Reflect on How Their Work is Re-Framing Classic Songs – and Breaking Down Cultural Barriers in the Process', *Rolling Stone* (24 August 2020), at https://www.rollingstone.com/music/music-features/youtube-reaction-videos-interviews-in-the-air-tonight-lost-in-vegas-1046225/.

insignificant when popular channels might have between 80K and 250K plus subscribers. Through these back-end architectures, reactors such as Jayy of The Jayy Show, also sell merchandise from clothing to headphones. PinkMetalHead, for example, makes videos of her exercise routines and clothing try-ons available to paid subscribers, while Kae and Livy are using paid requests for songs for a GoFundMe fund to build their own house.

But what value are reactors adding that might encourage subscribers to invest in their various 'brands'? This is where notions of sincerity and authenticity come in, as well as a complex economy of affective labour. Whereas subscribers request reactions to material that they already know, and in some cases have strong fandom relationships to, reactors usually claim to have never heard the music before, or at least only in passing in a film or on the radio (which they will usually stop the video to admit to). So what subscribers are paying for, whether economically or just in terms of investing time and attention in the channel, is a first time and therefore 'authentic' reaction to a piece of music and/or video that they know and love, but which in most cases is no longer fresh or new. For their part, reactors are intuitive archaeologists following the suggestions of their subscribers for a variety of explicit motives from 'keeping music alive' (Jamel aka

**Table 1** Table showing the main channels discussed in this chapter, their numbers of subscribers and videos

| Channel name | Number of subscribers | Number of videos | Month and year started |
| --- | --- | --- | --- |
| PinkMetalHead | 98K | 440 | July 2017 |
| The Jayy Show | 86.1K | 1,031 | January 2020 |
| JayVee TV | 245K | 1,696 | July 2019 |
| Sincerely KSO | 94.4K | 680 | January 2020 |
| Brad and Lex | 163K | 1,083 | January 2021 |
| IndiaReacts | 256K | 2,192 | August 2018 |
| Dean Bros/Kae and Livy | 72.15K | 1,531 | March 2019* |
| Twins the New Trend | 876K | 1,422 | July 2019** |
| BillyYouSoCrazy | 280K | 3,353 | August 2018 |
| Jamel aka Jamal | 852K | 3,185 | February 2019*** |

\* Channel began in 2017 but featured other content-like pranks and reactions to sports videos until 2019.
\*\* Channel began in 2017 but featured other content until 2019.
\*\*\* Not all reactions are to music videos in the beginning.

Jamal 'My Favourite Music Era', [video description], August 2020) to going on a 'music journey' (IndiaReacts, Channel home page, March 2018), or being 'Your heavy metal princess in training' (PinkMetalHead, Channel About page, 2021) or some other version of an expressed love for music and the desire to extend their musical experience via this socially networked assemblage. Paradoxically this authenticity needs to be performed, usually through emotional and visceral response, some examples of which will be examined soon. Although some reactors may just bop along to the music and give some indication as to whether or not they like it, many of the reactors are more performative and visibly embody a range of affective and energetic responses to these acts of listening. In one of the few articles on the emotional labour of these reaction videos to date, Byrd McDaniel sums this up as embodying various layers of reactivity:

> [Reactivity] describes the approach that creators take to listening, as they heighten and exaggerate their visceral experience of music media. In these reaction videos, performers treat their individual sensitivity to music as an asset, giving them unparalleled access to music's power. [...] Regardless of how they react to the music, they treat their affective experience of music as a kind of asset or skill, something that yields profit, visibility and authority for them as listeners. Second, reactivity describes their goals for creating these videos, which creators hope will provoke subsequent reactions among viewers and subscribers. Reaction videos ideally create more reactions.[13]

So reaction videos are really complex, affective chain reactions from the suggestions of the subscribers to the reactors, and then from the reactors through performative acts of listening to the viewers/listeners, thereby encouraging them to react to the channel by supporting it through likes and subscriptions, if not financial support. However, despite the name 'reaction videos', I would see this more in terms of responsiveness than reactivity; the responsive capacities of these performative acts of listening, generating feelings, meaning and value for the subscribers and constituting not only an affective economy but also a mode of sociality that may explain the exponential increase of reaction videos during the period of Covid lockdowns.

One important aspect of this recent wave of reaction videos is the way they cut across social lines, especially racial ones. Of course, musical genres have never been exclusively defined along racial lines, and there are rich and complex

---

[13] Byrd McDaniel, 'Popular Music Reaction Videos: Reactivity, Creator Labor, and the Performance of Listening Online,' *New Media and Society* 23, no 6 (2020): 2–3.

histories of musical genres. such as rock and roll, blues and jazz that have incorporated and combined forms of music originally coded as predominantly black or white. And although a lot of this movement is coded as the white appropriation of black music, the reverse has also occurred, as black artists appropriate elements of rock, psychedelic or punk music usually seen as largely white, whether in the case of an artist such as Prince, or participation in punk music by groups such as Bad Brains. However, especially where it comes to classic rock, or in a different way 1980s synthpop, these forms of music have largely been seen as coded as white, both in terms of their producers and their audiences. These are just the lines that music reaction videos tend to cross, adding up to an intervention in modes of listening to and participating in popular music and culture.

In a 2020 article for *Flow* Journal, María Elena Cepeda breaks down some of these issues, beginning with what she calls the relatively rare phenomenon in the era of algorithmically enhanced taste cultures of the 'opportunity for highly fragmented media audiences to engage each other over their shared appreciation for a common media text'.[14] What this amounts to, in the context of the escalation of racial conflicts in the form of police murders of African-Americans and resistance to this in the intensification of the Black Lives Matter movement, is 'an alternative view of Blackness, one marked by an emphasis on one of the most pleasurable of human acts: listening to music'.[15] Although keen to point out the political ambivalences at play with reaction videos, such as whether they are truly breaking down racially coded music genres and listening practices, or are overdetermined by racial power relations, in the relations that black creators have with the musical producers and with their subscribers who are assumed to be largely older and white, it is necessary to keep these complexities open, and neither make utopian claims for reaction videos as ushering in a post-racial era of music listening nor as merely re-inscribing existing relations of power. Certainly, as Jonathan Bernstein suggests, the almost complete indifference to music genres and the ways they are conventionally coded and contextualized is certainly changing the way popular music is being listened to, and raising important questions about who it is produced by and for, while challenging racialized assumptions about the answers to these questions.[16] PinkMetalHead

---

[14] María Elena Cepeda, 'Race and the Unintended Consequences of Musical Reaction Videos,' *Flow* (25 October 2020), at https://www.flowjournal.org/2020/10/musical-reaction-videos/.
[15] Ibid.
[16] Bernstein, 'How YouTube Reaction Videos Are Changing the Way We Listen.'

(Mona Platt), for example, grew up listening to Nu Metal, so exploring artists such as Black Sabbath, Slayer or Metallica was not such a great leap for her, even if it was seen as initially surprising on the part of the subscribers attracted to her channel.

In the rest of the chapter, I examine some of the specific strategies and affective performances of listening of reactors, organized not according to music genres or individual channels but rather affects. It will be impossible to discuss in detail all of the channels and reactors mentioned, so I have also assembled a YouTube playlist of reaction videos that can be consulted for further examples (this can be accessed via the QR code for this chapter). This list also includes some additional examples that operate quite differently, such as the 'React' channel, which organizes reactions of different demographic groups, and 'expert' review channels that trade on various forms of 'subcultural' capital, such as 'Album Review TV (ARTV, Beyond ARTV)' or even more obviously the 'Punk Rock MBA' or 'The Color Fred', the channel of former member of Emo band Taking Back Sunday who typically reacts both to his own and other emo videos. Although covering reactions to several different genres of music, the focus is on forms of alternative rock music conventionally coded as white, such as pop punk or emo, as well as some classic rock. This is because although classic rock has often been seen as making claims to universality, even if this was often in reality a very white form of universality based on appropriating black popular music genres, punk related genres are usually perceived as made by and for highly specific subcultures, and arguably have only circulated beyond this because of the affordances of digital platforms such as YouTube.

## Sadness/Tears/Nostalgia

One of the affects most at work for YouTube reaction videos subscribers is nostalgia, not only for specific songs, but also periods of their lives, which also often implies feelings of sadness and loss. It is therefore unsurprising that one of the key affects performed in reaction videos involves various degrees of sadness. This can be shown in everything from crying emojis in thumbnails, and titles such as 'Pink Floyd – Wish you were here (1985) Reaction (they made me cry again)' (PinkMetalHead), or 'I Cried like a Baby, Blink 182 "Adam's Song" REACTION!' (IndiaReacts). In the former, PinkMetalHead dedicates the song to a patient of hers who recently passed away, welling up in the process of talking about him, while the somewhat light treatment of suicide in Blink-182's 'Adam's Song' (1999) results in an even more personal performance of confessional emotion on the part of IndiaReacts, including talking about her own experiences of feeling suicidal (5.00).[17]

Similar reactions can be found to songs as different generically as REM's 'Everybody Hurts' (1992) or Tracy Chapman's 'Fast Car' (1988). Regardless of the genre of music, this form of reaction ratchets up the authenticity level by both affective performance of the body overwhelmed by emotion while listening, and the divulging of highly personal experiences, which in turn enable viewers who perhaps felt these intense emotions when they first heard the tracks in question, but after decades these resonances have inevitably faded away, to fully feel them once again. Several reactors describe themselves as empaths and vehemently deny that anything about their live emotional reactions to music is fake. Reactors, therefore, through their own performances of affective embodied listening, give back to viewers their own past affectivity through these prosthetic acts of listening and feeling. Here the racialized aspects of these affective ecologies as emotive reactions of largely younger people of colour for largely older, largely white users, could be raised but it would be a mistake to over generalize and see this as simply a paid or unpaid servicing of nostalgia – clearly the reactors get more out of these experiences than simply economic compensation, or the sense of giving subscribers what they want – they instead have a cathartic experience that many of them refer to in terms of 'love' that they feel both for their subscribers and from them.

It is important to point here to the seeming contradiction of contemporary digital platforms being a vehicle for nostalgia, a paradox recently explored by Grafton Tanner. Pointing to the nostalgia mobilized in the rise to presidency of Donald J. Trump, Tanner points out that this is hardly surprising, given that nostalgia frequently arises in periods of 'social, political and even personal unrest'.[18] But this is not merely a phenomenon external to technological platforms, but one that they actively produce and circulate so much so that he argues that the attention economy of social media is complemented or expressed

---

[17] India Reacts, 'I CRIED Like a Baby! Blink-182-Adam's Song REACTION!,' *YouTube video*, 00:08:24, 2December2020,https://www.youtube.com/watch?v=CCzrpvQHVKw&list=PLJT_IMCv7TkgrNVeG8-331xLh4ZVbSerp&index=4&t=359s.

[18] Grafton Tanner, *The Circle of the Snake: Nostalgia and Utopia in the Age of Big Tech* (Winchester: Zero Books, 2020), 8.

via a 'nostalgia industry'.[19] In addition to there being many incentives to escape into an imaginary past, essentially the Internet is a vast repository of artefacts from the past, of which music videos on YouTube would be a prime example, given that it is the videos from the late-twentieth century, the era of the ascendancy of music television, that tend to recirculate the most on reaction channels. But nostalgia is not just the intersection of the desire to escape the present into an imaginary better past and archival platforms, but, as Tanner writes, is also actively cultivated by algorithmically driven platforms:

> The structures of social media and online advertising encourage nostalgia to circulate. Recommender systems and predictive analytics – the very tools that allow our contemporary media to function – zero in on quick reactions, such as a flash of anger or a swell of nostalgia. These reactions are noted by algorithms, which then make recommendations based on them [...] the result is a nostalgic feedback loop wherein old ideas travel around.[20]

Like most writing on nostalgia, of which there is a rich tradition, including authors such as Fredric Jameson, it is generally seen as inherently reactionary, hence the indexing of nostalgia to the Trump phenomenon, for example. Other authors use terms such as 'retromania' (Simon Reynolds),[21] or the cancellation of the future (Mark Fisher),[22] to point to similar phenomena of popular music and culture in digital contexts having abandoned any form of 'progress' and reverting to the mere empty recycling of the past. Nevertheless, music reaction videos also prompt us to call these notions of nostalgia into question, especially the idea of whether nostalgic relations between the present and the past are necessarily so many forms of cultural amnesia and the annulment of historical awareness. Instead, it could be argued that the relations between the present and the past that reaction videos set up could in certain instances constitute non dialectical constellations in a Benjaminian sense, capable of undoing the certainties of the present through the unexhausted potentialities of fragments and artefacts of the past: perhaps music videos are our equivalent of Walter Benjamin's outmoded arcades, and reactors intuitive media archaeologists of these popular culture ruins.[23] As a

---

[19] Ibid., 9.
[20] Tanner, *The Circle of the Snake*, 10.
[21] Simon Reynolds, *Retromania: Pop Culture's Addiction to its Own Past* (London: Faber and Faber, 2012).
[22] Mark Fisher, *Ghosts of my Life: Writings on Depression, Hauntology and Lost Futures* (Winchester: Zero Books, 2014).
[23] Walter Benjamin, *The Arcades Project*, trans. Howard Eiland and Kevin McLaughlin (Cambridge, Mass.: Harvard University Press, 1999).

counter-example that fully embodies the reactionary nostalgia that critics in the Jamesonian tradition identify, we could look at the reaction channel created by Cat Sarai, 'Gen X Rewind.' The problem here is not the ethnicity of the reactor but the fact that she is reacting to the same music she loved and enjoyed twenty years earlier. There is no element of surprise or discovery here, just the presentation of an historical era of popular music from the 1980s and 1990s as intrinsically superior to music produced today. This form of nostalgia comes across as smug and elitist, as well as empty of anything but a comfortable and unchallenging exercise in reactionary nostalgia. The music might overlap considerably with that reacted to in the channels discussed in this chapter, but it is the relay and affective exchange between these reactors and their subscribers that changes everything; yes cross-cultural reaction channels do activate nostalgia, but it is not based on the reactors' long entrenched tastes, but rather on a process of mutual discovery between the reactors, their subscribers and the network that makes nostalgia function differently, as part of an assemblage of cross-cultural remediation.

## Humour/Laughter

Humour is another key affect performed by reactors, and several reactors who respond to music videos also respond to televisual or stand-up comedy, sometimes on a separate channel. But it is not necessary to go to explicitly defined comedy genres when there are videos by pop punk bands, such as The Offspring that receive a disproportionate number of reactions considering their significance in popular musical history. Although this applies to several of their videos, the vast majority of reactions are to 'Pretty Fly (for a White Guy)' (1998) whose humorous roasting of a white 'wannabee' could be seen as problematic for multiple reasons, such as its use of African-American and Latino/a stereotypes in both the song and the video. In fact, a recent article in *The Quietus* by J R Moores re-evaluated the band's output, especially songs like this from the *Americana* album, as so many expressions of 'punching down' claiming that the group is punk's equivalent to the contemporaneous TV series *Friends*:

> They may not have been so guilty at first, but by the time of their fourth album (1997's *Ixnay On The Hombre*), The Offspring had adopted the rich's undignified habit of sneering down at those less fortunate and far weaker than themselves. [...] 1998's *Americana*, is practically a concept album on how [...] implicitly loathsome sad sacks need to snap out of it, get a grip, sort themselves out, pull

their fingers out and their socks up, stop whining, pull themselves together, etc., etc., etc.[24]

Instead of this difficult to dispute re-evaluation of the band, which is only made more evident in its music videos, such as the one for 'Pretty Fly (for a White Guy)', most reactors seem to fully appreciate its humour, and tend, if anything, to feel sorry for the white wannabe protagonist's failed attempts to appropriate black culture. Certainly the idea that The Offspring's critical presentations of white 'wannabe' behaviour might be no less racist in its reproduction of stereotypes is something that is not generally mentioned. Rather than being about critique of racial representations (which does appear in some reaction videos, but more often in hip-hop related ones like to Joyner Lucas's 'I'm not Racist'(2017)), this video is usually responded to as pure comedy. But this avoidance of critique is more to do with the affective functions of reaction videos than any naivete on the part of the reactors. Although 'review' channels, such as *The Punk Rock MBA* point to similar shortcomings as at best cheesy both musically and conceptually, reaction videos are not there to pass judgement but respond affectively to a first-time listening and viewing experience. And Offspring videos do definitely lend themselves to a response of humour and laughter, however problematic their lyrics might be on closer investigation.

In general, pop punk as a genre is fairly suitable for this kind of response, for example, reactions to most Blink-182 videos, such as their boy band parody video for 'All the Small Things' (2000). As the band has pointed out in the video 'Blink-182 Reacts to Kids Reacting to Blink-182', this video has outlived the objects of its parody such as N' Sync, so that the absurd costume choices and onscreen behaviour will now be read as if they were themselves a boy band or at least scramble the differences between them. Another good example of this is the track by 2000s pop punk band The All-American Rejects, 'Gives you Hell' (2008), which BillyYouSoCrazy reacts to. In this video the lead singer and would-be Hollywood actor Tyson Ritter plays two roles of both an uptight straight suburbanite and a louche rock star inexplicably living next door who come into conflict and taunt each other in various ways before sleeping with each other's wife or girlfriend. But the heart of the song is based on bitterness about a previous relationship while pretending not to care about it, disguising feelings of loss

---

[24] J R Moores, 'The One With The Conservative Agenda: Why The Offspring Is Punk's Equivalent Of Friends,' *The Quietus* (November 2018), at https://thequietus.com/articles/25686-offspring-americana-review-anniversary.

through condescension and ridicule: 'Tomorrow you'll be thinkin' to yourself/ Yeah, where'd it all go wrong?/But the list goes on and on' (2008). In this reaction video, Billy sees right through the light-hearted video and the bittersweet humour of the lyrics, which is also reflected in its relatively pop musical style, and points out how this surface humour is a thin disguise for deep feelings of loss and resentment, describing it in the video subtitle as 'THE MOST BITTER SONG I EVER HEARD LMAO'. This can be seen in reactions to other music videos, for example to the B52s, which although not meant or reacted to as mere comedy, nevertheless communicate across genre differences by incorporating humour both into the musical style and especially the lyrics and their delivery, as well as music videos. As these contrasting examples show, the communication enabled by humour can just simply end there or promote the reading of deeper underlying meanings in the course of the reaction.

## Shock/Surprise

Another key affect performed by reaction video is shock or surprise. While this can be on the level of having expectations from the name of a group or song, and then the track turning out to be quite different, more dynamically it is when a song changes dramatically at a given moment. No song is perhaps more dramatic in this regard than Ukrainian metal band Jinjer and their song 'Pisces' (2016). Beginning as a mellow jazzy tune with emotional and strong but sweet feminine vocals on the part of vocalist Tatiana Shmailyuk, at a given moment a rising squall of feedback gives way to heavy metal riffage and an extraordinary vocal performance of growling vocals by the female singer that has caused more than one reactor to virtually fall out of their seat, as can be seen in the example on the playlist from Brad and Lex who began their reaction channel by most often reacting to hip-hop, including UK hip-hop but also selected other rock music groups such as Tool (they have now considerably expanded their range and cover the full spectrum of different rock genres as well as other popular music genres). This kind of reaction video in a way harks back to early more prank-like reaction videos on early YouTube or even television shows such as *Candid Camera*, especially when reactors then subject other family members, such as siblings and especially parents to this music video, in order to enjoy their shocked reactions.

Something similar if less dramatic happens when JayVee of JayveeTV reacts to Weezer's 'Say it Ain't So' (1994), which he had turned up because it was so quiet, only to be floored by the sudden explosion of power pop noise after the first verses. Or alternatively Kae and Livy's reaction to My Chemical Romance's 'Welcome to the Black Parade' (2006) is one of being energized synaesthetically by all the elements from the vocals to the *mise-en-scène* of the video, to the dramatic 'switch up' of the music into a more punk style in the bridge, leading to multiple interruptions of the video and listening accompanied by energetic movement and even singing along to the chorus despite this supposedly being a first experience of the music video. These reactions and more generally these reactors, although very different, share a tendency to react less in terms of emotion than energy, whether or not this is accompanied or triggered by shock or surprise. However, this is no less affective labour than crying or laughing, and similarly translates music associated with a specific largely white subculture, in this case, emo, to a differently racialized act of listening, informed by a previous history of reactions.

## Areas for Further Research

Having sketched out some but by no means all of the key affective registers deployed in reaction videos across the reaction channels I have focused on, what kind of conclusions can be drawn and what further areas for research can be identified? I would first make the caveat that I have not yet even researched these channels systematically, and the reaction videos I have seen and selected for analysis are as much about my own musical tastes and preferences as any claim to represent any individual channel in an exhaustive way. It is also important to point out that the nature of reaction videos is to be quite fluid, and reactors have often made substantial changes to their whole approach, whether in terms of the genres of music selected, strategies to evade issues of intellectual property and censorship by the platform, or finding different way to communicate with and include audiences, whether through live reaction shows or off platform Patreon and other secondary platforms, or through the selling of merchandize. All of these strategies and their modulation over time are complex and can lead to some reactors becoming more and more popular, while others disappear entirely or reduce their activity drastically. Nevertheless, it is possible to isolate several key areas for further investigation as itemized below:

**Techniques of reactivity:** this covers everything from verbal introductions to the décor and setting of the reaction, to the use of graphics by some reactors, to the incorporation of secondary material, such as Wikipedia or Genius lyrics information about the music. Sincerely KSO, for example, pays a lot of attention to colour in terms of both décor and her outfits, accessories and make-up, which are all part of the reaction. Even the two paintings on the wall of a yellow flower and a bee are there specifically to refer to her subscribers who she refers to as 'my hunnies'. Kae and Livy, who are much younger, have a kind of call and response catchphrase 'the grind don't stop till it hits the top, to the what, to the top, to the tippety tippety top', accompanied by a graphic explosion to hype up their viewers, while others such as JayVee TV and The Jayy Show have quite professional audiovisual opening sequences with music, graphics and in the latter case, the highlighting of material also available as merch. Although IndiaReacts will supplement her intuitive 'homegirl' interpretations of the meanings of songs through Wikipedia or Genius Lyrics, Sincerely KSO does performative readings of the lyrics of every song she reacts too, using these readings as a springboard for interpretation.

**Cross-cultural border crossings:** Although I gave some indication of the crossing of racialized generic boundaries of music listening, this was somewhat generalized as African-Americans with hip-hop and R and B backgrounds listening to 'white' music genres. In fact, even in my examples there is much more diversity; KSO is of a Nigerian background and is living in Canada, with no hip-hop background, as an African-American teenager, PinkMetalHead was a nu metal fan, so her reactions only built on this background, and other reactors give a truly global perspective to reaction videos such as Enoma (easygoing native outsiders making assessments), an Indian couple who often preface their reactions with an extreme emphasis on unedited authenticity, as well as listing their multiple degrees, or AfricaReacts who describes herself as 'an African girl responding to music, comedy and stories from around the globe'. More recently, a Pakistan based channel called 'Trybals' present subjects who are situated as 'tribal people' with a range of mostly Western musical phenomena from classical opera to Rammstein. But boundaries can also be closer to home, for example in Brad and Lex's reaction to UK hip-hop artist LowKey's 'Ghosts of Grenfell', which, while still ostensibly within a familiar genre, involves a local historical tragic fire taking place within the borough of Kensington and Chelsea in London. This video and its sequel therefore becomes an impetus for learning more about this tragedy, and what it represents in terms of multiple forms of inequality. As such, these videos and the reactions to them can function as a form of citizen journalism, even if this is a relatively rare phenomenon in the world of reaction videos.

**Affective ecologies and economies:** This is really the main theme of this whole chapter – there is a lot more to reaction videos than meets the eye; from complex relations between reactors and subscribers that are both affective and economic, to the performance of authenticity as a value adding brand, to the battles that reactors engage in with the algorithmic governance of the YouTube platform. The view of this presented by the *Rolling Stone* article is quite misleading in this regard: yes a few of the most popular reactors might catch the attention of some music, fashion or other companies, and be offered some kind of more legitimate career path, but this is a tiny minority. Even reactors who are very productive and might produce three videos a day, and have approaching 100K subscribers, get little or no corporate support or income from the platform, and are just as likely to see the results of their work subject to take downs, silencing or other punitive actions on behalf of purported copyright holders for what is on one level the sharing of advertising (for example, the famous 'Twins the New Trend' Phil Collins 'Something in the Air Tonight' reaction led to a 1,000 per cent spike in sales of the track). They therefore develop a whole range of strategies to avoid detection and blocking by the algorithm from smaller windows, or windows with distracting framings, or multiple windows within windows, etc.

At the very least, reaction videos are a complex phenomenon of digital remediation of music and listening, which, as the *Rolling Stone* article does get right, are changing the online landscape of popular music by crossings and even complete indifference to genre, as well as contesting ideas that specific musical genres belong to racially delineated listeners, whether that be of classic rock, metal, punk, indie music or even hip-hop and R and B. Although not explicitly political beyond this, reaction video makers have frequently been politicized by the lack of support and outright interference from the platform in wholly siding with copyright holders against their creative practices in unjust and arbitrary ways. This has been expressed through videos directly addressing viewers (see also in the playlist), but also YouTube as well, and both calling out the unfairness of its practices and underlining the value of these channels for the appreciation and circulation of a wide variety of popular music. Underlying this are utopian aspirations for alternative forms of sociality, made possible by digital platforms in which there is not only a post-racial sharing and circulation of music and affects, but the formation of a sense of community or family embodied in many of the reactors' discourses. The role and significance of reaction videos is only likely to increase in the future, in tandem with new modes and platforms of digital remediation.

# Bibliography

Arnold, Gina, Daniel Cookney, Kirsty Fairclough and Michael Goddard (eds). *Music/Video: Histories, Aesthetics, Media*. London: Bloomsbury, 2017.

Benjamin, Walter. *The Arcades Project*, trans. Howard Eiland and Kevin McLaughlin. Cambridge, Mass.: Harvard University Press, 1999.

Bernstein, Jonathan. 'How YouTube Reaction Videos Are Changing the Way We Listen: After a Viral Reaction to a Phil Collins Hit, Channel Creators Reflect on How Their Work is Re-Framing Classic Songs – And Breaking Down Cultural Barriers in the Process.' *Rolling Stone,* 24 August 2020, at https://www.rollingstone.com/music/music-features/youtube-reaction-videos-interviews-in-the-air-tonight-lost-in-vegas-1046225/.

Bolter, Jay David and Richard Grusin. *Remediation: Understanding New Media*. Cambridge, MA: MIT Press, 1999.

Cepeda María Elena, 'Race and the Unintended Consequences of Musical Reaction Videos.' *Flow*. 25 October 2020, at https://www.flowjournal.org/2020/10/musical-reaction-videos/.

Cunningham, Stuart and David Craig. *Social Media Entertainment: The New Intersection of Hollywood and Silicon Valley*. New York: NYU Press, 2019.

Cunningham, Stuart and David Craig (eds). *Creator Culture: An Introduction to Global Social Media Entertainment*. New York: NYU Press, 2021.

Fisher, Mark. *Ghosts of my Life*: *Writings on Depression, Hauntology and Lost Futures*. Winchester: Zero Books, 2014.

Lovink, Geert. *Networks Without a Cause: A Critique of Social Media*. Cambridge: Polity, 2011.

McDaniel, Byrd. 'Popular Music Reaction Videos: Reactivity, Creator Labor, and the Performance of Listening Online.' *New Media and Society*. [Online First], 2020.

Moores, J R. 'The One With The Conservative Agenda: Why The Offspring Is Punk's Equivalent Of *Friends*.' *The Quietus,* November 2018, at https://thequietus.com/articles/25686-offspring-americana-review-anniversary.

Park, Jaimie Y. et al. 'Exploring the User-Generated Content (UGC) Uploading Behavior on YouTube.' *World Wide Web Conference* 14 Proceedings, 2014.

Reynolds, Simon. *Retromania: Pop Culture's Addiction to its Own Past*. London: Faber and Faber, 2012.

Tanner, Grafton. *The Circle of the Snake: Nostalgia and Utopia in the Age of Big Tech*. Winchester: Zero Books, 2020.

Terranova, Tiziana. 'Free Labour.' In *Network Culture: Politics for the Information Age*, 73–97. London: Pluto Press, 2004.

Warren-Crow, Heather. 'Screaming Like a Girl: Viral Video and the Work of Reaction,' *Feminist Media Studies* 16, no 6 (October 2016): 1,113–17.

4

# Internet Archiving: The Many Lives of Songs in the YouTube Age

Henrik Smith Sivertsen

In the early spring of 2013, Danish singer and songwriter, Lukas Graham Forchhammer and his band, Lukas Graham, wrote a new song, '7 Years'.[1] Inspired by his father's sudden death in 2012, it was a song about life. Starting with the lines 'Once I was seven-years-old my mama told me go make yourself some friends or you'll be lonely', Graham structured the song over a line of impact points from his life, from 7 to 60 (7–11–20–30–60). As Graham was only twenty-two at the time of writing, most of the song outlines how he imagined the rest of his life would unfold. Since its Danish release on 16 June 2015, the song moved through various countries, first topping the charts in Scandinavia, before reaching number two on America's Billboard Hot 100 on 4 April 2016.[2] Within three years, '7 Years' had become a massive global hit.[3]

Although the 'Lukas Graham story' has been widely relayed, most notably in René Sascha Johannsen's 2020 documentary *7 Years of Lukas Graham*, the rapidity with which versions and covers of the song spread through YouTube, and the impact that this spread has had on the song's sensational success, is rarely considered. This is the story that I will tell. Here, I use '7 Years' to explore how hit songs have many lives in the brave new world of fan engagement, participatory culture, reappropriation and remediation, a world that has

---

[1] Here, I use his shortened name, Lukas Graham.
[2] Stuart Dredge, '7 Years: How Streaming Fuelled the Rapid Rise of Lukas Graham,' *Music Ally*, 23 March 2016, https://musically.com/2016/03/23/7-years-streaming-lukas-graham/.
[3] Billboard Hot 100, 'Chart History – Lukas Graham,' *Billboard*, https://www.billboard.com/artist/lukas-graham/chart-history/hsi/.

fundamentally changed the possibilities for music circulation. From an archival perspective, I trace the variety of musical versioning practices on YouTube to explore how recent and significant shifts in musicking have challenged what we might traditionally have considered to be a musical work. To do this, I have tracked down and registered as many versions of '7 Years' as possible, dividing them into two categories that run parallel to each other:

1. The versions performed and controlled by Lukas Graham and / or their music company.
2. The versions produced and / or performed by others.

This research began in 2015, after two related archival projects (in 2012 and 2014) threw into relief the various issues with analyzing online content: the first examined an early Danish case of a song going viral through cover versions in 2008;[4] the second focused on saving the 2014 European Song Contest (ESC) as an online event.[5] Comparing the two cases, it was clear that engagement with online material had changed radically within these six years. The material from 2008 was primarily amateurish cover versions, mostly in the shape of answer songs, while material from ESC 2014 was, although multifaceted, often in the form of high-quality video productions. It was obvious that what Axel Bruns calls 'produsage' was no longer an underground practice.[6] Not only had the idea of manipulating, covering and mashing up official moving-image content become a key phenomenon across Cybermedia, it was now built into the ESC's core as the slogan for the annual TV-show became 'Join us!'. In the months preceding the final events, fans were encouraged to record their own performances of the Danish 2013 winning song 'Only Teardrops' by Emmelie de Forest (2013) and upload them to the event homepage. These recordings were then integrated into the opening act at the first semifinal.[7]

Although this phenomenon presented new ways of engaging and interacting with screen media, it also problematized existing methods of audiovisual

---

[4] Henrik Smith-Sivertsen, *Et vaskeægte Myspace-fænomen – Sys Bjerre I Netarkivet* (Copenhagen: Danish Royal Library, 2014).
[5] Thomas Hoffmann, 'Eurovision Song Contest to be Part of Denmark's Cultural Heritage,' *ScienceNordic*, 8 May 2014, https://sciencenordic.com/culture-denmark-eurovision/eurovision-song-contest-to-be-part-of-denmarks-cultural-heritage/1400969.
[6] Axel Bruns, *Blogs, Wikipedia, Second Life, and Beyond: From Production to Produsage* (New York: Peter Lang, 2008).
[7] Eurovision Song Contest, 'Opening of the first Semi-Final of the 2014 Eurovision Song Contest with Emmelie de Forest,' *YouTube video*, 00:05:55, 7 May 2014, https://www.youtube.com/watch?v=3B0KLCPYc68. Archived at www.archive.org.

analysis. Research into the interactive possibilities of the ESC project, revealed that only a fragment of musical culture is acknowledged if only 'official recordings' are considered, even when these include live TV performances.[8] And yet, engaging with the fan-generated paratexts became difficult almost immediately: within several weeks of the broadcast, many of the versions, including the most popular ones, had been deleted. The only evidence that they had ever existed were my screenshots of the YouTube pages and their noted URLs. Therefore, when Lukas Graham started crawling up the world charts in Autumn 2015, I started preparing a similar project with the archival methods in the foreground; and this time I was focusing primarily on YouTube and *musical versioning practices*.

The latter term was developed during my Ph.D. project on Danish versions of international songs from 1945 to 2007.[9] In this historical study, the focus was primarily on translating and covering, two processes reflecting the most relevant musical versioning practices in a mediascape defined by regionality (geographical, cultural and linguistic), physicality (records, CDs, tapes etc.), broadcasting (radio and TV) and 'rock ideology' (originality and authenticity).[10] I described how technological changes have led to innovations in the way that music is produced, distributed and received. In the twentieth century, the major changes were the advent of, and accessibility to, sound recording devices, broadcasting (radio from the 1920s and TV from the 1950s) and reproduction technology (the tape recorder in the late 1940s). Although all these innovations were instrumental in increasing access to music, it was tape recording and its capacity for multitracking that enabled the radical manipulation of sound and introduced the concepts of an *original recording* and a *cover version*.[11] After tracing, analysing and comparing covers of a large number of songs, I discovered that the practice of versioning

---

[8] In Denmark we only recently changed our focus from physical CDs to digital files from the online music services. In 2014 we collected about 100 videos from YouTube monthly, including genres from music and politics to entertainment and YouTubers, and so on. In 2022 we collected no videos.
[9] Henrik Smith-Sivertsen, 'Kylling med soft ice og pølser: populærmusikalske versioneringspraksisser i forbindelse med danske versioner af udenlandske sange i perioden 1945–2007' (Doctoral dissertation, Copenhagen, 2007).
[10] Ibid. For a firm introduction to ideology and popular music, see Keir Keightley, 'Reconsidering Rock,' in *The Cambridge Companion to Pop and Rock*, ed. John Street, Simon Frith and Will Straw (Cambridge: Cambridge University Press, 2001), 109–4.
[11] Albin Zak, '"The Tune Was Made By the Way It Was Played": Covers, Copies, and Recording Consciousness,' *The Musical Quarterly* 104, no. 1–2 (1 November 2021): 93–113; Marc Pendzich, *Von der Coverversion zum Hit-Recycling: historische, ökonomische und rechtliche Aspekte eines zentralen Phänomens der Pop-und Rockmusik* (LIT Verlag Münster, 2004); Michael Coyle, 'Hijacked Hits and Antic Authenticity: Cover Songs, Race, and Postwar Marketing,' in *Rock Over the Edge: Transformations in Popular Music Culture* (Duke University Press, 2002), 133–58.

contemporary songs declined drastically during the second half of the twentieth century, when the idea of an authentic, *original recording* gained a prominent position, both ideologically and institutionally. However, when I submitted my thesis in 2007, everything was changing because of YouTube. Within a few months, the practice of versioning was dominating social media's musical spaces. Although it initially seemed as though my research was already outdated, I was easily able to transport my methodological framework to the emergent platform.

Since 2007, a body of literature on musical versioning practices has emerged. And yet, despite Lassi Liikkanen's and Antti Salovaara's 2015 study that identified three main categories of YouTube versions – traditional, user-appropriated and derivative – there has been a tendency to analyse only one type of versioning at a time.[12] Here, I counter this tendency by working horizontally across the platform to track down every thinkable video relating to '7 Years', in order to explore the multiple ways in which people use YouTube as a primary archive for all kinds of musicking. This has revealed several things. First, is a new way of interpreting and exploring musical meaning. In the 1950s, when the international music industry was rebuilding after the Second World War, the translation of international hits into national languages allowed music to move between countries. The sub-rights to translated songs were transmitted from the songwriter's main publisher to local publishers.[13] Significantly, standard contracts included no clause concerning translational fidelity, which gave a great deal of interpretative power to the translators.[14] As a result, translated versions of popular music from 1945 to the early 1980s reveals a semantically complex collection of approaches, from strict word-by-word translations to brand-new lyrics that lack any semantic relation to the original. However, during the 1960s and 1970s, as English became the lingua franca of popular music, and because of a general shift towards artists performing their own music, songwriters and music publishers became keen to maintain the rights to their songs in order to preserve their 'original meaning'. By the end of the century, song translation generally required close retranslation to secure fidelity to the source text. By tracing '7 years' through YouTube's many spaces, I show that, when a song enters the public consciousness, it can be altered, sometimes dramatically, while still

---

[12] Lassi A. Liikkanen and Antti Salovaara, 'Music on YouTube: User Engagement with Traditional, User-Appropriated and Derivative Videos,' *Computers in Human Behavior* 50 (1 September 2015): 108–24.
[13] Pendzich, 'Von der Coverversion zum Hit-Recycling'; Smith-Sivertsen, 'Kylling med soft ice og pølse.'
[14] Ibid., 40ff.

remaining recognizable; and these changes can tell us a lot about the meaning and essence of a song as it travels through multiple voices.

Second, is a refreshed understanding of the *reference original* concept and its use as an analytical tool for musical analysis.[15] In his article on the musical work concept and popular music, Richard Middleton shows that although song covers need originating moments, the version being copied is not always the original recording.[16] For instance, country singer Johnny Darrell released the first recording of 'Green, Green Grass of Home' in 1965. A year later, Tom Jones released a cover of the song, which became the reference original for numerous subsequent versions, including Dean Martin's 1967 hit. As will be demonstrated below, the concept of the reference original is highly useful in relation to the present mediascape, where YouTube's peripheral and unofficial practices of covering, remixing and translating coexist with the original and professionally produced covers distributed via music companies on the same platform.

## '7 Years' in Six

The database of versions of '7 Years', collected between 2015 and 2021, includes videos from YouTube pages harvested by the national Danish Web Archive.[17] Although impossible, the goal to register every version online required pressing to the limits of the different search functions. The first crucial findings were that limits are quite arbitrary. For example, searching for '7 Years and Lukas Graham' via Google's search engine throws up approximately 694,000 hits under the search box, but only 138 of these are shown. Access, then, is limited to only a tiny fragment of the relevant material, and the criteria for Google's selection is withheld. On YouTube, more hits are revealed, but the dark numbers remain immense: no matter the search, only a limited number of videos are shown in the results. Confounding matters further, these restrictions are not stable but oscillate between

---

[15] Ibid; Smith-Sivertsen, 'Et vaskeægte Myspace-fænomen.'
[16] Middleton actually writes about 'covers' and not 'versions'.
[17] References to all '7 Years'-related YouTube videos and pages mentioned in this article are found in a dataset collection published on https://loar.kb.dk/: Henrik Smith-Sivertsen and Kristoffer Brinch Kjeldby, *The 7 Years dataset* (2022), distributed by the Royal Danish Library. I have used both Netarkivet and the Internet Archive in this project, particularly to build the chronologies. The harvested YouTube pages include the titles, descriptions, views and likes data, and the suggested links to related videos. When possible, I primarily refer to the Internet Archive, as their permanent links are publicly accessible. The Internet Archive URL's both contains the URL harvested and a precise timestamp.

550 and 600. A simple search for '7 Years' and 'Lukas Graham' using the citation marks to minimize the number of irrelevant results, still reveals a similar number of results, as does the use of a filter to search a specific time range.

In the case of '7 Years', the number of weekly uploads of related videos has remained quite stable at around 100 videos since 2017.[18] This means that even monthly searches risk being insufficient, and for yearly searches the results only represent about 10 per cent of the total output. Additionally, the percentage of deleted videos is quite high. For example, of the 108 videos produced during a search for '7 Years' + 'Lukas', performed 29 August 2019, thirty-seven uploaded that week were deleted by November 2020; by February 2022, this number had risen to fifty-seven. Therefore, the only way to get a more representative picture is to perform daily searches for new uploads and registrations and/or do very specific searches. I did both, but the dark numbers are still huge, not least for the time period when '7 Years' was a world hit (during the first half of 2016).

However, to compensate for the lack of data, I also retrieved information from social media, such as Facebook and Twitter, news sites, fan sites, etc.[19] These searches revealed regular reference to videos since deleted, including several versions that had themselves become hits. Thus, it has been possible to use data harvested from Facebook and YouTube to reconstruct the chronology of the song's life across cyberspace.

## The Original Version(s)

- 2013 to 2015: Pre-history

    '#LukasGraham played a Brand New Song tonight, called Seven Years! You will hear it very soon ;-)'[20]

In April 2013, Lukas Graham, by then a local Danish act with a solid fan base in Germany and a thriving Facebook fanclub page, set out on a tour of Germany.[21] On

---

[18] I performed the first weekly searches in 2017. Therefore, I have no solid data from before 2017 on that specific matter.
[19] In 2017, I pulled down all data from Lukas Graham-related Facebook pages (their own page, https://www.facebook.com/LukasGraham, and the fan club page, https://www.facebook.com/LukasGrahamSupport) using the tool 'Digital Footprints'. This data includes all posts and comments from 2011 to 2013. The Twitterdata was ripped via the Twitter API and transformed into structural datasets. Because of GDPR, I cannot publish these datasets, but they can be examined by request.
[20] https://www.facebook.com/LukasGrahamSupport/posts/126680600856668, retrieved 12 April 2022 but no longer available.
[21] https://www.facebook.com/LukasGrahamSupport.

13 April, the band performed their premiere performance of '7 Years' at the Deutsches Haus, Flensburg. Several people at the concert managed to record the song, and by the following day, the first three of five different videos of the performance were uploaded to YouTube.[22] Several of these videos contained Lukas Grahams' introduction to the 'brand new song', stating that they 'haven't even recorded it yet'. Although the video and sound quality was extremely lo-fi, it was nevertheless possible to get a good sense of the song, which, when it was officially recorded in 2015, was little changed: the lyrics, form and arrangement (from the piano intro to the energic climax and the outro) were the same. For the next twenty-six months, the song lived a hidden life as a live act at Lukas Graham concerts and on YouTube and social media, primarily Facebook. The audience's video recordings from Flensburg were never taken down, and during the following two years, several new audience recordings of the song were added to YouTube's collection. The fans regularly asked for the band to record and release the song properly, but they didn't. Until June 2015.

- 2015 to 2016: The Official Originals

The band released their second album (*Lukas Graham – Blue Album*) on 16 June 2015. '7 Years', the album's opening track, achieved instant virality. Even though not initially released as a single, it topped the Danish Spotify chart from day one with 95,428 streams by 16 June 2015, and stayed there for almost two months.[23] Although it was not officially released on YouTube until 18 September of that year, several unofficial still videos with the track were uploaded, and often removed again, before that. When it arrived, now as an official single, the YouTube track was also a still picture version, showing the cover, a picture of a man and his son lying on a cliff, watching the ocean (Figure 4.1a, upper left).[24] That was the only official video until November, when the band released the 'Official Lyric Video', based on collages of Lukas Graham's life with unfurling handwritten lyrics (Figure 4.1b, upper right).[25] The third, and last official release, was the

---

[22] Smith-Sivertsen and Kjeldby, 'The 7 Years dataset,' D_original_versions,csv.
[23] Data retrieved from https://spotifycharts.com/regional, retrieved 20-03-2017.
[24] Lukas Graham, 'Lukas Graham - 7 Years,' *YouTube video*, 00:03:58, 18 September 2015, https://www.youtube.com/watch?v=0Iaua2rO5Zk.
[25] The description 'lyric video' is commonly used for videos consisting simply of a still picture or a simple animated background, an audio track and a scrolling text: Lukas Graham, 'Lukas Graham – 7 Years [OFFICIAL LYRIC VIDEO],' *YouTube video*, 00:04:10, 18 November 2015, https://www.youtube.com/watch?v=jErJimwom94. See also Carol Vernallis, Laura McLaren, Virginia Kuhn and Martin Rossouw, 'm☺Re tH@n WorD$: Aspects and Appeals of the Lyric Video,' in *YouTube and Music: Online Culture and Everyday Life*, ed. Holly Rogers, Joana Freitas and Joao Porfirio (New York: Bloomsbury, 2023), 149–68.

**Figure 4.1: a–d** The four 'official' originals, chronologically from left to right. The screenshots are from the exact same part of the song, showing how the videos add different meanings to the song.

'official music video' (directed by René Sascha Johannsen), released on 15 December 2015, a black-and-white film recorded in a cinema in Christiania, the Copenhagen area where Lukas Graham grew up, and various concert settings (Figure 4.1c, lower left).[26] The number of hits for both the lyric and music video rose rapidly to 20.5 million and 23.6 million respective views by 1 March 2016. Although an animated music video by Japanese comic artist Yukihiro Tada, launched by Warner Music Japan, Lukas Graham's own record company (Figure 4.1d, lower right), could be considered an apocryphal original, it was the three official versions that pushed the song to the top of the charts.[27] And yet, it was the work done by the unofficial live-footage uploads in the years before that, that had paved the way for the song's rapid and substantial success.

- The promotional tour

When '7 Years' started climbing the charts outside Denmark, a wide-ranging promotion tour was launched. It started with a performance on the TV Show 'SWR3 latenight' (with the German broadcaster SWR) on 16 October 2015, and

---

[26] Lukas Graham, 'Lukas Graham – 7 Years [Official Music Video],' *YouTube video*, 00:03:59, 15 December 2015, https://www.youtube.com/watch?v=LHCob76kigAT.

[27] Lukas Graham, 'Lukas Graham – 7 Years [JAPANESE ANIMATED VIDEO],' *YouTube video*, 00:03:58, 9 May 2016, https://www.youtube.com/watch?v=kZKmmCIqN2Y.

then moved through numerous live shows, as well as more TV appearances ('Late Night with Seth Meyers', 27 January 2016; 'The Ellen Show', 4 April 2016; and 'The Late Late Show with James Corden', 5 May 2016), before closing on 11 June 2016 at the Capital FM's Summertime Ball at London's Wembley Stadion in front of 80,000 people. By July of that year, '7 Years' was still in the charts, but the monthly YouTube viewing numbers had started to decline.[28] As the year drew to a close, the monthly views of the official music video were 17 million; one year later 14 million; and by the end of 2018 12.5 million, where they have since stabilized.[29]

## All the Rest

- The Beginning

    'Finally I got the time to make a cover, and I HAD to sing this amazing song! I really hope u guys like it :)' Fie Karlskov Busch, 20 June 2015.[30]

Three days after '7 Years' was released in Denmark on streaming services (16 June 2015), the first links to YouTube videos featuring the song quickly started to appear on Twitter.[31] Although the first linked video was deleted and never archived, according to the title – 'Lukas Graham – 7 Years Old (Lyrics)' – it was a lyric video. As it preceded the official music video, this lyric video was shared widely through the first months of the song's official life. The track used was the official recording from the album, probably just ripped and uploaded to YouTube by an anonymous user. The next version to appear was the first cover version, by Danish teenager Fie Karlskov Busch, beating the Danish duo 'Bare os' (just us) by twenty-four hours.[32] The amateur video was simply entitled '7 Years – Lukas Graham – Fie singing'. Busch sang acapella to a handheld, shaky camera from the living room. During the recording, in which background noise can be heard, she

---

[28] Smith-Sivertsen and Kjeldby, 'The 7 Years dataset,' D_original_versions,csv.
[29] Lukas Graham, 'Lukas Graham – 7 Years [Official Music Video].' Archived at www.archive.org.
[30] Fie Karlskov Busch, '7 Years – Lukas Graham – Fie singing,' *YouTube video*, 00:03:36, 20 June 2015, https://www.youtube.com/watch?v=0q6QfFEah0g. Archived at Netarkivet.
[31] One of the first tweets linking to that video was a tip directed at Simon Cowell, British record executive and media personality: Noxie Nox Nox (@Noxuk), Twitter post, 21 June 2015, 2:45 AM, https://twitter.com/Noxuk/status/612420998688804864). As the video was never saved, the only knowledge of it was the above mentioned title and the link: https://www.youtube.com/watch?v=EQ_5nVd5vLc.
[32] Bare os, '7 Years – Lukas Graham (Bare Os Cover),' *YouTube video*, 00:03:25, 21 June 2015, https://youtu.be/K0ecB8u6PHg.

often looks down, presumably at a screen with the lyrics on. As of 29 December 2015, the video had garnered 26,350 views. For a local Danish amateur act, this was a significant number: but by then, the song was not local anymore. Multiple cover versions from Sweden, Germany and other countries where the song was climbing the charts began to appear, and the full list of versions also included the first nightcore versions (tracks sped up), remixes, karaoke videos, playing tutorials and even the first translated version, uploaded by German, Mara Hoppen to her YouTube channel.[33] By the new year, '7 Years' was a major European hit with UK audiences being the main driver, and the number of versions, representing different practices, continued to rise exponentially through January. But that was just the beginning. When the song hit the US and UK charts in February 2016, it all exploded.

- Going viral

    'HERE IT IS!! My brand new cover of "7 Years" by Lukas Graham!! ENJOY!!' https://youtu.be/vmgu4dRUoSQ RT RT RT!'[34] (Conor Maynard, Twitter, 16-02-2016).

Although it is virtually impossible to get a full picture of this explosion, by February 2016 the song was featured on TV-talk shows, the radio and playlists, was being used in supermarkets as muzak, and had begun to appear in streaming service playlists right across social media. By 1 March of that year, daily tweets involving the term '7 Years' and 'Lukas Graham' numbered above 1,100, and daily uploads of versions on YouTube were rising rapidly.[35] Later that month, three versions were released within a week that show the various ways in which media can spread through the cybersphere. The first was Conor Maynard's professional music video cover, uploaded 16 February 2016.[36]

At 2:12 minutes long, the version includes only the first two verses and choruses of '7 Years' before ending with the refrain from the Years & Years song

---

[33] Mara Hoppen, '7 Years – AUF DEUTSCH !,' *YouTube video*, 29 November 2015, www.youtube.com/watch?v=03w-HlZOK1U. Archived at Netarkivet. In this video, uploaded 29 November 2015, she first showed her handwritten German lyrics to the song and then sang it herself, to an instrumental track. The translation was literal.

[34] Conor Maynard (@ConorMaynard), Twitter post, 16 February 2016, 8:06 PM, https://twitter.com/ConorMaynard/status/699671088633028608.

[35] Because of to the lack of transparency, it is impossible to produce a number for the daily uploads, but judging from the searches performed from 2019 onwards, it must have been in the hundreds, if not thousands.

[36] Conor Maynard, 'Lukas Graham – 7 Years,' *YouTube video*, 00:02:12, 16 February 2016, www.youtube.com/watch?v=vmgu4dRUoSQ.

'Eyes Shut' (2015). Maynard, already an established singer with a British number one album and a number two single, had started his career in 2008 by uploading cover versions of hit songs to YouTube. By mid-February 2016, he had 1.2 million subscribers on YouTube and about 1.6 million followers on Twitter.[37] He was thereby a first generation YouTube star, and by 2016 his primary ground was still, in his own words, 'basically record[ing] covers of the latest big songs, and upload[ing] them to YouTube, and hop[ing] that all you guys love them! :).'[38] In the description under this particular mashup cover, entitled simply 'Lukas Graham – 7 Years', Maynard stated that the song was getting 'requested like crazy ...' so he felt he had to do a version.[39] The performance is emotional: Maynard sits in a beautiful garden, singing, for much of the time, with his eyes closed and delivers physical impactful, emphatic physical and vocal gestures. With his high number of followers, the video quickly gained a lot of attention, passing 1.1 million views by early March 2016. With 38 million views by the end of May 2021, Maynard's take on '7 Years' became a phenomenal hit in its own right.

The second example is a four-minute video called '"7 Years, The Honest Version". Lukas Graham Parody By Matt Edmondson', uploaded by BBC Radio 1 to their official YouTube channel on 19 February 2016.[40] The video starts with a shot of Matt Edmondson, the host of a popular weekend radio show, sitting in his studio explaining how he asked listeners to send in embarrassing true stories from their lives at seven, eleven, twenty, thirty and sixty years old to show what real life is about. He then plays a version of '7 Years' that has been constructed from these stories, sung by the listeners themselves to an instrumental track. The first story is about Hannah pooing in a bucket at the age of seven, the next about Lauren being pulled out of a sunroof by a camel and so on. The host ties it all together with brief, energetic monologues between the shifting stories. Created to generate content for the show and something of a gimmick, the video nevertheless racked up 238,000 views by November 2021. Despite this lower number of hits, the fact that a notable radio host used the song as a vehicle for

---

[37] Conor Maynard, 'Rihanna – Work ft. Drake,' *YouTube video*, 00:03:19, 9 February 2016, archived www.youtube.com/watch?v=nsSCl8UXlrY. Archived at www.archive.org; Connor Maynard (@ConorMaynard), Twitter profile, https://twitter.com/ConorMaynard, harvested 5 February 2016, 2:05 AM, Archived at archive.org.
[38] Conor Maynard, 'About', archived 4 August 2017, https://www.YouTube.com/user/skillzaisherebooya/about. Archived at www.archive.org.
[39] Conor Maynard, 'Lukas Graham – 7 Years,' *YouTube video*, 00:02:12, 16 February 2016, www.youtube.com/watch?v=vmgu4dRUoSQ.
[40] Matt Edmondson, '"7 Years, The Honest Version". Lukas Graham Parody By Matt Edmondson,' *YouTube video*, 00:04:05, 19 February 2016, https://youtu.be/7hWwdzMTrWk.

his show, clearly indicates that this was now a song 'everybody' knew so well that it could be used for parody and humour.

The third and most successful of the three examples, the '7 Years (Rewrite Cover) – Leah Guest' was uploaded on 21 February 2016 by 19-year-old Leah Guest to multiple platforms (YouTube, Facebook, Vimeo and Soundcloud).[41] With about 1,000 subscribers on YouTube, Guest was in another league than both Maynard and BBC1, and it took about a month before her version gained public attention. But then it really took off. As the title indicates, Guest's version was a 'rewrite cover', a term denoting the practice of writing new lyrics to the song in order to help personalize it (Figure 4.2). At the time, this label was not very commonly used, and from my datasets it is obvious that Guest's version of '7 Years' marks a turning point in its popularity: since then, the 'rewrite' label has become an established one on YouTube. For her version, she populates the 7–11–20–30–60– structure with a story told from her female perspective. Love and friendship remain central, but contrary to Graham's story, she replaces the desire to conquer the world with a desire to be 'the kindest girl that I could be' and, at sixty, watching 'a generation rise up to change the nation', knowing that God was always by her side. The song became extremely successful, generating its own range of versions from lyrics videos, covers, nightcores, translated lyric videos and fanvids.[42] The paratexts that arose from Guest's version, then, became a vehicle for further interpretation, the *reference original* to other versions. In the case of '7 Years', this version is only one of a large number of versions that serve as points of departure for yet further versions.

These three versions of Lukas Graham's hit, then, were the first indications that '7 Years' was going viral. Maynard's version is an example of a professional artist covering hits; Edmonson's parody shows how the song became popular enough to be used as a broadcasting hook; and Guest's folkloristic and unofficial

---

[41] Leah Guest, '7 Years (Rewrite Cover) – Leah Guest,' *YouTube video*, 21 February 2016, https://www.youtube.com/watch?v=8WRizF7X2DQ, archived at www.archive.org; https://vimeo.com/156176433; https://www.facebook.com/leahguestmusic/videos/1668406253376319; https://soundcloud.com/leahguest/7-years-rewrite-leah-guest (only sound file).

[42] By 22 June 2016, the video had gained 6.4 million views on YouTube.com (Leah Guest, '7 Years (Rewrite Cover) – Leah Guest'), *YouTube video*, 21 February 2016, archived 22 June, https://www.YouTube.com/watch?v=8WRizF7X2DQ. Archived at archive.org). Leah Guest's video was blocked for unknown copyright infringement issues in 2017. From a legal perspective, it is a clear-cut case, as writing a subtext, either in same or another language, requires permissions from the copyright holder. Such permissions were obviously not cleared. Generally, the violations are ignored, but the more popular a given unofficial version becomes, the more problematic it gets, and the Leah Guest version definitely approached the status of an independent 'original'. Since then, however, the version has been re-uploaded by several other YouTube-users and has therefore been online all the time. Sivertsen and Kjeldby, 'The 7 Years dataset,' B_Specificic_searches.csv (sheet 8, 'Top').

**Figure 4.2** The Leah Guest Rewrite Cover was the first version by someone other than Lukas Graham to become a hit in its own right. It was later deleted for unknown copyright reasons, but has been web archived as one of few examples of the multitude of versions and practices. However, the video is only found if you know the exact URL. '7 Years (Rewrite Cover) – Leah Guest' (21 February 2016).

approach demonstrates how amateur musicians can generate substantial interest through kids singing to shaky cameras.[43] By March 2016, the first 'Top 5 covers of 7 Years' meta videos were made,[44] as well as the first covers of rewrite covers (all referring to the Leah Guest version).[45] The rewriting practice itself became extremely popular and numerous remediating content via YouTube's participatory and democratized spaces.

---

[43] Captain Bucky, '| Steve Rogers – once I was 7 years old |,' *YouTube video*, 00:03:44, 5 March 2016, https://www.youtube.com/watch?v=uCyeGNqeOjw; Smith-Sivertsen and Kjeldby, 'The 7 Years dataset,' A_All_searches.csv.
[44] Ibid., B_Specificic_searches.csv (sheet 8, 'Top')
[45] Ibid., sheet 1, 'cover'/sheet 4, 'Rewrite'.

These three early examples were indeed instrumental in establishing the song's virality, but the branches of versions were growing rapidly in multiple directions. Other versions on YouTube included the first fanvid (March 2016), dedicated to Captain America from the Avengers franchise, as well as covers of all kinds, from professionally produced music videos to recordings of street musicians, and versions including new personal stories or a parody on the narrative structure;[46] then there are the translated versions[47] and those adapted to different genres, particularly hip-hop.[48] The three most-viewed hip-hop versions (by May 2021) illustrate this spectrum of practices. At one end, the Bars and Melody cover (16 million views by May 2021) is simply a hip-hop version in which the original lyrics are recited rather than sung.[49] American rapper Cryptic Wisdom, contrarily, rewrote the lyrics completely, using the age-structure to tell his own story of hardship (5.5 million views by May 2021).[50] The last example, by American rapper Sik World (17 million views by May 2021), only uses the instrumental track, and seems to completely suspend both lyrics and the original story.[51] However, by referring to his dreams for the future at seven years old at the end of the song, World actually makes a quite sophisticated intertextual reference to the original version, but this is the only firm link to the source text.

During this time, there were also daily uploads of new lyric videos (both for the original version and rewrites), including translation into numerous other languages. These early fanvids were complemented by many others, covering a variety of popular film franchises, such as *Harry Potter* (2001 to 2011), *The Avengers* (2008–) and *Star Wars* (1977–), and series ranging from Manga series *Naruto* (1999–) to *The Walking Dead* (2010 to 2022). In most cases, the original Lukas Graham track was used, but eventually fanvids using rewrites of '7 Years', including translations, also started appearing. The same was the case for most other versioning practices, including remixes, nightcores and mashups.[52] Another significant genre of response to '7 Years' is the music tutorial, of which the most watched in the dataset is a 'solo Fingerstyle Guitar Version'

---

[46] Ibid.
[47] Ibid., sheet 2, 'cover'/sheet 4, 'Translation'.
[48] Ibid, sheet 5, 'Genre'.
[49] Bars and Melody, 'Lukas Graham – 7 Years (Bars and Melody Cover),' *YouTube video*, 00:03:57, 11 March 2016, https://www.youtube.com/watch?v=SoTpKBRaBHc.
[50] Cryptic Wisdom, '7 Years (REMIX) [Prod. Life & Death Productions],' *YouTube video*, 00:02:57, 17 April 2016, https://www.youtube.com/watch?v=uu2sqUxfXQg.
[51] Sik World, 'Lukas Graham – 7 Years (Sik World Remix),' *YouTube video*, 00:02:03, 11 June 2016, https://www.youtube.com/watch?v=Ukhq8rmrKxw.
[52] Smith-Sivertsen and Kjeldby, 'The 7 Years dataset,' A_All_searches.csv.

with 7 million views (by 21 May 2021).⁵³ There are also song tutorials for almost any instrument, ranging from lengthy instruction videos by music teachers, to screen filmed videos of tutorial apps. In the old cover/original sense, they are all cover versions, but that does not tell us much about their functions and meanings.

One last example from 2016 perfectly illustrates how traditional conceptions of musical versioning practices are challenged in the brave new world of YouTube. By early May 2016, YouTube videos with split screen duets suddenly appeared, with Lukas Graham on one side, and amateur singers on the other. It turned out that Lukas Graham had signed a deal with popular karaoke-app, Sing! by Smule, and had recorded a live duet track for them, which quickly found its way to YouTube where it generated thousands of versions, some very professionally produced, others extremely DIY.⁵⁴ With 5.3 million views (by March 2021), the most successful duet was made by Lawrence Park, a Korean-American singer/songwriter from San Francisco (Figure 4.3).⁵⁵ Besides being a

**Figure 4.3** Screenshot from the Lawrence Park Duet, just after Park's hair joke. An almost perfect simulation of a dialogue that never happened.

---

⁵³ Gareth Evans, '7 Years – Solo Fingerstyle Guitar Version,' *YouTube video*, 00:04:28, 8 May 2016, https://www.youtube.com/watch?v=EAsm2CBkMoo.
⁵⁴ 'Sing "7 Years" with Lukas Graham on Sing!,' *Smule*, 6 May 2016, https://blog.smule.com/sing-7-years-with-lukas-graham-on-sing.
⁵⁵ Lawrence Park, '7 Years – Lukas Graham | Lawrence Park Duet,' *YouTube video*, 00:03:52, 13 May 2016, https://www.youtube.com/watch?v=Hb_XTrX3e2I.

strong singer able to add harmony to Graham's lines and including all the necessary verbal and nonverbal gestures, he includes a joke about his hair in the beginning of the video, timed perfectly to (seemingly) initiate a grinning response from Graham.

## Many Practices, Many Purposes

As established, the total number of '7 Years' videos on YouTube is unquantifiable. A qualified, and very conservative, guess, based on the stable numbers of uploads since 2017, would be more than 30,000, although the true number is probably significantly higher. And yet it is evident that '7 Years' has grown, developed and lived in many different ways since its official release. One of the sheets in the dataset is a list of the most watched '7 Years' videos that have emerged beyond the control of Lukas Graham (or their music company) up to 21 May 2021.[56] As shown here, even a video produced in 2018 could go viral: in this case a Fortnite fanvid, viewed 36 million times in 2.5 years.[57] When a song becomes part of a shared cultural memory, it can always be activated in new contexts. Also notable from this data is the number of views. In total, the top 100 reach the same view level as the official music video (excluding the many videos found in other searches that, for unknown reasons, were not included in the count). The use of these videos is also unexpected. Three of the most watched are simple lyrics videos. The most viewed video in this category received 167 million views, eclipsing Lukas Graham's own 'official lyric video', which received only 124 million views (by April 2022).[58] However, this is understandable as the handwritten lyrics in the official video are quite hard to read, which in practice makes it almost unusable if the purpose of watching it is to use it as a singing guide. Taken together, the lyric videos and the karaoke video (in fifth position) show that four of the five most watched videos promote musical activity by the user, pointing to YouTube's promotion of interactive engagement. That perfectly sums up the differences to the 'original recording era' preceding the present and leads back to my introductory reflections.

---

[56] Smith-Sivertsen and Kjeldby, 'The 7 Years dataset,' E_Most_Watched.csv.
[57] Ibid.
[58] Ibid.

## Once I was 7 Years Old (outro)

It all started with Lukas Graham Forchhammer mourning the sudden loss of his father in September 2012. The grieving process resulted in a line of song that eventually generated '7 Years'. It is a very personal song, but, as we have seen, it has touched many people. Judging from the versions, the meaning of '7 Years' is the lifespan story, structured by the chronology of years (7, 11, 20, 30, 60). Some may listen carefully to the lyrics, but from the fanvids and rewrites, parodies and translations, it is clear that the core meaning is the continuation of life, not the specific life of Lukas Graham. And it is this combination of the personal and the translatable that prompted such significant musical versioning practices on YouTube.

The case of '7 Years' is unusual for several reasons. First, it produced a rare example of a local Danish act bursting onto the world stage via a single song, a move that was generated primarily through online activity; and second, this online activity began the process of international dissemination several years before its official release. On the other hand, it has become representative to how many major hit songs now spread through the contemporary mediascape. During this research and dataset creation, I have done regular tests with chart-topping songs, and the result is usually the same. When a song hits the top of the charts, especially in the Anglophone world, the number and variation of versions explodes. The same exercise of tracing the growth from a single song to a universe of remediated play, showing how spreadable media is now the centre of our mediascape, can be carried out with the same result with most global hit songs. And yet, so long as YouTube remains a messy and opaque archive, collecting and preserving data will be a time consuming and difficult process. That leads to my final points.

In her article on YouTube as a historical archive, Dutch media historian Susan Aasman directly questions whether the platform can be considered an archive or not. Her answer, although ambivalent, leans to the negative. The main problem, she argues, is that YouTube is a fully commercial service.[59] Google has no obligation to save anything, and if/when it decides to close down or relaunch the platform, everything will disappear. This is what happened when Myspace.com

---

[59] Susan Aasman, 'Finding Traces in YouTube's Living Archive: Exploring Informal Archival Practices,' *TMG Journal for Media History* 22, no. 1 (6 November 2019): 35–55.

was redesigned in 2013.[60] The fact that nobody actually knows how many videos YouTube contains, not least speaking of the number of videos deleted, perfectly illustrates the problem.[61] In the case of '7 Years', we now have a good idea about the song's online context and processes of remediation and strong data for further studies. And yet, if YouTube were to fold, we would lose most of the content that defines our present mediascape: all that would be left are fragments and traces in hard-to-access web archives. Source loss has always been a basic problem for archivists, and as Aasman correctly states, informal archival practices developed by specific online and offline communities can compensate for data losses to some extent. Still, if YouTube were to close down tomorrow, the scale of loss would be colossal. Although original and official versions will typically have been broadcast and therefore saved elsewhere, this uneven process of collecting offers a biased and outdated picture of our present mediascape.

## Bibliography

Aasman, Susan. 'Finding Traces in YouTube's Living Archive: Exploring Informal Archival Practices.' *TMG Journal for Media History* 22, no. 1 (2019): 35–55.

Billboard. 'Chart History – Lukas Graham,' at https://www.billboard.com/artist/lukas-graham/chart-history/hsi/.

Bruns, Axel. *Blogs, Wikipedia, Second Life, and Beyond: From Production to Produsage*. New York: Peter Lang, 2008.

Coyle, Michael. 'Hijacked Hits and Antic Authenticity: Cover Songs, Race, and Postwar Marketing.' In *Rock Over the Edge: Transformations in Popular Music Culture*, edited by Roger Beebe and Ben Saunders, 133–58. Durham, NC and London: Duke University Press, 2002.

Dredge, Stuart. '7 Years: How Streaming Fuelled the Rapid Rise of Lukas Graham.' *Music:)ally*, 23 March 2016, at https://musically.com/2016/03/23/7-years-streaming-lukas-graham/.

Hoffmann, Thomas. 'Eurovision Song Contest to be Part of Denmark's Cultural Heritage.' *ScienceNordic*, 8 May 2014, at https://sciencenordic.com/culture-denmark-eurovision/eurovision-song-contest-to-be-part-of-denmarks-cultural-heritage/1400969.

---

[60] 'In a Rush to Modernize, MySpace Destroyed More History,' *Active History*, 17 June 2013, https://activehistory.ca/2013/06/myspace-is-cool-again-too-bad-they-destroyed-history-along-the-way/.

[61] Aasman, 'Finding Traces in YouTube's Living Archive,' 40–1.

Keightley, Keir. 'Reconsidering Rock.' In *The Cambridge Companion to Pop and Rock*, edited by John Street, Simon Frith and Will Straw, 109–42. Cambridge: Cambridge University Press, 2001.

Liikkanen, Lassi A. and Antti Salovaara. 'Music on YouTube: User Engagement with Traditional, User-Appropriated and Derivative Videos.' *Computers in Human Behavior* 50 (2015): 108–24.

Middleton, Richard. 'Work-in(g) Practice: Configuration of the Popular Music Intertext.' In *The Musical Work: Reality or Invention?*, edited by Michael Talbot, 59–87. Liverpool: Liverpool University Press, 2000.

Milligan, Ian. 'In a Rush to Modernize, MySpace Destroyed More History.' *Active History*, 17 June 2013, at https://activehistory.ca/2013/06/myspace-is-cool-again-too-bad-they-destroyed-history-along-the-way/.

Smith-Sivertsen, Henrik and Kristoffer Brinch Kjeldby, *The 7 Years Dataset* (2022), distributed by Royal Danish Library, at https://loar.kb.dk/handle/1902/8116.

Smith-Sivertsen, Henrik. *Et vaskeægte Myspace-fænomen – Sys Bjerre I Netarkivet* (A Real Myspace Phenomenon – Sys Bjerre in the Danish Webarchive). Copenhagen: Danish Royal Library, 2014.

Smith-Sivertsen, Henrik. '*Kylling med soft ice og pølser: populærmusikalske versioneringspraksisser i forbindelse med danske versioner af udenlandske sange i perioden 1945–2007*' ('Chicken with Soft Cream Ice and Sausages – Versioning Practices within Popular Music Related to Danish Versions of International Songs 1945–2007'). Doctoral dissertation, Copenhagen, 2007.

Vernallis, Carol, Laura McLaren, Virginia Kuhn and Martin P. Rossouw. 'm☺Re tH@n WorD$: Aspects and Appeals of the Lyric Video.' In *YouTube and Music: Online Culture and Everyday Life*, edited by Holly Rogers, Joana Freitas and Joao Francisco Porfirio, 149–68. New York: Bloomsbury Academic, 2023.

Zak, Albin. '"The Tune Was Made By the Way It Was Played": Covers, Copies, and Recording Consciousness.' *The Musical Quarterly* 104 nos. 1–2 (2021): 93–113.

# 5

# Listening Through Social Media: Soundscape Composition, Collaboration and Networked Sonic Elongation

Holly Rogers

The affordances of new technology allow physical and aesthetic participation in the sonic resonances of our environment. Composers and artists of *musique concrète*, sound sonic art, noise music and electroacoustic music have long used technology to record and process real-world sounds, using them as compositional material for music composition and the remediation of our sonic environment. Audiovisual technology has enabled this form of sonic creativity to move into the moving image arts: creative sound design and soundscape composition in fiction and documentary film traditions have become increasingly common, thanks to the capabilities of the digital audio workstation and other technologies that enable the easy and imaginative combination of sound with music, and sound with image. Internet culture and social media have accelerated this move towards moving-image soundscape and its remediated afterlife. Mobile media with inbuilt cameras and microphones, online editing tools and compositional software, the promotion of user-generated and DIY content and the interconnection between platforms has led to new possibilities for the creation, remediation and consumption of the sonic arts. YouTube, in particular, has become a hub for sharing, manipulating and interpreting new ways of sounding and hearing our environment. According with the bodily turn in millennial musicology, which treats music as an embodied, situated practice, YouTube can be approached as a musical instrument that encourages refreshed creative activity, based on mobility, collaboration and open-ended process.

There is a video essay version of this chapter: the promo and link can be accessed via the chapter's YouTube channel.

Although moving image media is often a highly collaborative and decentralized space, with directors and composers working closely with actors, editors, sound designers, scriptwriters, costume and set stylists, cinematographers and a whole host of other creative forces, social media spaces have thrust the collective utterance into the foreground. The rise of peer production and participation has opened up opportunities for innovative forms of collaboration and open-ended work very different from the finished and discrete products we find in cinema and television.[1] Web 2.0 – Darcy DiNucci's term, later popularized by Tim O'Reilly (2004), for the increased move towards user-driven content, the idea of network as a platform, large-scale collaboration and the interoperability of technologies and software from the early 2000s onwards – has seen a move away from fixed and authored moving image material into a maelstrom of voices, perspectives and grass roots creativity.[2]

For music, this has had a profound effect on composition, performance, circulation, marketing, fandom and pedagogy, an influence I charted in the opening chapter to this volume's companion book, *YouTube and Music: Online Culture and Everyday Life*.[3] YouTube, as one of the first, and still one of the biggest platforms for music since its 2005 launch, has remained a pivotal space for refreshed modes of engagement with sonic material. And yet, in the age of post-media, audiovisual affect readily spreads across platforms and through devices, absorbing the subtle specificities of each and activating audiences in different ways. Although Twitter privileges text, Instagram static and, increasingly, moving images, and YouTube and TikTok video and sound, each hyperlinks and cross-references to the others in complex and entangled ways: in fact, since Instagram's introduction of reels and stories, this entanglement of platforms, format, style and content has become even more pronounced. This transmedial movement of moving images and sounds to, through and beyond YouTube allows us to see several things. First, how different platforms generate specific

---

[1] See Carol Vernallis, Holly Rogers and Lisa Perrott, *Transmedia Directors: Artistry, Industry and New Audiovisual Aesthetics* (New York: Bloomsbury, 2020).

[2] Webarchive.org, 'Web 2.0 Conference,' conference website, San Francisco, California (5-7 October 2004), at https://web.archive.org/web/20050312204307/, https://web.archive.org/web/20050312204307/http://www.web2con.com/web2con/; Darci DeNucci, 'Fragmented Future,' *Print* 32 (January 1999): 221–2; Tim O'Reilly, 'What is Web 2.0: Design Patterns and Business Models for the Next Generation of Software' (30 September 2005), at https://www.oreilly.com/pub/a/web2/archive/what-is-web-20.html.

[3] Holly Rogers, '"Welcome to your world": YouTube and the Reconfiguration of Music's Gatekeepers,' in *YouTube and Music: Online Culture and Everyday Life*, ed. Holly Rogers, Joana Freitas and João Francisco Porfírio (New York: Bloomsbury, 2023).

types of engagement with everyday sounds; second, how sound and its creative manipulation can adjust to different user requirements; and third, how sound can gather meaning and resonance as it passes through cyberspace. To explore the ways in which sound is mediated by social media technologies and users, I here extend my previous work into what I call networked sonic elongation.[4]

Sonic elongation is a compositional technique that has become common across moving image media over the past three decades. Appearing first in experimental films and documentaries, before moving into mainstream cinema culture, sonic elongation arises when real world, profilmic or foley sounds, synchronized with onscreen images and clearly emanating from the filmed world, undergo some sort of creative manipulation. Gradually, the recognizable sounds become muddled, move away from the images that originally generated them and shift into a different physical and conceptual space. Now unsynched and set adrift, sounds become compositional material that can be manipulated into musical rhythms, phrases, tonalites and textures, without the addition of any other sonic material. A good example can be found in Edward Artemiev's electro-acoustic score for *Stalker*, Andrey Tarkovsky's 1979 post-apocalyptic sci-fi. In one scene, the film's protagonists journey towards a mysterious Zone on a small train. At first, we hear sounds that seem to be realist sound effects, coming from the objects we are looking at. Gradually, though, the sounds become strange: they become unsynchronized and uncoupled from the image, and their textures become reverberant and unfamiliar, phasing in and out across the screen. Several minutes in and the sounds are almost entirely abstracted by electronic distortion, resulting in what Tarkovsky calls not sonic realism, but 'resonance'.[5] During this process, environmental sound is heightened and enlarged until it gathers together into a sort of musical flow. For the process to be successful, audiovisual fusion needs first to be established – we both see and hear a train – before the sounds undergo their transformation.

Elongated sounds demonstrate our fluency with cinematic vocabulary and the strength of the 'irresistible weld' between sound and image that Michel Chion attributes to the lure of 'synchresis' – a terminological mashup that refers

---

[4] Holly Rogers, 'Sonic Elongation and Sonic Aporia: Two Modes of Disrupted Listening in Film,' in *The Oxford Handbook of Cinematic Listening*, ed. Carlo Cenciarelli (Oxford: Oxford University Press, 2021), 427–49; Holly Rogers, 'Sonic Elongation: Creative Audition in Documentary Film,' *Journal of Cinema and Media Studies* 59, no. 2 (Winter 2020): 88–113.

[5] Andrey Tarkovsky, *Sculpting in Time*, trans. Kitty Hunter-Blair (Austin: University of Texas Press, 1986; 2003), 162.

to the natural and multimodal fusion of audiovisual components.[6] And yet, as the roles of sound and music become ambiguous and disjointed, soundscape begins to exceed image; and, as audiovisual gaps begin to open, they engender new processes of listening. The terminology here is significant: to elongate – to extend, broaden, enlarge – suggests a reconfiguration of audiovisual material. But unlike stretching, elongation does not imply distortion, or a thinning out of material as it is pulled through space and time, but rather a process of augmentation and growth from one thing to another: it indicates an accumulative, transformative process of sonic interpretation.

Reconfiguration, accumulation, transformation, interpretation. These four poles of sonic elongation feed into the core strategies of social media and over the past few decades, the manipulation of real-world sound through cybermedia's spaces has become increasingly prevalent. When uploaded, actuality sounds and images captured by amateur artists from all over the world can instantly become compositional material for other web users: and when what Jay Rosen has referred to as 'the people formerly known as the audience' treat these sounds creatively, the process of sonic elongation becomes communal, participatory, fluid and self-reflexive.[7] I call this multi-voiced elongation of noise from image 'networked sonic elongation' and define it as a technique that arises through multiple interpretations of an audiovisual event. As a practice of remediation, networked sonic elongation is related to, yet slightly different from, its cinematic cousin. Although it starts from a clear location and stretches the sounds gradually away from it, it is a creative progression achievable only through online collaborative processes. As a result, it has implications for how we listen to online culture and how online culture intersects with, extends, and, most radically, changes the world around us as it passes through the creative lens of multiple users. Original or existing sounds can be remediated in one of two ways. First, cyber-users employ the process of sonic elongation to respond in multiple ways to the original material. This generates numerous interpretations of the primary audiovisual object. Second, users can expand upon each other's versions to produce a chain of variations. This form of collaboration operates like Chinese whispers. Such produsage – Axel Bruns' term for a hybrid between producer and user – allows non-professional creators to employ cheap or free, easy-to-use

---

[6] Michel Chion, *Audio-Vision: Sound on Screen*, trans. Claudia Gorbman (New York: Columbia University Press, Second edition, 2019 [1994]), 5, 63.
[7] Jay Rosen, 'The People Formerly Known as the Audience,' in *The Social Media Reader*, ed. Michael Mandiberg (New York and London: New York University Press, 2012), 13–16.

technologies to remediate their environments and share their processes and perspectives in collaborative situations.[8]

To focus this exploration, I focus on networked sonic elongation during the first global lockdown, when quarantined populations across the world became more dependent than ever on online culture for communication, information and creativity: when the relationship between the real and the cyber became increasingly entangled; and when the democratized, networked potential of YouTube, with its accessible technologies, vast communities, established affinity spaces and potential for interaction became a vital place of sociability and information. Although YouTube and other social media platforms have always given a glimpse into, and interpretation of, current affairs, when familiar modes of social engagement were removed during the pandemic, their communicative capabilities augmented. I suggest that, during this time, YouTube became a postmedia nexus of sonic resonances that captured the fear, pleasure and anticipation of Covid-19. This chapter, then, is about the online mediation of sonic artefacts during the first wave of the 2020 pandemic. As the world retreated indoors, cyberspace became a significant space for creative expression and partnership, offering the opportunity for interactivity at a time of absolute inactivity.[9] But how were we asked to listen and how did the Internet mediate our access to the outside world? Social media sites such as YouTube gave us unprecedented and essential forms for sonic connection with others and with our forbidden surroundings; but through whose ears have we been listening? What processes of mediation have occurred and have these been recognized? And most importantly, can we believe what we hear?

## The Wave of Silence

As populations were locked indoors during the first wave of the Covid-19 pandemic, sonic recordings of the real world – particularly of pastoral spaces – became increasingly popular. On 19 April 2020, Oli Gudgeon, writing in the magazine *Contemporary Sound Art*, reported an increase in soundscape video

---

[8] Axel Bruns, *Blogs, Wikipedia, Second Life, and Beyond: From Production to Produsage* (New York: Peter Lang Publishing, 2008).
[9] The problems of terminology that surround cyberculture, cybermedia and cyberspace are discussed in detail in *Cybermedia: Explorations in Science, Sound, and Vision*, ed. Carol Vernallis, Holly Rogers, Selmin Kara and Jonathan Leal (New York: Bloomsbury, 2021).

views during early quarantine, with data from Google Trends showing a surge in what the author describes as 'search terms like "ocean soundscape", "nature sounds forest" and "rainforest soundscape", which became "Breakout" topics, meaning those search terms are experiencing new, significant growth', a trend particularly clear from YouTube's traffic data.[10] Johnnie Lawson's YouTube channel, for instance, which provides extreme long-form videos of natural sounds, experienced a 20 per cent increase in traffic between mid-February 2020 and the start of lockdown in early April of the same year; while other popular sites, such as the BBC archives, recontextualized their collections to directly attend to the sonic needs of a locked down population by promoting the calming soundtracks from nature programmes and field recordings from rural landscapes. The dedicated BBC's Covid-19 Collection claims that 'The power of music and sounds from the natural world are known to help during challenging times. To offer comfort and support during the current pandemic, BBC Archive, BBC Music and the Natural History Unit offer a selection of calming tracks and soundscapes for patients, care workers and families affected by Covid-19.'[11] This is not particularly surprising. Locked at home, entire populations were cut off from the physical world around them. Sites such as Johnnie Lawson's used the long-established soothing effects of bird song and running water to calm people's nerves and offer an alternative sonic space that could overlay the alarming realities of the pandemic. And yet, strangely, had people been allowed to venture outside, into the deserted streets and empty squares of capital cities and major towns, they would have encountered a soundscape that was not entirely different to those found on Lawson's YouTube channel.

The radical and abrupt reduction of global mobility as the coronavirus pandemic gathered pace during the world's first wave was unprecedented. News reports marvelled at the horror, but also the beauty of what's become known as the 'wave of silence' that engulfed most of the world's noisy urban centres. Human-derived sound in Paris, for instance, dropped by 90 per cent as the city moved into lockdown.[12] According to several accounts, the vibrations and

---

[10] Oli Gudgeon, 'Natural Soundscape Video Views Surge amid Covid-19 Quarantine,' *The Medium*, last modified 19 April 2020, at https://medium.com/contemporary-sound-art/natural-soundscape-video-views-surge-amid-covid-19-quarantine-4fb9bf8cabd3.

[11] BBC Archive, 'Archive for Wellbeing Collection,' *BBC*, at https://www.bbc.co.uk/archive/covid-19_collection/zrfq2sg.

[12] Abby Wendle, 'Human Life is Literally Quieter Due to Coronavirus Lockdown,' *npr.org*, last modified 14 April 2020, at https://www.npr.org/2020/04/14/834460094/human-life-is-literally-quieter-due-to-coronavirus-lockdown?t=1587480808639&t=1599641868346.

seismic waves sent deep into the earth by human modes of transport diminished to such an extent that geologists and geoscientists reported a reduction in seismic noise of almost 50 per cent. This, reported *Science Magazine*, 'is the longest and most prominent global anthropogenic seismic noise reduction on record', a drop, writes Elizabeth Gabney for *Nature Research Journal*, that has meant that 'the planet itself is moving a little less'.[13]

But silence is the wrong word here. As human-generated noise reduced, a plethora of other sounds came to the fore: the subtle sounds of nature, weather, creaking architecture, whispering trees. Amidst the chaos and horror, there were multiple reports of increased wildlife presence in the cities; goats, coyotes, foxes, but particularly birds, many of whom had adapted their songs to be higher and more varied in pitch, as well as louder, to compete with human noise, an adaptation that resulted in increased stress hormones. As the wave of silence crept over our urban environments, many birds found themselves shouting into a vacuum, able to expend less energy in their vocalizations and devote it instead to searching for food and boosting their immune systems.[14] Nature, it seemed, was wasting no time in reclaiming its territory. For some, this silencing of human noise and the re-energization of nature was nothing short of miraculous; for others, the absence of human presence was an eerie reminder of the virus' lurking hold over global movement, capital and freedom. In an interview on 10 April 2020, prominent sound artist and wildlife sound recordist Chris Watson noted an increase in the spatial depth of listening: 'You can hear into the distance, because normally a lot of the detail and subtle sounds – and that includes birdsong, of course – gets lost amidst a mush of traffic noise particularly in urban areas'. This, he reasoned, produced a strangely distorted sense of temporality: 'we're hearing the world like people heard it decades ago.'[15] The sounds of our near surroundings, in other words, became unfamiliar. What was once heard only as background noise, was suddenly positioned in the foreground by stint of its sudden otherness: taken away, forbidden and left with little human

---

[13] Elizabeth Gibney, 'Coronavirus Lockdowns have Changed the Way Earth Moves,' nature.com, last modified 31 March 2020, at https://www.nature.com/articles/d41586-020-00965-x?fbclid=IwAR1w JGGezt06Q5JqgxQqDPVnaNNRIPJcti3xsSwG2wpgzhL0dhL73ymVHjU.

[14] Nancy Eve Cohen, 'With Covid-19, Fewer Cars, Quieter Soundscape for Birds and Humans,' in *New England Public Radio*, last modified 31 March 2020, at https://www.nepr.net/post/covid-19-fewer-cars-quieter-soundscape-birds-and-humans#stream/0.

[15] Chris Green, '"You Can Hear Into the Distance": Wildlife Sound Expert on how Coronavirus has Changed the World,' inews.co.uk, last modified 10 April 2020, at https://inews.co.uk/news/coronavirus-lockdown-wildlife-expert-bird-songs-environment-nature-417130.

intervention, real-world noise suddenly became a common and highly desirable commodity.

And yet, not everywhere was quieter. Although the outside became hushed, home life became increasingly cacophonous as work and children were confined to kitchen tables and makeshift bedroom schools. For some, the unfamiliar noises of their new domestic workspaces made it difficult to concentrate, and it wasn't long before the Internet offered the chance for people to resound their alternative environments with familiar background hums. In his work on YouTube's 'domestic sonic videos', João Francisco Porfírio has noted how longform recordings of hoovers and fridges have become incredibly popular over the past decade.[16] During lockdown, these videos proliferated further, with apps such as Calm Office, an office sound generator tool that allows you to replicate the drones of a typical busy office space, gaining widespread use (Figure 5.1).[17] For others, however, the message to 'Stay at Home' increased local sounds, with the potential for emotional and physical harm. As Marie Thompson has previously written, the silence of leafy suburbs, quiet streets and safe neighbourhoods is a privilege only some can afford; during the pandemic, swathes of the population were locked into dense housing or dangerous domestic circumstances.[18] For people in such situations, lockdown bought a stressful excess of local human noise. During lockdown then, human-generated sound was distributed differently and unevenly through urban environments, becoming estranged from itself.

Online communities were quick to respond to the world's new sonic realities. As the urban streets became quieter, the noise of online content and activity gathered pace, increasing in volume and exploding with creative responses to the unprecedented situation. Although it's important to note that lockdown threw into relief global inequalities in terms of power provision, technological distribution, Internet connection and censorship, according to a report by *The New York Times*, social media sites and streaming services saw a marked increase in traffic during the pandemic, with Facebook seeing a 27 per cent upsurge and YouTube a 15 per cent growth compared to the months preceding

---

[16] João Francisco Porfírio, 'YouTube and the Sonification of Domestic Everyday Life', in *YouTube and Music: Cyberculture and Everyday Life*, ed. Holly Rogers, Joana Freitas and João Francisco Porfírio (New York: Bloomsbury, 2023), 209–20.
[17] Ir.S.Pigeon, Calm Office (website), at https://mynoise.net/NoiseMachines/openOfficeNoiseGenerator.php.
[18] Marie Thompson, *Beyond Unwanted Sound: Noise, Affect and Aesthetic Moralism* (London: Bloomsbury, 2017), 88.

Figure 5.1 Calm Office: Interactive Background Noise Generator.

lockdown.[19] However, according to statistics from the Pew Research Centre, YouTube's growth during pandemia was greater than any other social media app across America, increasing from 73 per cent of American adults in 2019 to 81 per cent two years later, while in India, the first forty-five days of lockdown resulted in 20.5 per cent new subscribers.[20] YouTube's own data reveals that the search terms 'at home' and '#withme' garnered 500 per cent increases on 15 March 2020 alone.[21] Significantly, the greatest increases in viewership were seen on laptops, while mobile media saw a marked drop in response to people spending more time at home and the reduced opportunity for mobility. Other notable successes can be found in online connecting sites, with Houseparty up 79 per cent, Zoom enjoying an unprecedented renaissance and apps such as

---

[19] Paul Harkins and Nick Prior, '(Dis)locating Democratization: Music Technologies in Practice,' *Popular Music and Society* 45, no. 1 (November 2021): 84–103; and Ella Koeze and Nathaniel Popper, 'The Virus Changed the Way We Internet,' *New York Times*, last modified 7 April 2020, at https://www.nytimes.com/interactive/2020/04/07/technology/coronavirus-internet-use.html.

[20] Salvador Rodriguez, 'YouTube is Social Media's Big Winner During the Pandemic,' *CNBC*, last modified 7 April 2021, at https://www.cnbc.com/2021/04/07/youtube-is-social-medias-big-winner-during-the-pandemic.html; India Partner, 'YouTube sees 20.5% Surge in Subscribers-Base During the 45 Days of the Lockdown,' *Business Insider*, last modified 21 April 2020, at https://www.businessinsider.in/advertising/ad-tech/news/youtube-sees-20-5-surge-in-subscribers-base-during-the-45-days-of-the-lockdown/articleshow/75268860.cms.

[21] Dennis Romero, 'YouTube Thrives as a Window for Those Isolated by Coronavirus,' *NBC News*, last modified 2 April 2020, at https://www.nbcnews.com/tech/social-media/youtube-thrives-window-those-isolated-coronavirus-n1173651.

Nextdoor coming to prominence as people sought to create local communities and become involved with their direct neighbourhoods, demonstrating a re-energized interest in local communities and environments. These increases show a clear desire for connection and companionship to go some way towards countering the instruction to 'Stay At Home', 'Shelter-in-Place'.

During this time, environmental sound, and its mediation through online culture, became an increasingly meaningful way for people to keep track of the outside, to share experiences and to react to the porous boundaries between what could once be clearly demarcated as physical and cyber realities. Confined to the home and unable to directly experience these newly audible sounds, people turned to the Internet as an ear to the outside world. Although many opted for the pre-recorded sounds of nature, such as Lawson's, others were ravenous for information about the outside, and the sharing of recordings of what our empty world now sounded like flooded cyberspace almost immediately. Government platforms and smaller, more creative initiatives launched projects to collect, archive, measure and assess sonic data in order to analyse the impact of confinement on our urban soundscapes.[22] The collaborative *Silent Cities Project*, for instance, created an open-access database of 35,000 hours of phonographic audio of the unique and ephemeral sounds of locked-down habitats from 161 locations around the world.[23] *The Sound and Memory* website, on the other hand, aimed to 'build a public archive of the sounds of pandemia, a collective testimony of the global crisis we are inhabiting'; here, the sounds and images could be captured on little more than a mobile phone; this project was about 'archiving as much data as possible for posterity'.[24] Although YouTube didn't issue an official call in the same way as these dedicated, research-based web pages, the platform was inundated with the videoed images and sounds of desolate spaces from around the world, many captured through illegal walks, from windows or via drones. This form of remote cyber-listening had a profound impact on the way that people engaged with everyday sounds. Now inaccessible,

---

[22] See, for example, César Asensio, Pierre Aumond, Arnaud Can, Luis Gascó, Peter Lercher, Jean-Marc Wunderli, Catherine Lavandier, Guillermo de Arcas, Carlos Ribeiro, Patricio Munoz and Gaetano Licitra, 'A Taxonomy Proposal for the Assessment of the Changes in Soundscape Resulting from the COVID-19 Lockdown,' *Internal Journal Environ. Res. Public Health* 17, no. 12 (2020): 4,205, at https://www.mdpi.com/1660-4601/17/12/4205/htm.

[23] 'THE SILENT CITIES PROJECT,' website, last updated 13 April 2022, at https://osf.io/h285u/.

[24] 'Sounds of Pandemia: Sound Archive Covid-19,' *Changing the Story Leeds*, Leeds University, at https://changingthestory.leeds.ac.uk/projects/sounds-of-pandemia-sound-archive-archivo-sonoro-covid-19/.

local and exotic locations could be experienced through a computer screen; and as we will see, these estranged sounds and disembodied images took on great importance. On YouTube, real-world sounds resonated in a particular way. Users want videos with the highest 'definition' of sound possible: the 'best' rain, the 'best' blackbird song, the 'best' waterfall sounds. As a result, real world sound recordings are often maximized. To achieve hyper clarity and definition – or 'crispiness', an adjective common in the comments sections of YouTube's real-sound videos – uploaders employ a range of sonic manipulation technologies to construct a fictional reality that is already quite distinct from its captured source sound. This maximization of sonic definition is one of the reasons that a video or a channel is more successful than others.

To listen to these recordings of absence, natural re-plenitude and hyper-definition takes a special kind of attention that seems at first to be at odds with what Nicholas Carr derisorily referred to as 'the shallows of distraction'. Engagement with the Internet, he argues, has rewired our brains to engage only superficially with material encountered.[25] John Palfrey talks more benevolently of an oscillation between 'grazing' and 'deep dive' for digital natives, or those born into a digital world.[26] These projects to collect the new sounds of urban life under pandemia trod the divide between grazing and deep dive engagement in interesting ways: hums, drones and the sounds of nature that ordinarily reside in the back of our perceptual awareness are here thrust into the foreground by both their strangeness and their physical in-accessibility.

## 'We're Gathering the Ambient Sounds of Isolation': Networked Sounds

These projects and YouTube uploads aimed to document, capture and preserve the current sonic environment through a form of acoustic ecology, that both archived and disseminated sonic content through open-access online processes to produce important forms of communality and significant historical sonic documents. But other projects encouraged users to not only capture their local

---

[25] Nicholas Carr, *The Shallows: How the Internet is Changing the Way We Think, Read and Remember* (London: Atlantic Books, 2011).
[26] John Palfrey and Urs Gasser, *Born Digital: Understanding the First Generation of Digital Natives* (Philadelphia: Basic Books, 2008).

sounds, but also to enhance, stretch and manipulate them through a process of sonic elongation: in other words, to *respond* to these new sonic environments. The creative responses to the captured sounds of quarantine could be produced by single artists or by teams of remote collaborators who passed content between users and platforms to make collective critical sonic responses to captured, real-world sounds. To those listening remotely to these mediated realities, the soundscapes included information not only about what was happening outside, but also about how the lack of human-generated sounds was affecting the global community; and about how people felt about these new soundscapes.

American experimental sound artist Drew Daniel, one half of electronic music duo Matmos, explored the creative potential of these phonograph recordings of locked down life in a particularly innovative way. Matmos have long been interested in composing with, and collaging, real-world sounds, often formed from samples such as 'the amplified aural activity of crayfish' that appears on their first album (*Matmos*, 1997), sounds from medical procedures (found on their 2001 album *A Chance to Cut Is a Chance to Cure)*, or the whir of their washing machine, which generated all the sounds for their 2016 album, *Ultimate Care II* (named after their Whirlpool Ultimate Care Washing Machine). Throughout their career, the duo have explored crowd-sourced composition and for *The Consuming Flame: Open Exercises in Group Form* (2020), they generated the entire album from samples, all recorded at 99 BPM, contributed by ninety-nine musicians. As the realities of quarantine unfolded, Daniel released a Twitter statement on 1 April about a new Kickstarter project. It said: 'we're gathering the ambient sounds of isolation' and will 'combine them into one collective track'.[27] The call generated sound clips from around 200 contributors from 'across the planet'; 'from Italy, Germany, Mexico, Czech Republic, India, Kenya and many others'. Once in Daniel's hands, the recordings were cleaned up and focused, but, he states in a recent interview, 'I did not otherwise process or manipulate these sounds. Sometimes, a single sound is heard in isolation. At other times, I decided to cluster and overlay the sounds into distinct areas (at its densest there are twelve separate layers playing simultaneously) ... Sometimes the threat of the coronavirus is front and centre; sometimes it's far in the background.'[28]

---

[27] Katheryn Thayer, 'Matmos' Drew Daniel Wants to Mix the Sounds of Your Quarantine,' *Kickstarter*, last modified 8 April 2020, at https://www.kickstarter.com/articles/matmos-drew-daniel-mixes-quarantine-sounds.

[28] Drew Daniel, 'Quarantine Supercut,' *Creative Independent*, 2020, at https://thecreativeindependent.com/events/tci-irl-1/.

On 4 May, the fifteen-minute track, 'Quarantine Supercut', went live on Kickstarter's Creative Independent arts site.[29] The piece moves from calm, domestic noises—a typewriter, a baby, a cat, an electric kettle, a girl 'not in the mood' for her homework—before increasing in anxiety as things become more glitchy; we hear someone sigh, more sounds are overlaid, there's an annoying squeaky swing, some drones, a voice yells 'I just want a couple of seconds to myself'; the sounds become less identifiable, more closely mixed, falling over one another. A cough, in reference to the virus, precedes the noise of rain from inside a car as the radio tells us about the COVID test; new sounds are added, the rain thunders down, louder and louder, overwhelming the voice.[30] Although these sounds can be detangled, with many of the original submissions uploaded to YouTube (see Video 1), the result is an egalitarian form of soundmaking that foregrounds the wonder of community in a time of dystopian crisis as recognizable real-world sounds are compiled to reveal the synergies in the differences.[31]

In itself, this process stems fluidly from the commonplace cultural processes that drive many areas of online life. The mediation of the world in which we live is one of the lynchpins of social media culture. Personal YouTube channels, Insta-vlogs and TikToks regularly stage content and make use of editing techniques and filters to manipulate the ordinary into something utopian and aspirational. This trickery has become an expected part of our virtual communications. 'Quarantine Supercut' also pulls into the participatory nature of Web 2.0. There have been examples of online participatory performance and composition in the past, of course, and musical produsage and collaborative creativity can be found throughout social media and other sites. During the pandemic, however, such examples took on a peculiar resonance, by portraying – or reimagining – a world we are no longer able to fully participate in. What we are hearing in Daniel's project is 'the people formerly known as the audience' activating to take creative production of sonic memory. We can think of this

---

[29] Peter C. Baker, 'Making a Supercut of the Sounds of Quarantine,' *New Yorker*, last modified 4 May 2020, at https://www.newyorker.com/culture/cultural-comment/making-a-supercut-of-the-sounds-of-quarantine.

[30] Drew Daniel, 'Quarantine Supercut,' *Creative Independent Soundcloud*, 00:15:02, uploaded 2020, https://soundcloud.com/user-597121341/tci-irl-the-sound-of-quarantine?ref=section-tci-irl-promo-open-call-quarantine-supercut-with-drew-daniel; Baker, 'Making a Supercut of the Sounds of Quarantine.'

[31] See, for example, Fabrizio Modonese Palumbo's contribution, 'Disintegrating Turin,' *YouTube video*, 00:06:00, 4 May 2020, https://www.youtube.com/watch?v=Vy-_pJXsboY.

process as a form of citizen journalism that reports and interprets current events. Referring to 'the everyday life of hundreds of millions of people who make and upload their media or write blogs became public', Lev Manovich notes that 'What before was ephemeral, transient, unmappable, and invisible became [with Web 2.0], permanent, mappable and viewable.'[32] With YouTube's early slogan of 'Broadcast Yourself', it is not a surprise that the Most Responded and Most Discussed categories are made up of two-thirds of user-generated content (UGC), as of 2019. Jean Burgess and Joshua Green recognized this early on in the scholarly engagement with social media, when they proclaimed that some of the most important content on YouTube resides in a different aesthetic space from the glossy nature of its professional content: they say, 'because so much of the symbolic material mediated via YouTube originates in the everyday lives of ordinary citizens, or is evaluated, discussed and curated by them, YouTube, in theory, represents a site of cosmopolitan cultural citizenship.'[33] Writing of 'cultural citizenship', Yoca Ermes identifies a 'process of bonding and community building, that is implied in partaking of the text-related practices of reading, consuming, celebrating and criticizing offered in the realm of (popular) culture.'[34] Michael Mandiberg reminds us that this process of citizen journalism destabilizes 'the one-directional broadcast from a reporter to an audience into a multivoiced conversation among participants.'[35] The multivoiced 'Quarantine Supercut' does just this. The piece does not give us an overlaid alterative to the wonder/ horror of the wave of silence: rather, it leaves a strong residue of its origins and places the process of its creative interpretation clearly in view.[36] We hear the original recordings, but they have now been placed alongside and over the top of each other so that we hear each differently: 'I want music that is a balm, or an alternative, or a different world,' he says.[37] On the one hand, the sounds in this piece clearly retain their source context: eating crisps, a cat meowing, the hushed city streets, rain falling on a car. But on the other, it mashes them together to convert these crowd-sourced personal moments into a global message. It moves

---

[32] Lev Manovich, 'The Practice of Everyday (Media) Life,' in *Video Vortex Reader: Responses to YouTube*, ed. Geert Lovink and Sabine Niederer (Amsterdam: Institute of Network Cultures, 2008), 38.
[33] Jean Burgess and Joshua Green, *YouTube: Online Video and Participatory Culture* (2009. Rep. Cambridge: Polity Press, 2019), 77, 126.
[34] Joke Hermes, *Re-Reading Popular Culture* (Malden: Blackwell, 2005), 10.
[35] Michael Mandiberg, 'Introduction,' in *The Social Media Reader*, 3.
[36] In this sense, networked sonic elongation comes close to the processes and aesthetics of video art, which can be performative and merge with its environment and visitors in entangled ways. See Holly Rogers, *Sounding the Gallery: Video and the Rise of Art-Music* (New York: Oxford University Press, 2013).
[37] Thayer, '"Matmos" Drew Daniel Wants to Mix the Sounds of Your Quarantine.'

from field recording towards soundscape composition, sonic art, music composition; from sonic document to a multi-authored musical remodelling. Each upload represents an important sonic moment or absence from numerous people: these chosen moments were curated and re-positioned against one another by Daniel, a facilitator rather than an author.

## YouTube's Pandemic Musicking

As I explored in the Introduction to our first volume of essays, YouTube has been a significant site for online musical activity since its launch, with music videos consistently prominent among the most favourited category and, by 2018, 47 per cent of all online music streaming coming through the platform.[38] During the pandemic, YouTube's circulation and remediation of music became more prominent than ever. In many ways, what was already happening to music online – in terms of composing, listening, playing and teaching – was bought into the relief – and even accelerated – and it was reported that, during the first few months of lockdown, 48 per cent of visitors to YouTube were seeking not information on the pandemic, despite its dedicated COVID homepage, but rather music-related content.[39] This content came in several forms (see Video 2).[40] Older songs received renewed viewership and new versions were uploaded with pandemic-appropriate lyric changes;[41] pandemic-bespoke festival and concerts, such as #SOSFEST, which saw the National Independent Venue Association partner with YouTube to run a three-day virtual benefit festival (see Video 3), and Andrea Bocelli's live-streamed concert from the Duomo di Milano – Music for Hope – received millions of views (see Video 4);[42] a renewed passion for

---

[38] Hugh McIntyre, 'Report: YouTube is the Most Popular Site of On-Demand Music Streaming,' *Forbes*, last modified 27 September 2017, at https://www.forbes.com/sites/hughmcintyre/2017/09/27/the-numbers-prove-it-the-world-is-listening-to-the-music-it-loves-on-youtube/.

[39] Lucas Matney, 'YouTube Launches Dedicated COVID-19 Home Page Section,' *TechnCrunch*, last modified 19 March 2020, at https://techcrunch.com/2020/03/19/youtube-launches-dedicated-covid-19-homepage-section/?guccounter=1; Channel Factory, 'Content Consumption and Consumer Sentiment Amid the Coronavirus Pandemic,' *Channelfactory.com* at https://channelfactory.com/content-consumption-sentiment-amid-covid-19channel-factory/.

[40] YouTube.com, 'The Year in YouTube Music,' *YouTube Culture & Trends*, last modified 9 December 2020, at https://www.youtube.com/trends/articles/2020-youtube-music-stats/.

[41] Eric T. Lehman, '"Washing Hands, Reaching Out" – Popular Music, Digital Leisure and Touch during the COVID-19 Pandemic,' *Leisure Sciences* 43, no. 1–2 (3 March 2021): 273–9.

[42] #sosfest, YouTube channel, at https://www.youtube.com/hashtag/sosfest; Andrea Bocelli, 'Andrea Bocelli: Music For Hope – Live From Duomo di Milano,' *YouTube video*, 00:24:56, streamed live on 12 April 2020, https://www.youtube.com/watch?v=huTUOek4LgU.

crowd-sourced collaborative videos developed, many of which quickly rose to the top of the most viewed lists; and a zeal for remixing well-known songs using editing tools such as YouTube's empty-spaces musical remixer, to let in a sense of isolation generated several viral memes.[43] Other musical activities aimed to transmit scenes of hope and unity into isolated bedrooms, and the platform blew up with grass-roots vernacular videos of apartment block singsongs (Figure 5.2)

**Figure 5.2a and b** A man plays the guitar and two men play guitar and flute from the balcony of their homes in the neighbourhood San Salvario during a flash mob launched throughout Italy to bring people together: 13 March 2020. (Photos by Nicolò Campo/LightRocket via Getty Images.)

[43] Meredith C. Ward, 'The Sounds of Lockdown: Virtual connection, Online Listening and the Emotional Weight of COVID-19,' *Sound Effects* 10, no. 1 (2021): 8–26, at https://www.soundeffects.dk/article/view/124195/171127.

and dancing doctors who used YouTube to spread messages of social distancing, hygiene and hope through song. These amateur clips of unedited real-life situations became a vital tool for maintaining and developing community across cities and countries, as Joana Freitas, João Francisco Porfírio and Júlia Durand note in their work on YouTube's pandemic surge of interest in video games, library music and sonic relaxation content, and the move from 'mobile' to 'immobile' listening'.[44]

For many professional artists, lockdown was a great creative opportunity to both explore new aesthetic forms and to tap into the vast potential of the locked in, furloughed global audience: Taylor Swift wrote her *Folklore* album during lockdown, premiering the first single, 'Cardigan' on her YouTube channel on 24 July 2020, for example. The song helped her to secure her sixth US number one, and propelled her to the top of the Digital Song Sales chart, with twenty number ones. It's difficult to say concretely that the song's success was down to more people having time at home to listen and view new content, or that her enforced stripped down pandemic aesthetic opened the doors to new ears, but streamed music and music videos were clearly booming. We need only look to BTS's release of their single 'Dynamite', released on 21 August, to see that Taylor Swift's success was not a one off. 'Dynamite' broke records when it became the most viewed video within the first twenty-four hours of its drop on YouTube with 101.1 million views. But there was also an increase in re-released content that ordinarily resided behind paywalls – music teachers, university module leaders, bands, venues and magazines released content for free in the spirit of comradery: over on TikTok, Prince's estate made his entire catalogue free to stream.[45]

---

[44] Gieson Cacho, 'Byproduct of a Pandemic: Coronavirus Parody Music Videos Flourish on YouTube,' *Mercury News*, 31 March 2020, at https://www.mercurynews.com/2020/03/31/byproduct-of-a-pandemic-coronavirus-parody-music-videos-flourish-on-youtube/; Michelle Langley and Leah Coutts, 'Why do we Turn to Music in Times of Crisis?' *World Economic Forum*, last updated 30 March 2020, at https://www.weforum.org/agenda/2020/03/coronavirus-music-covid-19-community/; Susannah Clapp, Kitty Empire, Laura Cumming, Michael Hogan, Sarah Crompton and Fiona Maddocks, 'Cancelled Culture: At-home Substitutes for Major Theatre, Art and Music Events,' *Guardian*, last modified 28 March 2020, at https://www.theguardian.com/culture/2020/mar/28/cancelled-cultural-events-alternative-online-theatre-podcasts-comedy-art-pop-music-books; Joana Freitas, João Francisco Porfírio and Júlia Durand, 'Listen, Watch, Play and Relax: YouTube, Video Games and Library Music in Everyday Life During the Pandemic,' *Sonic Scope: New Approaches to Audiovisual Culture* 3 (2021), at https://www.sonicscope.org/pub/jzu92u0h/release/2.

[45] Deidre Simonds, 'Prince's Entire Music Catalog Now Available on TikTok After the Late Icon's Estate Vows Inspire a "New Generation" of Fans,' *Daily Mail*, last updated 8 July 2020, at https://www.dailymail.co.uk/tvshowbiz/article-8464873/Princes-estate-makes-music-catalog-available-TikTok-inspire-new-generation-fans.html.

**Figure 5.3a** Screenshot from Trombonelus, 'LIVE Concert CORONAVIRUS ETUDE For Piano and Disinfecting Wipe (Jeff DePaoli)' (26 March 2020).
**Figure 5.3b** Dani Howard, '#Stay Home' on Logic Pro X (Twitter, 24 March 2020).
**Figure 5.3c** Screenshot from Matthew Shlomowich, 'Hexatonic Cycle with a Calm Stanley' (14 April 2020).

The pandemic also became a popular subject matter for music compositions. Within weeks, scientists translated the spikes of the virus directly into a strangely beautiful composition called 'Viral Counterpoint of the Corona Virus Spike Protein'.[46] It was also not long before the gestures of performance were merged with those becoming pandemic prevalent, often with a degree of humour, as in Jeff DePaoli's piece *Coronavirus Etude For Piano and Disinfecting Wipe (For Piano Teachers Everywhere*: Figure 5.3a; Video 5).[47] Hidden messages appeared encoded into Logic – as in Dani Howard's composition 'Stay Home' (Figure 5.3b), in which the visual interface spells #STAYHOME as the music unfolds across the screen.[48] Others offered bespoke services adaptable to each person's locked down circumstances: Matthew Shlomowitz, for instance, took commissions for his *Music For Cohabiters* project, offering compositions written especially for the instruments, players and abilities present in different quarantined homes (Video 6).[49] One of his pieces, 'Hexatonic Cycle with a Calm Stanley', shows a family performing a piece for piano, oboe and cello with the young Stanley trying (in vain) to stand still and play the djembe (Figure 5.3c).[50] In all these examples,

[46] Vineeth Venugopal, 'Scientists Have Turned the Structure of the Coronavirus into Music,' *Science Magazine*, 3 April 2020, at https://www.sciencemag.org/news/2020/04/scientists-have-turned-structure-coronavirus-music.
[47] A, 'Coronavirus Etude – for Piano and Disinfecting Wipe – WATCH UNTIL THE END!,' *YouTube video*, 00:01:28, 14 March 2020, https://youtu.be/whNICyl_et0.
[48] Dani Howard, 'A little musical message to the world,' Twitter post, 24 March 2020, at https://twitter.com/danihoward6/status/1242475804484763652?lang=en.
[49] 'University Lecturer Instrumental in Creating COVID Lockdown Compositions,' Southhampton.ac.uk, 16 April 2020, at https://www.southampton.ac.uk/news/2020/04/covid-compositions-shlomowitz.page.
[50] Matthew Shlomowitz, 'Hexatonic Cycle with a calmStanley (Music for cohabiters),' *YouTube Video*, 00:02:55, 14 April 2020, https://www.youtube.com/watch?v=1kPzdTeQ5f0.

compositions were uploaded straight from source with no middle man, no industry trail, no contracts, demonstrating a heightened presence of DIY grassroots music creation and distribution processes during the pandemic.

## Sonic Remediations

Once recorded and uploaded to YouTube, these ephemeral moments, new videos and responsive compositions became endlessly repeatable. Populated by ever expanding numbers of amateur and DIY users, rather than professional creators, social media's referencing, reuse and remixing of existing online content came to dominate its aesthetics to such an extent that O'Reilly identified a platform's potential 'hackability' and 'remixability' as one of the defining features of Web 2.0.[51] As we've seen in this book's introduction, musically, we can find the reuse and remixing of online material – particularly in song and dance form – everywhere, from the overt and continual referencing that drives musical versions and parodies, fanvids, reaction videos, bad lip-synching, lyric videos and music mashups on YouTube, to the majority of TikTok's re-versioned content.

YouTube's 'generative qualities' and the embrace of low-fi, amateur content became, for many, a significant means of creating social connections and escapism during the early days of lockdown. Versions became extremely popular during the pandemic, with parody songs, such as Chris Mann's 'Hello (From the Inside)' manipulating popular culture's most familiar works into humorous parodies of current events (Mann's version has received almost 15 million views and pages and pages of comments, see Video 7).[52] During the pandemic, this process of engaging in nostalgia through new ideas became extremely important. Starting from easily recognizable sonic or audiovisual material, memes knowingly embrace amateur aesthetics, using one cultural form to comment on another, by highlighting similarities and differences and de-centring authorship through participating audiences and citizen journalism.[53] However, this can result in complicated labour dynamics. We can see this happening in 'Quarantine

---

[51] O'Reilly, 'What is Web 2.0?'
[52] Chris Mann, 'Hello (from the Inside) An Adele Parody by Chris Mann,' *YouTube video*, 00:04:51, 26 March 2020, https://www.youtube.com/watch?v=M5azNpTwVk8.
[53] See for example, Barnaby Goodman, 'Amateur Content Creation as Compositional Practice: Viral Videos and Internet Memes in Online Participatory Culture,' *Sonic Scope: New Approaches to Audiovisual Culture* 2 (2021), at https://www.sonicscope.org/pub/m46tmp3s/release/1.

Supercut'. Created from natural sounds, this piece of sonic art both embraces the distributed authorship of Web 2.0's UGC *and* its zeal for retromania and remixing: 'I don't get to make any sounds' Daniel says, positioning himself as a curator rather than a composer: 'I just get to make the choices about their order and length':

> It's like a trust fall. I'm here to work with whatever I'm given, and to grow something from those submissions. I don't know how I'll feel about them, I'm not sure my feelings matter. I think what matters is what we all contribute, what everybody gives: 'Here's 30 seconds of my life. Take it and do something with it.' I think that memorial capacity of electronic music, to hold moments of time, and to make us care about them, and to dignify even very small and quiet things and say that they're worthy of attention, I think that's really powerful. It's not about me as a composer. It's just about the fact of what happens when you put a frame around everyday life and say, 'This is worth your time.'[54]

Here, field recordings are uploaded and recontextualized, collaged together to give a reading of current events that is both hopeful – we are all in this together – and terrifying – stay at home.

## Networked Sonic Elongation

If we now return to the idea of networked sonic elongation, we can see how the affordances of social media have encouraged participatory forms of sonic engagement. YouTube's mashups and memes offer musical community in the form of playing, exploring and creating together. However, in the earlier analysis of 'Quarantine Supercut', it was clear that this piece represents not only a more holistic and simultaneous process of compositional collaboration, but also a form of remediation where content is not taken from other online sources, but rather from the real world in a process of acoustic ecology; here, sound becomes a mediating device between users and their forbidden environments. And yet, whose reality are we hearing? The idea that a field recording can be objective and free from agency has been rejected by many in the sound art community.[55] For each piece of phonography (sound recorded in non-professionalized spaces

---

[54] Thayer, 'Matmos' Drew Daniel Wants to Mix the Sounds of Your Quarantine.'
[55] See Lawrence English, 'A Beginner's Guide to … Field Recording,' *Factmag*, n.d, at https://www.factmag.com/2014/11/18/a-beginners-guide-to-field-recording/.

with an emphasis on discovery rather than invention), many decisions have been made about what was worth capturing, where to place the microphone, when to press record and when to stop. And yet a condition of phonography is that the recorded sounds do not undergo any form of significant intervention after their capture; that the presence of the sounds remain as an historical artefact, or a portal into what once was. Although the framing belies a clear agential presence, the sounds rest undisturbed post-recording. And yet, they harbour a potential for temporal and interpretative intervention that can act as a powerful contemporary reaction to past events, as Paul Hegarty suggests in his work on the captured 'sonic real': 'Opening these recordings to constant and unlimited reconfiguration allows them to move into our present, to harbour not just what it was, but also what it means today.'[56] Key to all sonic arts is the refreshed and reinvigorated forms of listening it encourages – the ability to listen differently to our sonic environment, an aural engagement that has been rigorously theorized as reduced listening, deep listening, critical aurality, etc.[57] This form of engagement changes again when sounds are in some way manipulated. Once captured sounds are opened to more than an interpretative temporal fusion – once a source sound has been stretched, abstracted, augmented, heightened or otherwise manipulated – we enter the realms of *musique concrète* and soundscape composition.[58] From its emergence from R. Murray Schafer's 1970s World Soundscape Project, soundscape composers have used creative processes of sound combination and transformation to investigate how environmental noises influence and impact our creative and mental health.

In 2002, soundscape composer and theorist Barry Truax issued four useful characteristics of soundscape composition: 1. listener recognizability of the source material – this is achieved by making sure that the original texture and content of the recorded sounds are not obscured; 2. their knowledge of the context of the material, in terms of both environmental and psychological familiarity; 3. the composer's knowledge of these contexts and their ability to infuse the composition with these meanings, and '(4) The work enhances our understanding of the world, and its influence carries over into everyday

---

[56] Paul Hegarty, *Annihilating Noise* (London: Bloomsbury, 2020), 40.
[57] Pierre Schafer, *The Soundscape: Our Sonic Environment and The Tuning of the World* (New York: A.A. Knopf, 1977); Pauline Oliveros, *Deep Listening: A Composer's Sound Practice* (New York and London: Deep Listening Publications, 2005); John Drever, '"Primacy of the Ear" – But Whose Ear?: The Case for Auraldiversity in Sonic Arts Practice and Discourse,' *Organised Sound* 24, no. 1 (2019): 85–95.
[58] Barry Truax, 'Genres and Techniques of Soundscape Composition as Developed at Simon Fraser University,' *Organized Sound* 7, no. 1 (2002): 5–14.

perceptual habits,'[59] 'Quarantine Supercut' shows this process at work. The source material and its contexts remain easily recognizable for the listener. The sonic ambience gives clear clues as to location, and the psychological context can be gleaned from the tone of the voices, the urgency of the radio broadcast, etc. As the curator of the sounds, Daniel draws out the meanings and resonances between the disparate clips to create a powerful reading of life under quarantine.

But, although it shares many characteristics with soundscape composition, networked sonic elongation is slightly different. Sonic elongation is a process by which we stretch sounds away from a corresponding semantic sonic anchor: the object that produced them. Sound can remain close to the original material or become unrecognizable. So far, this mimics the process of soundscape composition. The difference, however, lies in the processes by which the sounds are transformed against an image and their afterlife. In networked sonic elongation, the original sounds are usually gathered from many sources; if they do come from one sound recordist, they are subsequently filtered through many voices. Either way, fundamental to the success of networked sonic elongation is the distribution of authorship and the use of online tools for its creation – from sound design apps to modes of social media distribution. Although Daniel's crowdsourcing Twitter call for 'Quarantine Supercut' generated peer-produced content, he, by his own admission, curated it into a fixed and final form that went live on Kickstarter, as we've seen. Other forms of sound mashup can be found in projects with a more collaborative, back and forth movement that builds on one another's ideas to develop a project simultaneously. The most liberating forms of networked sonic elongation, then, remain in flux. Each contribution acts as the launchpad for a new configuration, much like Instagram's memes or TikTok's infinite versions of the same dance, song or action. But crucially, the source material must be remixed and manipulated as it is in soundscape composition; with little added to transform the sounds from one user's interpretation to another's. And it must be understood as a continual process rather than the production of a discrete composition.

Although networked sonic elongation can occur through same-site remediation, at its most powerful, it remains a continual, open-ended and multi-platform process. Many of the examples noted so far began as bespoke, small projects, hosted on web pages with already-established sound-art communities. However, once in motion, the remediations migrated to YouTube, where they

---

[59] Barry Truax, 'The Aesthetics of Computer Music: A Questionable Concept Reconsidered,' *Organised Sound* 5, no. 3 (2000): 119–26.

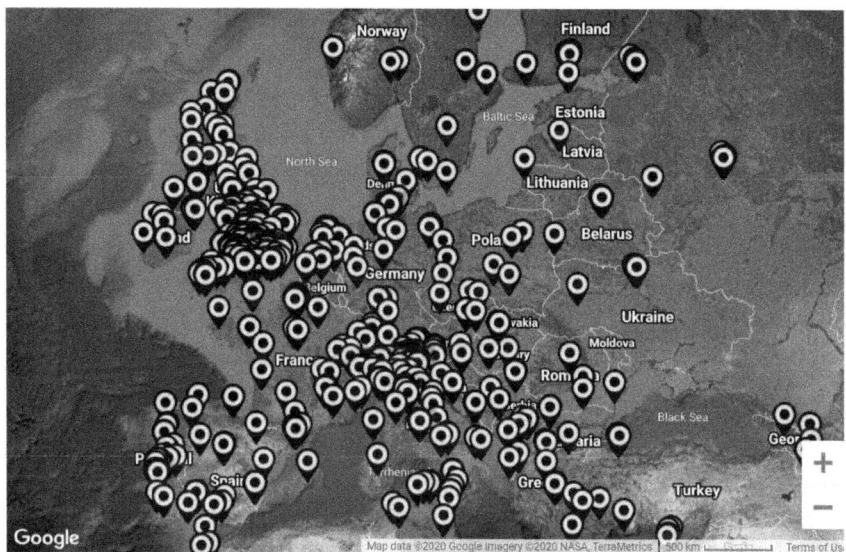

**Figure 5.4** Cities and Memories map.

drew in new audiences and kickstarted different types of collaboration and response. Cities and Memory, a field recording project that bills itself as 'a global, collaborative sound art and mapping project that remixes the world, one sound at a time', plays into these creative post-medial migrations. Every dot on an interactive Google map (Figure 5.4) marks a field recording. Click on any dot and the sounds from that location begin. The project's reach is astonishing, including more than 4,000 sounds recorded by 750 sound-artists in more than 100 countries. As the pandemic got underway, they launched #StayHomeSounds, with 'The desire to capture and compare. To share and marvel' at the pandemic's new global sounds.[60] Recordings came from all over the world, including the cacophony of locked-down homes, the silence of shopping centres, the rejuvenated sounds of nature, and new sounds, such as clap for carers, local bell ringing, balcony singing, etc. These field recordings of quarantine took on a peculiar and eerie resonance. If we think back to Truax's four points above, is it even possible for listeners to identify and empathize with source material that is so sonically strange?

The Cities and Memory team grappled with this strangeness by inviting straightforward field recordings, but also a sonically-elongated version of each: 'Every sound on the map is accompanied by a "memory" version, which is a

---

[60] Cities and Memory, 'Remixing the World, One Sound at a Time,' *citiesandmemory*, n.d, at https://citiesandmemory.com/.

recomposed, reimagined or remixed version of that sound through which our users can explore the sounds of the world as they are, or explore an alternative, imagined sound world created by the collective imagination of hundreds of artists. Remixing the world, one sound at a time – in short, proclaims the project's founder Stuart Fowkes.[61] The web page offers instructions, tutorials and links to online sound-making resources and software, which either the sound recordist or any other user can use to transform the uploaded recordings. These tools are ubiquitous and primitive: smart phone apps, free software; all easy to use and quick to share. Anyone with a recording device, however simple, could become involved. One notable example from this project is the re-imagined sounds of Grand Central Station in New York. The original phonography was recorded by Geoff Gersh on 30 March 2020, around 9.00 pm; it was then remediated through the Headliner app by another user, who manipulated the sparse and reverberant sounds of the cavernous hall to mimic train sounds with synths filling in the absent spaces.[62] With participation from all over the world, and by giving free licence for subsequent transformation, these pieces showed the power of transmedia to carry a story far and wide. Cross-platform community discussion on Facebook and Twitter allowed users to share content and collaborate on re-imagined sounds, sharing the results on YouTube, Kickstarter and bandcamp, and even receiving prominent airplay on London's Resonance FM (Figure 5.5).[63] Cities and Memory, then, is a project where content is not stable but constantly develops, undoing and redoing itself as people manipulate the work of others. And yet, like soundscape composition, it also remains pretty literal: the mapping element positions us in the exact location from which the elongated sounds were taken. And yet, it also provides access to the various ways that the global community reimagined and interpreted these eerie locked-down environments in myriad ways. We can even suggest that, by filtering the sonic strangeness of Covid-19's lockdown through the familiar processes of cyberculture, these re-imagined soundscapes provided a shared comfort to their listeners.

In this project, then, we can see the main themes of networked sonic elongation at play: the manipulation of real-world sounds via participatory, online culture; the blurring of producers and users, and the continual produsage

---

[61] Silvia Lacovcich, 'STUART FOWKES, Capturing the World into an Autonomous Network of Sounds,' *clotmag*, last modified 4 October 2020, at https://www.clotmag.com/interviews/stuart-fowkes-capturing-the-world-into-an-autonomous-network-of-sounds.

[62] Cities and Memory, 'Grand Central Interior,' *Audio Boom*, 3 April 2020, at https://audioboom.com/posts/7547462-grand-central-interior.

[63] Lanre Bakare, 'Art Project Captures Sound of Cities During Coronavirus Outbreak,' *Guardian*, 31 March 2020, at https://www.theguardian.com/world/2020/mar/31/art-project-captures-sound-of-cities-during-coronavirus-outbreak?CMP=share_btn_tw.

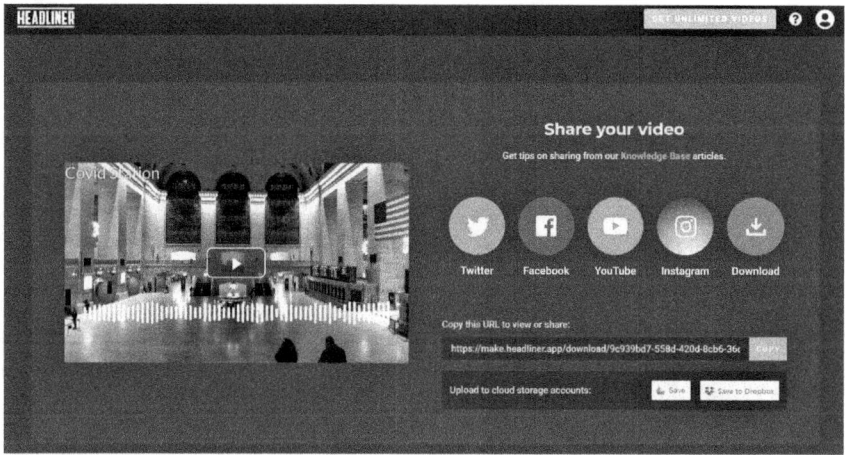

**Figure 5.5** 'Covid Station' sharing page from Cities and Memories.

of creative content; the remixing and remediation of both real and online source material; the interoperability of technologies; and the post-medial spread of sounds across various social media platforms.

## Remediating Silence

In the years since YouTube's launch, the process of sharing, collaborating and distributing have claimed ownership of many of our lives; our thought processes and modes of communication. The platform now sits within a tightly connected nexus of post-media potentialities, its content spreading across social media sites and out into everyday life. Experiencing, cataloguing, manipulating and disseminating music across this nexus has become entirely normal; and during the Covid-19 crisis, the social media vortex took on a particularly comforting and uniting role. YouTube sits at the centre of this vortex in several ways. First, with its ability to support a wide range of formats, it serves as a resource and a destination for sonic art practice. With millions of channels and videos dedicated to real-world soundscape recordings, it continues to provide ample raw material for composers to play with; and with well-established algorithms, search engines and communities, material can easily be passed between users. When uploaded, tags and comments provide a useful way to link between remixed works. But significantly, YouTube also acts as a vital conduit between various existing and bespoke online platforms.

Second, as we've seen, a major factor since YouTube's beginning has been to populate the online arena with content from our everyday lives. Scholars have long been interested in how, as social media grew to ever greater prominence, the boundaries between art and life – between networked and physical communication – became fragile. These examples of networked sonic elongation above throw this process into relief. Real-world sounds and images are uploaded to various platforms; other users download and re-compose them; these re-compositions are then available for others to work with. We are so well versed in remediated content, versions, mashups and remixed culture that we are used to this process of revisiting and re-evaluating content, however mundane, private, low fi and personal it may seem. The networked sonic elongation of real-world sounds plays into this embrace of the ordinary, the normal, the humdrum. Only during the pandemic, of course, the captured sounds and their cascading remediations were anything but ordinary.

Although some used cyberspace for total sonic escapism in the shape of long-form nature recordings, others sought more journalistic information through field-recording projects. But others still wanted to inject their feelings into these recordings, manipulating them to include their fears, frustrations and isolation, but also a joy at attentive listening to sounds abstracted from their locations. New sounds were generated, smaller sounds acquired greater significance, quieter sounds emerged from beneath louder ones and everything demanded greater aural attention. During lockdown, then, we heard less but we also heard more. But, to return to our original question, did we believe what we heard?

Unlike many forms of soundscape composition, networked sonic elongation is both a peer-produced and constantly evolving form. We can think of examples of networked sonic elongation not as compositions, but rather as ongoing sites of audiovisual activity that offer transitory snapshots into multiple local environments, while at the same time offering a commentary on the original sounds. It arises through multiple authors and encourages others to keep working with the material, taking sounds further and further away from their original destinations. Crucially, this activity is web-based, which enables each field recording to undergo successive forms of creative intervention though multiple voices. That it is streamed, matters. That sound artists can connect in real time, matters. And that free licence is given for subsequent transformations: that really matters. It's almost like a sort of post-human form of music-making that emerges through numerous, heterogeneous and sometimes clashing perspectives and identities; a form of sonic citizen journalism. As the real sounds become increasingly distant and abstracted, we hear a sonic remodelling of the emotional and psychological impact of the Covid-19 pandemic. And as it moves through and beyond YouTube, this impact is not stable, but is always emergent.

## Bibliography

Asensio, César, Pierre Aumond, Arnaud Can, Luis Gascó, Peter Lercher, Jean-Marc Wunderli, Catherine Lavandier, Guillermo de Arcas, Carlos Ribeiro, Patricio Munoz and Gaetano Licitra. 'A Taxonomy Proposal for the Assessment of the Changes in Soundscape Resulting from the COVID-19 Lockdown.' *Internal Journal Environ. Res. Public Health* 17, no. 12 (2020): 4,205.

Bakare, Lanre. 'Art Project Captures Sound of Cities During Coronavirus Outbreak.' *Guardian*, 31 March 2020, at https://www.theguardian.com/world/2020/mar/31/art-project-captures-sound-of-cities-during-coronavirus-outbreak?CMP=share_btn_tw.

Baker, Peter C. 'Making a Supercut of the Sounds of Quarantine.' *New Yorker*. Last modified 4 May 2020, at https://www.newyorker.com/culture/cultural-comment/making-a-supercut-of-the-sounds-of-quarantine.

Bruns, Axel. *Blogs, Wikipedia, Second Life, and Beyond: From Production to Produsage*. New York: Peter Lang Publishing, 2008.

Burgess Jean and Joshua Green. *YouTube: Online Video and Participatory Culture*. Cambridge: Polity Press, 2019 rep. [2009].

Cacho, Gieson. 'Byproduct of a Pandemic: Coronavirus Parody Music Videos Flourish on YouTube.' *Mercury News*, 31 March 2020, at https://www.mercurynews.com/2020/03/31/byproduct-of-a-pandemic-coronavirus-parody-music-videos-flourish-on-youtube/.

Carr, Nicholas. *The Shallows: How the Internet is Changing the Way We Think, Read and Remember*. London: Atlantic Books, 2011.

Channel Factory. 'Content Consumption and Consumer Sentiment Amid the Coronavirus Pandemic.' *Channelfactory.com*, at https://channelfactory.com/content-consumption-sentiment-amid-covid-19channel-factory/.

Chion, Michel. *Audio-Vision: Sound on Screen*. Translated by Claudia Gorbman. New York: Columbia University Press, Second edition, 2019 [1994].

Clapp, Susannah, Kitty Empire, Laura Cumming, Michael Hogan, Sarah Crompton and Fiona Maddocks. 'Cancelled Culture: At-Home Substitutes for Major Theatre, Art and Music Events.' *Guardian*, 28 March 2020, at https://www.theguardian.com/culture/2020/mar/28/cancelled-cultural-events-alternative-online-theatre-podcasts-comedy-art-pop-music-books.

Cohen, Nancy Eve. 'With Covid-19, Fewer Cars, Quieter Soundscape for Birds and Humans.' In *New England Public Radio*, 31 March 2020, at https://www.nepr.net/post/covid-19-fewer-cars-quieter-soundscape-birds-and-humans#stream/0.

Daniel, Drew. 'Quarantine Supercut.' *Creative Independent*, 2020, at https://thecreativeindependent.com/events/tci-irl-1/.

DeNucci, Darci. 'Fragmented Future.' *Print* 32 (January 1999): 221–2.

Drever, John. '"Primacy of the Ear" – But Whose Ear?: The Case for Auraldiversity in Sonic Arts Practice and Discourse.' *Organised Sound* 24, no. 1 (2019): 85–95.

English, Lawrence. 'A Beginner's Guide to ... Field Recording.' *Factmag*, n.d, at https://www.factmag.com/2014/11/18/a-beginners-guide-to-field-recording/.

Freitas, Joana, João Francisco Porfírio and Júlia Durand. 'Listen, Watch, Play and Relax: YouTube, Video Games and Library Music in Everyday Life During the Pandemic.' *Sonic Scope: New Approaches to Audiovisual Culture* 3 (2021): https://www.sonicscope.org/pub/jzu92u0h/release/2.

Gibney, Elizabeth. 'Coronavirus Lockdowns have Changed the Way Earth Moves.' *nature.com*, 31 March 2020, at https://www.nature.com/articles/d41586-020-00965-x?fbclid=IwAR1wJGGezt06Q5JqgxQqDPVnaNNRIPJcti3xsSwG2wpgzhL0dhL73ymVHjU.

Gibson, James J. *The Ecological Approach to Visual Perception*. Boston: Houghton Mifflin, 1979.

Goodman, Barnaby. 'Amateur Content Creation as Compositional Practice: Viral Videos and Internet Memes in Online Participatory Culture.' *Sonic Scope: New Approaches to Audiovisual Culture* 2 (2021): https://www.sonicscope.org/pub/m46tmp3s/release/1?readingCollection=d345dcdc.

Green, Chris. "You Can Hear into the Distance': Wildlife Sound Expert on how Coronavirus has Changed the World.' *inews.co.uk*, 10 April 2020, at https://inews.co.uk/news/coronavirus-lockdown-wildlife-expert-bird-songs-environment-nature-417130.

Gudgeon, Oli. 'Natural Soundscape Video Views Surge amid Covid-19 Quarantine.' *The Medium*, 19 April 2020, at https://medium.com/contemporary-sound-art/natural-soundscape-video-views-surge-amid-covid-19-quarantine-4fb9bf8cabd3.

Harkins, Paul and Nick Prior. '(Dis)locating Democratization: Music Technologies in Practice.' *Popular Music and Society* 45, no. 1 (2021): 84–103.

Hegarty, Paul. *Annihilating Noise*. London: Bloomsbury, 2020.

Hermes, Joke. *Re-Reading Popular Culture*. Malden: Blackwell, 2005.

Koeze Ella and Nathaniel Popper. 'The Virus Changed the Way We Internet.' *New York Times*, 7 April 2020, at https://www.nytimes.com/interactive/2020/04/07/technology/coronavirus-internet-use.html.

Lacovcich, Silvia. 'STUART FOWKES, Capturing the World into an Autonomous Network of Sounds.' *Clotmag*, 4 October 2020, at https://www.clotmag.com/interviews/stuart-fowkes-capturing-the-world-into-an-autonomous-network-of-sounds.

Langley Michelle and Leah Coutts. 'Why do we Turn to Music in Times of Crisis?' *World Economic Forum*, 30 March 2020, at https://www.weforum.org/agenda/2020/03/coronavirus-music-covid-19-community/.

Lehman, Eric T. '"Washing Hands, Reaching Out" – Popular Music, Digital Leisure and Touch during the COVID-19 Pandemic.' *Leisure Sciences* 43, no. 1–2 (3 March 2021): 273–9.

Mandiberg, Michael. 'Introduction.' In *The Social Media Reader*, edited by Michael Mandiberg, 1–12. New York and London: New York University Press, 2012.

Manovich, Lev. 'The Practice of Everyday (Media) Life.' In *Video Vortex Reader: Responses to YouTube*, edited by Geert Lovink and Sabine Niederer, 33–44. Amsterdam: Institute of Network Cultures, 2008.

Matney, Lucas. 'YouTube Launches Dedicated COVID-19 Home Page Section.' *TechnCrunch*, 19 March 2020, at https://techcrunch.com/2020/03/19/youtube-launches-dedicated-covid-19-homepage-section/?guccounter=1.

McIntyre, Hugh. 'Report: YouTube is the Most Popular Site of On-Demand Music Streaming.' *Forbes*, 27 September 2017, at https://www.forbes.com/sites/hughmcintyre/2017/09/27/the-numbers-prove-it-the-world-is-listening-to-the-music-it-loves-on-youtube/.

Minh-ha, Trin T. *Cinema-Interval*. Oxford: Routledge, 1999.

O'Reilly, Tim. 'What is Web 2.0: Design Patterns and Business Models for the Next Generation of Software.' *oreilly.com*, 30 September 2005, at https://www.oreilly.com/pub/a/web2/archive/what-is-web-20.html.

Oliveros, Pauline. *Deep Listening: A Composer's Sound Practice*. New York and London: Deep Listening Publications, 2005.

Palfrey John and Urs Gasser. *Born Digital: Understanding the First Generation of Digital Natives*. Philadelphia: Basic Books, 2008.

Partner, India. 'YouTube sees 20.5% Surge in Subscribers-Base During the 45 Days of the Lockdown.' *Business Insider*, 21 April 2020, at https://www.businessinsider.in/advertising/ad-tech/news/youtube-sees-20-5-surge-in-subscribers-base-during-the-45-days-of-the-lockdown/articleshow/75268860.cms.

Porfírio, João Francisco. 'YouTube and the Sonification of Domestic Everyday Life.' In *YouTube and Music: Cyberculture and Everyday Life*, edited by Holly Rogers, Joana Freitas and João Francisco Porfírio, 209–20. New York: Bloomsbury, 2023.

Rodriguez, Salvador. 'YouTube is Social Media's Big Winner During the Pandemic.' *CNBC*, 7 April 2021, at https://www.cnbc.com/2021/04/07/youtube-is-social-medias-big-winner-during-the-pandemic.html.

Rogers, Holly. 'Sonic Elongation and Sonic Aporia: Two Modes of Disrupted Listening in Film.' In *The Oxford Handbook of Cinematic Listening*, edited by Carlo Cenciarelli, 427–49. Oxford: Oxford University Press, 2021.

Rogers, Holly. 'Sonic Elongation: Creative Audition in Documentary Film.' *Journal of Cinema and Media Studies* 59, no. 2 (2020): 88–113.

Rogers, Holly. *Sounding the Gallery: Video and the Rise of Art-Music*. New York: Oxford University Press, 2013.

Rogers, Holly. '"Welcome to your world": YouTube and the Reconfiguration of Music's Gatekeepers.' In *YouTube and Music: Online Culture and Everyday Life,* edited by Holly Rogers, Joana Freitas and João Francisco Porfírio, 1–38. New York: Bloomsbury, 2023.

Romero, Dennis. 'YouTube Thrives as a Window for Those Isolated by Coronavirus.' *NBC News,* 2 April 2020, at https://www.nbcnews.com/tech/social-media/youtube-thrives-window-those-isolated-coronavirus-n1173651.

Rosen, Jay. 'The People Formerly Known as the Audience.' In *The Social Media Reader,* edited by Michael Mandiberg, 13–16. New York and London: New York University Press, 2012.

Simonds, Deidre. 'Prince's Entire Music Catalog Now Available on TikTok After the Late Icon's Estate Vows Inspire a "New Generation" of Fans.' *Daily Mail,* 8 July 2020, at https://www.dailymail.co.uk/tvshowbiz/article-8464873/Princes-estate-makes-music-catalog-available-TikTok-inspire-new-generation-fans.html.

Schafer, Pierre. *The Soundscape: Our Sonic Environment and The Tuning of the World.* New York: A.A. Knopf, 1977.

'Sounds of Pandemia: Sound Archive Covid-19.' *Changing the Story Leeds,* at https://changingthestory.leeds.ac.uk/projects/sounds-of-pandemia-sound-archive-archivo-sonoro-covid-19/.

Tarkovsky, Andrey. *Sculpting in Time.* Translated by Kitty Hunter-Blair. Austin: University of Texas Press, 1986; 2003.

Thayer, Katheryn. 'Matmos' Drew Daniel Wants to Mix the Sounds of Your Quarantine.' *Kickstarter,* 8 April 2020, at https://www.kickstarter.com/articles/matmos-drew-daniel-mixes-quarantine-sounds.

Thompson, Marie. *Beyond Unwanted Sound: Noise, Affect and Aesthetic Moralism.* London: Bloomsbury Press, 2017.

Truax, Barry. 'Genres and Techniques of Soundscape Composition as Developed at Simon Fraser University.' *Organised Sound* 7, no. 1 (2002): 5–14.

Truax, Barry. 'The Aesthetics of Computer Music: A Questionable Concept Reconsidered.' *Organised Sound* 5, no. 3 (2000): 119–26.

'University Lecturer Instrumental in Creating COVID Lockdown Compositions.' *Southhampton.ac.uk,* 16 April 2020, at https://www.southampton.ac.uk/news/2020/04/covid-compositions-shlomowitz.page.

Venugopal, Vineeth. 'Scientists Have Turned the Structure of the Coronavirus into Music.' *Science Magazine,* 3 April 2020, at https://www.sciencemag.org/news/2020/04/scientists-have-turned-structure-coronavirus-music.

Vernallis, Carol, Holly Rogers and Lisa Perrott. *Transmedia Directors: Artistry, Industry and New Audiovisual Aesthetics.* New York: Bloomsbury Press, 2020.

Vernallis, Carol, Holly Rogers, Selmin Kara and Jonathan Leal. *Cybermedia: Explorations in Science, Sound, and Vision.* New York: Bloomsbury, 2021.

Ward, Meredith C. 'The Sounds of Lockdown: Virtual Connection, Online Listening and the Emotional Weight of COVID-19.' *Sound Effects* 10, no. 1 (2021): 8–26.

Web.archive.org. 'Web 2.0 conference.' Conference website, San Francisco, California. 5–7 October, 2004, at https://web.archive.org/web/20050312204307/http://www.web2con.com/web2con.

Wendle, Abby. 'Human Life is Literally Quieter Due to Coronavirus Lockdown.' *npr.org*, 14 April 2020, at https://www.npr.org/2020/04/14/834460094/human-life-is-literally-quieter-due-to-coronavirus-lockdown?t=1587480808639&t=1599641868346.

YouTube.com. 'The Year in YouTube Music.' *YouTube Culture & Trends*, 9 December 2020, at https://www.youtube.com/trends/articles/2020-youtube-music-stats/.

# 6

## 'Only People With Good Imaginations Usually Listen to this Kind of Music':[1] On the Convergence of Musical Tags, Video Games and YouTube in the Epic Genre

Joana Freitas

What started as a common adjective for everything 'cool' during the first decade of the 2000s, quickly turned out to be yet another online trend that faded and gave way to other fads. During this period the term 'epic' – still used today – flooded the Internet, particularly between 2008 and 2013. A quick search for 'epic' on the platform *Urban Dictionary* produces 966 results between 2007 and 2021, showing different user-uploaded definitions in no defined order, which mirror general ideas and preconceptions shaped by this specific period.[2] In particular, entries dated 2008 to 2013 grasp the overuse of the word 'epic' to show 'impact' and applied to, basically, everything:

- 'An overly used word thats getting totally out of hand. Used WAY to much. *"that was epic"; "omg this movies epic"; "thats such an epic shirt"'* (sydney101, 16 January 2008);

---

[1] Comment from the user R F on the video Pandora Journey, '2-Hours Epic Music | THE POWER OF EPIC MUSIC – Best Of Collection – Vol.5 – 2019,' *YouTube video*, 02:03:42, 27 July 2019, https://youtu.be/KaXXVzGy7Y8.

[2] The platform's results for searching the word 'epic' can be found here: https://www.urbandictionary.com/define.php?term=Epic. The definitions mentioned here are direct quotes. For the sake of this search and the objective at hand, I limited the data to the first five pages of results, thus verifying thirty-five definitions in total that mainly focused on the period between 2007 and 2012. Other results, which are much scarcer, are dated between 2018 and 2021, and represent a different type of discourse, i.e. rational/non-memetic.

- 'A word that used to be used to describe a book, a movie or other work as timeless, great, and meaningful. Is now used by douchebags who combine it with "win" or "fail" to describe everyday things.' (watto17, 6 January 2010);
- 'The most freaking overused word in the english language. It has in fact been used so much that there is really no reasonable definition for this word.' (Lochnessoon, 28 May 2009);
- A word that every virgin, non action getting, video game loving, mama's boy, still living at home person uses to describe something awesome.' (meowmeowfuckyou, 30 April 2009);
- 'The band "Two Steps From Hell"' (Mememememememememe12345654321, 17 July 2011).
- 'Epic is currently used by most groups of people to describe anything extraordinary. Most of these people fail to recognize that Epic started in World of Warcraft referring to the highest level of loot gear you could normally get (I know legendary is higher but the only people you see with that shit are fucking crazy). Most people look down at those who play World of Warcraft but ironically use many of the terms that they came up with.' (Pakawakajaka, 21 October 2010).[3]

These examples, amongst others along the same lines, show how common tropes of humour, parody and other *memetic* media are interlinked with the general discourse portrayed by these definitions.[4] From terms directly associated with gaming and its stereotypes of nerds living in their basements, to music groups with an 'epic' repertoire, or just a general adjective for everything that can be either 'just cool' to 'out of this world', the word 'epic' was, in fact, present in many corners of the Internet, mainly in 'epic fails' videos. However, and for the purpose of this chapter, the understanding of the background of this term is important in order to perceive what 'epic' can mean when applied to music and media, its particular relation to video games and its central place on YouTube.

In the digital universe of audiovisual content production, YouTube is a major platform for the upload, consumption and sharing of millions of videos in a wide range of formats. Among these, we can find moving images, static images, videos without images, videos with or without music, videos with lyrics, etc. that, when uploaded on this platform, are automatically labelled as 'videos', whatever

---

[3] All grammar and spelling peculiarities are in the original.
[4] Limor Shifman, *Memes in Digital Culture* (Cambridge: The MIT Press, 2014).

their format and presentation may be. In their pioneering analysis of YouTube (both as a platform and as a phenomenon), Jean Burgess and Joshua Green found that, even in 2009, music video was one of the categories preferred by users, a fact they found surprising at the time but that has remained true ever since.[5] The cultural patterns and trends that collect videos together according to musicians, musical genres and so on, helps to gather users into complex social and interactive networks and communities. These processes of cataloguing and collecting – fuelled by artists, labels, studios, agents, fans, YouTubers and algorithms – are key to contemporary musical practices and have become one of the dominant modes of content diffusion and circulation on YouTube. In fact, the platform, which functions as an agent of aggregation rather than the production of videos, subsists almost exclusively on the practices underlying participatory culture; as Kevin Allocca,[6] Henry Jenkins and others have shown, such interactive processes of aggregation and organization have fostered new forms of media power that underpin the circulation of current videographic practice, and represents a move away from traditional capitalist business models.[7]

Among the constantly evolving platforms for music diffusion and consumption – Spotify, Soundcloud, Tidal, Pandora, Shazam and iTunes, for example – the big companies, such as Apple Music or Amazon Music, tend to centralize their market in the world of music, as does YouTube Music. However, apart from small video loops, or album art stills, these other applications provide pure sound rather than audiovisual content or visualized music. Even with YouTube Music, millions of users have used – and still use – 'regular' YouTube for the consumption and sharing of music, with or without associated images. And yet, unlike the other music platforms, YouTube allows the user to decide how to listen to, and /or watch, their music in several ways: first, with or without a video; and second, through official, amateur or remediated visualization. This (apparent) embrace of user agency is important for epic music. The direct relationship between video games and the epic category, now notorious in online spaces, is governed by gaming narratives and their commercialization in franchises underlined by a transmedia logic. During the past few decades, the

---

[5] Jean Burgess and Joshua Green, *YouTube: Online Video and Participatory Culture* (Cambridge: Polity, 2009).
[6] Kevin Allocca, *Videocracy: How YouTube Is Changing the World ... with Double Rainbows, Singing Foxes, and Other Trends We Can't Stop Watching* (New York: Bloomsbury, 2018).
[7] Henry Jenkins, *Fans, Bloggers, and Gamers: Exploring Participatory Culture* (New York: New York University Press, 2006).

term has broken its original semantic roots as it circulated through YouTube comments, forums and social networks, becoming a common descriptor for genres, styles and quality, as well as a common adjective for something that is impressive, awesome or timeless. It has also become a staple of transmedial storytelling, whereby a recognizable theme and musical style moves through platforms in fragments, thus relating back to the etymological roots of the term, as James Buhler explains:

> One reason franchising is drawn to developing epic tales, then, is because franchising works best when the world is immersive, when it can overlay our world with another fictive one. (...) The ideal franchise thus has an inherent epic quality, since the world represented in the story both encompasses the tale and exceeds its telling. Epic, here, means not simply big and spectacular but also harkens back to the literary meaning of the term as a story told in episodes and aimed at relating mythical tales of heroic acts.[8]

Through the use of codes and musical conventions in the composition of these soundtracks, audiovisual literacy is consolidated in the representation of the imaginaries conveyed by interactive narratives, thus structuring a compositional formula that migrates from Hollywood blockbusters to the latest hits in video games.

Music and sound are fundamental parts of a transmedial franchise's coherence, with consistent themes and textures helping to draw together film, game and social media worlds into a single immersive space.[9] In this chapter, I examine how YouTube has become an important, yet distinctive, component of this creative cluster. Here, the transmedial franchise is not established in advance. Instead, users navigate through thousands of videos and playlists, sharing different filters and tags that converge to form what we can call the sonic *epic brand*. This idea of the epic in relation to music, is collectively formed through user participation, and reflects a growing homogenization in the compositional logic by major studios for video games and other screen media that has been appropriated by users – whether fans or not – to soundtrack their daily lives. Besides 'epic', terms such as 'aggressive', 'hybrid', 'dramatic', 'power' and even 'war' connect epic music to a uniform set of musical textures. Although there is little

---

[8] James Buhler, 'Branding the Franchise: Music, Opening Credits, and the (Corporate) Myth of Origin', in *Music in Epic Film: Listening to Spectacle*, ed. Stephen C. Meyer (New York: Routledge, 2016), 4–5.
[9] On immersion, see Isabella van Elferen, 'Analyzing Game Musical Immersion: The ALI Model,' in *Ludomusicology: Approaches to Video Game Music*, ed. Michiel Kamp, Tim Summers and Mark Sweeney (Sheffield, UK: Equinox Publishing, 2016), 32–52.

variation in the musical content itself, it is fragmented by the multiplicity of these tags, which results in new forms of collage and the branding together of similar videos. In addition, 'epic' music is dependent on converting otherwise 'paywalled' music tracks to an accessible format on YouTube, and applying a specific selection of artwork, tags and other visual elements that quickly form numerous digital phenomena on this platform. This process remediates an 'epic affect', thus perpetuating the creation and circulation of seemingly 'new genres', when, in fact, what users require is a comfortable and familiar sonic imagery represented by its paratextual and pictorial descriptions. Just like a warehouse or a mall, YouTube turns into a never-ending shelf of neatly arranged and designed packages of music that correspond with one's 'musical self', from 'bardcore' to 'lo-fi fantasy', categories shared both by fans and specialized channels that reach out to several mediated online communities. As long as there is a minimal orchestral atmosphere and other identifiable tropes, 'epic music' is most often used to accompany the transformation of something menial to something great, even if it is already great to begin with.

## *BRAAAM*: A Brief Overview of 'Epic Music' in Contemporary Media

The connection between the idea of 'epic-ness' and video games is not new. In fact, not long after the 'epic' trend emerged, many video game websites introduced the term as a marketing tool for their own articles and reviews: from charts to recommendations, the most *epic* games of a specific genre, year or task were often listed and shared across several online spaces.[10] In this sense, using 'epic' to signify quality became a notion shared by companies, developers and users when producing content: from narrative standpoints to interactive elements, video games and their creative agents reach out to certain aspects of story design, mechanics, agency and audiovisual components to convey a potential 'epic' experience. Music has played an important role in structuring this entire process, through specificities developed first during gameplay, before moving *outside* the

---

[10] The use of this term can still be found in recent entries: as an example, *The Guardian* lists fifteen epic video games for people who are socially isolating a few weeks after the first lockdown because of the COVID-19 pandemic: Keith Stuart, 'Now's the Time – 15 Epic Video Games for the Socially Isolated', *The Guardian*, 30 March 2020, at https://www.theguardian.com/games/2020/mar/30/epic-video-games-self-isolating.

virtual experience in the form of soundtrack listening in different contexts or as an identifiable mark for the game's advertising, as we shall see later. As Buhler argued above, the immersive quality of a given universe on screen is amplified through its overlay with our own reality, be it through franchising or the construction of a specific brand.[11] Well-defined musical themes help to fill in the gaps between those two realities, as we can see in John Williams' score for the *Harry Potter* world and it's appropriation through its various paratexts.

In previous work, I have followed the prominent compositional and semiotic codes that Anahid Kassabian has identified as the key drivers of audiovisual media, to trace the direct connection between musical style and a player's immersion in the virtual world of interactive narratives.[12] This immersion relies on the alignment of the soundtrack with familiar romantic / Hollywoodesque tropes in order to engage the audiovisual literacy and familiarity that is expected from the listener. By looking at the audiovisual devices used in Role Playing Games (RPGs) with fantasy / Medieval settings, such as the *Elder Scrolls* franchise (Bethesda Softworks 1994–), I found that immersion arose best if the soundtrack was consistent across the virtual universe, i.e. an orchestral accompaniment with recognizable themes and motifs that perfectly suits both exploration and combat in Nordic landscapes with dragons and magic no matter the platform. The identification of these games and their narrative as epic recalls Tim Summers' definition of 'epic musical texturing' in gaming culture: that is, the use of musical references that instigate the production of meaning able to create referential links to other media that reinforce the personal experience of the player:

> Aside from denoting the appropriation of elements (plots, settings, musical styles, etc.) from epic Hollywood film, the use of the term may reveal an important aspect of game music . . . it is clear that the term 'epic' in the context of games and game music is not limited to the canon of classical epics. Instead, it is closer to the wider sense of the word, referring to an artistic genre that stems from classical epic poetry through to modern epic novels and epic film.[13]

Like the development of the epic game tradition, epic music shares and contributes to the consolidation of a 'blockbuster canon' through the same

---

[11] Buhler, 'Branding the Franchise,' 12–13.
[12] Anahid Kassabian, *Hearing Film: Tracking Identifications in Contemporary Hollywood Film Music* (New York: Routledge, 2001); Joana Freitas, '"The Music Is the Only Thing You Don't Have to Mod": The Musical Composition in Modification Files for Videogames' (Master's Thesis, Lisbon, NOVA FCSH, 2017).
[13] Tim Summers, *Understanding Video Game Music* (Cambridge: Cambridge University Press, 2016), 14.

musical codes and stereotypes to convey a set of ideas, emotions and ambiences that fit with the narrative, the world and the player's agency, and this can be seen operating at different levels on YouTube.[14] Much like a player who aims to be a hero on a grand quest in a certain video game, I want to investigate the connection between the 'epic' and the requirement for greatness, heroism, emotion and overachievement, among other things, that comprises much of YouTube's musical content and respective compilations. As mentioned, this content undergoes a careful selection by the channels responsible for its production: its upload actively contributes to a shared process of appropriating and constructing meanings and ways of customizing the listener's interaction with these sonic landscapes. A vast number of videos in the world of 'epic music' have multiple tracks combined with imagery. Both sound and image are extremely homogeneous and repetitive, and share the same type of comments and user activity. Nevertheless, uniform sounds are transformed into something highly – 'epically' – personal. But where does the online trend of 'epic' music come from?

Responsible for coining the term 'corporate classicism', Nicholas Reyland identifies a key trait of this style in contemporary Hollywood cinema: although films in the twentieth-century golden age had memorable thematic melodies (by composers such as Alan Silvestri and John Williams, for example), nowadays melody is often replaced by other compositional parameters, such as sonic texture, timbre and rhythmic pattern.[15] This stylistic trend endures through current scoring practices, despite more collaborative strategies of production as music composition is outsourced to large companies such as Remote Control Productions (RCP), a film-score production studio run by Hans Zimmer, which oversees many of the musical works that make their way to the big screens. Like Reyland, Stadoff uses RCP to show how both commercial film and AAA video games share a robust, hybrid orchestral-electronic soundworld – what he calls a 'hyperorchestral cinematic sound' – shaped by an editorial apparatus in corporate settings, a style that has been developed and honed over many years.[16] Benjamin Wright has also focused on Zimmer's work with RCP to show how 'the synergy

---

[14] I have discussed this in regard to the *Soulsbourne* franchise, particularly the third instalment, *Dark Souls III* (2016). See Joana Freitas, 'From Epic Fail to Epic Music: Music, Silence and Failure on "Dark Souls 3,"' *Journal of Sound, Silence, Image and Technology* 3 (December 2020): 55–74.

[15] Nicholas Reyland, 'Corporate Classicism and the Metaphysical Style: Affects, Effects, and Contexts of Two Recent Trends in Screen Scoring,' *Music, Sound, and the Moving Image* 9, no. 2 (2016): 115–30.

[16] Ronald H. Sadoff, 'Scoring for Film and Video Games: Collaborative Practices and Digital Post-Production,' in *The Oxford Handbook of Sound and Image in Digital Media*, ed. Carol Vernallis, Amy Herzog and John Richardson (Oxford: Oxford University Press, 2013), 662–81.

between electronic and orchestral music structures help to create a distinct house style (...) of contemporary film practices'.[17]

Aside from several hits spanning the 1990s and 2000s – *The Lion King* (Allers and Minkoff 1994), *Pirates of the Caribbean* (Verbinski 2003 to 2007), *Batman/ The Dark Knight* (Nolan 2005 to 2012), to name a few – Christopher Nolan's 2010 film *Inception* can be singled out as an example that changed the way we *listen* to movies. The 'BRAAAM' sound, a very loud mix of brass and piano with a synthetic feel, pervades Hans Zimmer's soundtrack and rapidly became a notable sonic marker that helped to consolidate the Zimmer style and enable listeners to instantly identify the authorship of a given soundtrack. According to Adrian Daub, no sooner was *Inception* released than this 'BRAAAM' sound invaded Hollywood and its soundtracks; and it has been adapted, copied and remediated ever since, appearing everywhere from trailers to teasers, from memes to playlists.[18] Along similar lines, Chloé Huvet writes that:

> (...) most [scientific] publications emphasize the masculine and epic characters of Zimmer's music, the massive and powerful sound of his scores, and the omnipresence of a strong rhythmic pulse. Several elements of this model, well identified by these authors, can be applied to many of the composer's scores – particularly the musical frameworks designed for action films – and creates the illusion of a relatively homogeneous musical language in Zimmer's work, which can be found almost identically from film to film.[19]

Although Huvet's research aims to differentiate Zimmer's typical musical idiom by analyzing *Interstellar* (Nolan 2014) and its atypical score, she recognizes and stresses the association between an 'epic' and 'masculine' feel. Although this raises problematic questions about gendered musical discourses, stereotypes and toxic binary roles, several other authors have also placed Zimmer's music within a framework of 'masculine' signifiers when analysing certain elements of his

---

[17] Benjamin Wright, 'Music and the Moving Image: A Case Study of Hans Zimmer,' in *The Routledge Reader on the Sociology of Music*, ed. John Shepherd and Kyle Devine (New York: Routledge, 2015), 319.

[18] Adrian Daub, '"BRAAAM!": The Sound That Invaded the Hollywood Soundtrack', *Longreads* (blog), 8 December 2016, at https://longreads.com/2016/12/08/braaam-inception-hollywood-soundtracks/. The multiplicity of possible uses given to this effect can be summarized in the website *INCEPTION*, where a big red button can be clicked to play (or download) the BRAAAM sound, thus 'adding drama to a certain situation' according to the clip assistant that shows up in the screen. Available here: https://inception.davepedu.com/.

[19] Chloé Huvet, '*Interstellar* de Hans Zimmer: plongée musicale au coeur des drames humains, par-delà l'infiniment grand. Pour une autre approche de l'esthétique zimmerienne,' *Revue musicale OICRM* 5, no. 2 (2018): 103–24. Translation by the author.

compositional style.[20] Frank Lehman, for instance, uses Zimmer's style to show its role in 'manufacturing the epic' in Hollywood action and sci-fi films. In fact, he discusses the epic codes that make up the composer's epic style, identifying a 'maximization of minimalism' and how this relates to masculinity. According to him, the use of 'Zimmermisms', such as the *marcato motto*, percussion loops and 'abstract anthems', can be seen as elements of fusion between the ideas of the 'epic' and the 'male', aiming to effectively portray and infuse a sense of 'huge force', 'virility' and 'spectacle' to contemporary multimedia texts:

> (...) the musical gendering is so over-the-top that it cannot help but suggest that Zimmer's sense of maleness is one that is 'in crisis', as American masculinity has been so frequently characterized since the mid-1990s. Many Zimmermisms, like the marcato action motifs and percussion loops, are manifestly aimed at injecting a scene with as much testosterone-infused energy as technologically possible. Others, such as the minor dominants and heavily abstracted leitmotifs, seem tailored to harden the edge of his music, giving it a darker, more serious tone.[21]

As Lehman points out, this does not mean that Zimmer's music can be reduced to a single domain of meaning and representation, as it is well able to depict and convey soundscapes of subtlety, complexity and, indeed, *non-maleness*. Even if it frequently falls into other highly coded categories that organize outdated feminine and Eurocentric musical devices – particularly the 'sacred', 'exotic' or 'ethnic' – that doesn't necessarily mean there's a corresponding representation on screen or, rather, a gendered musical writing/listening. Even so, most of the time, the *minimalist maximization* of the score accords with the binary opposition of musical categories into masculine and feminine that have underpinned many mainstream audiovisual narratives.[22] In fact, as William Wehrs points out, the minimal style of Zimmer's music seeks to reduce any potential narrative nuances by underscoring 'the immediate action' and evoking 'felt bodily states'.[23]

---

[20] Several authors pioneered the field of gender and musicology during the 1990s by focusing their attention on the analysis and deconstruction of various patterns and matrixes that are deeply rooted in the Western Art Music tradition, thus looking at systemic gender inequality, discrimination and socio-cultural structures of power. For more on this, see Joana Freitas, 'A (Silent) Game of Words: Notes on Jeremy Soule's Accusations and the *Elder Scrolls* Online Community,' *Journal of Sound and Music in Games* 3, no. 1 (1 January 2022): 50–9.

[21] Frank Lehman, 'Manufacturing the Epic Score: Hans Zimmer and the Sounds of Significance,' in *Music in Epic Film: Listening to Spectacle*, ed. Stephen C. Meyer (New York: Routledge, 2016), 46–7.

[22] Ibid., 47.

[23] William Wehrs, 'Affect and Film Music: A Brief History' in *The Palgrave Handbook of Affect Studies and Textual Criticism*, ed. Donald R. Wehrs and Thomas Blake (Cham: Springer International Publishing, 2017), 735–52.

Shifting this immediacy from moving images on the big screen to our own laptops and smartphones, the rich musical production aligned with Zimmer's aesthetic and its resounding 'epic' universe has secured a strong presence on YouTube; and many of the videos categorized under epic music follow the set of codes established by Zimmer to convey a relatively homogeneous sound. Taking into account the elements that have already been noted as key aspects of today's score writing for audiovisual media, particularly cinema and video games, the following section dives into the multiple forces that act on the processes of circulation, re-mediation and consumption of musical texts in the form of videos/playlists, thus creating an 'epic' musical brand that is free to access and used to transform the listener's daily life.

## 'The Fact That There are no Ads is Truly Epic'[24]: YouTube, *Epic Music* and (Extra)Ordinary Daily Lives

YouTube is a central hub for the convergence of creativity and participation, and the remediation of audiovisual content. When considering what Daniel Muriel and Garry Crawford describe as the 'videoludification' of society and the undeniable influence of video games in today's contemporary culture, it is not surprising that fragments, styles and aesthetics from video games have seeped into other screens and contexts.[25] YouTube has actively promoted this paratextual spread by including gaming as one of its main categories, along with music, sport and other dominant genres. Video game music has been key to merging game culture with the worlds of social media in two ways: first, by enabling fans to listen to it *outside* of its original virtual context; and second, by gathering together many different types of related aural content. However, as stated before, 'epic' music may sit in a grey area, as it can ultimately be regarded as an umbrella term for music with several possible tags, and it uses video game imagery to create an easily identifiable set of video thumbnails that make up a potential music genre.

The meme depicted in Figure 6.1 efficiently gathers many of the common elements that 'epic' music videos and their comments share. From the selection

---

[24] Comment from the user Mysho on the video Pandora Journey, '2-Hours Epic Music | THE POWER OF EPIC MUSIC – Best Of Collection – Vol.4,' *YouTube video*, 02:02:20, 14 August 2018, https://youtu.be/aBxLgW9lE64.

[25] Daniel Muriel and Garry Crawford, *Video Games as Culture: Considering the Role and Importance of Video Games in Contemporary Society* (New York: Routledge, 2018).

Figure 6.1 A meme from the popular 'Starter Pack' category shared by user ArcadeTheGreat on the subreddit r/starterpacks. Taken from: https://www.reddit.com/r/starterpacks/comments/a0050n/epic_music_on_youtube_starter_pack/.

of words and formatting in the titles, to what users say happens to them when listening to this music, this meme points out the exaggerated character of this type of content. It is worth noting the comment about 'either gaming wallpaper or stolen ArtStation images', as this aspect is directly related to the video game imagery that was just being discussed. With these ideas in mind, what is, in fact, 'epic' music and how do YouTube's users and channels engage with it?

Among the 300+ million search results generated when searching for 'epic music' on YouTube, patterns and trends quickly become evident, both in the videos and in the channels responsible for their availability. For clarity, it is important to point out the parameters of this research. It is both impossible and unfruitful to verify millions of entries. To better grasp the similarities of videos or playlists between different channels with equivalent titles, keywords, imagery and other aspects, and to make sure that what distinguishes them is taken into account, it is effective to use the platform's own search engine, along with several search combinations to select the objects. To do this, I use a separate profile on the Chrome browser exclusively for this research, which is similar to using incognito mode. I match and search different keywords, using the filters 'relevance' and 'decreasing number of views', to verify the results and identify the potential main differences. When searching for 'epic music', 'epic', 'orchestral music', 'epic orchestral music' and other similar terms, the results do not vary significantly (except for 'orchestral music' as it is a wider term). Although there are several methods for conducting digital research and ethnography, the individuality of each process means that a specific method may not function in the same way for another person. It is clear, however, that the digital and technological character of daily life poses a number of challenges, and researchers are required to innovate in response to the constantly expanding methodological repertoire.[26]

In this range of content, which can vary from a single piece of music to compilations of dozens of tracks that make up two to ten hours of video runtime, the cluster of adjectives/tags, as well as their formatting, is a requirement for easy identification and respective filtering by users, depending on the type of setting/style/aesthetic. Amid the most relevant/more viewed results, it is possible to proceed with a selection of the main channels responsible for the production of this content, namely: Epic Music World, Pandora Journey, Epic Music VN, HALLVARD, EpicMusicChannel, Epic Music Mania, Premium Music HQ, etc. Several of these channels are associated with or related to Epic Music World, which is the longest-running channel (active since 2010) and has the most subscribers and regular weekly activity; advertising on its social media platforms has the feel of an 'epic music family' because of the community of listeners and fans.[27] At first glance, the descriptive elements of the channel and its production are simple to grasp: music videos are divided by categories that can be reduced to 'epic' and 'beautiful'. These two categories can function separately, and sometimes also use other adjectives, like the ones mentioned earlier, or they can overlap in the same clip. All videos feature either single tracks with specific titles or multiple-track uploads (described in various ways, such as collections, volumes or compilations), and each has their own thumbnail addressing that same sonic setting, the illustration of what is sounding 'epic' or 'beautiful'.

If YouTube grew to be characterized as an example of a hybrid commercial space, developing advertising methods for new forms of monetization based on user engagement, as Jane Arthurs et al. have argued, then processes underlying

---

[26] See Helene Snee, Christine Hine, Yvette Morey, Steven Roberts and Hayley Watson, 'Digital Methods as Mainstream Methodology: An Introduction,' in *Digital Methods for Social Science*, ed. Helene Snee, Christine Hine, Yvette Morey, Steven Roberts and Hayley Watson (London: Palgrave Macmillan UK, 2016), 1–11.

[27] At the time of writing this chapter, the channel had 1.8 million subscribers, more than 1,906 uploads in total and activity such as livestreams or new music three times a week. The tab 'Community' on the channel features regular posts and the tab 'Channels' lists other channels/users associated with this 'family': https://www.youtube.com/c/EpicMusicWorldII/channels.

these epic music channels do not stray far from these profitable models.²⁸ Despite the fact that many of the videos have no ads – or a very reduced amount as mentioned in the comments – the tracks that are featured come from a wide range of sources, spanning from professional library music catalogues to individual portfolios of composers trying to make it online. Compiling tracks, or dedicating single videos to a particular piece to accord with terms such as 'epic', 'powerful', 'aggressive' or other terms prominent in platforms and studios such as Audiomachine, Cézame or Atom Music Audio and in the work of artists such as David Chapelle or Two Steps from Hell, makes this otherwise limited access music free to listen to on YouTube.²⁹

In interviews with the managers of these channels, I found that, in most cases, an upload is a carefully designed *final* product of an epic soundscape, constructed by taking into consideration not only the music but also its accompanying imagery.³⁰ After curating and organizing the most epic tracks into 'subgenres', each piece is then illustrated by a specific artwork with minimal animation and movement, generally from artists on DeviantArt and with recurring themes, characters or settings from video games and other screen media. The description section credits all the featured artists, tracks and other agents with direct links and timestamps. The *Orchestral Music Mix* from the first volume of the compilation THE POWER OF EPIC MUSIC is an example of one of the most popular videos by Epic Music World.³¹ In it, forty tracks are seamlessly shuffled with a corresponding animation, ranging from designs from video games, such as *The Elder Scrolls V: Skyrim* (Bethesda Softworks 2011), *Dark Souls III*

---

[28] Jane Arthurs, Sophia Drakopoulou and Alessandro Gandini, 'Researching YouTube', *Convergence* 24, no. 1 (1 February 2018): 3–15.
[29] Júlia Durand has been researching library music and the contemporary developments being conducted in its production and use across several platforms, including YouTube. See Chapter 9: 'Library Music as the Soundtrack of YouTube' in this volume.
[30] I have been able to conduct structured interviews via email with some of the individuals that make the relevant YouTube videos and playlists: it became clear that the process includes, among other elements, the selection of tracks from open submissions (alongside their own research) and establishing partnerships with artists for their promotion. So far, I have received feedback from the channels Epic Music Empire (31 March 2020), L'Orchestra Cinématique (27 October 2020), Spirit of Orchestral Music (26 April 2021) and Epic Music World (26 January 2022); others, such as Epic Music VN and Pandora Journey channels have been contacted several times with no response, and I am currently waiting for the Epic Music Mania channel interview responses. Although this is beyond the main scope of this chapter, it is important to mention the background work that results in these videos and how this is yet another model of creative production based on musical imaginaries, tropes, media trends and other aspects that constitute the current online panorama in a highly capitalized cultural industry.
[31] Epic Music World, 'Orchestral Music Mix | THE POWER OF EPIC MUSIC – Vol.1', *YouTube video*, 02:00:42, 9 September 2016, https://www.youtube.com/watch?v=Lo3rrP8u7Mw.

(FromSoftware 2016), *Mass Effect* (Bioware 2007 to 2021) and *Nier* (Square Enix 2010 to 2021), to the *Star Wars* franchise (1977–) and the anime series *Dragon Ball* (Toei Animation 1986–). These cross-textual elements share the main inspirations from fiction and fantasy by following a particular framework, where a solo figure – with feminine or masculine traits; in heroic or ponderous pose; after battle or experiencing an enemy encounter – is musically represented by a given track. A description of these possible scenarios was shared in a Q&A in the 'Community' section of Epic Music World's YouTube channel by the manager Kai Rathsack:

> I like tracks which just speak to my heart (it is hard to explain): 'Why do you like the music you like?' :D. My favorite genre is the 'Emotional Heroic' style, tracks starting slow (like the hero is nearly at his end watching over the battlefield and see all the destruction and death out there, his last mates falling, he nearly gave up), and then it turns to something more faster more dramatic and heroic (the hero summons his last power to fight for all who can't fight anymore and finally wins or die). Also every other style is working, which you can find on the channel (Hybrid, Action, Piano, Vocal, Fantasy, . . .) the tracks just have to be good when hearing the first time. They have to feel special when hearing. :)[32]

Translating into words what is one of the most used tropes in media, and particularly in video games, Rathsack shows that the construction of a hero / saviour is made easier when paired with an identifiable 'subgenre' of epic music such as the 'Emotional heroic' one.[33]

For many users, the multiple uses and purposes afforded these videos on YouTube, privileges the platform over other specialized streaming services as a place to listen to music. In the same Q&A, Rathsack explained that 'At the beginning there wasn't a site like Spotify or so, and I just wanted to have my own little channel where I can hear the music which I love while studying, gaming, reading and so on. So it just started in 2010 :).' Indeed, even in 2022, with the now well-established Spotify in full flow, music(al) videos remain one of the most viewed and *produced* content on YouTube, statistics in which epic music plays a large part.[34] Reception, then, is one of the main reasons that epic music

---

[32] The full thread can be verified here: https://www.youtube.com/channel/UC9ImTi0cbFHs7PQ4l2jGO1g/community?lb=Ugw6MTOEV31QDvSo4IN4AaABCQ.
[33] Stephanie C Jennings, 'Only You Can Save the World (of Videogames): Authoritarian Agencies in the Heroism of Videogame Design, Play, and Culture,' *Convergence* (27 February 2022): 13548565221079156a.
[34] Axel Bruns, *Blogs, Wikipedia, Second Life, and Beyond: From Production to Produsage* (New York: Peter Lang, 2008).

has established itself so strongly on YouTube. Able to engage with – and determine – epic music through likes, shares, subscriptions and comments, the multiple voices of YouTube's users have become an important part of the genre's construction. Comments are a particularly rich source of information, and can be summarized in two ways: first, are comments that demonstrate a general appreciation of the work done for a particular upload based on personal taste; and second, are the ones that reveal the uses to which these clips have been put in users' daily life, such as cooking, doing homework or going to the bathroom. Both types of remarks show that the epic character of the featured tracks have improved various aspects of their lives by allowing them to become whatever they 'imagine' or to turn something mundane, like an omelette, into the most wonderful meal they ever had:

- 'I accidentally let my pet bird listen to this, now he's one of the eagles in Lord of the Rings.'
- 'This is the most intensely I've ever drank my morning coffee. With every sip, I am slowly becoming immortal.'
- 'i'm listening to this while i'm reading, and i can tell: i can feel the words coming out of the book as the story goes.'
- 'For homeworks, cleanning room and running : IT'S WHAT YOU NEED.'
- 'My cat listened to this ... Now it is a lion.'
- 'Once, I listen to this while washing dishes ... Now, we have to buy a new set.'
- 'Listened to this while making a sandwich. Most epic tasting sandwich EVER !'[35]

It is clear from these quotes that these epic music videos have been used to soundtrack their fans' daily lives, musically renegotiating the *self* to regulate, enhance, remediate and construct meaning: in other words, to forge a *personal epic bubble*.[36] When used as a streaming platform, YouTube emphasizes the act of *listening* to epic music over its visualization. And yet, despite that, their visual designs are central to determining what the music 'should sound like' or what it can represent at different levels of meaning. However, as we have seen, they

---

[35] Following the same order, these comments are from the users Kaylin Hutson, tinman652, Késia Leite, Freitas MARC-ELIE, Luke Wolfe, ToyyArts and Ryan on the videos Pandora Journey, '2-Hours Epic Music Mix | THE POWER OF EPIC MUSIC – Full Mix Vol. 2,' *YouTube video*, 01:59:09, 31 July 2014, https://youtu.be/DeXoACwOT1o and Pandora Journey, '2-Hours Epic Music | THE POWER OF EPIC MUSIC – Best Of Collection – Vol.5 – 2019,' *YouTube video*, 02:03:42, 27 July 2019, https://youtu.be/KaXXVzGy7Y8.

[36] Tia DeNora, *Music in Everyday Life* (Cambridge; New York: Cambridge University Press, 2000).

present some problematic, gendered relationships. If the solo characters represented in the animations are deemed heroic, powerful or strong, the adjectives used to identify a certain video provide clues to what is expected to be heard (and seen) in the tracks. Tags such as 'orchestral', 'action', 'battle' or 'dark' are often linked to male figures, while it is rare to find the tags 'dramatic', 'emotional' or 'beautiful' attached to thumbnails that don't portray a woman-like figure, either warrior or angel-like. It is notable that a masculine aura is linked with energetic musical tropes, while a feminine aura engenders beauty-related codes. This binary division reinforces gender stereotypes concerning artistic production and consumption, and raises questions about how users perceive these musical codes, even without recourse to an image or narrative suggestion. The more masculine the positioning, the more likely it is that the tags accord with an orchestral, or as Sadoff puts it, 'orchestral-electronic hybrid' sounds.[37] The more 'masculine' and 'aggressive' the music becomes, the more dominant the drums, guitars and synthesizers. Conversely, 'beautiful' and 'emotional' tags feature music compilations that are 'epic' in emotion but do not fit the conventional parameters of epic music: rather, they tend to be characterized by piano, female voices and a less 'technological' sound and a more 'natural' and introspective feel.

## Fifty Shades of 'Epic Music' or an Epic *Everyday Life*

Carol Vernallis has noted that 'The most prevalent prosumer YouTube aesthetic is insistent reiteration.'[38] Indeed, repetitive and hyperintensified forms of rapid production for both professional and DIY content quickly adds to the immensity of YouTube subgenres, filling web pages with very similar little boxes in terms of design, paratexts and visual symbols. Whereas this can be seen as the most efficient form of consolidating specific content and making evident its place in each segment, for users and their personal engagement, it's a highly individualized way of exploring and transforming media texts. Building familiarity through their personal and collective engagement with 'epic music' videos is crucial for

---

[37] Sadoff, 'Scoring for Film and Video Games,' 670–1.
[38] Carol Vernallis, *Unruly Media: YouTube, Music Video, and the New Digital Cinema* (New York: Oxford University Press, 2013), 130.

the longevity and success of the channels that produce them, keeping this cycle in a constant flow of interdependence.[39]

This process of reiteration is also a reflection, following the words of Vernallis, of compulsive consumption encouraged by late capitalism and the loop cycle of 'enjoying' and 'starting over'.[40] Epic music channels thrive on this complex process of interactivity: although each uploaded clip presents itself as 'new', it actually contributes to the growing homogenization and standardization of this genre into one of orchestral singles, lasting on average three to four minutes, with certain instrumentation choices and compositional tropes. This, in turn, simplifies the act of searching and listening.

These channels transform and capitalize on the term 'epic' without the circulation of economic capital. Instead, the capital is symbolic; epic becomes a brand that, regardless of context, a user can easily integrate into their daily lives. This multi-layered process of musical production on YouTube shows a new and collaborative mode of production for contemporary media styles. Be it 'epic aggressive' or 'emotional', epic music compilations convey a set of tropes pre-established in other media to activate audiovisual memory. These tropes are so engrained that the videos can be coherently consumed with or without images. If they are associated with moving images, these are mainly heroes, protagonists, villains or other individual figures from the world of fantasy fiction. Even so, the voices and perspectives that have helped to develop this genre are manifold. Moving from major production studios, big-budget film and video games, the epic music style has been fragmented, remediated, copied and parodied by social media users, who have drawn on its tropes and semiotic codes to forge a standardized musical genre. First developed in conjunction with moving images, the music has taken on a life of its own and can now be consumed with or without images; this allows the music to move out into the real world and be used to soundtrack the everyday lives of its listeners. Epic music, then, is an important example of the power of transmedial convergence and user-generated practices: from *producing* to *prosuming*, YouTube has played a key role in the spread and augmentation of a key contemporary musical practice.

---

[39] Emma Keltie, *The Culture Industry and Participatory Audiences* (New York: Palgrave Macmillan, 2017).
[40] Vernallis, *Unruly Media*, 133.

# Bibliography

Allocca, Kevin. *Videocracy: How YouTube Is Changing the World . . . with Double Rainbows, Singing Foxes, and Other Trends We Can't Stop Watching*. New York: Bloomsbury, 2018.

Arthurs, Jane, Sophia Drakopoulou and Alessandro Gandini. 'Researching YouTube.' *Convergence* 24, no. 1 (2018): 3–15.

Brett, Philip, Elizabeth Wood, and Gary C. Thomas, eds. *Queering the Pitch: The New Gay and Lesbian Musicology*. New York: Routledge, 1994.

Bruns, Axel. *Blogs, Wikipedia, Second Life, and Beyond: From Production to Produsage*. New York: Peter Lang, 2008.

Buhler, James. 'Branding the Franchise: Music, Opening Credits, and the (Corporate) Myth of Origin.' In *Music in Epic Film: Listening to Spectacle*, edited by Stephen C. Meyer, 3–26. New York: Routledge, 2016.

Buikema, Rosemarie, and Iris van der Tuin, eds. *Doing Gender in Media, Art and Culture*. New York: Routledge, 2009.

Butler, Judith. *Gender Trouble: Feminism and the Subversion of Identity*. New York: Routledge, 1990.

Burgess, Jean and Joshua Green. *YouTube: Online Video and Participatory Culture*. Cambridge: Polity, 2009.

Carter, Cynthia, Linda Steiner, and Lisa McLaughlin, eds. *The Routledge Companion to Media and Gender*. New York: Routledge, 2015.

Daub, Adrian. '"BRAAAM!": The Sound That Invaded the Hollywood Soundtrack.' *Longreads* (blog), 8 December 2016, at https://longreads.com/2016/12/08/braaam-inception-hollywood-soundtracks/.

DeNora, Tia. *Music in Everyday Life*. Cambridge; New York: Cambridge University Press, 2000.

Elferen, Isabella van. 'Analyzing Game Musical Immersion: The ALI Model.' In *Ludomusicology: Approaches to Video Game Music*, edited by Michiel Kamp, Tim Summers and Mark Sweeney, 32–52. Sheffield, UK: Equinox Publishing, 2016.

Freitas, Joana. 'From Epic Fail to Epic Music: Music, Silence and Failure on "Dark Souls 3".' *Journal of Sound, Silence, Image and Technology* 3 (2020): 55–74.

Freitas, Joana. 'A (Silent) Game of Words: Notes on Jeremy Soule's Accusations and the Elder Scrolls Online Community'. *Journal of Sound and Music in Games* 3, no. 1 (1 January 2022): 50–59. https://doi.org/10.1525/jsmg.2022.3.1.50.

———. '"The Music Is the Only Thing You Don't Have to Mod": The Musical Composition in Modification Files for Videogames.' Masters Thesis, NOVA FCSH, 2017.

Gomes-Ribeiro, Paula, Júlia Durand, Joana Freitas, and Filipe Gaspar, eds. *Música, Género, Sexualidades: Musical Trouble . . . After Butler*. Vila Nova de Famalicão: Edições Húmus, 2021.

Hesmondhalgh, David. *The Cultural Industries*. 4th edition. Thousand Oaks, CA: SAGE Publications, 2018.

Huvet, Chloé. '*Interstellar* de Hans Zimmer : plongée musicale au coeur des drames humains, par-delà l'infiniment grand. Pour une autre approche de l'esthétique zimmerienne.' *Revue musicale OICRM* 5 2 (2018): 103–24.

Jenkins, Henry, Sam Ford and Joshua Green. *Spreadable Media: Creating Value and Meaning in a Networked Culture*. New York ; London: New York University Press, 2013.

Jenkins, Henry. *Fans, Bloggers, and Gamers: Exploring Participatory Culture*. New York: New York University Press, 2006.

Jennings, Stephanie C. 'Only You Can Save the World (of Videogames): Authoritarian Agencies in the Heroism of Videogame Design, Play, and Culture.' *Convergence* 27 (2022): 13548565221079156.

Kassabian, Anahid. *Hearing Film: Tracking Identifications in Contemporary Hollywood Film Music*. New York: Routledge, 2001.

Keltie, Emma. *The Culture Industry and Participatory Audiences*. New York: Palgrave Macmillan, 2017.

Krijnen, Tonny, and Sofie van Bauwel. *Gender and Media: Representing, Producing, Consuming*. London : New York: Routledge, 2015.

Lehman, Frank. 'Manufacturing the Epic Score: Hans Zimmer and the Sounds of Significance.' In *Music in Epic Film: Listening to Spectacle*, edited by Stephen C. Meyer, 27–55. New York: Routledge, 2016.

Leppert, Richard D., and Susan McClary, eds. *Music and Society: The Politics of Composition, Performance, and Reception*. Cambridge: Cambridge University Press, 2001.

McClary, Susan. *Feminine Endings: Music, Gender, and Sexuality*. Minneapolis: University of Minnesota Press, 1991.

Muriel, Daniel and Garry Crawford. *Video Games as Culture: Considering the Role and Importance of Video Games in Contemporary Society*. New York: Routledge, 2018.

Reyland, Nicholas. 'Corporate Classicism and the Metaphysical Style: Affects, Effects, and Contexts of Two Recent Trends in Screen Scoring.' *Music, Sound, and the Moving Image* 9, no. 2 (2016): 115–30.

Sadoff, Ronald H. 'Scoring for Film and Video Games: Collaborative Practices and Digital Post-Production.' In *The Oxford Handbook of Sound and Image in Digital Media*, edited by Carol Vernallis, Amy Herzog and John Richardson, 662–81. Oxford University Press, 2013.

Shapiro, Eve. *Gender Circuits: Bodies and Identities in a Technological Age*. 2nd ed. New York: Routledge, 2015.

Shifman, Limor. *Memes in Digital Culture*. Cambridge: The MIT Press, 2014.

Snee, Helene, Christine Hine, Yvette Morey, Steven Roberts and Hayley Watson. 'Digital Methods as Mainstream Methodology: An Introduction.' In *Digital Methods for*

*Social Science*, edited by Helene Snee, Christine Hine, Yvette Morey, Steven Roberts and Hayley Watson, 1–11. London: Palgrave Macmillan UK, 2016.

Solie, Ruth A., ed. *Musicology and Difference: Gender and Sexuality in Music Scholarship*. Berkeley: University of California Press, 1993.

Stuart, Keith. 'Now's the Time – 15 Epic Video Games for the Socially Isolated.' *The Guardian*, 30 March 2020, sec. Games, at https://www.theguardian.com/games/2020/mar/30/epic-video-games-self-isolating.

Summers, Tim. *Understanding Video Game Music*. Cambridge: Cambridge University Press, 2016.

Vernallis, Carol. *Unruly Media: Youtube, Music Video, and the New Digital Cinema*. New York: Oxford University Press, 2013.

Wehrs, William. 'Affect and Film Music: A Brief History.' In *The Palgrave Handbook of Affect Studies and Textual Criticism*, edited by Donald R. Wehrs and Thomas Blake, 735–52. Cham: Springer International Publishing, 2017.

Wright, Benjamin. 'Music and the Moving Image: A Case Study of Hans Zimmer.' In *The Routledge Reader on the Sociology of Music*, edited by John Shepherd and Kyle Devine, 319–28. New York: Routledge, 2015.

# Of Clouds and Vapours: Transcending Ironic Distance in Networked Composition

Jonas Wolf

Ironic distance is still widely regarded as a common denominator for postmodern strategies of re-appropriation and parody, ranging from subversive hyper-affirmations and bitextual interventions to (self-)vulgarizing 'trash'. However, it must be noted that the omnipresence of ironic expression across the whole spectrum of pop-cultural aesthetic production often entails issues of decoding regarding its differential or negatory intent. Although first-century Roman rhetorician Quintilian's fundamental definition of irony as 'something which is the opposite of what is actually said' could without a doubt pass as a dictionary entry for irony today, it does not adequately address the complexities of ironic expression in postmodern art and music engaged with an ever-expanding nexus of references.[1] In this context, Claire Colebrook points out that '[w]e live in a world of quotation, pastiche, simulation and cynicism: a general and all-encompassing irony. Irony, then, by the very simplicity of its definition becomes curiously indefinable'.[2] As a dominant mode of cultural production, ironic expression runs the risk of perpetuating a non-critical negativity that is not aimed at a positive complement anymore and thus, because of its distancing effect, merely results in de-subjectivized creation. Such a nihilistic ironic expression for its own sake knows no reality beyond itself that it could refer to – there is no positive content or stance it chooses to highlight; rather, the deployment

---

[1] Quintilian, *Institutio Oratoria*, trans. Harold Edgeworth Butler (London: William Heinemann Ltd., 1921), IX.2.44.
[2] Claire Colebrook, *Irony: The New Critical Idiom* (London and New York: Routledge, 2014), 1.

of ironic distance frees the subject from formulating any definite meaning on its own, disguised by a tongue-in-cheek attitude. Regardless of whether or not today's experimental and flexible play with representations and references within socio-technical infrastructures of networked aesthetic individualism is conceived of as symptomatic for a postmodern crisis of historicity, the resulting continual fragmentation and blurring of overarching referential codes is apparent. In this context, Fredric Jameson questions whether the postmodern individual has come 'to be a kind of linguistic island, separated from everyone else', concluding that 'in that case, the very possibility of any linguistic norm in terms of which one could ridicule private languages and idiosyncratic styles would vanish, and we would have nothing but stylistic diversity and heterogeneity'.[3]

Fuelled by the digital principles of media convergence and modularity, combinatorial and selective approaches to circulating media objects, and texts on online platforms and beyond, take place in an accelerated fashion. As Andreas Reckwitz notes, online practices of the postmodern 'computer subject' are characterized by their electivity, experimentality and playful aesthetic imagination. They take place within a hypertext that forms an uncontrollable web of references via signs, which are lacking fixable causal or temporal links. At the same time, the semiotic excess of our oversaturated informational space forces users to generate symbolic connectability by way of selection, re-arrangement and re-combination.[4] Hence, the fluid and flow-like processes of self-positionings in the context of Internet culture seem to further reinforce and perpetuate the fragmentation of linguistic and stylistic norms. Consequentially, the arbitrariness and ambiguity of ironic expression is increased, further entailing the deployment of ironic distance as a rhetorical mechanism that helps avoid a strong subjective stance. Undirected irony has come to be a fundamental accompaniment of online communication processes – and, at its worst, can serve as a mechanism of camouflaging otherwise unacceptable utterances: cases of deliberate disguises of (politically charged) ridicule and hate speech under the veil of irony in Internet-mediated communication are all-too familiar by now. For instance, such a cynical approach can be found with respect to comments and memes in online communities based on trolling and/or political activism

---

[3] Fredric Jameson, *Postmodernism, or, The Cultural Logic of Late Capitalism* (Durham, NC: Duke University Press, 1991), 17.
[4] See Andreas Reckwitz, *Das hybride Subjekt: Eine Theorie der Subjektkulturen von der bürgerlichen Moderne zur Postmoderne* (Weilerswist: Velbrück Wissenschaft, 2006), 577–80.

that attempt to territorialize, steer or destabilize online discourse – and evade counter attacks by finding refuge in claims of irony.⁵

Of course, ambiguous and undirected irony is not an exclusively postmodern issue, as Søren Kierkegaard's thematization of irony in his 1841 master's thesis illustrates: 'In irony, the subject is continually retreating, talking every phenomenon out of its reality in order to save itself – that is, in order to preserve itself in negative independence of everything. [...] For irony, everything becomes nothing, but nothing can be taken in several ways.'⁶ However, within a (pop-) cultural domain of ever-accumulating (meta-)references, 'where immanence and its self-reflexive transgression, where authentic and virtual utterances can no longer be distinguished from one another, but where any communication also gets lost in an ever more complex web of signs,' Tobias Janz asserts irony's new quality as a form of (post-) authenticity: 'What was earlier thought to be authentic can now be communicated only in the mode of irony, while irony itself becomes a new form of authenticity, the only form of communication still adequate in a situation where what is hybrid becomes what is real.'⁷ As an answer to the often cynical and de-subjectivizing nature of postmodern existential irony in contemporary artistic expression, *post*-ironic approaches have been proclaimed within the fields of literature and the visual arts. For example, Lee Konstantinou paradigmatically used the notion of post-irony with regard to postmodern literature, which is focused on transcending irony. However, this does not mean that a return to 'pre-ironic' times is wished for or even deemed possible by 'post-ironic' authors. Thus, different from a turn to 'new sincerity', irony is integrated as a speech act while overcome as an ideology. To strengthen his concept, Konstantinou asks critically why sincerity would be 'the aspired state one might want to attain if one was concerned about irony? Why not commitment, or passion, or emotion, or decision?'⁸ A call for a turn towards

---

⁵ In an article for *Wired*, Emma Grey Ellis links the fundamental problem of decoding irony in a disembodied and socially fragmented sphere of online communication to our accelerated informational space of today, thereby drawing lines from trolling subcultures on 4chan to recent (Trumpian) phenomena of post-factual politics. See Emma Grey Ellis, 'Can't Take a Joke? That's Just Poe's Law, 2017's Most Important Internet Phenomenon,' WIRED (5 June 2017), at https://www.wired.com/2017/06/poes-law-troll-cultures-central-rule/.

⁶ Søren Kierkegaard, *The Concept of Irony, with Continual References to Socrates*, trans. Howard V. Hong and Edna H. Hong (Princeton: Princeton University Press, 1989), 257.

⁷ Tobias Janz, 'Goodbye 20th Century: Sonic Youth, John Cage's "Number Pieces" and the Long Farewell to the Avant-Garde,' in *The Metareferential Turn in Contemporary Arts and Media: Forms, Functions, Attempts at Explanation*, ed. Werner Wolf (Amsterdam/New York: Rodopi, 2011), 543.

⁸ Lee Konstantinou, *Cool Characters: Irony and American Fiction*, (Cambridge, MA: Harvard University Press, 2016), 38.

affectivity, immediacy and positivity can also be noted with regard to the 'first post-ironic manifesto' (2008) by the Swiss artist duo *Com&Com*, founded by Johannes Hedinger and Marcus Gossolt. Here, the rejection of ironic doubt – criticized as 'dissatisfaction elevated into a lifestyle' – is coupled with a call for temporal and tactical affirmation – 'truth [...] changes to fit the demands of the moment' – and the equation of post-irony with 'total imaginative and creative freedom'.[9] As Hedinger and Gossolt are aware that post-ironic art can only build on the remains of an ironic *zeitgeist*, the manifesto itself, besides being stylized in rainbow colours, includes passages with potentially ironic undertones that are in need of interpretation by the recipient. Both post-ironic stances by Konstantinou and *Com&Com* argue for the inclusion of aesthetic modes of irony within an overall text that is supposed to render the inner stance and decision-making of the artist/author readable. However, the potential ambiguity of irony cannot and shall not be dissolved, as Sebastian Plönges notes:

> According to the hereby proposed reading [of the first post-ironic manifesto], the endurance – not the elimination! – of contingencies is the strong suit of the post-ironist, who thus offers a free and productive option for unfolding the ironic paradox. [...] The post-ironic manifesto enables us to float in contingencies and, at the same time, offers a productive way of dealing with this – if one is willing to read it that way and to argue in its favour.[10]

The resulting semiotic excess is obvious: although the rejection of ironic doubt is clearly conveyed by the post-ironist through affective renderings and changes of perspective within their work, the contingency of the included ironic forms is irreducible. Ironic patterns appear to be completely detached from any binary logic of affirmation or negation; furthermore, pre-existent differentiations

---

[9] The complete text of the manifesto reads as follows: '1. WE ARE LIVING IN A POSTIRONIC AGE. IRONIC DOUBT IS JUST DISSATISFACTION ELEVATED INTO A LIFESTYLE. 2. WE HAVE BEGUN TO HAVE DOUBTS ABOUT THE PROCESS OF DOUBTING. 3. TRUTH IS NO LONGER UNCONDITIONAL, BUT RATHER CHANGES TO FIT THE DEMANDS OF THE MOMENT. 4. THE WORLD IS MORE THAN WHAT IT IS. 5. EVERYDAY LIFE PROVIDES A PROVING GROUND FOR THE HUMAN SPIRIT. 6. EVERYTHING IS FILLED WITH MAGIC AND BEAUTY. 7. BEAUTY CAN INSPIRE US TO BECOME BETTER PEOPLE. 8. BEAUTY CAN GROW INTO LOVE. 9. OUT OF LOVE, TRUTH CAN EMERGE. 10. WE ARE STANDING AT THE VERGE OF SOMETHING WONDROUS: THE REBIRTH OF OUR SELFCREATION. POST-IRONY MEANS TOTAL IMAGINATIVE AND CREATIVE FREEDOM.' Marcus Gossolt und Johannes M. Hedinger (*Com&Com*), 'First Post-Ironic Manifesto' (2008), at https://postirony.files.wordpress.com/2009/01/postirony-web1.jpg.
[10] Sebastian Plönges, 'Postironie als Entfaltung,' in *Medien und Bildung: Institutionelle Kontexte und kultureller Wandel*, ed. Torsten Meyer, Wey-Han Tan, Christina Schwalbe and Ralf Appelt (Springer: Wiesbaden 2011), 444 (my translation).

between authenticity and artificiality are not considered relevant for post-ironic approaches anymore[11] – and, anyway, argues Plönges, 'the problem which post-irony could be an answer for stops being a problem as soon as one has learnt to deal with paradoxes.'[12]

Plönges correctly hints at the home-born, vernacular qualities of post-ironic playfulness in digitally situated forms of communication and creativity by pointing out the need for 'a selective approach to selectivity, which is something natural and intuitive for many a native of ubiquitous Internet culture with its instantaneous communication options'.[13] A look into visual self-representations on social media platforms such as Instagram confirms his observation; although one does not even need to look that far, as the mere use of emojis, abbreviations and Internet slang already represents potential post-ironic operations. A new realm of selectivity has opened up, which can flourish best in the simulative space of social media. As one of many emergent websites that focused on aspects of sharing and networking, the launch of YouTube in 2005 falls into the time of an overall diagnosis of a 'Web 2.0' – a term that denotes the new networked and participatory condition of the World Wide Web, enabled by the emergence of sites and applications focused on user-led creativity and sharing.[14] Instant access to freely circulating media objects, as well as the material affordances of transforming digital files, stand in a synergetic relationship to the participatory ethos fostered by social media platforms. With regard to video content, YouTube became the central platform to curate, interlink and encourage user participation. Because of its archival function – although the platform rather resembles a barely framed 'jumbled attic' than an archive, as Simon Reynolds notes – it is itself oversaturated with media objects and thus 'naturally' suggests and perpetuates performative combinatorial approaches to pre-existing audiovisual figurations.[15] With particular respect to audiovisual media environments such as YouTube, a prominent mashup character can be attributed to creative transformations of media objects. In processes of creative relay and referential

---

[11] See Johannes M. Hedinger, 'Postironie: Geschichte, Theorie und Praxis einer Kunst nach der Ironie (Eine Betrachtung aus zwei Perspektiven),' *Kunstform International* 213 (February 2012): 117.
[12] Plönges, 'Postironie als Entfaltung,' 445 (my translation).
[13] Ibid.
[14] See Tim O'Reilly, 'What Is Web 2.0: Design Patterns and Business Models for the Next Generation of Software' (30 September 2005), at https://www.oreilly.com/pub/a/web2/archive/what-is-web-20.html.
[15] Simon Reynolds, *Retromania: Pop Culture's Addiction to its Own Past* (New York: Faber and Faber, 2011), 62.

(re-)composition, the most heterogeneous sources can become performatively recombined, conveying meaning only in the form of associative montage. Here, the term of mashup is not only used to concretize the heterogeneity and simultaneity of pre-existing material in referential practices, but also to denote the fundamental shift from historical forms of remix that lie in the performativity of continual re-contextualization and re-combination of media objects – and their less privileged status as discursive objects, as Thomas Wilke notes: 'Media objects are not exclusively steering the discourse anymore but become a constituent of the discourse's productive conditions of possibility. The radical shift lies in the realization of a possibility, the continuation of which leads to an extensive pluralisation.'[16]

In face of this irreducible symbolic multiplicity and polyvalency, it comes as little surprise that musical forms and formats that emerged in dependence on the socio-technical infrastructure of social media platforms – or engage with subjective experiences and affective stimuli linked to the state of 'being online' – incorporate post-ironic attitude and (self-)expression in an often intuitive manner. The chosen examples bear witness to the fact that post-ironic *modi operandi* have never been exclusive to practices and discourse within the high arts; rather, conceptualizations of post-irony emerged in the wake of an already existing post-ironic *zeitgeist* in (networked) pop-cultural (re-)production and communication.[17] The following examined forms and formats of networked and platform-situated *musical* composition delineate a wide range of potential affective renderings driven by selective approaches to ironic ambiguities – illustrating the fact that the tactical optimism proclaimed by *Com&Com*'s 'first post-ironic manifesto' is but one way of transcending the de-subjectivizing effects of existential irony in postmodern forms of aesthetic (self-)expression. Most importantly, however, the analyses make describable the accelerating effects digital environments of platform-situated distribution, consumption and iteration have on post-ironic compositional approaches and methods. YouTube's important role within this media ecology cannot be overstated. For one, the

---

[16] Thomas Wilke, 'Kombiniere! Variiere! Transformiere! Mashups als performative Diskursobjekte in populären Medienkulturen,' in *Mashups. Neue Praktiken und Ästhetiken in populären Medienkulturen* (Wiesbaden: Springer, 2015), 37 (my translation).
[17] (Academicized) post-ironic artworks and literature thus need to be regarded as *faits sociaux*. According to Theodor Adorno, 'aesthetic form as sedimented content' can historically and culturally be traced back; moreover, 'aesthetic relations of production' only exist as 'sedimentations or imprintings of social relations of production'. Theodor W. Adorno, *Aesthetic Theory*, trans. Robert Hullot-Kentor (Minneapolis: University of Minnesota Press, 1997), 5.

platform serves as an all-absorbing distribution channel in its functionality as a 'total archive'. What is more, it affords the (inter-)creative development of impactful post-ironic audiovisual aesthetics and practices of self-representation that are exclusively situated on the platform, and help increase the artists' individual prestige and communal belongingness. Thus, in the following reflections, the video platform shall serve as a pivotal example that helps highlight the interrelations and synergies between platform-specific forms and manifestations of Internet-mediated post-ironic composition.

## Self-Destruction and Melancholia in SoundCloud Rap and Beyond

In the early-to-mid 2010s, new Internet-mediated genre formations informed by post-ironic approaches to self-expression experienced a general rise in popularity. For example, early Cloud Rap can be attributed to these genres. In its early stages, before becoming commercialized, Cloud Rap subculture was primarily driven by social media interaction and a DIY ethos, thereby embracing a gift logic based on free distribution and sharing. On a musical and sonic level, the genre is often associated with lo-fi sound production, atmospheric synths, trap beats and extensive use of voice manipulation. However, Peter Wikström and Erik van Ooijen argue that the label 'Cloud' functions as the most effective denominator for characterizations of the genre and name 'three distinguishing characteristics: its "hazy", ethereal aesthetic both in terms of aural and visual expression; its nebulousness as a genre without clearly defined borders; and its Internet-mediated emergence, being primarily self-distributed through Cloud services (Sound Cloud, YouTube, Twitter) rather than through traditional and analog media.'[18] This notion of Cloud rap does not help define the scope of the genre; however, the last point hints at the crucial moment that entails the genre's post-ironic potential, namely the complete transfer of analogically developed traditions of lyrical output and (oral) presence into the realm of the digital. The new environment of continually remediated signs entailed a break with what Wikström and Ooijen describe as 'most previous forms of hip-hop, which have

---

[18] Peter Wikström and Erik van Ooijen, 'Post-Authentic Digitalism in Cloud Rap' (summary), paper presented at the conference *Popular Music Discourses: Authenticity and Mediatization*, Karlstad University, Karlstad, Sweden, 13 November 2018. https://www.researchgate.net/publication/333422124_Post-authentic_digitalism_in_cloud_rap.

tended to privilege presence, immediacy and origins. For example, rappers were long expected to write their own rhymes; to be able to rap without the help of technological aids or digital post-production; and to actively represent, and "stay true" to their geographical origins.[19] Early Cloud rap, often referred to as 'SoundCloud rap' because of its origins on the platform, is a musical genre primarily defined by its mediation through vernacular forms of digital communication and creativity on platforms such as SoundCloud and YouTube – and less so by its quite heterogeneous stylistic features. By way of selective reiteration and cumulation of lyrical and compositional tropes, SoundCloud rap artists deal with symbolic and informational oversaturation, thereby rejecting claims for realness or originality in the traditional sense. But, the digital 'post-authenticity' of Cloud rap does not necessarily result in a lack of intimacy or emotionality. Rather, to the contrary, SoundCloud rappers in the early-to-mid 2010s – particularly artists who would later also be labelled as 'sad rap' or 'emo rap', such as Yung Lean, Bones, XXXTentacion or $uicideboy$ – used their music as a vehicle for conveying their sentimentality and emotional fragility. The general anti-virtuosic attitude – especially in terms of lo-fi sound and video production, rapping styles, lyrical output and vocal post-production – is coupled with a range of visual or lyrical topics, encompassing (pseudo-)philosophical issues, depression, surreal nonsense and profanities, seemingly random pop-cultural references, and almost caricatural fetishizations of status symbols and drug abuse. The awareness of the simulacric symbolic sphere they are operating in, or, more generally, the perceived lack of immediate self-awareness, seems to be at the basis of many performances by SoundCloud rap artists. However, there is no oppositional use of irony, which would be directed at perforating or 'unmasking' the hyperreal imagery they are reproducing. Contrary to de-subjectivized and distanced interferences, the use of dreamy, moody and melodic soundscapes and hooks serves as a way of affectively rendering feelings of melancholia, new-found inwardness or nihilistic 'no future' attitudes. In other words, the audiovisual aesthetic of SoundCloud rap is characterized by the post-ironic affirmation of insurmountable indifference, enabling the artists' and recipients' indulgence in states of floating, longing or self-loathing.

In some cases, the elevation and romanticization of suicidal thoughts not only functions as a mere lyrical option, but as a red thread for the artists' self-narration. The rap duo $uicideboy$, who started their musical career with self-

[19] Ibid.

produced beats on SoundCloud, was supposedly even formed on the basis of a 'suicide pact': in case their music career should fail, $crim (Scott Arceneaux Jr.) and Ruby Da Cherry (Aristos Norman Petrou) planned to take their lives.[20] This story is paradigmatic for the impenetrable merging of hypermedialized, quasi-mythological personal branding and sincere self-conceptions of the two artists, who quickly gained a cult following that expanded from niche online communities into the wider rap underground. Their music itself is characterized by booming basses, trap influences, ethereal instrumental tracks and lyrical content informed by suicidal ideation, violence and substance abuse. These lyrical tropes are hyper-affirmed and often enriched by genre-untypical occult and anti-Christian messages, as can be seen in the track 'FUCKTHEPOPULATION' on their self-released mixtape *My Liver Will Handle What My Heart Can't* (2015):

[…]
Smoking and drinking I ain't never thinking
Popping them pills till I'm under the cement
Six hundred sixty-six, smoking that reefer
If you looking for dope, boy I got it for cheaper
New Orleans crypt keeper, the killer the creeper
Believe me that demons are real once you see us
Fuckboys wanna be us, the hoes wanna please us
Ask in yo city, they'll tell you I'm Jesus
The motherfuckin anti-Christ, $uicide we anti life
Bitch don't make me tell you twice that I can't go to Heaven nah[21]

From the very beginning, $uicideboy$' musical output was accompanied by their self-produced music videos. Since they joined YouTube in 2013, as many as seventy music videos have been uploaded to their channel. The rap duo's visual output is a prime example for the new-found possibilities of self-performance in the form of DIY music videos, which the platform affords in its function as an intermediary that facilitates and fosters user participation. However, $crim's and Ruby Da Cherry's videos are YouTube-specific products not only because of the platform's affordances in terms of access and distribution. Rather, as the videos are carried by a no-budget production and a corresponding DIY ethos, a

---

[20] Kristin Robinson, 'How $uicideboy$ Became the Multi-Million Dollar Brand You Never Heard Of,' *Billboard*(22October2021),athttps://www.billboard.com/music/music-news/suicideboys-new-album-headlining-tour-2021-interview-9649488/.
[21] $UICIDEBOY$, 'FUCKTHEPOPULATION', SoundCloud audio, 00.02:30, 21 September 2015, https://soundcloud.com/g59/fuckthepopulation.

non-institutional ordinariness and carelessness is performatively invoked. The use of found footage and collage aesthetics, grainy lo-fi imagery, shaky handheld camera shots, pseudo-documentary smartphone videos and selfie angles, split-screens and computational visual interfaces performatively imbricates the videos within the screenic repertoires of vernacular content creation on social media, thereby meta-referentially signalling their 'home-born' status as YouTube-mediated forms of cultural expression. The videos are dominated by recurring or resembling sequences that serve as visual gestures or moods rather than concise narratives. Their self-made music video for 'FUCKTHEPOPULATION', for instance, stages a hostage video situation: in alternating order, $crim and Ruby Da Cherry can be seen wearing a ski mask and holding a gun to the head of their bandmate, who kneels on the ground, impersonating the hostage (see Figure 7.1). The shock value of the video is increased by a reversed US flag in the background (displaying a large sprayed-on '666') and the VHS video aesthetic (with a tape overlay set to the date of 11 September 2001).[22] Despite the obvious 'poser' attitude in both their lyrical and bodily performance, bolstered up by references to drugs, violence and anti-Christian ideas, the song and video serve

**Figure 7.1** $crim is holding a gun to Ruby Da Cherry's head while the latter offers him a joint, '$UICIDEBOY$ – FUCKTHEPOPULATION' (11 September 2015).

[22] $uicideboy$, '$UICIDEBOYS – FUCKTHEPOPULATION', *YouTube video*, 00:02:22, 11 September 2015, https://www.youtube.com/watch?v=Qj0eCoc0ii4.

as vehicles for affective renderings of the artists' self-loathing and their gloomy reflections on their impulsive behaviour. Meta-narratives and clichés are not merely embraced for the sake of generating extraordinary performances based on phantasies of stardom (such as 'sex, drugs and rock'n'roll'). Rather, beyond turning the artists into objects of consumption-oriented demands, $uicideboy$' tracks and music videos take on confessional forms, in which the navigation of hyperreal referential webs serves as a means to drastically convey $crim's and Ruby Da Cherry's personal battles with mental health issues.

In general, the frontiers between hyperreal imagery and existential reality, as well as between rap personas and real-life persons, are blurred in many musical careers hailing from a SoundCloud rap background. By way of networked reception and reproduction, afforded by the storage and communication options of online platforms, the aesthetics and ethos of SoundCloud rap have become socialized quickly and helped establish a thriving rap subculture. Both a result of and a precondition for formations of networked communal communication, SoundCloud rap's 'ideological products' – such as the glorification of excessive drug consumption and suicidal tendencies – materialized not only in lyrical and visual repertoires (as well as in many rappers' stage names), but also became integrated in everyday communication, shaping the lifestyle of young artists and fans. Our postmodern condition, according to which the hybrid and hyperreal becomes the new 'real', seems to be radically accelerated and reinforced by the post-authentic performance of SoundCloud rappers – with devastating ramifications: many rappers with a Cloud rap background – among them Lil Peep (age 21), XXXTentacion (age 20) and Juice WRLD (age 21) – have died at a shockingly young age, prompting the notion of a '21 Club', in reference to the famous '27 Club', which includes Brian Jones, Jimi Hendrix, Janis Joplin, Jim Morrison, Kurt Cobain and Amy Winehouse (among others).[23]

Complementary to nihilistic and self-destructive attitudes, the musical and visual reproduction of affective stimuli of melancholia played a significant role in SoundCloud rap production in the early-to-mid 2010s – and, since then, has informed musical approaches beyond the stylistic constraints of rap. Spooky Black, nowadays better known as Corbin, gained mass exposure through his

---

[23] The idea of the '21 Club' goes back to a line in Juice WRLD's track 'Legends' on his EP *Too Soon ..*: 'What's the 27 club? We ain't making it past 21.' In the following year, Juice WRLD died at the age of 21 as a result of a drug overdose. See @Juice WRLD, 'juice wrld – legends,' SoundCloud audio, 3:11, 20 June 2018, at https://soundcloud.com/uiceheidd/juice-wrld-legends?in=uiceheidd/sets/too-soon.

early SoundCloud and YouTube uploads, which places him in a SoundCloud rap context, although his music from 2014 onwards is stylistically oriented towards alternative, 'hazy' R&B. His music video for 'Without You', which he released in 2014 at the age of sixteen, received immediate attention and became a source of inspiration for fellow Internet artists because of its uncompromising and genre-defying post-ironic attitude.[24] The non-ironic and at times bizarre combination of visual and musical elements is held together by a VHS video aesthetic and an ethereal instrumental track. The latter drenches the track in melancholia and carries Spooky Black's R&B-stylized singing. His idiosyncratic self-display adds another level: imagery of Spooky Black in a snowy forest – a scenery one would rather expect in a black metal video – alternates with footage of the artist at home. His bodily expressions, ranging from thinker's poses and hip-hop hand gestures, to relaxed lounging on his couch, are accompanying his performance of the song's lyrics, which are thematizing heartbreak and longing. The text itself offers inner discrepancies, shifting from passages such as 'Thinkin' I'mma flip and fill my brain with lead, I'mma end my life without you' to 'Don't you know you're so sexy the way you move your body up and down'. Despite seeming exaggerative, generic or even out of place, the lyrical patterns are embedded in the consistent overall 'flow' of the song, and never conveyed in an ironically distanced manner. With 'Without You', Spooky Black aims at musically conveying a sense of proximity and affectivity, far from any use of irony that could serve him as a shield from notions of sentimentality or ridiculousness. However, his choice of wearing a durag throughout the entire video entails some questions with respect to the artistic intention, as it represents an uncommented appropriation of a fashion item rooted in Afro-American culture. In an article for the online magazine DJ Booth, Nathan Slavik writes:

> So a white kid naming himself Spooky Black and dressing in durags and FUBU? Either it's a hell of a coincidence and he's just a weird kid dumbly unaware of the racial implications of his whole artistic vision, or it's an intentional, self-aware provocation intended to get attention on the Internet, which worked astoundingly well, in which case fuck him.[25]

In any case, the example of this early Spooky Black video proves that the de-differentiating potential of post-ironic selectivity does not entail the erasure

---

[24] Gabe Broderick, 'SPOOKY BLACK – WITHOUT YOU (PROD. GREAF).' *YouTube video*, 00:05:03, 28 February 2014, https://www.youtube.com/watch?v=dT2YDdZdE-I.

[25] Nathan Slavik, 'Spooky Black: Dope, Wack or Kinda Racist? (All of the Above),' *DJ Booth* (30 July 2014), at https://djbooth.net/features/spooky-black-dope-wack-or-kinda-racist.

of pre-existent contexts and can – and sometimes should – be critically approached from an outside perspective.

## Reflective Nostalgia and Self-Development: Post-Ironic Pattern Aesthetics and Post-Genre Fusions

Another Internet-mediated microgenre, which is of particular interest in this context because of its post-ironic approach to historicity, is vaporwave. Vaporwave is one of many labels that formed in the context of emerging self-reflective musical approaches to nostalgia and collective popular memory since the late 2000s – other genre labels include hypnagogic pop, chillwave or glo-fi, to name just a few. Arguably, all these microgenres represent specified offshoots from the broad musical trend of hauntology, which developed in the UK during the 2000s. As the name suggests, hauntological music draws on Jacques Derrida's concept of Hauntology. In his book *Spectres de Marx*, Derrida lays out his concept of a present – or rather 'non-present present'[26] – which is continuously haunted by linguistic and ideal constructs from the past, thereby questioning the finiteness of history as such. Through performative acts, Derrida asserts, the

> frontier between the public and the private is constantly being displaced [...] And if this important frontier is being displaced, it is because the medium in which it is instituted, namely, the medium of the media themselves (news, the press, tele-communications, techno-tele-discursivity, techno-tele-iconicity, that which in general assures and determines the spacing of public space, the very possibility of the res publica [...]), this element itself is neither living nor dead, present nor absent: it spectralizes. It does not belong to ontology, to the discourse on the Being of beings, or to the essence of life or death.[27]

Derrida's thought, derived with respect to the 'haunted' history of political and philosophical Marxism, can be transferred to any context, as the spectralizing linguistic and ideational traces pre-form any human-made concept before it even comes into being – including concepts concerned with interpreting our past. At the same time, every interpretation is performative, as it 'transforms the

---

[26] Jacques Derrida, *Specters of Marx*, trans. Peggy Kamuf (New York: Routledge, 1994), 5.
[27] Ibid., 63.

very thing it interprets'.[28] Hauntological music takes up this Derridean term by reanimating past musical periods through a present-day lens. The trend is focused on the use of analogue media and recording devices from the 1960s and 1970s, thereby drawing on samples from a vast spectrum of authentic sound sources from the past.[29] This array of musically disparate outcomes prompted the emergence of several microgenres with their own specific musical and sonic approaches to cultural memory, vaporwave arguably being the first one to emerge and stay entirely situated within the fabric of digitally mediated co-creation. The genre label's formation, further negotiation and circulation on Internet boards, such as Last.fm or Reddit in the early 2010s secured a wide online audience – and further inevitable offshoots. Similar to musical precursors, vaporwave builds on what Adam Trainer refers to as the 'reappropriation of the cultural detritus of a media-saturated capitalist social order' by sonically invoking corporate mood music from the 1980s and 1990s, including elevator music, lounge jazz or synth pop.[30] It thereby relies entirely on samples, often entire pieces, which are slowed down, looped, pitch-shifted or otherwise manipulated. Despite the pioneering effort and influence of artists such as James Ferraro and Daniel Lopatin, vaporwave is characterized by a pointedly communal spirit with respect to individual creation, which does not aim at attaining stylistic distinction. Communal participation is thereby facilitated by low technological thresholds in terms of attaining the distinctive 'vaporwave sound'.[31] Moreover, online platforms serve as ever-expanding archives for audiovisual repertoires. Particularly YouTube's options of storage, communication and content curation afford the diffusion of vaporwave through user-curated playlists and 24/7 radio

---

[28] Ibid.
[29] Simon Reynolds and Mark Fisher wrote extensively about hauntological music, thereby appropriating Derrida's term more widely. Musical Hauntology is not guided by an 'archeological' ethos or aspirations for accurate historicity, but rather aims at generating a sense of nostalgia that disrupts time through aesthetic renderings of faded memories and collective imaginations of alternate pasts or failed futures. See, for instance: Reynolds, *Retromania*; Mark Fisher, *Ghosts of My Life: Writings on Depression, Hauntology and Lost Futures* (Winchester: Zero Books, 2014).
[30] Adam Trainer, 'From Hypnagogia to Distroid: Postironic Musical Renderings of Personal Memory,' in *The Oxford Handbook of Music and Virtuality*, ed. Sheila Whiteley and Shara Rambarran (Oxford: Oxford University Press, 2016), 414.
[31] Besides slowing down the entire track, the 'vaporwave sound' is attained by simple additions of surreal reverb effects, subtle pitch shifts or high and low pass filters, which can be added via free plug-ins in digital audio workstations – or, even easier, by using free apps such as the 'Vaporwave Music Maker' (previously known as 'CD-ROMantic'), which automatically generates entire vaporwave albums based on the uploaded original tracks. See MAA FOR APPS, 'Vaporwave Music Maker,' Google Play, version 3.2.2b (last update 14 February 2022), https://play.google.com/store/apps/details?id=maa.slowed_reverb.vaporwave_music_maker.

channels based on not only exhibiting *musical* but also *visual* 'vaporwave aesthetics' – the latter including motifs from late 1990s web design, 3D renderings, Greek statues, classic video games, skylines, company logos and many more, often composed in collage form.

Usually, the audiovisual surface of vaporwave is either described as an attempt at creating a critically directed *détournement* of symbols that represent late capitalist fantasies or are, quite simply, regarded as a joke. However, any simplified attribution of ironic de-familiarization disregards the fundamental self- and media-reflexivity underlying these contributions. Vaporwave exists because of – and despite – the artists' awareness of the 'hauntedness' of our pop-cultural memory. Fittingly, the genre label itself is a nod to the term 'vaporware', which is used for computer hardware or software that has been officially announced but never actually manufactured or released nor cancelled. This disappearance without a trace is analogous to the bygone era vaporwave supposedly represents. Similar to the status of 'vaporware', it remains unclear whether the times and places vaporwave takes us to have ever existed. In a medial environment that continually accumulates images and styles, the 'new spatial logic of the simulacrum', as Jameson puts it, can fully unfold, condemning us 'to seek History by way of our own pop images and simulacra of that history, which itself remains forever out of reach'.[32] Vaporwave artists post-ironically float within this all-encompassing spectral simulacrum, evoking descriptions of the vaporwave sound as a sonic rendering of 'a future which never was' or of 'memories we never had'. It can be seen as a manifestation of an overarching postmodern tendency towards communally mediated practices of reflective nostalgia, which, according to Svetlana Boym 'thrives in *álgos*, the longing itself, and delays the homecoming – wistfully, ironically, desperately'.[33] However, the main fascination of vaporwave is not its ironic character – although patterns of irony are easily detectable – but the communal reproduction of what Alison Koc refers to as 'melancholy affect through an aesthetic representation of the depthlessness, waning of affect, new technologies, pastiche and collapse of high/low categories into consumer culture'.[34]

---

[32] Jameson, *Postmodernism*, 18, 25.
Ibid., 25.
[33] Svetlana Boym, *The Future of Nostalgia* (New York: Basic Books, 2001), xviii.
[34] Alican Koc, 'Do You Want Vaporwave, or Do You Want the Truth? Cognitive Mapping of Late Capitalist Affect in the Virtual Lifeworld of Vaporwave,' *Capacious: Journal for Emerging Affect Inquiry* 1, no. 1 (2017): 40–1.

In the wake of networked generic approaches to community-oriented media-reflection and meta-reference such as vaporwave, highly idiosyncratic post-ironic forms, which defy any genre attributions and stylistic constraints, have emerged and continue to proliferate. Artists who are influenced by Internet-mediated forms of collaborative musicking often attain visibility by fostering an intimate and interactive relationship with musical niche communities, which they address as their 'imagined' (and real) audience through social media's various communication channels. For Chicago-based artist Angel Marcloid, for instance, self-representation on YouTube plays a big role in shaping her public profile as an artist. With her web series 'Behind the Muzak', she makes use of the communication options of YouTube's socio-technical infrastructure. In episodes of thirty minutes or more, Marcloid extensively talks about her musical, worldly and spiritual inspirations for her artistic vision, and positions herself in relation to pre-existing vernacular forms and repertoires of networked audiovisual composition and (post-)digital aesthetics. In general, formats based on self-representation and self-thematization – be it make-up tutorials, unboxing videos, Let's Plays or diary vlogs – shape the overall 'platform vernacular' of YouTube, as they dynamically constitute a grammar of communication between aspirational YouTubers and their audience through shared and continually developing forms and conventions of interaction that allow for the achievement of individual prestige and communal belonging. In 'Behind the Muzak', Marcloid cultivates her artistic online persona, thereby aiming at generating intimacy to an (imagined) fannish audience – for example through the sharing of inside knowledge, authenticating confessional moments and (post-ironic) conveyances of sincerity (see Figure 7.2). Her musical output itself is characterized by a deeply personal engagement with our computationally accelerated simulacric (pop-)cultural space. Taking the idea of 'post-genre' to its extremes, Marcloid relentlessly blends musical patterns into psychedelic amalgams that never rest in one place or time, but radically represent the ahistorical spatial montage and experiential compression in today's online environments, where any possible affective stimulus is only a mouse-click away. For example, the music of one of her many one-woman projects, Fire-Toolz, is characterized by a deliberately accelerated oversaturation with musical signifiers: in the track 'mailto:spasm@swamp.god?subject—ind-Body Parallels' from her 2019 album *Field Whispers (Into The Crystal Palace)*, Marcloid navigates the most diverse musical textures and patterns that encompass, among others: elevator music licks, black metal screams and blast beats, kitsch electronica, MIDI instruments, 8-bit sound effects, samples of virtuosic metal guitar sweeping and soothing synth layers. On her Tumblr page, she describes her inspiration for the track as follows: 'The body-mind is a unified unit. I love walking in nature. Being with animals. Being where I am. Waking up out of some bullshit. I tried to nod to my fav no-treble octave smooth jazz guitarist. Imo the beat & bass slams.'[35] Both inspired by everyday epiphenomena and banalities, as well as by religious, philosophical and mystical themes, Marcloid regards her music as 'melodramatically sincere' expressions of her personal and spiritual journey.[36] Generally, her Fire-Toolz records follow overarching thematic threads: for example, the title of her newest album *Eternal Home* (2021) not only refers to the experience of confinement and isolation during the COVID-19 pandemic at the time of its production and release, but more importantly, on a spiritual level, it addresses her compositional engagement with ideas of belonging and self-fulfilment, as Marcloid underscores in her liner notes:

> Our Eternal Home is Heaven. Heaven is the ultimate reality of our shared Being, but the conscious experience of it is a state of mind (a dimension we are meant for). [...] In all of the grief, fear and stinging emotional pain I have endured in this incarnation, despite the richness and miraculous unfolding that is my beautiful life, it turns out: I am always Home, and Home is always safe. The album is what settled in the sink after I wrung myself dry. It is full of sensory memories, love of nature, spiritual deliberation and relating childhood experiences to my present-day psychology, but it is also a metamorphosis. It engulfs the vast darkness in more light than it can handle.[37]

Beyond defining her musical output by way of genre attributions, which seems inevitably futile, it seems more productive to regard Marcloid's music as a meta-referential musical rendering of our oversaturated informational space, characterized by a post-ironic hyper-affirmation of its principles of acceleration.[38]

---

[35] @Fire-Toolz, Tumblr post, 8 September 2019. https://fire-toolz.tumblr.com/post/187584231189/%C3%ADn-th%C3%ADs-thr%D1%94%CE%B1d-%C3%AD-w%C3%ADll-d%C3%ADscuss-tr%CE%B1ck-%D0%B2%D1%87-tr%CE%B1ck-%CE%B1.
[36] See Angel Marcloid, 'Infinity and "I": An Interview with Fire-Toolz', by Audrey Lockie, *Slug Mag*, (7 May 2020), https://www.slugmag.com/music/interviews/music-interviews/infinity-and-i-an-interview-with-fire-toolz/.
[37] Angel Marcloid, liner notes for Fire-Toolz, *Eternal Home*, Hausu Mountain Records, 15 October 2021, digital album.
[38] 'Avant-vaporwave' and 'cyber prog metal' are but two of the many genre labels applied to *Fire-Toolz*' music, demonstrating the disparity of attributions. See Fire-Toolz, review of 'Fire-Toolz – Rainbow ∞ Bridge (official music video)', by Jeff Cubbison, *Impose Magazine* (1 April 2020), at https://imposemagazine.com/bytes/new-music/fire-toolz-rainbow-%E2%88%9E-bridge; see Fire-Toolz, review of *Eternal Home*, by Kristoffer Cornils, *musikexpress* (15 October 2021), at https://www.musikexpress.de/reviews/fire-toolz-eternal-home/.

**Figure 7.2** Marcloid talks extensively about her music in her YouTube video series 'Behind the Muzak', which, on a visual level, is characterized by post-ironic video editing: *Behind The Muzak #3: Fire-Toolz – Skinless X-1* (@Fire-Toolz).

The eclectic free fall through an endless array of musical references without fixed symbolic anchorage becomes a motor of musical growth and self-discovery, in tune with her spiritual journey: 'I'm on a journey; steadily growing every day, until my body no longer works. I'm not even saying I'm getting better and better, but I'm always changing. I'm constantly falling, and there is no ground.'[39]

## Outro: The Irony of Post-Ironic Transcendence

Procedures of networked composition are afforded by platform-specific socio-technical infrastructures and carried out by networked subjects that do not act autonomously but in adherence with the platform's communication options and in anticipation of the upload's potential algorithmic diffusion. Over the course of creative relay by aspirational and co-creative artists, communally recognized repertoires and conventions of musical re-composition and self-representation emerge and develop. The concrete modalities and affective charge of an artist's musical output may shift according to the functionality of the used platform. For

---

[39] Marcloid, 'An Interview with Fire-Toolz.'

instance, YouTube, as a video hub and a participatory communicative environment, empowers artists to prove their creativity and relevance with respect to music video production and communicative formats of strategic self-display and self-thematization. These audiovisual vehicles of Internet-mediated artistic (self-)expression exist complementarily to their content on other social media platforms and distribution channels. Moreover, they inspire the ongoing development, resignification and personification of audiovisual forms and formats of musical (self-)expression within YouTube and across social media platforms in general.

The circulating and materially repeatable themes and aesthetic patterns of Internet-mediated music genres can be understood as constituents of the productive conditions of possibility regarding discursive formations of musical vernaculars, which serve to integrate socio-aesthetics and ethe into subcultural everyday communication and creativity. Across a web of modal interrelations between platform-specific forms and formats of content creation, musical, visual and performative conventions of conveying communally shared post-ironic attitudes emerge, transcending the distancing and often cynical effects of irony by way of navigating the hyperreal 'tissues of quotation' with a new-found sense of proximity and affectivity. SoundCloud rap's 'post-authentic' subject positions or vaporwave's affective embracement of disorientation are but two ways in which emotional distance can be reduced in favour of a new-found immediacy that denies the possibility of cynically seeking refuge in absolute negative independence through ubiquitous irony. Post-irony in Internet-mediated music genres appears to be an intuitive accompaniment of (often openly confused) compositional engagement, with the all-engulfing symbolic multiplicity of popular culture. In contrast to the utopian and optimistic impulse of post-ironic postulates in the fields of literature and the visual arts, a turn toward responsibility and commitment appears as a potential incentive or concomitance, not as a precondition for post-ironic aesthetics in general. After all, as the examples in this article have demonstrated, post-ironic composition aimed at transcending the distancing and de-subjectivizing effects of irony affords for a wide range of affective stimuli and ethical stances, from affirmations of nihilistic indifference and depression over melancholia and reflective nostalgia, to optimistic approaches aimed at self-awareness and spiritual self-fulfilment.

It needs to be pointed out that the post-ironic *zeitgeist* does not solve but rather accelerates postmodern issues of encoding and decoding, as the establishment of (often community-exclusive) post-ironic competencies within the digital sphere further blurs overarching referential codes. Against the backdrop of previous conceptualizations of post-irony in the 'high arts', this development comes across as ironic, as the crisis of ironic readability was the actual issue that led to proclamations of post-ironic attitudes in the first place. All in all, digitally mediated post-ironic (re-)composition on YouTube and beyond serves as a playground for new forms of subjectively channelled aesthetics. However, although the reduction of emotional distance in favour of a new-found immediacy denies the possibility of cynically seeking refuge in absolute negative independence, the transcendence of 'traditional subject positioning in lieu of an affective rendering of experiential vagueness' entails a de-differentiation and de-politicization of the used or reappropriated musical material, as any notion of aesthetic or ideological hurdles in need to be overcome is removed.[40]

## Bibliography

Adorno, Theodor W. *Aesthetic Theory*. Translated by Robert Hullot-Kentor. Minneapolis: University of Minnesota Press, 1997.

Boym, Svetlana. *The Future of Nostalgia*. New York: Basic Books, 2001.

Colebrook, Claire. *Irony: The New Critical Idiom*. London and New York: Routledge, 2014.

Derrida, Jacques. *Specters of Marx*. Translated by Peggy Kamuf. New York: Routledge, 1994.

Fire-Toolz. 'Review of 'Fire-Toolz – Rainbow ∞ Bridge (official music video).' by Jeff Cubbison'. *Impose Magazine*, 1 April 2020, at https://imposemagazine.com/bytes/new-music/fire-toolz-rainbow-%E2%88%9E-bridge.

Fire-Toolz. 'Review of *Eternal Home*, by Kristoffer Cornils,' *musikexpress*, 15 October 2021, at https://www.musikexpress.de/reviews/fire-toolz-eternal-home/.

Gossolt, Marcus and Johannes M. Hedinger (Com&Com). 'First Post-Ironic Manifesto,' 2008, at https://postirony.files.wordpress.com/2009/01/postirony-web1.jpg.

Grey Ellis, Emma. 'Can't Take a Joke? That's Just Poe's Law, 2017's Most Important Internet Phenomenon.' *Wired*, 5 June 2017, at https://www.wired.com/2017/06/poes-law-troll-cultures-central-rule/.

Hedinger, Johannes M. 'Postironie: Geschichte, Theorie und Praxis einer Kunst nach der Ironie (Eine Betrachtung aus zwei Perspektiven).' *Kunstform International* 213 (2012): 112–25.

---

[40] Trainer, 'From Hypnagogia to Distroid', 422.

Jameson, Fredric. *Postmodernism, or, The Cultural Logic of Late Capitalism*. Durham, NC: Duke University Press, 1991.

Janz, Tobias. 'Goodbye 20th Century: Sonic Youth, John Cage's "Number Pieces" and the Long Farewell to the Avant-Garde.' In *The Metareferential Turn in Contemporary Arts and Media: Forms, Functions, Attempts at Explanation*, edited by Werner Wolf, 525–47. Amsterdam/New York: Rodopi, 2011.

Kierkegaard, Søren. *The Concept of Irony, with Continual References to Socrates*. Translated by Howard V. Hong and Edna H. Hong. Princeton: Princeton University Press, 1989.

Koc, Alican. 'Do You Want Vaporwave, or Do You Want the Truth? Cognitive Mapping of Late Capitalist Affect in the Virtual Lifeworld of Vaporwave.' *Capacious: Journal for Emerging Affect Inquiry* 1, no. 1 (2017): 40–1.

Konstantinou, Lee. *Cool Characters: Irony and American Fiction*. Cambridge, MA: Harvard University Press, 2016.

Marcloid, Angel. 'Infinity and "I": An Interview with Fire-Toolz.' By Audrey Lockie. *Slug Mag*, 7 May 2020, at https://www.slugmag.com/music/interviews/music-interviews/infinity-and-i-an-interview-with-fire-toolz/.

Marcloid, Angel. Liner notes for Fire-Toolz, *Eternal Home*. Hausu Mountain Records, 15 October 2021, digital album.

Plönges, Sebastian. 'Postironie als Entfaltung.' In *Medien und Bildung: Institutionelle Kontexte und kultureller Wandel*, edited by Torsten Meyer, Wey-Han Tan, Christina Schwalbe and Ralf Appelt, 439–46. Springer: Wiesbaden 2011.

Quintilian, Marcus Fabius. *Institutio Oratoria*. Translated by Harold Edgeworth Butler. London: William Heinemann Ltd., 1921.

Reckwitz, Andreas. *Das hybride Subjekt: Eine Theorie der Subjektkulturen von der bürgerlichen Moderne zur Postmoderne*. Weilerswist: Velbrück Wissenschaft, 2006.

Robinson, Kristin. 'How $uicideboy$ Became the Multi-Million Dollar Brand You Never Heard Of.' *Billboard*, 22 October 2021, at https://www.billboard.com/music/music-news/suicideboys-new-album-headlining-tour-2021-interview-9649488/.

Slavik, Nathan. 'Spooky Black: Dope, Wack or Kinda Racist? (All of the Above).' *DJ Booth*, 30 July 2014, at https://djbooth.net/features/spooky-black-dope-wack-or-kinda-racist.

Trainer, Adam. 'From Hypnagogia to Distroid: Postironic Musical Renderings of Personal Memory.' In *The Oxford Handbook of Music and Virtuality*, edited by Sheila Whiteley and Shara Rambarran, 409–27. Oxford: Oxford University Press, 2016.

Wikström, Peter and Erik van Ooijen. 'Post-Authentic Digitalism in Cloud Rap' (summary). Paper presented at the conference *Popular Music Discourses: Authenticity and Mediatization*, Karlstad University, Karlstad, Sweden, 13 November 2018, at https://www.researchgate.net/publication/333422124_Post-authentic_digitalism_in_cloud_rap.

# 8

# Performing Beyond the Platform: Experiencing Musicking on and Through YouTube, TikTok and Instagram

Juan Bermúdez

On one occasion, after a long day at the university, I took the train home. The train was crowded with young people. In the middle of an orgiastic sound mix, I recognized that a brief but striking melody, which was currently being used for TikTok performances, was being repeatedly played. Four youngsters were sitting around a table on the train; a smartphone was lying on the table. They were all staring at the screen as the striking TikTok melody played. I observed a typical practice of TikTok musicking: just as in my own experience, these youngsters were watching a performance, but, unlike me, they were watching it as a group. What happened next took me by surprise. These young people started to analyse the performance, imitate the sequences and criticize its aesthetic properties. They played the same musical TikToks repeatedly and correlated them to other versions elsewhere on the platform, as well as on YouTube. Then they started to explore different possibilities of making individual or group versions of the same TikTok, a discussion that would end thanks to a WhatsApp message from 'Julia' from school saying that it would be better if they met the next day to do a duet after class.

This story shows us that the interactions and interrelations of TikTok musicking do not just occur through the TikTok app, but also on and amongst other digital platforms and out into the physical world. The (musical) practices that these young people – like many of us – carry out are developed on and through digital platforms, which have become an inseparable part of our daily lives. We search for the closest restaurant on Google Maps while chatting through WhatsApp with friends who could be in the same region or any other country. We *like* some pictures shared by our family or friends on Instagram, and we show our shopping tours or a concert *live* via Facebook or YouTube. The use of digital media and devices sharpens our daily lives; and it also influences our musical practices. Although musicians employ social media and other digital technologies to represent and market themselves, other stakeholders participate in the discourse on digital music practices in a range of different ways.

However, many of these practices are carried out in an interactive space that goes beyond a specific platform or physical location. In my opening story, I recalled four youngsters with a smartphone practising choreography, analysing a video and spending time together, but I could not perceive the other participants (like 'Julia'), who joined the conversation through asynchronous and mediatized routes. But they were all present at that moment on the train. Although my encounter occurred in a physical setting, it was part of a much larger network of interactions and interrelations constructed by different participants using a range of devices able to connect de-territorialized and asynchronously-experienced spaces.[1] Using music and dance as the connective strand, this interactive network interlaced various physical, everyday places (e.g. schools, parks) with digital spaces (e.g. TikTok, YouTube, Instagram, etc.). These interlocking spaces, platforms and technologies can be understood as multimedia.

Today, it is not easy to imagine any mainstream musical practice without acknowledging the role that digital platforms, especially YouTube, play in its creation and articulation. Although the specificities of each platform have established certain individual musical and performative peculiarities, many musical practices move and develop across platforms and through cyberspace. This transmedial flow has fostered the development of networked creativity and practice. Here, I apply ethnographic research methods to explore cross-platform musicking through TikTok, YouTube, Instagram and beyond, from an Austrian context. What is the interrelation between musical practices through these platforms? How does music change as it moves into different social media spaces? And how do these changes encourage us to conceptualize amateur

---

[1] Juan Bermúdez, '"It's All About 'Being There'": Rethinking Presence and Co-presence in the Ethnographic Field During and After the COVID-19 Pandemic,' in 'Oral Traditions and Participatory Music Practices in Times of Pandemic: Scenarios and Perspectives', Special Issue, *Journal of World Popular Music* (forthcoming).

creative networks in a way appropriate to the digital age? Based on examples of cross-platform performance practices, I propose different facets of multimedial musical performance, and suggest that digital platforms are not closed spaces, but rather interconnected ones that encourage fluid and malleable networks of sonic creativity.

## Musicking Beyond A Single Platform

The rise and expansion of the Internet and the development of new devices, forms of communication and platforms, have developed significant connections between physical and virtual multilocal and multimedia spaces. As seen with the introduction of new technologies in the past, the current appropriation of digital spaces in the globalized world, as well as the continual development of digital music platforms (YouTube, Spotify, etc.) and devices, has not only shaped and augmented the interactive possibilities between users, it has also enabled and reinforced the adaptation and development of new forms of musical practice.[2] Musicians use social media and other digital technologies both as a tool to represent and promote themselves, and as an active part of their artistic creation and exploration: they use platforms such as YouTube, in other words, for their broadcasting and participatory, process-driven qualities.[3] In his work on Web 2.0, Axel Bruns notes that this double role has made the borders between digital production and reception fragile.[4] We can extend his observation to suggest that the dissolving borders between musical articulation and experience have forged new and radical relationships between digital environments and daily life.

Music's creation, articulation, processing and experience may occur autonomously at different times and in separate digital or physical spaces. Nowadays, we no longer have to be in front of musicians to listen to and experience music, as we would have just 100 years ago. Now, in the contemporary globalized world, it is possible for us to listen to practically any recorded music of the world – performed long ago or in current times – simply by taking out a

---

[2] See Alfred Smudits, *Mediamorphosen des Kulturschaffens: Kunst und Kommunikationstechnologien in Wandel* (Vienna: Braumüller, 2002).
[3] See Holly Rogers, "'Welcome to your world': YouTube and the Reconfiguration of Music's Gatekeepers," in *YouTube and Music: Cyberculture and Everyday Life*, ed. Holly Rogers, Joana Freitas and João Francisco Porfírio (New York: Bloomsbury, 2023), 1–38.
[4] Axel Bruns, *Blogs, Wikipedia, Second Life, And Beyond: From Production to Produsage* (Wien-New York: Peter Lang, 2008), 9–36; 227–58.

small device – maybe no larger than a couple of centimetres – which allows us to connect through the Internet to a particular platform (such as YouTube Music, Spotify or Apple Music) and access a discography so vast that no one person could live long enough to listen to it all. Critics such as Tia DeNora, Anahid Kassabian and Michael Bull have shown how such accessibility and portability have enabled the conscious and unconscious embedding of musical practices throughout our daily lives.[5] We listen to music while we go from one place to another or perform various activities: we share music videos that we like with friends and family through YouTube and other platforms; we make and share playlists that reflect our tastes and moods and become an essential part of our personalities. In short, we frame many of our daily activities with our own personal soundtrack(s).

Beyond this, anyone can actively participate in one way or another in the generation of content around or about the musical performance itself. Thanks to the development and expansion of Web 2.0, the ways in which we can interact with various platforms changed from the consumption of online data to a more active and direct participation in its creation and circulation through likes, comments, shares, playlisting and remediation. Growing technological development, as well as the increasing accessibility to it, has also enabled users to actively participate in content creation by producing original compositions or remixing, parodying and mashing-up pre-existent work. This participation in YouTube's creative forums can be done alone or in cooperation with other people. Cheap and easy-to-use technology means that users no longer need a professional recording studio to generate a track or video: music and music videos can now be produced at home with outstanding quality, and shared, as Patricia Lange has shown, through YouTube's vast amateur networks.[6]

The creation and sharing of music and media through YouTube and TikTok accelerated with the development of portable devices, especially the smartphone, which allowed access to the Internet – and therefore to digital music platforms

---

[5] See Tia DeNora, *Music in Everyday Life* (Cambridge: Cambridge University Press, 2000); Anahid Kassabian, *Ubiquitous Listening: Affect, Attention, and Distributed Subjectivity* (Berkeley: University of California Press, 2013); Marta García Quiñones, Anahid Kassabian and Elena Boschi (eds.), *Ubiquitous Musics: The Everyday Sounds That We Don't Always Notice* (Farnham: Ashgate Publishing, 2013); Michael Bull, *Sound Moves: iPod Culture and Urban Experience* (New York: Routledge, 2007).
[6] See Patricia Lange, *Thanks for Watching: An Anthropological Study of Video Sharing on YouTube* (Louisville: University Press of Colorado, 2019).

– and provided the hardware and software necessary for the quick generation and dissemination of content.[7] Taking a photo, making a video, recording a sound or a song; all these activities can now be done using the same handheld device. It is no longer necessary to carry a computer, a camera and a video recorder with us to create, frame and share our daily lives or to generate our own personal soundtracks almost instantly. As a result, platforms such as YouTube and, later TikTok, have become a fundamental part of everyday life, creating a musicking based on multimedia networks of creativity and practice.

Amateur short music videos that move through YouTube, TikTok and Instagram show how this everyday multimedia musicking has produced new audiovisual forms based on interdisciplinary networks of creativity and practice. An example of such phenomenon can be found in the choreographic remediation of 'Jerusalema' (2020) by Master KG and Nomcebo. Like Pharrell Williams' 'Happy' (2013), 'Jerusalema' became an instant viral hit, with the dance moves replicated in a variety of performance situations (Figure 8.1). But although 'Jerusalema's' choreography and music remain constant, the creative means of reproducing the trend – the ways in which it was performed on each of the platforms, as well as on the street as part of everyday popular culture – were highly changeable. On YouTube, versions tend to be videos of dance collectives, filmed with long, extensive camera shots; on TikTok and Instagram, short, individual performances dominate, with cameras focused primarily on the dancer; and in live performances located in real-world settings, the choreography is often performed in small fragments as a joke during conversations or when listening to the song in the street. These short performances, made as part of people's daily lives, provide a framework through which users can express their joys, sorrows and concerns; and afford a space for others to share and comment on these experiences. As they spread across platforms, the videos can generate bonds and friendships between creators.[8] 'Happy' and 'Jerusalema', then, evidence the ways in which TikToks, Reels and Shorts have extended beyond the

---

[7] For a much more detailed and in-depth overview of these processes see Nicholas Cook, Monique M. Ingalls and David Trippett (eds.), *The Cambridge Companion to Music in Digital Culture* (Cambridge: Cambridge University Press, 2019); Sumanth Gopinath and Jason Stanyek (eds.), *The Oxford Handbook of Mobile Music Studies, Volumes 1 & 2* (Oxford: Oxford University Press, 2014).

[8] The word *creator* is used here as an emic concept, and the performers of these videos can be understood under Bruns' concept of *produsers* (see Bruns, *Blogs, Wikipedia, Second Life, And Beyond*).

**Figure 8.1** Choreographic remediation of 'Jerusalema' (Master KG and Nomcebo 2020).

smartphone landscape. Although both videos initially appeared on YouTube, they generated millions of reinterpretations on other platforms and through live flashmobs.

This integration of video creation and experience in everyday life, as well as the occurrence of these practices through diverse spaces and platforms, has generated cultural discourse and knowledge that goes beyond local context into the glocal cultural imaginary. This allows musical styles and trends to influence cultural practices and behaviours far beyond the original platform or geographical locale. A sound/track made by a teenager in their house can become a world hit, and later accompany the day-to-day of young people around the world, as in the case of Justin Bieber. A video of someone dancing in the street, shared on YouTube, can become the next viral trend on TikTok. Beyond this, dances and memes are also taken up by popular culture and appropriated in other contexts, from music videos to television shows and movies. However, videos of tragic events, like those of @valerisssh about her experiences fleeing the Russian-Ukrainian War, or protest actions shared through these networks, can also become the spark that ignites social movements, such as #BlackLivesMatter, leaving a mark on the memory of our generation. YouTube, as well as TikTok, has not only become part of contemporary mainstream popular culture; it also operates as a portal into the social, political and cultural spectrums of everyday life. But how do creative interrelations between platforms work? How do they make possible the creation of a larger glocal cultural imaginary?

## From One Platform to The World and Back Again

Like YouTube before it, TikTok quickly become one of the most widely used video creation and viewing apps. Users create new TikToks and appropriate and remediate existing ones; they participate in the discourse around these practices by commenting on other videos; and, as our opening story reveals, engagement with TikToks occurs not only on their home platform, but also across YouTube and Instagram, in real, physical spaces and through digital and physical magazines and web pages.[9] Increasingly, audiovisual practices developed on YouTube are readapted to the aesthetic contexts and languages of TikTok and Instagram, thus enabling the creation and renegotiation of common multimedia practices able to take advantage of the specificities and style of different platforms.

Transmedia movements reveal much about user behaviour, and tracing TikToks across platforms reveals information about how interrelationships are created between accounts and / or creators: although TikTokers create profiles on YouTube and / or Instagram to represent and market themselves, YouTubers and Instagrammers expand their performance networks through TikTok and other platforms. German twins Lisa and Lena (@lisaandlena), for example, became famous on the Musical.ly app, before developing successful careers on YouTube and Instagram and conquering TikTok in German-speaking countries after its merger with Musical.ly, while American Charlie D'Amelio, one of the most followed TikTokers globally, also enjoys massive success on YouTube and Instagram. As we follow creators across platforms, experiencing their performances and sharing a joint space with them, relationships and friendships can develop that can bleed into real life.[10]

These interrelationships encourage the development of specific performative identities and musical persona able to manifest coherently across different contexts. Philip Auslander, in his work on liveness and the performance situation, notes the importance of music's physicality: 'What musicians perform first and foremost is not music, but their own identities as musicians, [...] Seen this way, the object of musical performance is the successful presentation of an identity, a musical persona, in a defined social context, rather than the execution of a text.'[11]

---

[9] The German-language magazines *Bravo* and *Cool*, among others, are clear examples of physical magazines that dedicate space to the performative and aesthetic practices of digital platforms such as TikTok. In addition, these magazines and other newspapers and television programmes have chosen to make their own accounts on YouTube, Instagram and TikTok.

[10] See Lange, *Thanks for Watching*; Bermúdez, 'It's All About "Being There"'.

[11] Philip Auslander, 'Musical Personae,' *The Drama Review* 50, no. 1 (2006): 102–4, 118. See also Philip Auslander, *In Concert: Performing Musical Persona* (Ann Arbor: University of Michigan Press, 2021).

Digital media musicians forge their musical persona by establishing their specificity as a YouTuber, TikToker or Instagrammer, while simultaneously adapting to the aesthetic fluidity between platforms. In this way, they are able to create a recognizable meta-musical persona through different performance networks. Fundamental to this inter-platform mediation is the process of stylistic and aesthetic convergence, a transference of affect that has formed the basis of my ethnographic research into the on- and offline musicking practices on TikTok from an Austrian perspective.[12] TikTokers no longer only create and experience videos on TikTok, but also use YouTube to search for new dances, performative forms, trends and other related trends, using and creating YouTube tutorials that teach particular dance routines that can then be remediated into new TikToks. One can find countless tutorials on YouTube showing relatively simple steps such as 'floss' or much more complicated ones like 'renegade', for instance. However, one can also find countless compilations of these or other dances and trends. Dances such as 'renegade' help young people to articulate their identities within a communal space as part of a larger conversation: they can respond to an existing dance routine and, in turn, their version can be remediated by other creators to form a complex audiovisual landscape of adaptations and translations that are then subject to the negotiation of aesthetic and racial discourses by yet other users who compile the 'best' and 'worst' versions of these dance steps.[13] These practices of creation, copying, sharing and cataloguing influence how new dance videos are created and experienced later on TikTok. In addition, the practice of commenting and rating various aspects of TikToks through videos on YouTube has become common, as in the case of the YouTubers TwoSetViolin.[14] This musical duo, like many other creators, bring local performances, knowledge and aesthetics to a more heterogeneous public, spreading particular cultural discourses and knowledge beyond their local context and thus situating themselves within a larger glocal cultural imaginary.

Although some of the dances and sounds used in TikTok videos have been taken up by other creators and brought into new cyber contexts, the

---

[12] See Juan Bermúdez, 'Ethnographing TikTok: Towards an E3thnomusicological Approach to a Multimedia Musicking,' in 'TikTok-Music-Cultures: Perspectives on the Study of Musicking Practices On & Through TikTok,' Special Issue, *Musicologica Austriaca – Journal for Austrian Music Studies* (forthcoming); Juan Bermúdez, 'Virtual Musical.ly(ties): Identities, Performances & Meanings in a Mobile Application. An Ethnomusicological Approach to TikTok's Musicking,' PhD. diss., University of Vienna, 2022.

[13] Trevor Boffone, *Renegades: Digital Dance Cultures from Dubsmash to TikTok* (New York: Oxford University Press, 2021).

[14] TwoSetViolin's YouTube Channel is here: https://www.youtube.com/c/twosetviolin.

cross-platform influence and interconnected practice may run deeper, as the creation process of the music hit 'Savage Love (Laxed – Siren Beat)' by Jawsh 685 (Joshua Nanai) and Jason Derulo demonstrates.[15] This immense popularity drew the attention of various record labels, and Jawsh 685 signed with Columbia Records, releasing 'Laxed (Siren Beat)' on various streaming platforms in April 2020. As a result, 'Laxed' became the musical base for developing various trends on TikTok during the start of the COVID-19 pandemic, reaching numerous social groups around the world. One of these users was the singer Jason Derulo who uploaded his own TikTok, in which he danced to the rhythm of 'Laxed'.[16] On 11 May 2020, Derulo published another TikTok announcing his new song, which he had just composed: 'Savage Love'.[17] However, 'Savage Love' used the 'Laxed' sample available on TikTok without crediting Jawsh 685. After much criticism and legal issues, Derulo and Jawsh 685 reached an agreement and ended up releasing 'Savage Love (Laxed – Siren Beat)' together in June 2020. Although this example reveals some of the unethical practices that have plagued social media, it also shows the influence and interconnection between users and practices across various digital platforms, and how a video or song can regenerate practices, performances and meanings in different technological settings.[18]

As cultural practices and aesthetics spread through popular Internet culture, refreshed artistic realms are generated, a rejuvenation seen in the movement of the video 'Don't Lie to Me' by German singer Lena released in March 2019 on YouTube.[19] Recorded in portrait mode with and from the perspective of an iPhone, (Figure 8.2). 'Don't Lie to Me' thus exemplifies the multimediality that exists in the practices that we carry out in our day-to-day activities, and the influence that these practices generate in the production of new multimedia aesthetics within what Carol Vernallis has called the 'media swirl'.[20]

---

[15] Jason Derulo, 'Jason Derulo & Jawsh 685 – Savage Love (Studio Music Video),' YouTube video, 00:02:52, 9 June 2020, https://www.youtube.com/watch?v=gUci-tsiU4I.
[16] @jasonderulo, 'Is this a trend?,' 17 April 2020, TikTok video, https://vm.tiktok.com/ZML6ue4Ds/.
[17] @jasonderulo, 'Made this song last night,' 11 May 2020, TikTok video, https://vm.tiktok.com/ZML6uMSuq/.
[18] In his work on the 'renegade' dance, Trevor Boffone (see Boffone, *Renegades*) extensively exposes the problems that black artists experience in being stripped of credit for the choreography they create. Although in the past year, TikTok has tried to change this situation by running information campaigns to create an awareness of authorship in the application, BIPOC artists continue to contribute choreography and performances to the TikTok community without being recognized for it.
[19] Lena, 'Lena – Don't Lie To Me (Official Video),' YouTube video, 00:03:28, 15 March 2019, https://www.youtube.com/watch?v=B_BLi76JPqA.
[20] Carol Vernallis, *Unruly Media: YouTube, Music Video, and the New Digital Cinema* (Oxford: Oxford University Press, 2013); See also Carol Vernallis, Holly Rogers and Lisa Perrott (ed.), *Transmedia Directors. Artistry, Industry and New Audiovisual Aesthetics* (London: Bloomsbury Press, 2020).

**Figure 8.2** Scenes from Lena's 'Don't Lie to Me' (2019).

So far, we've seen how affect and style can transfer between platforms, how content can refer to the aesthetics and specificities of other forms of social media, and how everything can flow into the real world. But dances and memes have also bled into other audiovisual contexts, such as movies and television series. The dialogue between Jodi and her parents, Helaine and Richie Kreyman, in the Netflix movie *Tall Girl 2* (Emily Ting, 2022), for instance, addresses TikTok in such a way as to demonstrate the generational differences in the articulation of multimedia practices:

**Helaine**  Dr. Seeger probably saw me on the Tok.

**Richie**  Huh?

**Helaine**  The Tickety Tok. I was doin' all of that. I was plugging your show, though.

**Jodi**  You're on TikTok?

**Helaine**  You don't follow me? (twenty-eight minutes)

Although this movie embeds the platform within its cultural setting, other cinematic examples play on social media's constant recontextualization of sounds, memes and routines. An example of this can be seen during the performance of the song 'Surface Pressure' by Luisa in the Disney movie *Encanto* (Byron Howard and Jared Bush, 2021).[21] Luisa's dance performance not only refers to the dance culture on TikTok, but has also influenced the development

---

[21] DisneyMusicVEVO, 'Jessica Darrow – Surface Pressure (From 'Encanto'),' *YouTube video*, 00:03:30, 24 December 2021, https://www.youtube.com/watch?v=tQwVKr8rCYw.

of new trends on this platform. TikTokers make versions of Luisa's dance, imitating her steps or creating new versions of her choreography. They do duets with her and other TikTokers, and share these performances and other compilations through YouTube and Instagram. By becoming part of popular culture, these moves, which could previously have been shared on TikTok itself, are recontextualized and performed (in a new way) on other platforms, only to be taken up on TikTok and re-adapted to this environment.

These are not just processes of reinterpretation and recontextualization, but also of appropriation, with the potential of going viral, and are used by various artists to promote their work. Because of the different audiences that each platform can reach, some artists include aesthetics from these platforms in their performances, as we saw happening in Lena's 'Don't Lie to Me' video. On the other hand, however, some artists use the specific practices of a particular platform to help their music go viral. Austrian singer Andreas Gabalier's song 'LIEBELEBEN' is a good example of this.[22] Before launching his song in June 2021, Gabalier published various Stories through his Instagram account. These Stories did not explicitly announce the release of his next single but invited his followers to learn a particular choreography, step by step, Story by Story. After the official launch of the song through YouTube in commemoration of Pride Month, it was clear that these dance steps would turn out to be the choreography for the song's chorus. The prelude to the video offers different Reels showing young girls performing the choreography, and, in the official video, Gabalier performs the moves with a group of dancers each time the chorus is heard. In the weeks following the release, Gabalier encouraged fellow users to join the #LIEBELEBEN Dance Challenge, inviting people to dance the choreography and share their Reels under that hashtag through Instagram. Although this request was not particularly successful, the choreography and its sound went viral on TikTok.

## Multimedia Practices – Musicking Through TikTok, YouTube and Instagram

Although 'Don't Lie to Me' shows how social media aesthetics have begun to influence, and be influenced by, the professional sphere via film and television,

---

[22] Andreas Gabalier, 'Andreas Gabalier – LIEBELEBEN (Offizielles Musikvideo),' *YouTube video*, 0:03:57, 4 June 2021, https://www.youtube.com/watch?v=ECG72etNlsQ.

various musical traditions, such as electronic dance music, Argentinian tango and German Schlager, have merged and continue to merge these digital environments and platforms into their performance, representation and/or communication practices.[23] In fact, for many, the experience and performance of music and dance on and through YouTube, TikTok and Instagram has become necessary for the economic survival of young artists and cultural institutions in a hyperconnected world. The search for new formats and scenarios for the diffusion of music has led to live-streamed concerts across different platforms, as well as the development of partnerships with a range of non-traditional institutions. One example is *Tiger King 2 The TikTopera* (Figure 8.3), collaboratively produced by Netflix and The English National Opera in 2021, and launched on TikTok and YouTube as a preamble and promotion to the launch of the second season of Netflix's *Tiger King 2*.[24]

Alongside these new collaborations are experiments with new performance formats.[25] The adaptation of Mozart's *Die Entführung aus dem Serai* (K384, 1782) into '#FREE_Constanze' in 2021 and Bizet's *Carmen* (1875) into 'Carmen by Carmen' in 2022, for instance, were made on TikTok by Hamburg's Opernloft team as part of their strategy to attract new audiences to its theatre, taking advantage of the financial support provided through TikTok's #CreatorsForDiversity campaign in Germany (Figure 8.4).[26] These TikTok-Operas not only experimented with new formats and dramaturgical strategies, but also used various practices and aesthetics widely spread on TikTok, YouTube and Instagram to forge vernacular modes of expression more accessible to a younger generation. In response to the use of various trends and challenges

---

[23] See Alejandro L. Madrid, *Nor-tec Rifa! Electronic Dance Music From Tijuana to the World* (New York: Oxford University Press, 2008); Kendra Steputtat, 'Tango Musicality and Tango Danceability: Reconnecting Strategies in Current Cosmopolitan Tango Argentino Practice,' in *Choreomusicology II: Translocality / Local Ontology*, Special Issue, *The World of Music (new series)* 9, no. 2 (2020): 5–30; Julio Mendívil, *Ein musikalisches Stück Heimat: Ethnologische Beobachtungen zum deutschen Schlager* (Bielefeld: transcript Verlag, 2008).
[24] Netflix, 'Tiger King 2 The TikTopera Netflix,' *YouTube video*, 00:05:14, 15 November 2021, https://www.youtube.com/watch?v=lnh1UD8t_nA.
[25] See Monika Voithofer, '"DENKEN, HÖREN, DA CAPO": Konzeptuelle Musik im 20. und 21. Jahrhundert: Eine Studie zu Genealogie, Materialität, Form und Semantik,' PhD diss., University of Graz, 2021. A more current example of this type of exploration can be seen in the multimedia compositions of Belenish Moreno-Gil, Óscar Escudero, Nik Bohnenberger and Karel Stulens among others.
[26] @opernloft, 'That escalated quickly,' 8 October 2021, TikTok video, https://vm.tiktok.com/ZMLrbnAQ9/; @opernloft, 'Welcome to 'Carmen by Carmen'!,' 20 January 2022, TikTok video, https://vm.tiktok.com/ZMLrbwbRp/.

**Figure 8.3** Scenes from *Tiger King 2 The TikTopera* (2021).

existing on TikTok, they created their own challenges, such as the #TikTokDanceChallangeMozartEdition.

Even though the growing popularity of digital platforms has generated radical new musical and performative worlds, many of the creative practices once unique to each platform now flow through the contemporary 'media swirl' and beyond the digital world altogether. When I witnessed four youngsters viewing, analysing and copying a video on TikTok and YouTube on their smartphones, it was clear that they were deftly navigating between different online and physical spaces, combining and superimposing one on the other to forge a new hyper-real mode of communication. To explore mediatized musical practices across social media, it is necessary to conceptualize digital and analogue media as practices that are created, negotiated and experienced in everyday multimedia situations and contexts synchronously or asynchronously.[27] These interrelationships, enabled by the interoperability of platforms, have fostered the development of exciting forms of networked creativity and practice, a multimedia network that emerges through the articulation of joint musical and dance practices experienced through the interlacing of physical and digital spaces; a multimedia network in which we live and experience our day-to-day lives.

---

[27] Juan Bermúdez, '¿Qué música? Si nadie toca... si nadie sabe...: Reflexionando el etnografiar de un musicking digital,' *Boletín Música* 52-3 (Julio 2019-Junio 2020): 51-60; Bermúdez, 'Ethnographing TikTok.'

**Figure 8.4** Scenes from '#FREE_Constanze' (2021) and 'Carmen by Carmen' (2022).

# Bibliography

Auslander, Philip. 'Musical Personae.' *The Drama Review* 50, no. 1 (2006): 100–19.
———. *In Concert: Performing Musical Persona*. Ann Arbor: University of Michigan Press, 2021.
Bermúdez, Juan. '¿Qué música? Si nadie toca … si nadie sabe …' Reflexionando el etnografiar de un musicking digital.' *Boletín Música* 52–3 (Julio 2019–Junio 2020): 51–60.
———. 'Ethnographing TikTok: Towards an E3thnomusicological Approach to a Multimedia Musicking,' *Yearbook for Traditional Music* 54 (under review).
———. 'It's All About "Being There": Rethinking Presence and Co-presence in the Ethnographic Field During and After the COVID-19 Pandemic.' In 'Oral Traditions

and Participatory Music Practices in Times of Pandemic: Scenarios and Perspectives', Special Issue, *Journal of World Popular Music* (under review).

——. 'Virtual Musical.ly(ties): Identities, Performances, and Meanings in a Mobile Application. An Ethnomusicological Approach to TikTok Musicking'. PhD. diss., University of Vienna, 2022.

Boffone, Trevor. *Renegades: Digital Dance Cultures from Dubsmash to TikTok*. New York: Oxford University Press, 2021.

Bruns, Axel. *Blogs, Wikipedia, Second Life, And Beyond: From Production to Produsage*. New York: Peter Lang, 2008.

Bull, Michael. *Sound Moves: iPod Culture and Urban Experience*. New York: Routledge, 2007.

Cook, Nicholas, Monique M. Ingalls and David Trippett (eds.). *The Cambridge Companion to Music in Digital Culture*. Cambridge: Cambridge University Press, 2019.

DeNora, Tia. *Music in Everyday Life*. Cambridge: Cambridge University Press, 2000.

Gopinath, Sumanth and Jason Stanyek (eds.). *The Oxford Handbook of Mobile Music Studies*, Volume 1 & 2. Oxford: Oxford University Press, 2014.

Kassabian, Anahid. *Ubiquitous Listening: Affect, Attention, and Distributed Subjectivity*. Berkeley: University of California Press, 2013.

Lange, Patricia. *Thanks for Watching: An Anthropological Study of Video Sharing on YouTube*. Louisville: University Press of Colorado, 2019.

Madrid, Alejandro L. *Nor-tec Rifa!: Electronic Dance Music From Tijuana to the World*. New York: Oxford University Press, 2008.

Mendívil, Julio. *Ein musikalisches Stück Heimat: Ethnologische Beobachtungen zum deutschen Schlager*. Bielefeld: Verlag, 2008.

Quiñones, Marta García, Anahid Kassabian and Elena Boschi (eds.). *Ubiquitous Musics: The Everyday Sounds That We Don't Always Notice*. Farnham: Ashgate Publishing, 2013.

Rogers, Holly. '"Welcome to your world": YouTube and the Reconfiguration of Music's Gatekeepers'. In *YouTube and Music: Cyberculture and Everyday Life*, edited by Holly Rogers, Joana Freitas and João Francisco Porfírio, 1–38. New York: Bloomsbury, 2023.

Smudits, Alfred. *Mediamorphosen des Kulturschaffens: Kunst und Kommunikationstechnologien in Wandel*. Vienna: Braumüller, 2002.

Vernallis, Carol, Holly Rogers and Lisa Perrott (eds.). *Transmedia Directors. Artistry, Industry and New AudioVisual Aesthetics*. London: Bloomsbury Press, 2020.

Vernallis, Carol. *Unruly Media: YouTube, Music Video, and the New Digital Cinema*. Oxford: Oxford University Press, 2013.

Voithofer, Monika. '"DENKEN, HÖREN, DA CAPO": Konzeptuelle Musik im 20. und 21. Jahrhundert: Eine Studie zu Genealogie, Materialität, Form und Semantik'. PhD diss., University of Graz, 2021.

# 9

# Library Music as the Soundtrack of YouTube

Júlia Durand

'Is this stuff actually safe to use?', asks a member of a Facebook group frequented by YouTubers, referring to a music track advertised as being free to use in YouTube videos. Like many of his peers, this videographer sought first and foremost to find out how legally 'safe' it would be for him to use this track in his content. Wary of navigating the tricky waters of intellectual property and of sinking their videos with a copyright claim by using music that isn't properly licensed for online media, many YouTubers seek library music that can be specifically licensed for YouTube and other video sharing platforms of Web 2.0. Also known as stock or production music, library music is composed for future use in all kinds of media and audiovisual creations. It is currently found in online catalogues, where it is categorized by mood, emotion, instrumentation and genre, among other possibilities.[1] Traditionally, library music was mainly licensed for television broadcasting and corporate videos. However, it is also now becoming inescapable in online media: across all types of content that is tirelessly uploaded onto video sharing platforms and social networks today, from cooking lessons and makeup tutorials to travel vlogs and political commentary, more often than not we encounter the much heard – but little heard of – library music.

---

[1] Júlia Durand, '"Romantic Piano" and "Sleazy Saxophone": Categories and Stereotypes in Library Music Catalogues,' *Music, Sound, and the Moving Image* 14, no. 1 (2020): 23. See also Carlo Nardi, 'Library Music: Technology, Copyright and Authorship,' in *Issues in Music Research: Copyright, Power And Transnational Musical Processes*, ed. Salwa El-Shawan Castelo-Branco, Susana Moreno and Pedro Roxo (Lisbon: Colibri, 2012), 74.

Indeed, the industry of library music is rushing to meet the rapidly growing demand of music for audiovisuals that are exclusively disseminated online. This has initiated a slew of new licensing models, with increasingly marked differences between, on the one hand, libraries that deal with higher-end clients, such as television productions and trailers, and, on the other, those that offer so-called 'royalty-free' licences with greatly reduced prices that target online content creators such as YouTubers, Twitch streamers and Instagram influencers, among others. This new market is vastly different from the professional audiovisual producers who make up the conventional client base of the library music industry: these hobbyists and semi-professional videographers have different concerns, budgets, experiences and skill sets, as well as a limited understanding of the legal intricacies of licensing music for media.

Nevertheless, content creators such as YouTubers now represent a considerable portion of library music's users, warranting a closer look at how they interact with this music and for what purposes they include it in their videos. From full-time YouTubers to those who view their channels as a hobby, these videographers resort to library music for a variety of reasons: although some can be traced to well-established conventions in cinema and television, others are motivated by the specific constraints and dynamics of Web 2.0. In addition, the unprecedented growth of YouTubers who seek music for their videos has dramatically altered the face of the library music industry, prompting its transformation from a once relatively homogeneous field with standard practices and licences, to a far more fragmented industry with significant tensions between its competing players. Furthermore, a new type of library music has emerged in tandem with the rise of Web 2.0: tracks that are published under Creative Commons licenses and that can be freely used across online media.

This chapter surveys key developments in the production, licensing and use of library music that is targeted at video sharing platforms, chief among them YouTube. Although library music in general is finally attracting more academic attention, there is yet to be any research that specifically addresses the ways in which this music is used in online content, especially in what concerns audiovisual material created by hobbyists or semi-professionals. In order to provide a greater understanding of this phenomenon, and taking into account the growing number of individuals who interact with library music and work it into their online videos, this chapter departs from two central questions: what are the most noteworthy tendencies in how and why library music is used in YouTube videos, and what changes has this prompted in its production and licensing? An examination of YouTube content that uses library music allows us to identify old habits and strategies that have, in fact, long been present in the synchronization of music to moving images, alongside new practices that are specific to Web 2.0. Moreover, it brings to light the importance of library music's role in how YouTubers shape the meanings and messages of their videos. These lines of enquiry are best pursued with an approach that encompasses the perspectives of both library composers and the videographers who go on to use their music. I will therefore be drawing data from interviews I conducted with these different agents, as well as from a participant observation of two Facebook groups dedicated to YouTubers, carried out over a period of four years, between 2017 and 2021.[2]

## Redactive Creativity

An increasing number of authors have highlighted how cultural production and consumption in Web 2.0 is defined by an inextricable coexistence of professional and amateur creations, capitalist and gift economies, and the remix, mashup and recycling of pre-existing texts. Music and media scholars have partly based their analysis of these processes on the concept of what Henry Jenkins refers to as 'participatory culture', a theoretical perspective that is essential to an understanding of how library music comes to be used and reused in a wide range of online videos: far from being a linear transmission of a 'closed' music piece that is meant to be received 'as is' by passive consumers, library music is first and foremost regarded as a musical material that undergoes multiple transformations at the hands of audiovisual creators who have an active role in its remediation, by working it into an unpredictable variety of media and messages.[3]

Authors such as Nicholas Cook and David Hesmondhalgh have also pointed to the growing accessibility of digital tools as a vital factor in the exponential

---

[2] Interviews were based on a semi-structured script and took place in person or over video calls (the interviewees' names were here replaced by pseudonyms). Permission was obtained from the administrators of the Facebook groups to conduct participant observation, under the condition of obscuring the names of the groups and their members in a maximum cloaked situation. See also Robert Kozinets, *Netnography: Doing Ethnographic Research Online* (London: SAGE Publications, 2010), 155.

[3] Henry Jenkins, Sam Ford and Joshua Green, *Spreadable Media: Creating Value And Meaning in a Networked Culture* (New York/London: New York University Press, 2013), 2.

increase in individuals who produce and upload audiovisual content onto online platforms, stressing the ease with which such tools enable practices of collage, mashup and remix of all kinds of media.[4] The platforms of Web 2.0 thus yield an abundance of content that is based on the reshaping and repurposing of pre-existing materials, in a process that strays far from conventional notions of 'creativity' as the creation of what Miguel Mera describes as 'something from nothing',[5] and that is more closely aligned with John Hartley's concept of 'redactive creativity'.[6] Cook identifies precisely that form of creativity in the wealth of audiovisual content hosted by YouTube, seeing in the platform an epitome of 'digital participatory culture'.[7] Cook is by no means the only author who has referred to YouTube as an illuminating example of Web 2.0's cultural production: Martin Scherzinger describes it as the *locus classicus* of Web 2.0, for instance, and of the 'produsage' that many of its platforms depend on, while Hesmondhalgh and Dave Elder-Vass have pointed to the predominance of user-created videos that nevertheless increasingly intermingle with commercially-produced content.[8]

The production and use of library music on YouTube is also entangled in this interweaving of professional and amateur creation: just as YouTube videos themselves can range from highly-polished, professionally-produced videos, to ten-second clips of cats filmed with a phone camera, the library music heard in these audiovisual examples can be sourced from prestigious libraries with higher prices, newer royalty-free catalogues with more affordable licences, or even personal websites of composers who authorize the free use of their music under Creative Commons licenses. These last two licensing models are largely targeted at the ever-growing demographic of hobbyist videographers who have neither

---

[4] Nicholas Cook, 'Digital Technology and Cultural Practice,' in *The Cambridge Companion to Music in Digital Culture*, ed. Nicholas Cook, Monique M. Ingalls and David Trippett (Cambridge: Cambridge University Press, 2019), 5–28. David Hesmondhalgh, *The Cultural Industries* (London: Sage Publications, 2019). See also Helene Snee, Christine Hine, Yvette Morey, Steven Roberts and Hayley Watson, 'Digital Methods as Mainstream Methodology: An Introduction,' in *Digital Methods for Social Science: An Interdisciplinary Guide to Research Innovation*, ed. Helene Snee, Christine Hine, Yvette Morey, Steven Roberts and Hayley Watson (New York: Palgrave Macmillan, 2016), 2–3.

[5] Miguel Mera, 'Screen Music And The Question Of Originality,' in *The Routledge Companion to Screen Music and Sound*, ed. Miguel Mera, Ronald Sadoff and Ben Winters (New York: Routledge, 2017), 38.

[6] John Hartley, *Television Truths: Forms of Knowledge in Popular Culture* (London: Blackwell, 2008).

[7] Cook, 'Digital Technology and Cultural Practice,' 17.

[8] Martin Scherzinger, 'Toward a History of Digital Music: New Technologies, Business Practices and Intellectual Property Regimes,' in *The Cambridge Companion to Music in Digital Culture*, 45; Hesmondhalgh, *The Cultural Industries*, 117; Dave Elder-Vass, *Profit and Gift in the Digital Economy* (Cambridge/New York: Cambridge University Press, 2016), 493.

the budget nor the understanding of the complexities of intellectual property that would be necessary to resort to more 'traditional' libraries. It is worth noting that it is not the first time that library music has deviated from its traditionally 'business-to-business' model: Liz Czach presents a fascinating account of library albums that were marketed to individual consumers between the 1960s and 1980s with music to accompany their 'home movies', for instance.[9] These attempts were commercially unsuccessful, partly because of the difficulty of editing and synchronizing music to films in a home setting. With the expansion of digital technologies, however, the number of hobbyist video creators who use library music in their projects has now reached unprecedented levels.

The library music licences that were originally designed for television broadcasting do not transition well to the multiplatform reality of Web 2.0. Although some libraries were relatively slow in adapting to the specificities of online media, new libraries cropped up with licensing models based on a one-time payment that allows a track to be used in perpetuity in all platforms, thus addressing the unpredictability and fluidity of the circulation of audiovisual content on the Internet. In an interview I conducted with 'Bertha', a professional videographer who specializes in weddings, she criticizes what she deems to be 'archaic' library music licences that fail to take into account the profoundly uncontrollable spread of audiovisual material online. 'Bertha' professes a preference for the royalty-free library Artlist because its licences are tailored to online usage:

> [With other libraries] I'm not sure which [licence] applies to me, because they mention a number of copies and how many people will watch the video. But how can I know how many people will see it before I publish it online? What if it goes viral? I think those licences are archaic. I'm not going to show it on cinemas! And when they ask how many copies – we're not gonna burn a CD, I don't know how many copies it'll be! So it's all a bit old fashioned. In my case, my end clients are two people, and the video is for them, but it's also for the whole world when they post it online – it's really complicated. Artlist includes all those uses, posting it online, me having it in my portfolio ... I feel safer with that.

If 'Bertha', a professional videographer, claims to feel legally 'safer' with library music licences designed for online media, the same is especially true of hobbyists

---

[9] Liz Czach, 'Now – For Even Greater Enjoyment ... The Home Movie Soundtrack Album,' in *The Soundtrack Album: Listening to Media*, ed. Paul N. Reinsch and Laurel Westrup (New York: Routledge, 2020).

who are not versed in the legal intricacies of licensing music, and who are merely looking for a track to synchronize to a 'homemade' video that they will then upload onto YouTube with no (initial) intentions of monetizing it. In an episode of the podcast Synchronized!, produced for and by members of the library music industry, Alex Black, CEO of Sonoton Music, points to the swift growth of royalty-free licensing models, and the apprehension it has caused in more traditional sectors of this industry. Black claims a significant number of libraries are still focused on 'servicing the professional videomakers' needs', thereby neglecting 'newer media and newer platforms'. For Black, this inevitably puts royalty-free libraries at an advantage, for, as he states, 'there are a finite number of professionals working and choosing music in audiovisual, but there's an infinite number of hobbyists'.[10]

It is this 'infinite number of hobbyists' that has prompted the development of libraries such as the Swedish company Epidemic Sound, whose founder claimed, in a 2018 interview for *Forbes* magazine, that 'when the explosion of vlogging and online video took off (...) we created an offering for these types of storytellers too (...) and we hit the point where our music was consistently being played 20 billion times a month on videos across YouTube and Facebook'.[11] This subscription-based library is tremendously popular on YouTube, and its use by notorious YouTubers such as PewDiePie and Zoella contributes to its frequent recommendations in vlogs and online forums as a source of 'good' and 'safe' music for videos.[12] However, Epidemic Sound's business model (which pays composers a single buy-out fee for a track, but withholds subsequent royalties) is deeply controversial within the library music industry.[13] During interviews I conducted with composers, many criticized this licensing system, but a few nonetheless admitted to publishing some of their music through this or other royalty-free libraries because they deemed YouTube too vast a market to ignore. This is the case with 'Simon', who claims to have submitted a few of his tracks to a royalty-free library that primarily targets YouTubers, despite some initial reluctance:

---

[10] Simon Webb and Ferry van Beek, 'Ep. 17 With Alex Black,' *Synchronized!* (Podcast), 14 May 2021, https://podcasts.apple.com/gb/podcast/ep-17-with-alex-black/id1522203564?i=1000521706422.

[11] Alastair Dryburgh, 'Reinventing The Music Industry – Again,' *Forbes*, 3 March 2018, https://www.forbes.com/sites/alastairdryburgh/2018/03/03/reinventing-the-music-industry-again/#d068944739bb.

[12] Peter McKinnon, 'How to find MUSIC for YOUR VIDEOS!!,' *YouTube video*, 00:07:48, 2 March 2017, https://www.youtube.com/watch?v=hb0EGNVtFLc&ab_channel=PeterMcKinnon.

[13] Dan Graham, *A Composer's Guide To Library Music* (N.p.: Gothic Storm, 2018), 90.

They are royalty-free, and I was like ... 'well royalty free, I don't know about that'... [it's] a set fee for the YouTube user or whoever ... So someone goes 'yes I want to use it', and it's not like, if you're gonna show it to this many people you pay this fee, because you don't know if something will go viral, if it'll end up having millions of views... (...) So even if it's going out to a 100 different countries to be broadcast, it's still a set fee. Which sounds bad if that were the case, but the user base is more like YouTube users wanting background music.

In another interview, 'Kurt', composer and founder of a library, condemns Epidemic Sound's business model, but also criticizes the more 'traditional' sectors of the industry for, in his perspective, not adapting swiftly enough to the new demand of library music for YouTube, stating, 'They're too slow (...) you can't bury your head in the sand, you need to get to YouTube fast (...) YouTube aren't bad guys, let's try to figure out stuff that's good for everyone.' That being said, a growing number of libraries today promote their services by claiming they are specially tailored for online media – and, although their licences encompass everything from hours-long Twitch streams to one-minute TikTok videos, libraries' advertisements often expressly mention YouTube, hinting at its importance among their client base.[14]

YouTube's Content ID system has also become a recurring topic in libraries' promotional texts, with repeated assurances that their music will not cause any copyright strikes when used on YouTube. YouTuber Tim Schmoyer, whose company Video Creators offers consulting services and 'expert advice to grow YouTube channels faster', posted a video in 2015 that was sponsored by the library, Audio Blocks: in the video, Schmoyer promotes the library by presenting it as a solution to the problems that YouTubers face when the music they use is incorrectly flagged by Content ID as copyright infringement ('A common issue that goes with using music on YouTube is all the copyright issues and the Content ID, even if it's 100% your original music that you made, sometimes you still have issues with it on YouTube.[15] So that's why I've been using a site called Audioblocks. com. I have had no issues with any of their music').[16] An awareness of YouTubers' anxiety over potential issues duly or unduly caused by the Content ID system,

---

[14] We find an example of this in the royalty-free website Artlist: 'From YouTube monetization to commercial use worldwide, we've got the right plan for you.' 'Homepage,' in *Artlist*, at https://artlist.io/.
[15] 'YouTube Certified Consultant,' in *Video Creators*, at https://videocreators.com/youtube-certified-consultant/.
[16] Video Creators, 'How to Use Background Music to make Engaging Videos,' *YouTube video*, 00:08:37, 3 June 2015, https://www.youtube.com/watch?v=b3t8UTWHHek.

has thus become a significant factor in the promotional efforts of libraries, pointing to the growing interconnection between the library music industry and the specific affordances and obstacles of video sharing platforms, in particular YouTube: the more the former adapts to the latter, the greater its chances of commercial success with videographers who publish their creations online.

The categories and thematic playlists with which libraries organize their music also play a vital part in their marketing strategies to target YouTubers. Many libraries offer playlists directed at online content creators: while the titles of some are rather broad (such as a playlist called 'Vlog & Social Media' on the royalty-free library SoundStripe), others explicitly mention YouTube. For example, on the website of British library music company, Audio Network, a page called 'Playlists for YouTube Creators' presents tracks under themes such as 'Comedy', 'Fashion and Beauty', 'Food', 'Gaming', 'Kids', 'Sport & Fitness', 'Parenting', 'Tech' and 'Travel', thus covering a thorough variety of popular video genres on YouTube. Similarly, the website Stockmusic.net offers a playlist for 'YouTube instructional and how-to videos', advertising it with: 'You know those videos with no dialog you can't stop watching? Perfect music for today's modern HowTo genre.' To give yet another example, the library PremiumBeat displays a selection of tracks under the header 'Royalty-Free Music for YouTube Videos', describing it with 'No matter the genre of your YouTube video content, PremiumBeat's vast library of royalty-free music is sure to have the tracks you need to raise the volume on your viewer engagement'.[17] In some cases, the word 'YouTube' has even become a library category in and of itself: for instance, the website Icons8, under the category 'Themes', combines 'Meditation', 'News' and 'Trailer' with 'Streaming' and 'YouTube'.

In addition, many libraries have associated blogs and social media pages where they post articles with advice on how to become a full-time YouTuber, edit and promote videos, and attract more subscribers: for example, Epidemic Sound's and Artlist's blogs regularly publish articles with titles such as 'How to Create a YouTube Channel' or 'How to Make and Monetize YouTube Shorts'.[18] Unsurprisingly, such articles are part of the marketing approaches of these companies as they present library music as an indispensable element of

---

[17] 'Royalty-Free Music for YouTube Videos,' in *PremiumBeat*, at https://www.premiumbeat.com/royalty-free/music-for-youtube.
[18] 'How to Create a YouTube Channel,' in *Epidemic Sound*, at https://www.epidemicsound.com/blog/how-to-create-a-youtube-channel/; 'How to Make and Monetize YouTube Shorts,' in *Artlist*, at https://artlist.io/blog/youtube-shorts/.

YouTubers' success strategies, either by casting it as a 'safe' solution to their concerns over copyright strikes, or as a 'magical ingredient' that can instantly convey the intended emotion and message to their viewers.

Besides prompting noteworthy changes in the ways libraries produce, market and licence their tracks, the demand for library music for YouTube videos has also given rise to a phenomenon that, although not subsumed into this music industry, runs parallel to it. A growing number of composers publish their tracks on personal websites and authorize their free use in media through Creative Commons licenses (often with the sole condition of being credited as the authors of the music). In so doing, they replicate many of the distinctive characteristics of library music (such as tracks that are purposefully composed and structured for future synchronization with moving images, their categorization by mood or emotion, etc.), but the logic that governs the use of their music falls under the gift economies that coexist with capitalistic and hybrid Web 2.0 economies.

## Music For Content Creators

YouTube itself, in its Studio Area where creators can manage their channel, offers a large number of tracks in a section called Audio Library. The tracks (which are not exclusive to the library) are published with Creative Commons licenses and can be freely used in videos. Many of them are by Kevin MacLeod, a North-American composer whose free library music, as will be discussed in greater detail later, is astoundingly ubiquitous in YouTube videos. In addition to the Audio Library, YouTube hosts several channels that to all effects fulfil the same function, by aggregating music tracks that can be freely used by YouTubers (so long as their composer is credited). Some examples are the channels 'Audio Library – Music for Content Creators' and 'NoCopyrightSounds', described as 'a channel dedicated to releasing free music for the sole purpose of providing creators with the finest sounds to enhance the creativity and popularity of their content, safe from any copyright claims or infringement'.[19] Some of these channels have staggering numbers of subscribers (as of 2022, for instance, 'NoCopyrightSounds' boasts nearly 32 million subscribers), and have become go-to providers of background music for YouTubers.

---

[19] 'About', in *NoCopyrightSounds*, at https://www.youtube.com/channel/UC_aEa8K-EOJ3D6gOs7HcyNg/about.

Although some of these channels belong to a single musician and exclusively publish their tracks, others present a varied selection of pre-existing music, based on a curation process that is firstly motivated not by aesthetic criteria, but rather by the legal 'safety' of using a track in a video – in other words, whether or not its use will constitute a copyright violation. For example, the 'About' section of the channel 'Music For Content Creators' states 'We work hard to test each song to make sure it won't get a copyright claim. We find the best music that sounds good AND is free to use'.[20] These channels constitute a particularly fascinating example of how YouTube became a vital site not only of library music usage, but also of library music production and curation. The channels have no ties to library music companies (although they mirror some of their standard practices, namely with the categorization of tracks), and they specifically address the needs and concerns of YouTubers who search for music for their content. In that respect, when it comes to free-to-use music for videos, YouTube is, in a way, becoming self-sufficient, by hosting both video creators *and* those who produce or curate music for them.

Between these selections of free tracks and paid royalty-free libraries, creators are therefore well supplied with a wide variety of music that they can safely licence for YouTube videos. One source, in particular, of free library music, stands out in how profusely it has been used by YouTubers for more than a decade: the website Incompetech, founded by composer Kevin MacLeod. MacLeod's music is used so frequently in videos that it has achieved something quite rare for the usually inconspicuous library music: it has become notorious, at least among YouTubers and their audiences. The cult-following that MacLeod has earned on YouTube is perhaps best illustrated by user comments left on one of the many videos that reupload his music: 'This man literally has the power to shut down YouTube'; 'Petition to rename this video to "YouTube Official Soundtrack"'; 'This man created all of the meme Soundtracks ever known'; 'If YouTube had a soundtrack, this would be it!'; 'Nostalgia for the good ol' days when everyone used this music in Minecraft prank videos and animations'.[21]

This last comment hints at a fascinating phenomenon surrounding the use and reuse of MacLeod's music on YouTube. Some of the composer's tracks have

---

[20] 'About', in *Music For Content Creators*, at https://www.youtube.com/channel/UCRE4GJzmvJ0iziFWS6Yau_A/about.

[21] Kevin MacLeod Archive, 'Kevin MacLeod: BEST OF [Best known music by Kevin MacLeod]', *YouTube video*, 01:27:42, 7 October2015, https://www.youtube.com/watch?v=LbjcaMAhJRQ&ab_channel=KevinMacLeodArchive.

been so abundantly worked into the same type of videos, or for the same narrative purposes, that they have over time acquired specific meanings in the context of this platform, while becoming part of the editing and stylistic conventions of certain genres of YouTube videos. A clear example is that of his tracks 'Scheming Weasel' and 'Sneaky Snitch', which featured heavily in a genre of gaming content that was popular on the platform between 2010 and 2020: playing sessions in the video game Minecraft where one player pranks another. The recurring association between those two tracks and this genre of YouTube videos, more specifically with comedic sequences where players prank each other, has gradually strengthened and crystallized the tracks' meanings as being synonymous with 'sneakiness' and 'trolling' in the perspective of YouTubers: they have therefore become the sound of 'trolling' on YouTube, even finding their way to a video compilation of music called 'The Best Troll Songs'.[22] This phenomenon clearly illustrates the processes of 'redactive creativity' and remediation thanks to which these tracks, because of the actions of several YouTubers over a period of time, gain new meanings and connotations that were not necessarily intended by their composer.

Comments on the many videos that use MacLeod's music confirm the meanings these two tracks now hold on YouTube, pointing to the images and narratives with which they are typically associated, and reinforcing stereotypes that are fondly acknowledged and discussed by users of this platform. For instance, when 'Audio Library – Music for Content Creators' (one of the previously mentioned channels that curate free music for videos) reuploaded the track 'Sneaky Snitch', user comments followed two main lines: many claimed to have heard the track in several videos and to have searched for it for hours, days or even years, sometimes in order to use it in their own content ('I've been looking for this song all day, took hours to find it'; 'After many years, I have finally located this song', 'found this song after years'; 'I have been looking for this song for nearly three years, three long years!!!'); and others, in a playful tone, pointed to the track's omnipresence in Minecraft 'trolling' videos ('every Minecraft troll music'; 'every Minecraft trolling video'; 'the perfect troll gamer music lol'; 'this is always used when someone's bout to troll lmao').[23]

---

[22] PLAYBACK, 'The Best Troll Songs #1,' *YouTube video*, 00:05:05, 11 July 2015, https://www.youtube.com/watch?v=2J6y3zK2MS0&t=7s.

[23] Audio Library – Music for Content Creators, 'Sneaky Snitch – Kevin MacLeod (No Copyright Music),' *YouTube video*, 00:02:16, 15 February 2016, https://www.youtube.com/watch?v=7-rXQALDv-4.

Of course, these tracks draw on long-established Western musical conventions to evoke vague concepts such as 'mischief' and 'sneakiness', especially with the use of pizzicatos and staccato woodwinds.[24] However, the more specific meanings and connotations that they acquired, and the means and dynamics through which they acquired them, are particular to YouTube: they arose through the actions of the platform's content producers, and are reinforced by the discussions and interactions of their viewers, who at times go on to reuse the tracks in their own videos. In other words, free library tracks such as 'Scheming Weasel' and 'Sneaky Snitch', although based on familiar musical stereotypes, hold detailed meanings for YouTubers and their audiences, which emerged specifically in the context of this platform.

Therefore, if the copious use of MacLeod's tracks was initially because of the fact that they were free and easy to licence, their continued and assiduous presence in YouTube videos cannot perhaps be solely attributed to that factor anymore, especially considering that, since Incompetech's launch in 2005, plenty of other websites and YouTube channels have cropped up to provide free music for videos. None, however, have achieved the iconic status that MacLeod's tracks hold on YouTube, and which contributes to their reuse as a trope that is widely recognized by the platform's creators and viewers. Their cult following is also demonstrated by the fact that they are not merely used as background music in videos: they are also included in various music compilations, or transformed by users into a myriad of different versions, sped up, slowed down, looped and thoroughly remixed to suit every taste, from piano reductions to bombastic 'epic' orchestrations. For example, a search by 'Scheming Weasel' on YouTube yields, among many other results, a ten-hour version, several piano tutorials, electronic remixes and a heavy metal rendition. All of these illustrate the remixing culture that is so characteristic of Web 2.0's aesthetics, applied here to a free library music track that gained an unexpected notoriety on YouTube.

Interestingly, however, the immense popularity of MacLeod's music sometimes prompts YouTubers to avoid it for deeming it 'overused'. This is especially true when they look for library tracks to serve as the recurring music

---

[24] In addition, authors such as Philip Tagg and Anahid Kassabian, among others, have examined how musical formulas such as these come to acquire specific meanings throughout their frequent reuse in film and television, thus shaping a musical vocabulary that is shared by a wide audience. See Philip Tagg, *Music's Meanings: A Modern Musicology for Non-Musos* (New York: The Mass Media Music Scholar's Press, 2012); and Anahid Kassabian, 'Music, Sound and the Moving Image: The Present and a Future?', in *The Ashgate Research Companion To Popular Musicology*, ed. Derek B. Scott (Burlington: Ashgate, 2009), 43–57.

theme of their channel, and to build their distinctive sonic 'brand', turning instead to paid royalty-free libraries in order to find music that hasn't been reused too frequently. Indeed, the marketing texts of some libraries explicitly mention the usefulness of their music for YouTubers seeking to 'build their brand'.[25] This is just one of the various motives for which YouTubers use library music: some are derived from the widely theorized 'functions' of music in cinema and television, such as portraying a character or location, suggesting mood or emotion and indicating the genre and target audience of a video; whereas others are more specific to online platforms.[26]

For example, the use of library music is often presented as a strategic way of retaining viewers' attention or even altering their perception of time, making a video feel shorter than it actually is. This speaks to YouTubers' efforts of competing for attention in an increasingly saturated platform, especially given that YouTube's algorithm takes into account the amount of time that a viewer spends on videos in order to calculate several factors (such as how many view counts it will have, and who it will be recommended to). It is therefore unsurprising that this, too, is an important aspect in the promotion of royalty-free libraries that target YouTubers: '[Music] holds people's attention longer, which gets you more watch time, so your videos start performing better (...) use it strategically to hook [a] viewer and keep their attention.'[27] This ties clearly into Anahid Kassabian's remarks on the difficulties that face media makers whose revenue is based on advertising, and who therefore 'need to capture attention as their main commodity'.[28]

This notion of library music as an effective way of catching and keeping viewers' attention partly explains why it's often discussed by YouTubers in informal settings as an asset that their videos cannot dispense with. A regular observation over a period of four years of two Facebook groups where beginner YouTubers interact, reveals that library music is a frequent topic of conversation, with members of the group asking the same recurring questions to their peers: where

---

[25] 'How YouTube Analytics Can Help You Discover the Perfect YouTube Background Music for Your Videos', in *SoundStripe*, at https://soundstripe.com/blogs/youtube-analytics-helps-you-find-better-youtube-background-music.

[26] Claudia Gorbman, *Unheard Melodies: Narrative Film Music* (Bloomington: Indiana University Press, 1987), 73.

[27] Video Creators, 'How To Properly Use Background Music to Hook YouTube Viewers,' *YouTube video*, 00:08:20, 17 August 2017, https://www.youtube.com/watch?v=QuZ7TSzfDUc.

[28] Anahid Kassabian, 'The End Of Diegesis As We Know It?,' in *The Oxford Handbook Of New Audiovisual Aesthetics*, ed. John Richardson, Claudia Gorbman and Carol Vernallis (New York: Oxford University Press, 2013), xviii.

should they source library music from, how should they use it in videos and why. A few fundamental points can be gleaned from these discussions: firstly, music is seen as an easy way of adding production value to a video and making it appear more professional; secondly, as previously stated, it is recommended as a means of retaining viewers' attention; and thirdly, the most often mentioned reason by these YouTubers for using library music, it is praised for quickly setting the tone of a video and conveying its intended message. Given this view of library music as an essential tool for YouTubers, be it to polish a video or to influence its viewers' emotions, it is perhaps unsurprising that a member in one of these groups once asked their peers whether it was acceptable *not* to use music in a video.

However, most discussions around library music were based on these YouTubers' shared concern of having copyright claims on their videos. Several members report having had copyright issues after resorting to music that was supposedly free to use, and claim that the experience led them to opt for paid royalty-free libraries, such as Epidemic Sound. Members therefore frequently ask their peers for recommendations of library music that is 'safe' to use: in fact, in interactions in these groups, the word 'safe' features more prominently than other terms that might connote more aesthetic considerations in their search for library music (such as 'good' or 'quality' music). If many creators who upload videos on YouTube remain relatively unaware of the legal constraints that apply to the synchronization of music to moving images (at least until they are directly confronted with them), for others, avoiding having their video taken down or monetized by another party for copyright infringement is one of, if not the most significant criteria in their choice of music, prompting them to steer clear of any library tracks that they do not consider 'safe' for YouTube. The fact that this is a priority for many YouTubers in their selection of music indirectly determines which libraries get used the most and thereby provide a considerable portion of the 'background music' for content in this platform. The prevalence of tracks from libraries such as Epidemic Sound is therefore partly explained by the fact that its licences are fine-tuned to adapt to YouTube's monitoring of undue uses of copyrighted music, leading YouTubers to regard it as a 'safe' and 'trustworthy' source of library music – even as composers who write for more 'traditional' libraries denounce the company for what they deem to be the unethically low prices of its licences.[29]

---

[29] 'Music Authors And Performers Strongly Denounce *Epidemic Sound*'s Malpractices And Its Profound Disrespect For Their Rights,' in *ECSA*, at https://composeralliance.org/media/54-ecsa_epidemicsound.23.09.pdf.

This vital factor in how online content creators interact with library music and discuss it with their peers is specific to the context of Web 2.0's video sharing platforms. Nevertheless, as previously stated, some of the ways in which YouTubers select and wield library tracks are directly descended from old habits in film and television with which these videographers are profoundly familiar as media consumers. For example, YouTubers in the observed Facebook groups often express a view of library music as a necessary 'sonic wallpaper' for their videos that ought to be used at a low volume – loud enough to be perceptible and fill an undesirable silence, but not so loud that it will impede an understanding of the spoken voice. Comments in discussions frequently point to library music's role in 'improving a video' and in avoiding a silence that would be 'jarring', while remaining 'discreet' and 'not too noticeable'.

This rule for the use of library music is insistently pointed out by YouTubers in these groups, along with the importance of using tracks that 'suit' or 'match' the tone of a video. In that respect, it is interesting to note that YouTubers in these discussions claim they look for library music that will 'fit' or 'suit' the mood of their video, while simultaneously praising its usefulness for 'setting the tone'. This perspective is also manifested in online vlogs and articles that advise videographers on how to effectively use library music.[30] We encounter here the same contradictory terminology that has shaped both formal and informal discourse on music in cinema and television, where music is sometimes cast as both invaluable in suggesting mood or emotion (thus implying it plays a fundamental part in constructing the overall message of an audiovisual), and as merely 'fitting' what is somehow already present in the images to begin with – or, in Katherine Kalinak's words, a problematic terminology that 'assumes the image is the bearer of meaning and that music functions to modify that meaning in some way, heightening, reinforcing, or undercutting what is "in" the image'.[31]

The contradictory terms with which the role of library music in videos is discussed by YouTubers does however indicate that their understanding of this music's usefulness is strongly aligned with the functions assigned to music in mainstream Western cinema and television. A very telling example came from

---

[30] For example, 'One of the first things I learned about adding music to video was to have the music match the overall mood to characteristics of the video.' 'The Friday Roundup – Choosing Music, the Glitch Effect and Voiceovers', DIY Video Editor, https://diyvideoeditor.com/the-friday-roundup-choosing-music-the-glitch-effect-and-voiceovers/.

[31] Kathryn Kalinak, *Film Music: A Very Short Introduction* (New York: Oxford University Press, 2010), 17.

an interview I conducted with 'Bryan', whose YouTube channel specializes in videos debunking conspiracy theories. 'Bryan's' description of his use of royalty-free tracks falls into conventional functions of music in audiovisual productions that have long preceded online media, but which heavily inform the ways in which YouTubers incorporate music into their videos. 'Bryan' starts by explaining that he chooses tracks that are 'appropriate' to the video's theme and that 'suit' it, giving as an example, 'for videos with scientific themes, I use a lot of electronic music'. He also takes into account the music's potential to shape the pace of a video, stating, 'when I start talking about something more complex or exciting, or laying out my main conclusions, I switch to faster music with a more marked rhythm'. He does nonetheless end with the comment that 'the music is there to create an ambiance, but not really to be noticed'.

'Bryan' uses royalty-free music that is specifically marketed for YouTube videos, but he wields it according to typical functions of music in audiovisual productions, from the clichéd association of electronic timbres with a vague concept of 'science', to the role of music as a 'sonic wallpaper' that must remain mostly unheard, while contributing to a video's overall tone and message. YouTube videos such as 'Bryan's' may be shorter and less polished than professional productions, displaying a more jarring editing style where library tracks are predominantly treated as musical 'blocks' to be copied and pasted with abrupt cuts and transitions.[32] Despite such differences, non-professional videographers on YouTube are guided in their use of library music by a set of conventions with which they have a profound familiarity because of a lifetime of exposure to cinema, television and other audiovisual media.

YouTube hosts an astonishing variety of content with a broad spectrum of editing styles, subject matters and intents, from short films with highly-skilled post-production to barely edited videos of household pets. If there is one element that this wide array of content has in common, it is the use of library tracks by individuals who, before the advent of Web 2.0 and of digital tools of video and sound editing, did not come into contact with this type of music. The widespread popularity of video sharing platforms created a demand for tracks that could cheaply, easily and legally be licensed for online media, prompting the library music industry to expand from its traditional client base of audiovisual professionals to encompass a vast market of hobbyists and semi-professional

---

[32] For more on this, see Jean Burgess and Joshua Green, *YouTube: Online Video and Participatory Culture* (Cambridge/Malen: Polity Press, 2009), 53.

videographers with different skill sets and budgets. This new demand – which shows no signs of abating – fundamentally fragmented the library music industry into an ever-expanding number of libraries with differing prices and licences. Many of these now target online content creators, in particular YouTubers, by implementing licensing models that are better suited to the consumption and circulation of media online, but which have caused significant consternation among library composers who deem it a threat to their long-term income by lessening or outright cutting their future earnings with royalties.

In addition to the royalty-free libraries that emerged to meet the demand of YouTubers, a new type of library music arose outside the bounds of this music industry: tracks that are published under Creative Commons licenses and that can be freely used in videos. This phenomenon is indissociable from the specific practices and dynamics of cultural production across Web 2.0, with non-professional creators seeking all kinds of pre-existing material to use in their own projects. Although some of this free-to-use music is published in the personal websites of composers, increasingly we find YouTube channels that function as 'libraries' within the platform to provide YouTubers with music. The most noteworthy example of free library tracks used in YouTube videos is doubtlessly that of MacLeod: its constant reuse in certain genres of videos, the creation of remixes and alternative versions by fans, and the interactions between commenters in videos with MacLeod's music, has contributed to the meanings and connotations that some of his tracks have acquired specifically in the context of this platform. However, YouTubers who mistrust the legal 'safety' of music tracks presented as being free-to-use, opt instead for paid libraries, not necessarily motivated by aesthetic preferences, but mostly out of pragmatic considerations, chief among them the wish of avoiding future issues with YouTube's Content ID system.

That being said, whether paid for or free, library music is increasingly the go-to source of music for YouTubers: it is cast as an invaluable tool, be it to build their 'brand', retain their viewers' attention, improve the editing of their video or merely as a necessary 'sonic wallpaper' to fill an undesirable silence. The interactions of YouTubers with library music are both shaped by the new possibilities and constraints of Web 2.0, and rooted in well-established conventions: although their preference for certain libraries is tied to the audiovisual formats and legal requirements of video sharing platforms, their synchronization of music to the moving image is also informed by the typical functions of music in cinema and television. In the brave new world of library music designed and marketed specifically for YouTube videos, not everything is new: old habits and new practices converge as a growing number of YouTubers turn to library music to fashion their videos, making this often-overlooked music an inescapable and constantly remediated 'soundtrack' of YouTube.

## Bibliography

Burgess, Jean and Joshua Green. *YouTube: Online Video and Participatory Culture.* Cambridge/Malen: Polity Press, 2009.

Cook, Nicholas. 'Digital Technology and Cultural Practice.' In *The Cambridge Companion to Music in Digital Culture*, edited by Nicholas Cook, Monique M. Ingalls and David Trippett, 5–28. Cambridge: Cambridge University Press, 2019.

Czach, Liz. 'Now – For Even Greater Enjoyment ... The Home Movie Soundtrack Album.' In *The Soundtrack Album: Listening to Media*, edited by Paul N. Reinsch and Laurel Westrup, 211–28. New York: Routledge, 2020.

DIY Video Editor. 'The Friday Roundup – Choosing Music, the Glitch Effect and Voiceovers,' at https://diyvideoeditor.com/the-friday-roundup-choosing-music-the-glitch-effect-and-voiceovers/.

Dryburgh, Alastair. 'Reinventing The Music Industry – Again.' *Forbes*, 3 March 2018, at https://www.forbes.com/sites/alastairdryburgh/2018/03/03/reinventing-the-music-industry-again/#d068944739bb.

Durand, Júlia. '"Romantic Piano" and "Sleazy Saxophone": Categories and Stereotypes in Library Music Catalogues.' *Music, Sound, and the Moving Image* 14, no. 1 (2020): 23–45.

ECSA. 'Music Authors And Performers Strongly Denounce *Epidemic Sound*'s Malpractices And Its Profound Disrespect For Their Rights,' at https://composeralliance.org/media/54-ecsa_epidemicsound.23.09.pdf.

Elder-Vass, Dave. *Profit and Gift in the Digital Economy.* Cambridge: Cambridge University Press, 2016.

Epidemic Sound. 'How to Create a YouTube Channel,' 30 December 2021, at https://www.epidemicsound.com/blog/how-to-create-a-youtube-channel/.

Gorbman, Claudia. *Unheard Melodies: Narrative Film Music.* Bloomington: Indiana University Press, 1987.

Graham, Dan. *A Composer's Guide To Library Music.* N.p.: Gothic Storm, 2018.

Hartley, John. *Television Truths: Forms of Knowledge in Popular Culture.* London: Blackwell, 2008.

Hesmondhalgh, David. *The Cultural Industries.* London: Sage Publications, 2019.

Jenkins, Henry, Sam Ford and Joshua Green. *Spreadable Media: Creating Value And Meaning in a Networked Culture.* New York/London: New York University Press, 2013.

Kalinak, Kathryn. *Film Music: A Very Short Introduction*. New York: Oxford University Press, 2010.

Kassabian, Anahid. 'The End Of Diegesis As We Know It?' In *The Oxford Handbook Of New Audiovisual Aesthetics*, edited by John Richardson, Claudia Gorbman and Carol Vernallis, 89–106. New York: Oxford University Press, 2013.

Kassabian, Anahid. 'Music, Sound and the Moving Image: The Present and a Future?'. In *The Ashgate Research Companion To Popular Musicology*, edited by Derek B. Scott, 43–57. Burlington: Ashgate, 2009.

Kozinets, Robert. *Netnography: Doing Ethnographic Research Online*. London: SAGE Publications, 2010.

Mera, Miguel. 'Screen Music And The Question Of Originality.' In *The Routledge Companion to Screen Music and Sound*, edited by Miguel Mera, Ronald Sadoff and Ben Winters, 38–49. New York: Routledge, 2017.

Nardi, Carlo. 'Library Music: Technology, Copyright and Authorship.' In *Issues in Music Research: Copyright, Power And Transnational Musical Processes*, edited by Salwa El-Shawan Castelo-Branco, Susana Moreno and Pedro Roxo, 73–83. Lisbon: Colibri, 2012.

Peter McKinnon. 'How to Find MUSIC for YOUR VIDEOS!!' YouTube Video, 00:07:48. 2 March, 2017, at https://www.youtube.com/watch?v=hb0EGNVtFLc&ab_channel=PeterMcKinnon.

Scherzinger, Martin. 'Toward a History of Digital Music: New Technologies, Business Practices and Intellectual Property Regimes.' In *The Cambridge Companion to Music in Digital Culture*, edited by Nicholas Cook, Monique M. Ingalls and David Trippett, 33–57. Cambridge: Cambridge University Press, 2019.

Snee, Helene, Christine Hine, Yvette Morey, Steven Roberts and Hayley Watson. 'Digital Methods as Mainstream Methodology: An Introduction.' In *Digital Methods for Social Science: An Interdisciplinary Guide to Research Innovation*, edited by Helene Snee, Christine Hine, Yvette Morey, Steven Roberts and Hayley Watson, 1–11. New York: Palgrave Macmillan, 2016.

Tagg, Philip. *Music's Meanings: A Modern Musicology for Non-Musos*. New York: The Mass Media Music Scholar's Press, 2012.

Webb, Simon and Ferry van Beek. 'Ep. 17 With Alex Black.' *Synchronized!* (Podcast), 14 May 2021, at https://podcasts.apple.com/gb/podcast/ep-17-with-alex-black/id1522203564?i=1000521706422.

# 10

# Meme and Variations: How Video Mashups of John Coltrane's *Giant Steps* Became a Thing

Scott B. Spencer

The academic field of ethnomusicology has not been entirely successful at working with memes, or even music tied to moving image. Stemming from a historical split with the field of musicology over the location of musical culture, scholars in the field of ethnomusicology began to adopt tools from cultural anthropology (performance context, ethnography) rather than relying solely on texts (manuscripts, musical scores) for the creation of knowledge. Though my description of the fields here is both blunt and reductionist, it is worth pointing out that neither academic approach (ethnography or source studies) is set up well to delve into musical memes on YouTube, as this chapter will explore. So, here I build a case for the need to develop analytic tools through which to explore today's popular culture, though I will also end up borrowing from classic aspects of these fields as we approach the subject at hand: YouTube memes referencing John Coltrane's legendary 1960 recording, *Giant Steps* (Atlantic Records, 1960). We will find that the YouTube platform, as colloquially used, parallels the various layers of contextual, musical and social engagement inherent in the artform of jazz.

## John Coltrane's 'Giant Steps'

Before we investigate YouTube memes, it is best to understand some of the most important aspects of Coltrane's 'Giant Steps' as a composition, as well as his iconic performance on the 1960 Atlantic Records album. Coltrane, one of the towering figures of jazz saxophone and a developer of the jazz genre 'bebop' with trumpeter Dizzy Gillespie and others, was also a prolific composer of jazz pieces, and pushed the realm of jazz into new stylistic areas through many of his recordings and compositions. In 1959, Coltrane had been experimenting with a theoretic compositional style that embraced aspects of twelve-tone and modal music, and had just been working with Miles Davis on his *Kind of Blue* album (Columbia Records, 1959). Coltrane called a session for 5 May 1959 to record pieces for the upcoming album. He had assembled as an ensemble for this particular session, Tommy Flanagan on piano, Art Taylor on drum set and Paul Chambers on double bass.

In the usual fashion in jazz sessions, the musicians probably did not know in advance what pieces they would be playing that day. Legend has it that the musicians thought it would be a ballad session (slow, expressive pieces based on lyrical songs), but Coltrane instead handed them his new composition, 'Giant Steps'. The piece had a complex and incredibly difficult chordal structure (later referred to as the 'Coltrane changes') with a simple melody floating above. The chord progression was based on Coltrane's artistic interpretation of the mathematical relationships between musical scales called the 'circle of fifths', and presented his innovative systematic pathway through them.[1] Coltrane had been thinking through larger ideas of music and the human experience, and his thought experiments had often taken him deep into the roles of the musician in society (Video example 1).[2] As Ben Leubner wrote in his review of Chris DeVito's compendium of Coltrane interviews *Coltrane on Coltrane*, the composer was justified in undertaking such introspective work as a part of his compositional process, as he had ' … an unwavering confidence in the power of music and a humble self-awareness of his obligation, through his own talents, to develop and advance that power as far as he can, to touch and perhaps heal as many lives as possible by way of it.'[3] Coltrane's new work was representative of this sort of deep thought, and was not immediately approachable because of it.

[1] Rich Pellegrin spells out this complexity in a nuanced and comprehensive article 'Motive, Collection, and Voice Leading in John Coltrane's "Giant Steps"', *Jazz Perspectives* 12, no. 1 (2020): 7–49.
[2] In this piece for the animated series 'Blank on Blank', Frank Kofsky's tape-recorded interview with John Coltrane in November 1966 – recorded a year before Coltrane's death at age 40 – has recently been set to images. In it, we can hear Coltrane discussing some of the larger ideas about music and the role of the musician that he tried to convey in his compositions. Blank on Blank, 'John Coltrane on Giant Steps | Blank on Blank,' *YouTube video*, 00:04:57, 12 May 2015, https://www.youtube.com/watch?v=ZF0EvYd_Bgw.
[3] Chris DeVito (ed.), *Coltrane on Coltrane: The John Coltrane Interviews* (Chicago: Chicago Review Press, 2010); Ben Leubner, 'Coltrane on Coltrane: The John Coltrane Interviews,' *Critical Studies in Improvisation* 6, no. 2 (2010), 2.

When he composed 'Giant Steps', Coltrane placed onto his complex chord changes a melody that was more functional than lyrical. As jazz critic Nat Hentoff wrote for the album's liner notes, 'The bass line is kind of a loping one. It goes from minor thirds to fourths, kind of a lop-sided pattern in contrast to moving strictly in fourths or in half-steps.'[4] Or as pianist Tommy Flanagan later explained, 'I don't think there was any melody, just the chord sequence, which spells out the melody, practically.'[5] The melody was in service of the difficult chord progression – the opposite of most jazz pieces, in which a good melody would drive logical and expressive chording.

Again, jazz legend has it that in the recording session, Coltrane counted off the tempo for the piece – a blistering 300 BPM – and the musicians, having expected a ballad, suddenly had to dive in headfirst and scramble to keep up, as we can hear in Video example 2.[6] A jazz piece usually starts with the statement of the melody, or 'head' (often played two times), followed by a series of individual improvisations over the repeated structure of that melody, with a return to a statement of the melody just before ending the piece. In this recording, Coltrane plays the 'head' from the start of the recording to the 0:13 mark, and then repeats it, ending the repeat at 0:26. Flanagan backs him with chords (the Coltrane changes) on the piano, while Chambers plays through the changes on double bass and Taylor keeps time on the drums. After the second time through the 'head', Coltrane takes the first solo, playing immediately at a breakneck pace from the 26-second mark to 2:55 in a virtuosic series of improvisations that sticks strictly to the chordal structure and yet drives the piece forward with a fierce intensity. Tommy Flanagan is next to take a solo, and immediately is in over his head. By the 3:30 mark, he is clearly 'drowning' in jazz parlance (a term meaning floundering, or struggling to keep up), and switches back to chords to feebly end his solo at 3:44. Coltrane rushes back in with a second improvised solo, playing even more brilliantly than before from 3:44 to 4:10, wherein he returns to play the 'head', repeats it, and then ends the recording with a little outside-of-time saxophone flourish.

In jazz circles, this is one of the most revered pieces in the history of the genre – in part because of the difficulty of its chord changes (Video example 3),

---

[4] Nat Hentoff, 'Liner Notes,' John Coltrane, et al. *Giant Steps*. Atlantic Records, 1960.
[5] Lewis Porter, *John Coltrane: His Life and Music* (Ann Arbor: University of Michigan Press, 1998), 155.
[6] Jazzman 2696, 'Giant Steps,' *YouTube video*, 00:04:46, 30 September 2010, https://www.youtube.com/watch?v=30FTr6G53VU.

and in part because of the effervescent playing by John Coltrane in his improvised solos (jazz fans also love a good story, and the details behind Flanagan's botched solo is a lovely parallel narrative to this masterpiece).[7] Today's students of jazz – especially saxophone players – will transcribe, note by note, Coltrane's improvised solos on this recording as a rite of passage and as a means to better understand this important piece from Coltrane's musical perspective (Video example 4).[8] Tony Whyton, in his piece on Coltrane fandom, details this reverence for his compositions and recordings, writing that ' ... Coltrane is now firmly established as an iconic figure who reinforces the core values and mythologies of the jazz tradition ... Indeed, Coltrane's works, up to and including *A Love Supreme*, are idolized and presented as seminal and canonical.'[9]

Jazz musicians also tend to 'stand on the shoulders of giants' by quoting previous important works in their own improvisations through short referential (and reverential) homages. Predating and paralleling the 'sample' in rap and hip-hop, these short and familiar melodic lines are often dropped into an improvised solo, and function to illustrate that the soloist has 'done their homework' in learning the standard jazz repertoire, as well as to show off their cleverness and in-the-moment mental nimbleness to those listeners who are 'in the know'. This tradition of recontextualizing short referential snippets into other pieces is a hallmark of jazz, and as we will see shortly, also of meme culture.

## Meme ...

A meme is often referred to generically as a unit of cultural transmission, though in practice, today's users of social media platforms will better understand a meme as an easily-sharable short video or image, often with an intricate and fleeting web of cultural references. Most publications on memes suggest that the modern concept was inspired by the Italian geneticist L. L. Cavalli-Sforza working with biologist Marcus Feldman as they explored the idea of 'cultural

---

[7] In the Vox series 'Earworm', musicians Braxton Cook and Adam Neely discuss and demonstrate the compositional music theory behind the complex 'Coltrane changes'. Vox, 'The Most Feared Song in Jazz, Explained,' *YouTube video*,00:10:49, 12 November 2018, https://www.youtube.com/watch?v=62tIvfP9A2w.

[8] dancohen, 'Animated Sheet Music: "Giant Steps" by John Coltrane,' *YouTube video*, 00:04:51, 3 January 2007, https://www.youtube.com/watch?v=2kotK9FNEYU.

[9] Tony Whyton, 'Song of Praise: Musicians, Myths and the "Cult" of John Coltrane,' in *Popular Music Fandom*, ed. Mark Duffett (New York: Routledge, 2014), 109.

transmission and evolution'.[10] But Richard Dawkins' 1976 book *The Selfish Gene* had already presented some of the same ideas, built in part on concepts presented by George C. Williams in his 1966 book *Adaptation and Natural Selection*.[11] Elliott Oring's 1973 article 'Mimetics and Folkloristics', while also referencing Dawkins ideas, breaks down the influential factors of a meme for our purposes, while also giving us insight into its function:

> Memes are entities that can be imitated and copied, and thus constitute a new kind of replicator launching a new kind of evolution. However, they are selected for on the same basis as those first (genetic) replicators in the primeval soup – longevity, fecundity and copying fidelity. Thus, memes, like genes, are selfish and seek (again, using Dawkins' shorthand) to occupy as many brains as possible.[12]

Seeing the importance of video-based memes in my students' lives, I tried to learn about them through an emic perspective. University of Southern California student Navarro Peck walked me through the odd and often slippery history of popular memes, and the layers of referential meaning they build upon. As biologists and geneticists studying the genome of *drosophila melanogaster* (the common fruit fly) have noted, an organism that can reproduce and mutate in the course of a few days is difficult to keep up with, but also allows for quick insights and trackable trends. My field (as mentioned above) does not necessarily have the tools to actively engage with these fleeting cultural documents, as memes operate in a rather liminal space (or maybe as a non-Newtonian substance) – both as a recorded document, and as a living and changing cultural token and referent. As Steve Wixon has noted in his important article on representation in performance:

> The categories live and recorded can be usefully conceptualized in relation to their spectator-auditors (consumers). The live is characterized by the spatial co-presence and temporal simultaneity of audience and posited event. The recorded is characterized by the event's spatial absence and temporal anteriority.[13]

---

[10] Luigi Luca Cavalli-Sforza and Marcus W. Feldman, *Cultural Transmission and Evolution: A Quantitative Approach* (New Jersey: Princeton University Press, 1981).
[11] Richard Dawkins, *The Selfish Gene* (Oxford: Oxford University Press, 1976); George C. Williams, *Adaptation and Natural Selection: A Critique of Some Current Evolutionary Thought* (New Jersey: Princeton University Press, 1966).
[12] Elliott Oring, 'Memetics and Folkloristics – The Theory,' *Western Folklife* 73, no. 4 (Fall 2014): 438.
[13] Steve Wurtzler, 'She Sang Live, But the Microphone Was Turned Off: The Live, the Recorded, and the Subject of Representation,' in *Sound Theory, Sound Practice*, ed Rick Altman (New York: Routledge, 1992), 89.

In the case of memes, the 'live' and 'recorded' are in some way blurred, and the category of 'producer' should probably be added (or 'produser' as Axel Bruns writes), as the consumer is often also a producer, or at very least (as consumers 'like and share') a modifier and replicator.[14]

Recent scholars working with memes and virality have come up with various means through which one can study the digital life and human interface of a meme. Limor Shifman has theorized a more modern approach to Dawkins' initial ideas of longevity, fecundity and copying fidelity to include stages of viral dissemination, giving us tools through which to best understand a meme's circulation. 'Three main attributes ascribed to memes are particularly relevant to the analysis of contemporary digital culture: (1) a gradual propagation from individuals to society, (2) reproduction via copying and imitation, and (3) diffusion through competition and selection.'[15] Shifman goes on to suggest that the higher-level processes beyond simple propagation – imitation, repackaging, mimicry and remix – require a deeper engagement with the meme.[16] Ryan M. Milner suggests that these deeper engagements often rely on specialization in creative technologies – such as experience with and access to audio or video editing software - and that memetic responses incorporating multimodality are fundamentally more engaging:

> Multimodality – in its intense integration of word, image, audio, video and hypertext – facilitates the vibrant creative expression and conversation at the heart of memetic media. Some forms of this expression – like participating in a hashtag or uploading a photo – are widely accessible. Some forms – like Photoshopping or AutoTuning – are more specialized. Through these practices, mediated conversations are not just linguistic, or even just visual. Instead, these conversations rely on an array of communicative forms. And commentary spills out from these multiple sources.[17]

With all this in mind, I decided to approach the subject of video-based musical memes by enhancing the tools that I already have from the field of ethnomusicology: contextual research and personal ethnographic interviews, paired with the above ideas on process and circulation.[18] Together, Navarro and

---

[14] See Axel Brun's discussions on the changing role of the 'producer' and consumer in Web 2.0 in *Blogs, Wikipedia, Second Life, and Beyond: From Production to Produsage* (Bern: Peter Lang, 2008).
[15] Limor Shifman, *Memes in Digital Culture* (Cambridge Mass.: MIT Press, 2013), 18.
[16] Ibid., 19–20.
[17] Ryan M. Milner, *The World Made Meme: Public Conversations and Participatory Media* (Cambridge, Mass.: The MIT Press, 2016), 218.
[18] Though I am very much anticipating Paula Harper's forthcoming book, *Viral Musicking and the Rise of Noisy Platforms*.

I assembled a list of roughly forty video-based memes referencing John Coltrane's 'Giant Steps'. Though we noted that memes often spread through social media and person-to-person transfer, most of the longer-form video memes were hosted on YouTube. In a way, this platform is perfect for the study of musical memes, as it presents content with an upload date and account name, provides easy content links to share and facilitates a section for comment from viewers. With additional assistance from independent meme researcher Zev Spencer-Shapiro, we sorted them chronologically, and I reached out to the creators of each meme for an interview.

One of the earliest 'Giant Steps' memes, which was also the most referenced by other meme creators (and whose creator was by far the most difficult to track down) was a video entitled 'Giant Steps in C (Live)'. Originally posted on 22 January 2014, the GiantStepsInC YouTube account had posted no other content, and included no obvious means of contacting the creator. The video presented the audio of Coltrane's 'Giant Steps' with video from a different performance, but the audio had been manipulated to iron out every chord to C major – thereby rendering the Coltrane changes moot. In April 2020, the video had 475,000 views and more than a thousand comments ranging from disbelief to deep engagement with the aspects of jazz culture being referenced (Video example 5).[19] My research found mentions of 'Giant Steps in C (Live)' in various chat boards, with some extended discussions in a Facebook group called 'The Shitposting of Jazz to Come' and on various jazz subreddits.[20] With no leads on the creator, I left a hopeful note in the 'Giant Steps in C (Live)' YouTube comments with contact information, and waited.

Fortunately, Caleb Curtis saw my comment a few weeks later, and agreed to an interview on his work. Curtis is an active jazz instrumentalist working in New York City, and had made the original audio of 'Giant Steps in C (Live)' as an experiment with music manipulation software:

> I think I originally ... there are these videos that – I think it's called Major to Minor or something like that, where they're taking pop tunes or Beatles tunes and turning them minor. I found those somewhere and wanted to know how they did that – how that happened. I didn't understand what the technology was.

---

[19] GiantStepsInC, 'Giant Steps in C (Live),' *YouTube video*, 00:04:43, 22 January 2014, https://web.archive.org/web/20200408164342/https://www.youtube.com/watch?v=qTYzYpb1MY0&app=desktop.

[20] 'The Shitposting of Jazz to Come.' Facebook group: https://www.facebook.com/groups/745582758958047/.

Somehow I figured out that it was a plug-in from Zynaptiq called Pitchmap. I wanted to see what was possible. I made a handful of clips: like a whole tone version of 'Donna Lee'. Just trying to think of different things to map different melodies – like trying to map a major version of 'So What' . . . a major version of "Moanin".[21]

The Pitchmap software, created by the software company Zynaptiq, allows users to apply pitch-adjusting filters to recorded sound in much the same way that the familiar pitch-correcting software AutoTune functions for single notes (Video example 6).[22] Often used to shift songs between major keys and minor keys, Pitchmap-adjusted parodies (or recontextualizations) can be found across YouTube, with effects such as this version of Henry Mancini's 'Pink Panther Theme' (1963), which has been adjusted to a major key (Video example 7).[23]

Curtis explained that Coltrane's 'Giant Steps' was a perfect source for chordal recontextualization, and a jazz idol ripe for parody. As a jazz saxophone student in college, he 'learned the Coltrane solo on it, and spent time wrestling the progressions and trying to improvise within it. For a long time it was one of the most mysterious things.'[24] With Pitchmap software, he made a version in which every chord was ironed out to a C major, and every note of Coltrane's lauded solo was within the C major scale. Though he had been experimenting with other jazz standards and playing them to friends, Coltrane's piece 'elicited the greatest reaction. Because of course, think about it – it turns up the primary element of the song! I love the irreverence of the whole thing. There's a deep love for Coltrane and it wouldn't make this without that.'[25]

Curtis deliberately chose the most appropriate hosting site for his creation, realizing that it would have more impact if it was mapped with video (Video example 8; Figure 10.1):[26]

> I had the melody, and I had it in Dropbox – just the audio – and I sent it (in November or December 2013) to a couple of people and showed it to a couple of

---

[21] Personal interview with Caleb Curtis, 11 October 2019.
[22] Production Expert, 'Zynaptiq Pitchmap Review', *YouTube video*, 00:07:02, 16 November 2013, https://www.youtube.com/watch?v=O6T0S2D1dBU.
[23] Oleg Berg, 'Pink Panther Theme in Major Key', *YouTube video*, 00:02:14, 25 June 2013, https://www.youtube.com/watch?v=2BkEorFwJGg.
[24] Personal interview with Caleb Curtis.
[25] Ibid.
[26] Guillermo Arriagada R., 'John Coltrane Quartet – Impressions,' *YouTube video*, 00:14:05, 8 February 2013, https://www.youtube.com/watch?v=03juO5oS2gg.

people, then it started to make its way around. And then I was like, I want to be able to see what happens, how many times it gets listened to or whatever. I thought it would be funny to put a video to it. So I found a video from (John Coltrane's composition) '*Impressions*' and it was sort of a similar tempo, and so I downloaded the video of '*Impressions*' and threw it into Final Cut or Premier or something and started to try to edit. I spent an hour trying to make it look like they were playing – to try to line up the breath when Coltrane was breathing, and make the ride cymbal look sorta like it was right. I didn't want it to be on Vine, or a personal YouTube channel, because I just want attribution – I didn't want to incur anyone's wrath. I didn't want the attention if there was any kind of copyright issue.[27]

The jazz world and meme world overlapped in their reactions – with responses coming in the form of criticisms and applause on message boards, and uploads of video responses in the form of informed memes. Jazz purists called the piece

**Figure 10.1** Caleb Curtis' 'Giant Steps in C [Live]', originally uploaded to YouTube on 22 January 2014. Curtis edited historic footage from a performance of Coltrane's 'Impressions' to fit his chordal parody of Coltrane's 'Giant Steps', 'Giant Steps in C [Live]' (18 March 2022).

---

[27] Personal interview with Caleb Curtis.

everything from 'an abomination' to 'pure genius', while many tried to figure out who had posted the video – and why.[28] One video response that immediately stood out was in the form of a transcription of the 'Giant Steps in C (Live)' melody and solo – something that a jazz performer would do with any iconic Coltrane piece (Video example 9; Figure 10.2).[29] Curtis kept an eye on the responses, mentioning that:

> I love it when they think they know my motivations for it. There are a couple of things that happened that just bring me so much joy. The first one was the transcription. It's a scrolling video of the solo with the chord changes – a sendup of what everyone is doing, except with a C over every bar.[30]

He is still amazed that the video has had so much attention, especially as the videos he has posted in his personal YouTube account – many featuring his own performances on saxophone and trumpet – have had drastically fewer views:

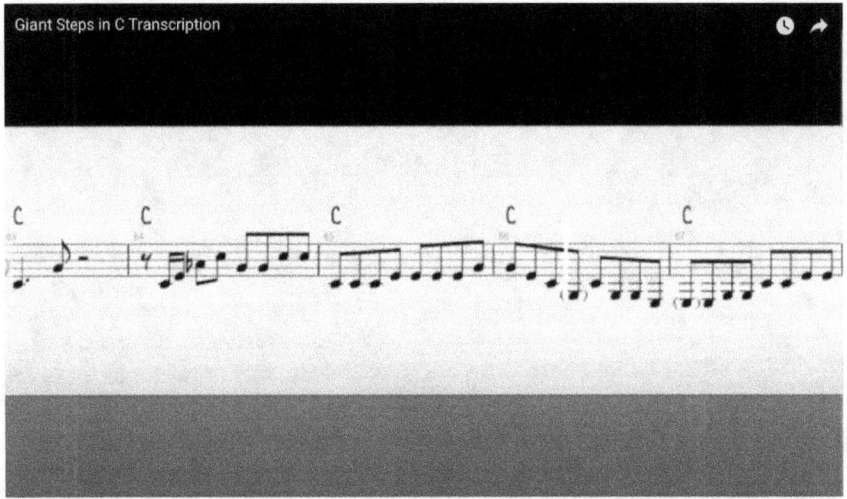

**Figure 10.2** Kaz Takasugi uploaded his 'Giant Steps in C Transcription' to YouTube on 1 January 2016. The single chord transcription is a sendup of a deep rite of passage in jazz – transcribing every note of an improvised Coltrane solo to understand its complexity, 'Giant Steps in C Transcription' (1 January 2016).

---

[28] GiantStepsInC, 'Giant Steps in C (Live)'..
[29] Kaz Takasugi, 'Giant Steps in C Transcription,' *YouTube video*, 00:02:57, 1 January 2016, https://www.youtube.com/watch?v=vPFh5_hTM28.
[30] Personal correspondence with Caleb Curtis, 11 October 2019.
[31] Ibid.

I was just fucking around. It was funny, and I realized that it might have some legs to it, and so I made it more available, and then just watched it go. I don't aspire to have 500,000 views on my videos. It would be nice, but it's not something I'm trying to design. And so it's sort of funny and interesting to see it do it on its own, with no effort.[31]

## ...And Variations

Curtis had sent his audio version around to friends more than a year before posting it with video on YouTube on 22 January 2014. With the enthusiastic discussions and comments on 'The Shitposting of Jazz to Come' Facebook page and elsewhere, a number of video responses began popping up, and the meme took off. We will be looking at those responses in a moment, but must mention two outlier videos first.

Brad Smith had posted a Nintendo Entertainment System (NES) transcription version of 'Giant Steps' almost two years before Curtis' 'Giant Steps in C (Live)'. The sound is distinctive to eight-bit music, as was used in video gaming consoles with low processing speed and memory – especially Nintendo systems. Smith uploaded to YouTube an NES version of 'Giant Steps' on 25 November 2012, complete with transcribed and recreated saxophone and piano solos (Video example 10).[32] Smith noted that he had come from both a jazz and computer science background, mentioning that 'yes you could call me a jazz fan. I played trombone in jazz bands throughout high school and university. At university I studied music and computer science'.[33]

His original idea was to transcribe the piece, and potentially use the transcription to generate similar version of Coltrane's solo through applied AI:

> I like to transcribe music, either to learn about it or learn how to play it. 'Giant Steps' seemed like a fun challenge; a little bit unusual compared to other transcriptions I had done before. The great density of notes, but also their strange uniformity made it a bit unique. I transcribed a lot of it sometime around 2002, and wondered if I could make a computer generate endless/infinite variations of that solo. I put a pin in that idea for a rainy day.[34]

---

[32] Brad Smith, 'Giant Steps – NES,' *YouTube video*,00:04:43, 25 November 2012, https://youtu.be/i5vyQO81qNc.
[33] Personal correspondence with Brad Smith, 16 September 2019.
[34] Ibid.
[35] Ibid.

Returning to it later, he incorporated the transcription into a project involving the Nintendo sound:

> A decade later I had become interested in the NES, and had been experimenting with programming games and demos and music for it. I remembered that idea I'd had for 'Giant Steps' and figured it could fit on the NES. I went back and finished my transcription, getting the bass and that very important and delicate piano solo as well, and then I wrote the NES program to play it.[35]

Smith does not think that his project fits into the recent history of 'Giant Steps' memes. He noted that 'Well, the question of it being a recent meme is not really my story', and suggested that many of the people who became interested in the phenomenon may have done so through exposure to the Vox video with Braxton Cook and Adam Neely (mentioned above), which was published on 12 November 2018.[36]

Another outlier video was created by Ilja Reijngoud, and references both 'Giant Steps' and the disco supergroup The Bee Gees (Video example 11).[37] Reijngoud's video, entitled 'Giant Steps Bee Gees' was uploaded to YouTube on 21 January 2014 – the day before 'Giant Steps in C (Live)'! Paralleling the comments by Curtis above, Reijngoud's video had more success than his other more 'serious' jazz videos:

> The funny thing is that I recorded this 'Giant Steps Bee Gees' thing as a joke. I even sang the vocals myself and played a one-take simple trombone solo over it. And shortly after that it became quite popular on YouTube (at least it had more success than my regular recordings as a jazz trombone player on YouTube .... haha).[38]

Many of the video memes that referenced 'Giant Steps' began to spring up in 2018, and often referenced other trends in meme culture. Diane Wong's 'Giant Step (Dubstep Remix)' was posted to YouTube on 29 March 2018, and referenced both the moon landing and the electronic dance music (EDM) subgenre called dubstep (Video example 12).[39] Wong mentioned that she made the video for her Electronic Writing & Production class while in music school. 'I did this mainly

---

[36] Ibid.
[37] Ilja Reijngoud, 'Giant Steps The BeeGees,' *YouTube video*, 00:01:04, 21 January 2014, https://youtu.be/wHV6gMLZkmY.
[38] Personal correspondence with Ilja Reijngoud, 16 September 2019.
[39] Wong Diane, 'Giant Step (Dubstep Remix),' *YouTube video*, 00:02:45, 29 March 2018, https://youtu.be/hDsIYGdYGps.
[40] Personal correspondence with Diane Wong, 17 September 2019.

because I had to do a dubstep project, and I thought of doing Giant "step" and included one small "step" – just as a joke and to have some fun with my assignment. Haha.'[40]

Wong even included in her video some footage from the 'Impressions' video that Curtis had used in creating his 'Giant Steps in C (Live)' video. Wong knew that 'Giant Steps' was an iconic tune in jazz circles, and though she didn't personally identify with it, she realized its potential for satire.

> It definitely was a tune that people talked about in harmony classes and like a staple tune that you would learn if you are a jazz musician – and thus some inside joke among music college students, I think, to poke fun at. I myself was not a performance major, so not as much of a mountain for me to climb personally.[41]

Ian Ostaszewski was not a stranger to mashups when he created 'Giant Steps/ Work', which was uploaded to YouTube on 15 January 2019. He noted that 'I'd definitely seen some similar videos and stuff like that before. I love mashups and I've made a lot of them.'[42] Ostaszewski combined the Coltrane changes with Rihanna's 'Work' (2016) to make a recontextualized mashup (Video example 13).[43]

> So I was just inspired by edits like these because I thought they were hilarious and wanted to try doing something similar. I'm not sure where I specifically got the idea for 'Work/Giant Steps', the only thing I can remember is one day I randomly noticed how the melody phrases are a little similar – the way 'Work' repeats the same word five times and 'Giant Steps' has five notes followed by a slight pause. That's when I realized I could just combine them, overlay one song with the other because it might be surprising and funny.[44]

Even pianist Tommy Flanagan did not escape meme attention, as the video entitled 'Tommy Flannagan [sic] Solos on Giant Steps (Rare Footage)' was uploaded to YouTube on 20 May 2018 (Video example 14).[45] In this piece, the creator uses images from the Japanese manga *Golden Boy* (a static visual meme in itself), while depicting Flanagan 'drowning' during his solo during the classic

---

[41] Ibid.
[42] Personal correspondence with Ian Ostaszewski, 16 September 2019.
[43] Ian Ostaszewski, 'Work by Rihanna but it's Giant Steps by John Coltrane,' *YouTube video*, 00:00:31, 15 January 2019, https://youtu.be/oqmVs2Orb-0.
[44] Personal interview with Ian Ostaszewski.
[45] andyydna101, 'Tommy Flannagan Solos on Giant Steps (Rare Footage),' *YouTube video*, 00:00:44, 20 May 2018, https://youtu.be/subUre6o_Qk.
[46] It is worth noting here that this article does not take on the rich and nuanced area of visual imagery

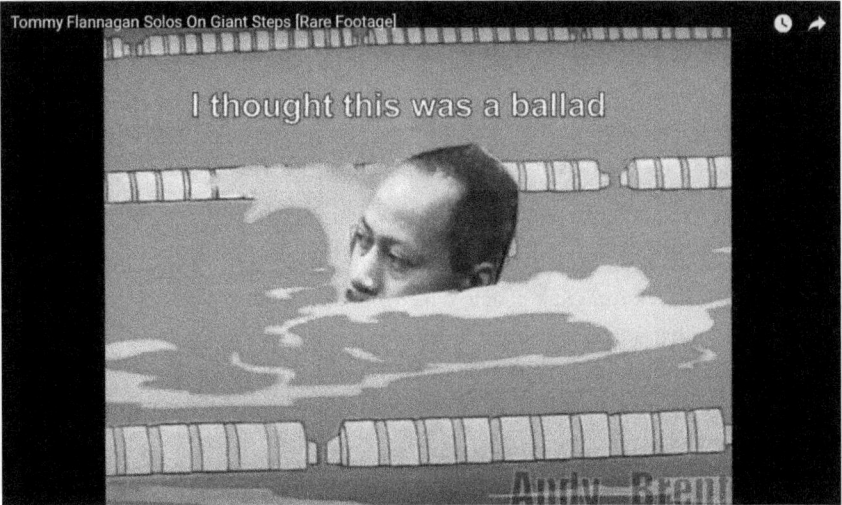

**Figure 10.3** A mashup of Tommy Flanagan's piano solo on 'Giant Steps' with images from the popular manga 'Golden Boy', uploaded to the YouTube account andyydna101 on 20 May 2018. Andy Brent plays on the jazz term 'drowning' (not being able to keep up) in the classic session where Flanagan had thought he would be recording slower and more esoteric ballads, 'Tommy Flannagan Solos On Giant Steps [Rare Footage]' (21 May 2018).

1959 recording session (Figure 10.3). Surrounding the floundering Flanagan are the other members of the ensemble, with Coltrane himself blowing a saxophone mouthpiece reframed to look like a lifeguard's whistle. At one point in the video, the words 'I thought this was a ballad' scroll past, indicating that the creator is steeped in jazz lore and the specific history of the 'Giant Steps' recording session. The visual references in this piece also mark an intersectional moment between jazz and meme worlds, as iconic images from *Golden Boy* are paired with homages to iconic instrumentalists.[46]

As meme culture began to drive video postings on the theme of 'Giant Steps' or the Coltrane changes in 2019, heady mashups became the predominant genre in uploads. Jasper Swunk quickly created and posted at least nine relevant videos – from a Baroque harpsicord performance with the 'Giant Steps' chord progression, to a mashup with the popular earworm 'Baby Shark' (Video example

in meme culture, as that could fill an entire book by itself!
[47] jasperiscool, 'Funky Swunk – Baby Steps,' *YouTube video*, 00:01:20, 28 February 2019, https://youtu.

15).⁴⁷ Swunk was very aware of trends in popular culture, and decided to take on 'Giant Steps' as the basis for a number of his projects:

> I heard the rumour about 'Giant Steps' being hard to play in a book. I think it was at that time that I rolled in the Facebook group 'the Shitposting of Jazz to Come', where 'Giant Steps' slowly became popular as a reference, which re-sparked my interest. With all the shitposting I got pieces of information about how to interpret the changes and I started practising the chords, now with some harmonic context.⁴⁸

Swunk had seen Curtis' work (among many others), and decided to try his hand at reworking another popular earworm for laughs:

> Somehow 'Giant Steps in C (Live)' grabbed my attention about then. I guess that must have been the moment I felt the urge to take 'Giant Steps' and do all sorts of things with it, just 'for the lolz'. And suddenly the popular meme was 'Baby Shark', turning up everywhere. Every Facebook music group, every discord guild, every classroom in elementary school ... It was the Rick Roll of the month I guess.⁴⁹

By 2019, 'Giant Steps' memes quickly took a strange turn and began to splinter into videos referencing multiple other parallel memes. Examples of this would include 'John Coaltrain – Thomas the Giant Engine (Rare) (1962)' posted to an account named The Cursed Recordings of the Spirit of Jazz (Figure 10.4), or Simon Fransman's 'Katy Perry's "Giant Steps" but it's John Coltrane's "Roar" but it's smooth jazz' in which the chords of Katy Perry's 'Roar' (2013) are transmogrified into the Coltrane changes, while also being recontextualized as smooth jazz (Video example 16).⁵⁰ Memes referencing 'Giant Steps' from this moment on seem to be reaching to meme culture for laughs and recognition, rather than to the jazz world. Many can be viewed on the accompanying YouTube playlist, though I personally advise you to restrain yourself.

---

be/fyPVSQBkVmM.
⁴⁸ Personal correspondence with Jasper Swunk, 23 September 2019.
⁴⁹ Ibid.
⁵⁰ Simon Fransman, 'Katy Perrys "Giant Steps" but it's John Coltrane's "Roar" but it's smooth jazz,' *YouTube video*, 00:01:28, 17 January 17 2019, https://youtu.be/0WiINuiVm6o.
⁵¹ Personal interview with Caleb Curtis.

**Figure 10.4** The musical theme from Thomas the Tank Engine set to the Coltrane changes was uploaded to the YouTube account 'The Cursed Recordings of the Spirit of Jazz' on 13 November 2016, 'John Coaltrain – Thomas the Giant Engine (Rare) (1962)' (13 November 2016).

# Coda

Meme culture, satire and parody are contextual, and are not always fully understood outside of their bounded ecosystem or echo chamber. Caleb Curtis mentioned a moment in which his 'Giant Steps in C (Live)' returned to him in a rather surprising fashion, giving light to non-contextual misunderstandings and the secret lives of memes. 'I was a guest on a concert. After I got off (stage) I had a message from a buddy of mine, and he said "Have you seen this?" and sent me this clip from Facebook.'[51] His friend had sent him a clip from an Italian documentary on jazz, in which the narrator was discussing the difficult chord changes in John Coltrane's 'Giant Steps', and playing video from 'Giant Steps in C (Live)' (Video example 17).[52]

> To be totally honest, I was done with the gig, and I got a little stoned, and I was like 'Is this real life?' I found out that what they were talking about in the clip was

---

[52] Scott Spencer, 'Giant Steps Italian Documentary,' *YouTube video*, 00:00:55, 17 March 2022, https://youtu.be/cRqiRl_1SUo.
[53] Personal interview with Caleb Curtis.

his harmonic innovation, and how important Coltrane changes are in jazz. I imagine the producer was like 'Go get me video of "Giant Steps". And there isn't video of 'Giant Steps' – there's really only that recording – from the record. I was not sure what I was seeing, because it was so bizarre. It was so far from anything I could have imagined. It had travelled over there and someone had gotten it and just because I called it 'Giant Steps in C (Live)'. I was totally taken aback. This exposed their deep ignorance on the topic.[53]

Curtis' creation, 'Giant Steps in C (Live)' was removed from YouTube in 2021. The original post is currently marked with 'Video unavailable. This video is no longer available due to a copyright claim by Michael B. Frisch' (Video example 18).[54] My research shows that Michael B. Frisch is a partner with the law firm Herbsman, Hafer, Weber & Frisch, LLP, an intellectual property firm based in New York City.[55] At the time of writing, my enquiries to Mr. Frisch and the firm remain unanswered.

## Flourish

YouTube has recently become a repository for layers of cultural knowledge, giving researchers the resources to puncture through strata of static documents in an attempt to contextualize certain moments in a dynamic popular culture. Academia has to play catch up to new developments, and so we must constantly recalibrate our existing research and analytic tools to adjust to the needs of any new use of media. A means to explore musical memes could, as demonstrated here, include a thorough media archaeology paired with a more fluid ethnographic approach to find glimpses of process and influence; meaning; timelines; personal agency and impact. But, a digital repository is inherently in flux: an important post may be removed, and the string of cultural referents would then be broken. But would the contemporaneous performativity of having posted then be rendered historically and culturally moot? Would a jazz player who quotes obscure tunes be irrelevant?

Jazz as an artform has a long history of performative riffing; improvisation and referencing; quotation and recontextualization; posturing, satire and

---

[54] YouTube. 'Video Unavailable,' at https://www.youtube.com/watch?v=qTYzYpb1MY0&app=desktop.
[55] Herbsman, Hafer, Weber & Frisch, LLP https://musiclaw.com.
[56] Damon R. Young. 'Ironies of Web 2.0,' *Post45* 2 (2019), at https://post45.org/2019/05/ironies-of-

positioning – all as a means for personal expression and placement in the history of the genre. Memes function as a similar form of cultural curation and personal performance, perfectly suited to today's creative climate and enabled by the ever-presence of technology and ease of access to and interaction with primary source documents. As Damon R. Young writes in the article 'Ironies of Web 2.0':

> For the idealist, the technologies of Web 2.0 embed a certain democratic potential, turning authorship into an open category and inviting a mode of reading that can participate in the revision of the text (as on Wikipedia), its evaluation ('thumbs up' or 'thumbs down') and an active responsiveness through the comments threads that are arguably Web 2.0's most ubiquitous feature.[56]

However, memes seem to live lives of their own, reproducing and mutating like laboratory fruit flies in a hotbox of interconnected media.

In jazz, the roles of performer, audience and reviewer have always been strictly separated – delineated by stage, seat and published critique. In YouTube meme culture, these roles have all been wrapped into one platform. Jazz-like riffing, referencing, improvisation, criticism and commentary are now all supported on a public platform in which culture is consumed and passed in our feverish and fleeting lacuna of tiny attention spans and ever-shifting digital spotlights.

## Bibliography

Cavalli-Sforza, Luigi Luca and Marcus W. Feldman. *Cultural Transmission and Evolution: A Quantitative Approach*. Princeton University Press, 1981.
Coltrane, John, et al. *Giant Steps*. Atlantic Records, 1960.
Curtis, Caleb. Personal interview with the author. 11 October 2019.
Davis, Miles, et al. *Kind of Blue*. Columbia Records, 1959.
DeVito, Chris (ed). *Coltrane on Coltrane: The John Coltrane Interviews*. Chicago: Chicago Review Press, 2010.
Leubner, Ben. 'Coltrane on Coltrane: The John Coltrane Interviews.' *Critical Studies in Improvisation* 6, no. 2 (2010): https://www.criticalimprov.com/index.php/csieci/article/view/1312/1904.
Oring, Elliott. 'Memetics and Folkloristics – The Theory.' *Western Folklife* 73, no. 4 (2014): 432–54.

web-2-0/.

Ostaszewski, Ian. Personal correspondence with the author, 16 September 2019.
Pellegrin, Rich. 'Motive, Collection, and Voice Leading in John Coltrane's "Giant Steps".' *Jazz Perspectives* 12, no. 1 (2020): 7–49.
Porter, Lewis. *John Coltrane: His Life and Music*. Ann Arbor: University of Michigan Press, 1998.
Reijngoud, Ilja. Personal correspondence with the author. 16 September 2019.
Smith, Brad. Personal correspondence with the author. 16 September 2019.
Swunk, Jasper. Personal correspondence with the author. 23 September 2019.
Whyton, Tony. 'Song of Praise: Musicians, Myths and the "Cult" of John Coltrane.' *Popular Music Fandom*, edited by Mark Duffett, 107–24. New York: Routledge, 2014.
Williams, George C. *Adaptation and Natural Selection: A Critique of Some Current Evolutionary Thought*. Princeton: Princeton University Press, 1966.
Wong, Diane. Personal correspondence with the author, 17 September 2019.
Wurtzler, Steve. 'She Sang Live, But the Microphone Was Turned Off: The Live, the Recorded, and the Subject of Representation.' In *Sound Theory, Sound Practice*, edited by Rick Altman, 87–103. New York: Routledge, 1992.

# 11

# 'Spinning Straw Into Gold': Nacho Video and the Exquisite Corpse of Fan-editing

Lisa Perrott

> 'Nacho is a magician, pulling Bowie gems from the vault for all of us to enjoy,'[1]

'Doing it, doing it right,' croons David Bowie.[2] That distinctive voice, the familiar sound of soul music, grainy black-and-white film footage – all combine to trigger a massive dose of nostalgia. Sucked into the vortex of YouTube, I'm transported to a rehearsal at a Los Angeles Studio in 1974. But this is not a typical video of an American soul band rehearsing. Ava Cherry, Robin Clark and Luther Vandross are grooving alongside a skeletal figure with blonde hair and translucent skin. This unlikely image looks wrong, yet it feels so right. Singing 'taking it all the right way, keeping it in the back', Bowie's voice slides effortlessly from baritone to falsetto and somewhere in-between. Notoriously establishing himself as the artist who invented 'plastic soul', Bowie may look like a white alien, but his vocal and lyrics fit seamlessly with the sound and feel of 1970s African-American soul music.[3]

Watching this video on Nacho Video's YouTube channel only a few months after Bowie's death in 2016, I wondered if someone had unearthed a long-lost official video for a song that was shamefully omitted from Bowie's audiovisual catalogue. Or was I watching a remnant of *cinéma verité*, stitched together by a

---

[1] Comment from YouTube user Pleasant Valley Picker CA to Nacho Video, 'David Bowie | John, I'm Only Dancing | Promo | Unreleased Mick Rock Outtake Footage Re-edit | 1972,' *YouTube video*, 00:02:54, 5 March 2017, https://www.youtube.com/watch?v=adhFZr6VDes.
[2] See the YouTube playlist for this chapter.
[3] For more on this, see: Simon Mashaun, '"Plastic Soul": David Bowie's Legacy and Impact on Black Artists,' *NBC News*, 12 January 2016, https://www.nbcnews.com/news/nbcblk/plastic-soul-david-bowie-s-legacy-impact-black-artists-n494241.

fan who'd stumbled across a secret vault filled with archive footage? Seemingly rekindled out of Bowie's ashes, Nacho's fan-made video for 'Right' (1975) fills a gap in the *oeuvre* of publicly available Bowie videos.[4] Although the online collection of videos is extensive, there's never been an officially released music video to accompany any of the songs on Bowie's 1975 studio album, *Young Americans*. Generating the satisfaction of stumbling upon a freshly excavated relic, Nacho's archive video for 'Right' provides fans with a privileged peek behind the scenes of a momentous recording session. It also reveals a unique process of collaboration and the birth of a new form of soul music. Although Bowie fans may have seen fragments of this footage in the documentaries *Cracked Actor* (1975) or *David Bowie: Five Years* (2013), this footage had not previously been available in the form of a coherent music video.[5] Nacho's video for 'Right' was received by grieving Bowie fans as a magical gift from the vault. Inspired by my first experience of a Nacho video, I became an instant YouTube fan of this Bowie fan.

This story of my discovery and appreciation for Nacho's videos is incomplete without acknowledging that not only am I a fan of Nacho, I am a long-term Bowie fan who accidentally became an 'aca-fan' – an academic whose research includes examining the artistic and cultural contributions of Bowie, along with other subjects of my fandom.[6] Although academics have debated the legitimacy and value of researching from the subjective position of fandom, I argue that such a position can contribute a unique perspective and a richness of engagement. As we shall see, this is similar to the type of unique contribution that Nacho is also able to make as a fan with integrity, commitment and connections. But his repurposing projects are not without challenges, and they raise questions about the role of fans in relation to creative integrity and authorship. This chapter examines how such processes play out across a selection of Nacho's videos, while allowing his words to open a window in to the broader issues related to 're-presenting' the work of dead musicians, music video directors and filmmakers on YouTube.[7]

---

[4] Nacho Video, 'David Bowie . Right . Promo [Take Four] . 1975,' *Nachovideos.com*, 00:04:38 (n.d), https://www.nachosvideos.com/bowie-videos.

[5] *Cracked Actor* (1975) [documentary film]. Director Alan Yentob, United Kingdom: BBC; *David Bowie: Five Years* (2013) [documentary film]. Director Francis Whately, London: BBC.

[6] The term 'aca-fan' refers to an academic who is undertaking scholarly research focused on the object of their fandom. For more on this, see: Henry Jenkins, 'Confessions of an aca-fan,' *Henry Jenkins*, 22 October 2011, http://henryjenkins.org/blog/2011/10/acafandom_and_beyond_will_broo_1.html.

[7] Nacho, Interview by Lisa Perrott, 23 September 2022. I would not have been able to write this chapter without the generous input of Nacho.

By 2022, Nacho had established a popular YouTube channel exhibiting numerous remastered and re-edited Bowie videos, along with several videos featuring the work of other musicians. Although the YouTube channel description says he's 'just a fan, making videos for other fans', his playlists are titled 'Bunnymen Chronology' and 'A Batch of My Best Bowie's'. Apart from these artists, his channel features repurposed videos for his favourite bands, such as Roxy Music, Joy Division, The Clash, Iggy Pop, Kraftwerk, Wilco, Simple Minds and The Verve.

At the time of writing this chapter, Brett Morgen's newly released film, *Moonage Daydream* (2022) was triggering vigorous debate among the most ardent of Bowie fans, and some suggested that Nacho could have done a better job if he had directed such a film. After contributing a comment about this on social media, I was fortunate to secure an interview with the enigmatic 'magician' known as Nacho Video.[8] Looking at the photo on his website, I was wrong to assume I'd be zooming with a hooded and secretive Banksy-esque figure.[9] With a warm smile and humble demeanour, Nacho explained the story behind his pseudonym. His mysterious online persona creates intrigue and maintains separation from his private life. Out of respect for his privacy I won't divulge his real name, but will note that Nacho is a British video editor and yoga teacher living in Hong Kong. After teaching his early morning yoga class, Nacho spends the remainder of his day working on video-editing projects, described by him as 'research and restoration and creation of archive music videos'.[10] Although a small portion of these projects are commissioned projects, much of Nacho's time is spent working on his own fan-made video-editing projects for which he receives no payment. He's now a well-respected figure within a community of fans who re-purpose, restore and re-edit videos and other archive materials pertaining to the musicians they admire. Despite uploading their videos to a variety of Internet platforms, websites and social media pages, many of these fan video editors rely predominantly on YouTube as a platform to share their videos. Those who share their re-edited videos using footage of dead musicians face

---

[8] Ibid.
[9] Banksy is an elusive street art activist who had become an international icon because of the subversive and secretive nature of his public art works. For more on this, see: Will Ellsworth-Jones, 'The Story Behind Banksy,' *Smithsonian Magazine* 2013, http://www.ribar.com/UserFiles/2m-2015.pdf.
[10] Nacho Video, correspondence with Chuck Braverman. Nacho Video, 'David Bowie | Young Americans | Remastered U.S. TV Ad | 1975,' *YouTube video*, 00:00:44, 25 September 2016, https://www.youtube.com/watch?v=kjh25cgnpFk.

particular challenges, such as accessing archive materials, ethics around assemblage processes and perceived copyright infringements. In the face of such challenges, some editors have responded collaboratively and creatively in order to keep their practice alive. For Nacho, keeping his practice alive is entangled with the process of reinvigorating the buried and neglected archival footage of various artists. Bowie is a key inspiration in terms of collaborative assemblage, and the sense I get from Nacho's work is that life emerges from death. This chapter examines how such processes play out in Nacho's videos, while allowing his words to open a window in to the broader issues related to 're-presenting' (as he describes it) the work of dead musicians, music video directors and filmmakers on YouTube.[11]

## Out Of The Ashes

> After Bowie died. I was just sort of dabbling, I discovered a love for video editing … In the beginning it was part tribute. It was a desperate need to join the worldwide suffering or whatever we were going through … I don't think I set out to make a tribute video.[12]

Though he'd been a Bowie fan since he was a child, Nacho had lost interest during the eighties and hadn't listened to his music for a long time. Seemingly, by some force of divine intervention or 'the universe that gave me this blessing', Bowie's death in 2016 triggered a chain of events that led to Nacho becoming a video editor with his own YouTube channel.[13] Out of the ashes of Bowie, his fandom was rekindled, and he was about to find his calling. Finding himself mesmerized by the 1974 section of the documentary *David Bowie: Five Years* (2013), Nacho recalls 'when I saw that footage it was that Eureka moment, oh f---, this could *be* something':

> It was like, they're singing 'Right' and that's one of my favourites … I chucked it into iMovie, erased the sound, got the album track, started moving things around. And I was like wow, I could almost make a promo video! At the end of the day I'd made quite a respectable video. The ideas had somehow come *to* me rather than *from* me. So that's how it started, it was just a kind of accident. It was

---

[11] Nacho, Interview by Lisa Perrott.
[12] Ibid.
[13] Ibid.

that grief pouring through me, but it was an accident. When that 'Right' video kind of rolled itself out, especially at the end, and that beautiful thing when Bowie's singing 'never need no', you know it's so beautiful, and then I found a way that I could ... although he's not saying those words, you know he's, you feel that he's kind of thinking them or directing the session.[14]

This concluding section of his video for 'Right' exemplifies what Nacho does really well. The inserted footage creates the impression that Bowie is processing the lyrics and directing the band from the side-line as they rehearse (Figure 11.1). A closer look reveals that, although eclipsed by Luther Vandross, Bowie is there in the footage of the rehearsing band, so he couldn't have been in two places at once (Figure 11.2). Despite this potential to rupture verisimilitude, the cross-cut footage works remarkably well. Bowie had once described this aspect of the song as a type of 'mantra'.[15] According to Nicholas Pegg, the sonic call-and-response between the backing singers and Bowie 'lends an air of immaculate sophistication to the lyric's paean to positive thinking'.[16] Nacho's cross-cutting method of editing visually mimics the vocal call-and-response that underpins the song. But the video is also extraordinary for the way it merges music video aesthetics with a *vérité* documentary style to create a hybrid audiovisual form with a time travelling dimension. Nacho's video achieves something akin to Peter Jackson's TV mini-series *The Beatles: Get Back* (2021), an officially recognized, award-winning example of a fan re-edit of archive footage.[17] Although differing in terms of length, status, monetization and platform, both of these examples offer an experience of being transported back in time, to be immersed in the intimacy and spontaneity of the rehearsal process.

Although partly triggered by his response to Bowie's death, Nacho's first accidental YouTube video for 'Right' was also prompted by a frustrating experience while on a date. Nacho and his new friend were getting to know each other by trawling through YouTube and sharing their 'musical loves'. He was trying to communicate his appreciation of Bowie's less-known material and became frustrated at the dearth of quality videos available on YouTube:

> That got me thinking and I realized, there's a massive deficit ... most artists there's a massive deficit in their video legacy. It's shameful actually. You've got

---

[14] Ibid.
[15] Bowie, cited in Nicholas Pegg, *The Complete David Bowie* (London: Titan Books, 2016), 226.
[16] Pegg, Ibid., 226.
[17] For more on this, see: The Beatles, 'Peter Jackson Gives an Inside Look at Making The Beatles: Get Back,' YouTube video, 00:02:18, 28 November 2021, https://www.youtube.com/watch?v=YBtxzVWD7sY.

**Figure 11.1** The inserted footage creates the impression that Bowie is directing the band from the side-line as they rehearse, 'NACHO'S 45th ANNIVERSARY RIGHT REDUX' (25 September 2020).

**Figure 11.2** Bowie is there in the footage of the rehearsing band, so he couldn't have been in two places at once, 'NACHO'S 45th ANNIVERSARY RIGHT REDUX' (25 September 2020).

these crappy 360 pixels, 480 pixels at best, low definition video, terrible sound, they've been transferred at the wrong speed . . . then I began to notice that some fans were already trying to remedy that, so I joined those ranks . . . I just felt like – somebody needs to remedy this. Somebody needs to represent these things better. So that was another starting point.[18]

Although Nacho may be describing a familiar experience, his recollection of this starting point as an archive video editor is instructive. Not only did he experience frustration over the difficulty in adequately communicating his love for music, he perceived the poor quality of the videos to be shameful. YouTube was full of gaps and he wanted to fill those gaps for other fans. Nacho was not alone.

## The World-Building Role of Fan-Creators

The phenomenon of fans re-editing the archives of dead musicians is not entirely new, but it raises new questions around creative process, authorship and representation. The advent of the Internet and the proliferation of file sharing platforms such as YouTube has led to the emergence of niche communities,

[18] Nacho, Interview by Lisa Perrott.

participatory cultures and fan-creators. Individual participants within these communities experience the benefits of heightened connectivity and access to materials collected by similarly interested fans. Those who are creatively inclined and technically adept are using the latest technological advancements to capture and manipulate archive materials in ways not previously possible. Platforms such as YouTube have given rise to a proliferation of 'behind the scenes' networks comprised of savvy fan-creators and collectors whose videos are produced from archival footage. Scholars express differing perspectives about the functions of these videos and the authorial status of their creators. They provoke a range of perspectives about auteurism, collaborative authorship, participatory culture, assemblage and intertextuality. These issues of fan participation and dispersed authorship have been explored by Henry Jenkins, who has explained how the process of 'media convergence' has enabled fans to participate in creating and disseminating spreadable media and engaging in world-building activities.[19] On one hand, Jenkins uses a pejorative phrase to describe fans as 'poachers who get to keep what they take and use their plundered goods as the foundations for the construction of an alternative cultural community'.[20] On the other hand, he emphasizes the creative processes involved in cultural borrowing, arguing that fan-generated texts:

> cannot simply be interpreted as the material traces of interpretive acts, but need to be understood within their own terms as cultural artifacts. They are aesthetic objects that draw on the artistic traditions of the fan community, as well as on the personal creativity and insights of individual consumers/artists. If there is an art of 'making do'... that art lies in transforming 'borrowed materials' from mass culture into new texts. A fan aesthetic centres on the selection, inflection, juxtaposition, and recirculation of ready-made images and discourses. In short, a poached culture requires a conception of aesthetics emphasizing borrowing and recombination as much or more as original creation and artistic innovation.[21]

Although writing in 2012 about the 'ready-made images and discourses' of television series that preceded YouTube, Jenkins provokes a useful consideration of assemblage as creative process. His subsequent writing on fandom explores

---

[19] Henry Jenkins, *Spreadable Media: Creating Value and Meaning in a Networked Culture* (New York: New York University Press, 2018), 39.
[20] Henry Jenkins, ed., *Textual Poachers: Television Fans and Participatory Culture* (New York: Routledge, 2012), 223.
[21] Ibid.

how fans engage in creative activities that elaborate canonical transmedia worlds.[22] As we shall see, Nacho provides a pertinent example of an elaborationist fan whose creative process exemplifies Jenkins's view of 'an alternative model of authorship . . . one where authorship is collective rather than individual, and one where artworks are appropriative and transformative rather than original'.[23] I use this alternative model of authorship as a springboard for considering how a fan might borrow from the ready-made sonic forms, images and discourses of a musician, who may in many instances serve as the primary object of a fan's admiration.

## The Exquisite Corpse of Fan Re-Editors

Before interviewing Nacho, I had imagined he worked in isolation and that he may not wish to share information about his process. To the contrary, I discovered that he is driven by a desire to communicate, and by the sense of community and comradery at the heart of his practice as a video editor. Soon after he posted his first few videos on YouTube, Nacho was embraced by various fan-communities devoted to Bowie and other artists. As an off-shoot of his video uploads and fan-networking, he also became part of a community of likeminded practitioners:

> I got some of these deep fans wanting to correspond with me. And some of them were collectors. They'd say 'I've got much better quality versions than you, you shouldn't be doing your work based on these crappy things you've downloaded from YouTube, they're all really crappy. I've got a copy of the master, and I'm going to send it to you.'[24]

These 'deep fans' were devoted collectors who were interested in archiving and trading their materials. This particular subset of the fan community was not only drawn together by their shared fandom of Bowie, but by a desire to collect and preserve Bowie's work in the highest possible quality; some of them wanted to redress what they perceived as a paucity of quality videos on YouTube. Those who had access to quality materials such as master tapes were also driven by a

---

[22] Henry Jenkins, 'The Aesthetics of Transmedia: in Response to David Bordwell (Part One),' *Henry Jenkins*, 10 September 2009, http://henryjenkins.org/blog/2009/09/the_aesthetics_of_transmedia_i.html.
[23] Henry Jenkins, '"Art Happens Not in Isolation, But in Community": the Collective Literacies of Media Fandom,' *Cultural Science Journal* 11, no.1 (2019): 78.
[24] Nacho, Interview by Lisa Perrott.

desire to represent Bowie with integrity, and they were discerning about who they would share their materials with. According to Nacho's description of events, it appears that he was chosen as a 'safe pair of hands' – a person who they believed would handle their collected archive materials with integrity:

> There's a network of fans in England, about seven of them, they've got loads of video. Between them they had everything. Those guys, they were all communicating. Because of me, one of them decided, 'I'm going to put all my stuff on an external hard-drive and send it to the next guy. He's going to put all of his stuff, and the next guy and the next guy and the next guy. And then, we're going to send it to you, and you'll have everything.' And so, after a couple of years of doing that stuff I got this hard drive ... I haven't even finished going through it. That's an amazing collaboration.[25]

Nacho's description of this strong communal aspect of fan collaboration shattered my preconceptions of a Banksy-esque 'lone wolf' video editor working in isolation, and of YouTube video editors being entirely competitive and protective of their materials and claims to authorship. I learnt from Nacho that behind the scenes there exists a lively community of practitioners who may be competitive, but are also able to collaborate to obtain materials, some of which may result in YouTube uploads; also, that such communal foraging and sharing of materials is at the very heart of Nacho's creative process. Such a process can be understood in terms of the collaborative authorship illustrated by the surrealist parlour game, the 'Exquisite Corpse'.[26] This game involves creating a collaborative poem or drawing, with each person adding their word or image and passing it on to the next person, until the multi-authored work forms a whole sentence or depiction of a 'body' that is then shared. Drawing attention to the collaborative authorship activated by variants of the Exquisite Corpse, Kanta Kochhar-Lindgren explains how 'the pastiche of images created' through the exquisite corpse:

> ...forms a living tissue of disparate bits and bodies in which politics and aesthetics are built into the process rather than as something added on to a previously established subject. In this sense, the various models of the Exquisite

---

[25] Ibid.
[26] For more on this, see: Anne Kern, 'From One Exquisite Corpse (in)to Another: Influences and Transformations From Early to Late Surrealist Games,' in *The Exquisite Corpse: Chance and Collaboration in Surrealism's Parlor Game (Texts and Contexts)*, ed. Kanta Kochhar-Lindgren, Davis Schneiderman and Tom Denlinger (Nebraska: University of Nebraska, 2009), 3–28.

Corpse are anti-Kantian and anti-Romantic, dispensing with the notion of artwork created by the individual genius that forms an enclosed and teleological whole.[27]

In order to fully appreciate the role played by video editors such as Nacho, it's important to critique the notion of sole authorship as a romanticized view of an author with purely original ideas, working in isolation from social and cultural influences. Although authors tend to imbue their creations with something unique of themselves, they cannot help but inflect their creations with the influences, symbols and residues of the people, cultures, places and texts they come in contact with. In the case of Nacho's videos, the form of each fragment of archive material is altered during its transit from one collaborator to another, the passage through video editing technology and through the decisions of the various authors within the network. Such refracted authorship forms the interstices of the visual and sonic intertexts associated with Nacho's reassembled videos.

Before examining these videos, it's important to distinguish between the processes of collaboration, dispersal and 're-authorship'. The collaborative aspect is apparent by the way in which fan-editors share materials and ideas through various networks of fandom. There's also the collaborative act of each person altering the archive materials as they're passed along the chain in Exquisite Corpse fashion. The notion of dispersed authorship is more relevant when considering the way a specific text (video or piece of footage) travels through time, with several authors having represented it in different ways. The videos available on YouTube for different versions of Bowie's song 'Space Oddity' (1969, 1972, 1979) exemplify this dispersion of authorship across time and space, while showing how many fans have elaborated upon the storyworld of this song, which Bowie himself modified across his *oeuvre*. This extensive development of a transmedia storyworld can be traced across five decades, beginning with official videos directed by Malcolm J Thomson (1969), Mick Rock (1972) and David Mallet (1979).[28] This dispersal of authorship is extended further with fan-made

---

[27] Kanta Kochhar-Lindgren, 'Towards A Communal Body Of Art: The Exquisite Corpse and Augusto Boal's Theatre,' *Angelaki: Journal of Theoretical Humanities* 7, no. 1 (2002): 219.

[28] David Bowie, 'David Bowie – Space Oddity,' *YouTube video*, 00:03:46, 10 March 2019, https://www.youtube.com/watch?v=tRMZ_5WYmCg; David Bowie, 'David Bowie – Space Oddity (Official Video),' *YouTube video*, 00:05:04, 10 July 2015, https://www.youtube.com/watch?v=iYYRH4apXDo; Nacho Video, 'David Bowie • Space Oddity • Will Kenny Everett Make It To 1980? Show • 31 December 1979,' *YouTube video*, 00:04:54, 1 January 2020, https://www.youtube.com/watch?v=63qvJoQLumw.

videos, including Commander Chris Hadfield's performance of the song, which was shot on board the International Space Station (2013),[29] an acapella cover version directed by Soren Lundvall Danielsen (2017),[30] a tribute video directed by Tim Pope (2019),[31] an interpretation of the song performed by the Kingston University Stylophone Orchestra (directed by Leah Kardos and Tony Visconti, 2019)[32] and a digital youth chorale performance by the Silverlake Conservatory of Music Choir, where each performer contributed their vocal via video-link (2020).[33] To this dispersed collection of authors and inter-texts, Nacho contributed his own re-edited version of the 'Space Oddity' video, which was originally screened on Swiss television in 1969.[34] Aiming to address the poor sound quality of the existing video, Nacho re-edited the footage to sync up to the 2019 Tony Visconti album mix of the original 1969 version of 'Space Oddity', thereby creating what he describes as a 'marriage of the two sources'.[35] Although this video exemplifies Nacho's contribution to the dispersed authorship associated with re-editing and reinterpreting 'Space Oddity', his other videos are less indicative of such broadly dispersed authorship. Rather, they better exemplify processes of collaborative foraging and re-authorship, or what Nacho describes as 're-presentation'.

## From Restoration To Re-Authorship

Nacho collaborated with another fan to come up with the idea to create a re-authored music video for Bowie's promotional film 'John I'm Only Dancing', which was originally shot and directed by Mick Rock in 1972.[36] Nacho explains

---

[29] Rare Earth, 'Space Oddity,' *YouTube video*, 00:05:30, 13 May 2013, https://www.youtube.com/watch?v=KaOC9danxNo.

[30] DunkelDirks, 'Space Oddity acapella cover,' *YouTube video*, 00:03:59, 23 August 2017, https://www.youtube.com/watch?v=gLA5URPoWNo.

[31] David Bowie, 'David Bowie – Space Oddity (2019 Mix) [Official Video],' *YouTube video*, 00:04:43, 21 July 2019, https://www.youtube.com/watch?v=ptVbk7r4IcA.

[32] KUSO, 'Space Oddity (Cover) – Kingston University Stylophone Orchestra,' *YouTube video*, 00:04:54, 17 December 2019, https://www.youtube.com/watch?v=LzejkGiK64A.

[33] Silverlake Conservatory of Music, 'Silverlake Conservatory Youth and Master Youth . . . still bringing on the music!,' *YouTube video*, 00:04:35, 22 April 2020, https://www.youtube.com/watch?v=qMtMkZOoRQE.

[34] Nacho Video, 'David Bowie, Space Oddity (2019 Tony Visconti Full Length Mix), 1969,' *YouTube video*, 00:05:19, 19 November 2019, https://www.youtube.com/watch?v=PbNsWll5ufw.

[35] Ibid.

[36] David Bowie, 'David Bowie – John, I'm Only Dancing (Official Video),' *YouTube video*, 00:03:02, 10 July 2015, https://www.youtube.com/watch?v=lmVVyhpuFRc.

how a fellow collaborator from the fan-network proposed, 'I've got a copy of the master reel of the "John, I'm Only Dancing" outtakes from Mick Rock ... so there's twenty minutes of outtakes never seen. You could make your own alternate version.'[37] Nacho explains how this sharing of archive materials and ideas eventually led to a process of restoration and re-editing, in which he had an opportunity to have a go at re-authoring Rock's music video:

> Why that appealed to me is because I remember seeing that video when I was a kid and I remember being horrified by those hideous dancers in this fishnet green ... you get to the chorus and then you've got these creepy dancers. I don't want to see this creepy stuff, I want to see *my* Bowie. And so what appealed to me was, I could make the 'John, I'm Only Dancing' video that *I* would like to see. So that idea kind of came from him and I invested my thing in it, and of course by the time its finished, its mine, I made it.[38]

Although acknowledging the collaborative aspect of accessing archive materials and generating the impulse for this video, Nacho confidently claims authorship of the new video he has created by editing together the outtakes shot by Rock for 'John, I'm Only Dancing'. Nacho explained that whenever he uploads one of his re-edited videos, he's careful to acknowledge all his sources, including the original director of the music video. This is evident on his YouTube channel; for each video uploaded, he acknowledges his sources in a respectful and accurate manner. The act of creating a new version of this video and publishing it on YouTube may potentially trigger debate about authorship and the integrity of fans engaged in re-assemblage of archive materials perceived by some as sacrosanct. It is therefore helpful to evaluate the extent of Nacho's creative contribution to the inter-texts that exist for 'John, I'm Only Dancing'.

Unlike his other videos, Nacho has created a coherent music video comprised of footage not used in a prior video or seen by the public. As he explains, his video is comprised entirely of outtake footage that had been shot by Rock for the purpose of the 1972 video, but had not been used in that video:

> The silent 30 minute, 16 mm reel of 'John, I'm Only Dancing' outtakes was transferred to video by Mainman in 1995. It has been in the hand of collectors since then ... Having acquired a copy of the transfer myself ... I started investigating it, checking out the different silent scenes of Bowie and the boys miming and pouting, and in Bowie's case, profusely smoking. I saw so many

---

[37] Nacho, Interview by Lisa Perrott.
[38] Ibid.

gorgeous moments that were not used in the original 'John, I'm Only Dancing' promo, and I became attracted to the idea of creating my own video for the song.[39]

Nacho's transitions make use of shot overlays, which create texture and depth within the frame. One salient example of this is an extreme close-up of Bowie's eye, including the anchor tattoo high on his cheekbone. This is overlaid with an image of Bowie clapping his hands in the foreground and the band playing in the background (Figure 11.3: timecode: 00:01:30). This audio-visual synchronization of the clapping triggers a moment of revelation; since Rock's video had not included this shot, it wasn't previously obvious that this repeated rhythmic motif was created by human handclaps. To accentuate the third handclap, Nacho aligns each cut to

**Figure 11.3** An extreme close-up of Bowie's cheekbone is overlaid with an image of Bowie clapping his hands in the foreground and the band playing in the background, 'David Bowie | John, I'm Only Dancing | Promo | Unreleased Mick Rock Outtake Footage Re-edit | 1972' (4 March 2017).

[39] Nacho Video, 'David Bowie | John, I'm Only Dancing | Promo | Unreleased Mick Rock Outtake Footage Re-edit | 1972,' *YouTube video*, 00:02:54, 5 March 2017, https://www.youtube.com/watch?v=adhFZr6VDes.

create a visual analogue with each of the sonic claps (timecode: 00:01.44), resulting in a sequence of fast cuts that portray a strong sense of rhythmic editing and audio-visual correlation. With the benefit of hindsight, Nacho's emphasis on handclapping draws attention to Bowie's innovative use of handclapping as a percussive instrument in several of his songs.[40] In this light, Nacho's video could be interpreted as a celebration of Bowie's broader use of the instrumental handclap.

Aside from the revelation around the source of the clapping sounds, Nacho's edit is also notable for the absence of the green-lit, fishnet-clad dancers that he found so creepy as a child. Devoid of these cut-away shots, Nacho gives much more screen time to Bowie's band members, The Spiders. As the video winds up, each band member is featured with a lingering image comprised of a foreground close-up and a background long-shot. A particularly glamorous close-up of Mick Ronson lingers as we see his face spontaneously burst into a radiant smile (Figure 11.4). The shot gradually dissolves, morphing into a close-up of Bowie's face (Figure 11.5). This foreground shot then dissolves to reveal a bust-shot of Bowie in the mid-ground and a long-shot of Ronson in the background. Ronson appears in strobe effect, which mimics the repetitive beeping sound of the electric guitar. He raises his guitar above his head as we hear the penultimate note. In unison with the final lingering note, the guitarist lowers his instrument to the floor, just as Bowie raises his middle finger in the foreground (Figure 11.6).

Not only does this outrageous finale provide an appropriate visual analogue to the music, it also ends with a gesture reinforcing Bowie's performance of a proto-punk attitude and a reminder of his subversive humour. The effect of the final sequence is aptly expressed by a YouTube user:

> What a great f----n' video Nacho, that final scene – where Ronno smiles and then Bowie's face appears underneath – is probably one of the best things I've seen on your channel yet mate. If it was part of the original promo then that's cool, but if you cut that in yerself then massive kudo to you mate. And the attitude at the end... absolute genius![41]

Such applaud for Nacho's videos is abundant in the comments sections of his YouTube channel. This is not only because he exhumes previously unseen footage,

---

[40] Bowie uses handclapping as a percussive instrument in several of his songs, including: 'Uncle Arthur' (1967), 'All the Madmen' (1970), 'Andy Warhol' (1971), 'Starman' (1972), 'Soul Love' (1972), 'The Prettiest Star' (1973), 'Golden Years' (1975), 'Fashion' (1980), 'Under Pressure' (1981) and 'Love is Lost' (2013).

[41] Nacho Video, 'David Bowie | John, I'm Only Dancing | Promo | Unreleased Mick Rock Outtake Footage Re-edit | 1972,' *YouTube video*, 00:02:54, 5 March 2017, https://www.youtube.com/watch?v=adhFZr6VDes.

**Figure 11.4** Mick Ronson is featured in a background long-shot overlaid with a foreground close-up, 'David Bowie | John, I'm Only Dancing | Promo | Unreleased Mick Rock Outtake Footage Re-edit | 1972' (4 March 2017).

**Figure 11.5** Mick Ronson's smiling face gradually morphs into a close-up of Bowie's face, 'David Bowie | John, I'm Only Dancing | Promo | Unreleased Mick Rock Outtake Footage Re-edit | 1972' (4 March 2017).

**Figure 11.6** In unison with the final lingering note, Mick Ronson lowers his guitar to the floor, just as Bowie raises his middle finger in the foreground, 'David Bowie | John, I'm Only Dancing | Promo | Unreleased Mick Rock Outtake Footage Re-edit | 1972' (4 March 2017).

but also because of the creative manner with which he re-presents previously seen video materials. Although Nacho's video for 'John, I'm Only Dancing' presents us with an example of re-authoring, it might also be considered as a form of collaborative authorship. Rock directed the performance and shot the footage that Nacho later edited. This was not collaboration in the sense of knowingly working together and communicating about creative decisions, as Nacho and Rock never met or communicated with one another. But the final product is the result of creative decisions made by Rock, Bowie and eventually Nacho, with footage and ideas provided by Nacho's colleagues. In this sense, there's an element of collaboration in the creative process, even if it is unsolicited – and if two of the authors are no longer alive to share that sense of collaborative authorship. Rock and Bowie may have been interested to see that the final shot of Nacho's video revealed a long-forgotten piece of footage that perfectly expresses the protopunk attitude and subversive humour they shared.[42]

---

[42] For more on this, see: Lisa Perrott, *David Bowie and the Art of Music Video* (New York: Bloomsbury, 2023).

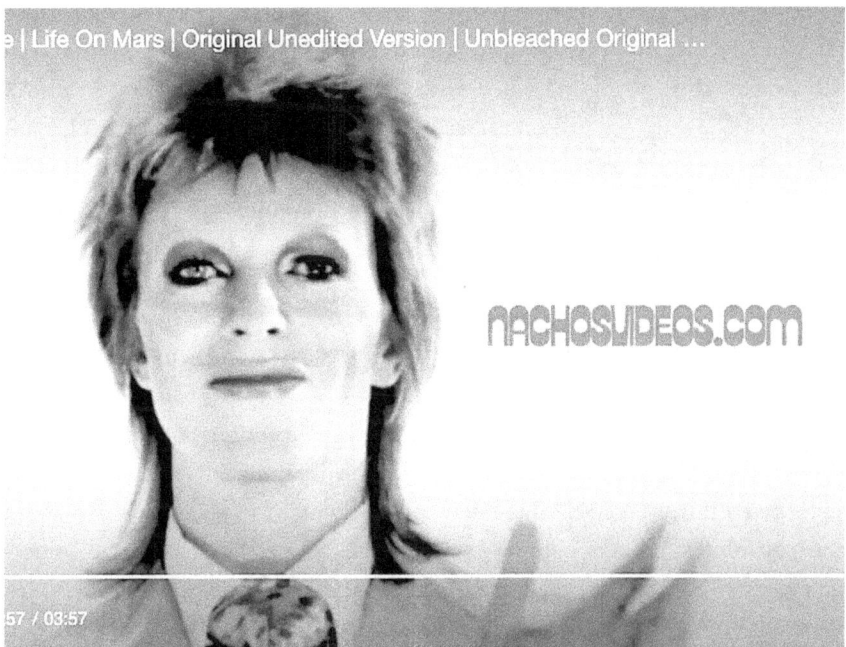

Figure 11.7 Nacho's remastered version includes outtake footage, showing Bowie expressing his disappointment of the prospect that the recording had been ruined by the sound of the phone ringing in the back of the recording studio, 'David Bowie – Life On Mars? (Original Unedited Version, Remastered by Nacho)' (2021).

In a similar vein, these transgressive artists may have been fascinated to see Nacho's re-edit of the original unbleached version of Rock's promo for Bowie's song 'Life on Mars?' (1973).[43] Nacho's remastered video has revelatory impact for fans, since it includes previously unseen outtakes, along with the accidental ending that had only existed on the original recording of the song.[44] In Nacho's video, this epic song concludes, only to be followed by Bowie gesturing disappointment (Figure 11.7) and Ronson verbally cursing; both expressing frustration by the prospect that the recording had been ruined by the sound of the phone ringing in the back of the recording studio. Nacho's inclusion of these

[43] David Bowie, 'David Bowie – Life On Mars? (Official Video),' *YouTube video*, 00:04:09, 10 July 2015, https://www.youtube.com/watch?v=AZKcl4-tcuo.
[44] Nacho Video, 'David Bowie | Life On Mars | Original Unedited Version | Unbleached Original Promo | Remastered by Nacho,' *Nachosvideos.com*, 00:03:57 (n.d), https://www.nachosvideos.com/bowie-videos.

audio and visual outtakes reveals moments of spontaneity – 'flickers of authenticity' that rupture the artifice of both Bowie's performance and the overall visual style, thus giving the video a *vérité* feel that was not present in Rock's original 1972 video for 'Life on Mars?'.[45] In this way, Nacho's re-edited video not only re-presents the original footage, it exemplifies a form of re-authorship that portrays his interest in blending the codes and conventions of music video and documentary.

## From Promotional Video To Documentary

Nacho often experiments with the aesthetics and conventions of different genres, sometimes creating unexpected fusions from disparate materials. In 2020 he uploaded a thirty-seven minute documentary along with an explanation about the convoluted process behind its inception. He describes how the project emerged from the initial idea of re-purposing a 1980 radio advertisement for *The Elephant Man* theatrical performance, but then developed into a much bigger, hybrid documentary that was 'culled from over fifty sources':[46]

> The idea for this film originated in 2016 out of desperation to see / create a video for the Bowie '80 era. I toyed with using *Elephant Man* footage to make a video for the track 'Scary Monsters'. Those experiments proved fruitless. But when telling a Bowie collector mate about them, he suggested making a 'fake' TV ad, based on the real 1980 radio ad for Bowie in the *Elephant Man* play. Whilst working on that, it occurred to me that there should be a documentary about Bowie in the play. And then the 'fake' ad morphed into a hybrid of ad and trailer for an imaginary forthcoming documentary, then called: 'David Bowie is The Elephant Man.' Well, four years and about 500 editing hours later, here is the documentary.[47]

---

[45] 'Flickers of authenticity' is a term coined by Jane Roscoe to describe a moment in Reality TV shows when participants unexpectedly let down their guard to show rare moments of emotional authenticity. This momentary 'flicker' breaks their coded performance, which often involves acting as though they are unaware of the presence of camera. For more on this, see: Derek Paget and Jane Roscoe, 'Giving Voice: Performance and Authenticity in the Documentary Musical,' *Jump Cut: A Review of Contemporary Media* 48 (2006): https://www.ejumpcut.org/archive/jc48.2006/MusicalDocy/.
[46] Nacho Video, 'David Bowie in New York 1980 The Elephant Man, Scary Monsters & Other Strange People | 2020,' *YouTube video*, 00:37:48, 5 December 2020, https://www.youtube.com/watch?v=F1fTtwGqdQw&t=46s.
[47] Ibid.

Although the completed documentary portrays Nacho's skill as a documentary editor, his explanation of his creative process shows how many of his projects are triggered by a desire to fill a gap, and then stumbling upon a piece of archive material. Once he had begun experimenting with sonic and visual relationships, the project would often take on an organic life of its own.

## David Bowie Is The Man Who Fell To Earth

The experimentation with audio-visual materials and genre conventions described above is also apparent in Nacho's 2017 documentary titled *David Bowie is The Man Who Fell To Earth*, which he revised and re-published on his YouTube channel in 2021.[48] Describing this project as an exploration of Nicolas Roeg's 1976 film *The Man Who Fell to Earth*, Nacho adds that his documentary also contemplates Bowie's involvement in this film, and the enduring impact this experience had on him and his music.[49] The documentary provides context about Roeg's directorial intentions while allowing Bowie and Candy Clarke to voice their reflections about the film and its impact on them personally. By drawing together these diverse perspectives, the documentary fills gaps in the publicly available knowledge about this film. Going beyond the gap-filling role that Jenkins ascribed to fandom, Nacho's editing creatively elaborates on the canon of *The Man Who Fell to Earth*.[50] By stitching together found fragments from multiple authors and sources, Nacho has experimented with the artistic strategy of bricolage to create a coherent feature-length documentary that is greater than the sum of its parts. Although multiple authors can be attributed to each part, Nacho's authorship as director and editor of this documentary is indicated by his signature at the lower right corner of the frame, much like a painter would sign their canvas. Given this artisanal approach to indicating authorship, it's interesting that Nacho says his documentary 'tries to paint a small portrait of Bowie and his music during the era – from 1974 up to the 1977 album, *Low*. The film also ruminates on Bowie's missing soundtrack for *The Man Who Fell To Earth*'.[51] The mythology around this missing soundtrack indicates that

---

[48] Nacho Video, 'David Bowie is The Man Who Fell To Earth . Redux . Documentary . 2021,' *Nachosvieos.com*, 01:04:02, 18 March 2021, https://www.nachosvideos.com/db-is-tmwfte.
[49] *The Man Who Fell to Earth* (1976) [film] dir. Nicolas Roeg, United Kingdom: British Lion Film Corporation.
[50] Jenkins, *Textual Poachers*, 165.
[51] Ibid.

after the film had been shot, Bowie worked on music that he intended to be used for the soundtrack. Although that music was not used, Bowie later incorporated elements of the unused music into his subsequent albums. According to legend, Bowie sent a copy of his album *Low* (1977) to Roeg, with a message saying 'this is what I wanted to do for the film'.[52] Nacho explains that 'as part of the story telling' in his documentary, 'some of Bowie's music from the era is used with re-edits of scenes from the movie, worked in with the interviews and commentary'.[53] The missing soundtrack presented a gap-filling opportunity for Nacho, who responded by taking the creative liberty of removing the original music from sections of Roeg's film and editing these shots together with pieces of Bowie's music. This is a significant act of creative liberty on Nacho's part, which may have started as an experiment with audio-visual relations, but eventuated in a fan playing with the notion of revising history and re-authoring a cult film. By doing so, Nacho is giving the audience a sense of how this film could have been experienced if Roeg had chosen to use Bowie's music. The result is much like the revelatory impact of his re-edited music videos, since sections of the film are re-contextualized with an entirely different tone. To emphasize Bowie's comment that acting in the film had influenced the music on *Station to Station*, Nacho has overlaid the song 'Station to Station' (1976) with the scene from Roeg's film that inspired the album cover (Figure 11.8). In the middle of the

**Figure 11.8** Nacho has overlaid the song 'Station to Station' (1976) with the scene from Roeg's film that inspired the *Station to Station* album cover, 'David Bowie is The Man Who Fell To Earth (Redux – A Nacho Documentary – 2021)' (2021).

[52] Sean Doyle, 'Video Essay: The Soundtracks of the Man Who Fell to Earth,' *Film Comment*, n.d, https://www.filmcomment.com/video-essay-the-soundtracks-of-the-man-who-fell-to-earth/.
[53] Nacho Video, 'David Bowie is The Man Who Fell To Earth . Redux . Documentary . 2021,' ibid.

documentary, Nacho includes an imaginative audio-visual re-coupling that appears as a re-authored video for Bowie's version of 'Wild is the Wind' (timecode 00:38:57–00:41:25). By overlaying this song with the love-making scene in the film, both the sex scene and the song take on a completely new tone. Throughout Nacho's documentary, similar instances of audio-visual re-coupling produce a combined sense of nostalgia and defamiliarization, but the result feels eerily right. Perhaps because Bowie's performance is wrapped in his own music, which was partially generated from his experience of acting in the film. For many Bowie fans, Nacho has filled the gap of the missing soundtrack by reuniting it with its rightful partner.

## Artistic Integrity

There's a large dose of creative liberty undertaken in such acts of re-assemblage. Not all Bowie fans find such creative re-assemblage and re-authorship acceptable, as has been expressed in reviews of Morgen's film *Moonage Daydream*.[54] In contrast to some of the responses to Morgen's approach as a fan re-editor, fans have praised Nacho for being a 'magician' who pulls 'Bowie gems from the vault for all of us to enjoy'.[55] Such plaudits come from recognition among fan communities that Nacho re-assembles from a place of integrity and therefore is a 'safe pair of hands' with which to entrust with access to 'the vault'. Such trust has been earnt over time through the building of relationships and through demonstrating representational integrity. Although taking care to credit his sources and the owners of copyright, Nacho assures us that he does not monetize the videos he uploads on his YouTube channel: 'I don't monetize them ... I don't know if there's revenue I'm missing, it's irrelevant to me actually. And my conscience is clean because I don't get anything from that channel.'[56] Despite the liberation that goes with having a clean conscience, Nacho expressed an awareness of inadvertently being part of something he despises:

---

[54] For instance, see these contrasting reviews: Carl Wilson, 'The David Bowie Documentary Makes a Mess of a Velvet Goldmine,' *Slate*, 19 September 2022, https://slate.com/culture/2022/09/david-bowie-moonage-daydream-2022-documentary-movie-review.html?fbclid=IwAR2cyzLaXepQhS3 OFMrIUhLSLYu6E_GJSZ5zmDfzosb5k-9NA3zgrAj12AU; Lisa Perrott '*Moonage Daydream*: Brilliant Bowie Film Takes Big Risks to Create Something New,' *The Conversation*, 14 September 2022,https://theconversation.com/moonage-daydream-brilliant-bowie-film-takes-big-risks-to-create-something-truly-new-190347.
[55] Pleasant Valley Picker CA, YouTube User, ibid.
[56] Nacho, Interview by Lisa Perrott.

I'm part of what I call the 'dead Bowie industry', which is for the most part very tacky. It's kind of offensive to me. You know, Bowie Barbie-doll, Monopoly set, trainers, the endless unnecessary reissues, picture disc, coloured vinyl, not anything of any real value, doesn't add to the canon in any way that's desirable. I'm part of that industry. Except of course, I haven't made a penny from that industry, there's that big difference ... as the 'dead Bowie industry' gets ever more offensive to me and ever more tacky and gross, I feel that some of us are trying to hold up the other end of things, and say this is the *art* ... that's where I think I fit in it, I'm trying to present what I really like about Bowie.[57]

At this point in the interview, I had to acknowledge that as an 'aca-fan', I too cannot escape being unintentionally part of the 'dead Bowie industry'. I too share Nacho's impetus to try and 'hold up the other end of things' by exploring the art of Bowie from a place of integrity. Nacho's response to this dilemma indicates a level of awareness that is not always articulated by video re-editors on YouTube or by directors of official projects.

When considering issues of artistic integrity and authorship, it's important to critique the notion of sole authorship and consider the collaborative authorship that occurs among fans, often behind the scenes. By examining Nacho's videos, and listening to him describe his creative process, I was most surprised to learn of the Exquisite Corpse-like collaborative process that includes a string of foragers and assemblage artists. Bowie too, reassembled the work of artists he admired. He was a rampant forager who wove together strands of what I call 'loose continuity' across time and mediums.[58] Through a process of recontextualizing and re-authoring the work of other artists, the trope of alienation, the strategy of masking and the figure of Pierrot are loosely woven across five decades of sonic and visual art forms. Rather than tying these strands into sacrosanct knots of singular authorship, Bowie left them dangling so they could be picked up and extended by fans, artists and future generations.[59] By untangling and re-weaving these strands, Nacho serves as a transmedia elaborator who unintentionally mimics Bowie's penchant for foraging, re-assemblage and the alchemy of 'spinning straw into gold'.[60] To be accepted by

---

[57] Ibid.
[58] Lisa Perrott, 'The Alchemical Union of David Bowie and Floria Sigismondi: "Transmedia Surrealism" and "Loose Continuity"', in *Transmedia Directors: Artistry, Industry and New Audiovisual Aesthetics*, ed. Carol Vernallis, Holly Rogers and Lisa Perrott (New York: Bloomsbury, 2020), 196.
[59] For more on this, see: Lisa Perrott, *David Bowie and the Transformation of Music Video: 1984–2016 (and Beyond)* (New York: Bloomsbury, 2023).
[60] The Brothers Grimm, 'Rumpelstiltskin' [fairy tale], *Children's and Household Tales*, 1812.

fans as a descendent of Bowie's lineage requires a high level of artistic integrity. But does Nacho see himself as an artist?

> I'm an artisan I guess... I don't know if it's art, but it's how I'm expressing myself, if that's art. I don't want to make any false claims about myself. To me it's just a blessing that just came to me. I mean I'm a yoga-hippie man, it was the universe that gave me this blessing. It just came to me. I didn't apparently do anything.[61]

# Bibliography

Doyle, Sean. 'Video Essay: The Soundtracks of the Man Who Fell to Earth.' *Film Comment*, https://www.filmcomment.com/video-essay-the-soundtracks-of-the-man-who-fell-to-earth/.

Ellsworth-Jones, Will. 'The Story Behind Banksy.' *Smithsonian Magazine*, February 2013, at http://www.ribar.com/UserFiles/2m-2015.pdf.

Jenkins, Henry. '"Art Happens Not in Isolation, But in Community": The Collective Literacies of Media Fandom.' *Cultural Science Journal* 11, no.1 (2019): 78–88.

Jenkins, Henry. *Spreadable Media: Creating Value and Meaning in a Networked Culture*. New York: New York University Press, 2018.

Jenkins, Henry. 'Confessions of an Aca-Fan.' *Henry Jenkins*, 22 October 2011, at http://henryjenkins.org/blog/2011/10/acafandom_and_beyond_will_broo_1.html.

Jenkins, Henry. 'The Aesthetics of Transmedia: in Response to David Bordwell (Part One).' *Henry Jenkins*, 10 September 2009, at http://henryjenkins.org/blog/2009/09/the_aesthetics_of_transmedia_i.html.

Jenkins, Henry. *Textual Poachers: Television Fans and Participatory Culture*. New York: Routledge, 1992.

Kern, Anne. 'From One Exquisite Corpse (in)to Another: Influences and Transformations From Early to Late Surrealist Games.' In *The Exquisite Corpse: Chance and Collaboration in Surrealism's Parlor Game (Texts and Contexts)*, edited by Kanta Kochhar-Lindgren, Davis Schneiderman and Tom Denlinger, 3–28. Nebraska: University of Nebraska, 2009.

Kochhar-Lindgren, Kanta. 'Towards A Communal Body Of Art: The Exquisite Corpse and Augusto Boal's Theatre.' *Angelaki: Journal of Theoretical Humanities* 7, no. 1 (2002): 217–26.

Mashaun, Simon. '"Plastic Soul": David Bowie's Legacy and Impact on Black Artists.' *NBC News*, 12 January 2016, at https://www.nbcnews.com/news/nbcblk/plastic-soul-david-bowie-s-legacy-impact-black-artists-n494241.

---

[61] Nacho, Interview by Lisa Perrott.

Nacho Video. Interview by Lisa Perrott, 23 September 2022.

Nacho Video. correspondence with Chuck Braverman, 'David Bowie | Young Americans | Remastered U.S. TV Ad | 1975.' YouTube video, 25 September 2016, at https://www.youtube.com/watch?v=kjh25cgnpFk.

Paget, Derek and Jane Roscoe. 'Giving Voice: Performance and Authenticity in the Documentary Musical.' *Jump Cut: A Review of Contemporary Media* 48 (2006): https://www.ejumpcut.org/archive/jc48.2006/MusicalDocy/

Pegg, Nicholas. *The Complete David Bowie*. London: Titan Books, 2016.

Perrott, Lisa. *David Bowie and the Art of Music Video*. New York: Bloomsbury, 2023.

Perrott, Lisa. *David Bowie and the Transformation of Music Video: 1984–2016 (and Beyond)*. New York: Bloomsbury, 2023.

Perrott, Lisa. '*Moonage Daydream*: Brilliant Bowie Film Takes Big Risks to Create Something New.' *The Conversation*, 14 September 2022, at https://theconversation.com/moonage-daydream-brilliant-bowie-film-takes-big-risks-to-create-something-truly-new-190347.

Perrott, Lisa. 'The Alchemical Union of David Bowie and Floria Sigismondi: "Transmedia Surrealism" and "Loose Continuity".' In *Transmedia Directors: Artistry, Industry and New Audiovisual Aesthetics*, edited by Carol Vernallis, Holly Rogers and Lisa Perrott, 194–220. New York: Bloomsbury, 2020.

The Brothers Grimm. 'Rumpelstiltskin.' [fairytale] *Children's and Household Tales*, 1812.

Wilson, Carl. 'The David Bowie Documentary Makes a Mess of a Velvet Goldmine.' *Slate*, 19 September 2022, at https://slate.com/culture/2022/09/david-bowie-moonage-daydream-2022-documentary-movie-review.html?fbclid=IwAR2cyzLaXepQhS3OFMrIUhLSLYu6E_GJSZ5zmDfzosb5k-9NA3zgrAj12AU.

12

# Music Videos as Protest Communication: The Gezi Park Protest on YouTube

Olu Jenzen, Itir Erhart, Hande Eslen-Ziya, Derya Güçdemir, Umut Korkut and Aidan Mcgarry

## Introduction

Today music is an established part of political communication.[1] Yet, music is often marginalized in the theorization of politics. The use of music is one of the ways social movements 'gain a hearing to serve as vehicles of cultural change'[2] and among other cultural products, music 'facilitate[s] the recruitment and socialization of new adherents and help movements maintain their readiness and capacity for collective action'.[3] Music is an increasingly pivotal part of political communication across many political spheres, from election rallies to NGO media campaigns and street protests. Although some would argue that the heyday of the protest song is over,[4] the fact that the Gezi Park protests of 2013 in

---

This chapter first appeared as Jenzen, Olu, Itir Erhart, Hande Eslen-Ziya, Derya Güçdemir, Umut Korkut, and Aidan McGarry, '"Music Videos as Protest Communication: The Gezi Park Protest on YouTube," in *The Aesthetics of Global Protest: Visual Culture and Communication*, ed. Olu Jenzen, Itir Erhart, Hande Eslen-Ziya, Umut Korkut and Aidan McGarry (Amsterdam: Amsterdam University Press, 2020), 211-32.
It has been reprinted by permission of the publisher.

[1] John Street, *Music and Politics* (Cambridge: Polity, 2012).
[2] Verta Taylor and Nella Van Dyke, '"Get up, Stand up": Tactical Repertoires of Social Movements', in *The Blackwell Companion to Social Movements*, ed. David A. Snow, Sarah Anne Soule and Hanspeter Kriesi (Malden, MA: Blackwell Pub, 2004), 279.
[3] Bob Edwards and John McCarthy, 'Resources and Social Movement Mobilization', in *The Blackwell Companion to Social Movements*, 126.
[4] Dorian Lynskey, *33 Revolutions per Minute: A History of Protest Songs* (London: Faber, 2010); Peter Manuel, 'World Music and Activism Since the End of History', *Music and Politics* 11, no. 1 (2017): https://doi.org/10.3998/mp.9460447.0011.101.

Turkey produced an extraordinary number of protest songs and music videos suggests that the protest song as political communication is still relevant in the Internet era.[5] Challenging the view that 'the context in which protest music once thrived is no longer present',[6] we propose that if we look at protest music online, we would see a thriving production. Particularly, if we look at the case of the Gezi Park protest, a wealth of creativity is evident with its diverse YouTube video output, combining music and image to challenge the mainstream media message about protest (and protestors), to communicate what the struggle is about, and eventually to connect wider publics to the local protest.

Research on digital activism, social media and protest has mainly focused on social media as a tool for sharing information regarding activities and for raising awareness of a protest.[7] Less attention has been given to aesthetics and creativity. In this chapter, we explore the aesthetics and function of music videos as a specific protest expression and as a form of digital activism. This research, focusing specifically on YouTube videos that have been circulated on Twitter during the Gezi Park protests, forms part of the larger Arts and Humanities Research Council (AHRC)-funded 'Aesthetics of Protest' project which has explored visual protest culture and communication.[8] The protest music video, we argue, draws on already established genres of video activism such as witness documentation,[9] rally call, and political remix videos,[10] which, when combined with a musical soundtrack, communicates across intellectual and emotional registers.[11]

Using the highly mediated Gezi Park protest in Istanbul in 2013 as a case study, the chapter explores how digital technologies and social media offer new opportunities for protest music to be produced and reach new audiences. We argue that the affordances of digital media and Internet platforms such as

---

[5] An impressive catalogue of music dedicated to, or inspired by, Gezi was produced. It encompassed many genres, from traditional Turkish folk to hard rock, rap and pop. See, for example, the 'Artists in Resistance' blog or the 'Çapulcu Şarkılar' playlist on Bandcamp, with over 140 songs.

[6] Beate Kutschke, Noriko Manabe and John Street, 'Responses to Peter Manuel's "World Music and Activism since the End of History [sic]"' *Music and Politics* 11, no. 1 (2017): 12.

[7] W. Lance Bennett and Alexandra Segerberg, 'The Logic of Connective Action', *Information, Communication & Society* 15, no. 5 (1 June 2012): 739–68.

[8] See the 'Aesthetics of Protest' project, https://www.aestheticsofprotest.com, AHRC Reference: AH/N004779/1.

[9] Tina Askanius, 'Online Video Activism and Political Mash-up Genres,' *JOMEC Journalism, Media and Cultural Studies* 4 (2013): https://lucris.lub.lu.se/ws/portalfiles/portal/4197460/4180639.pdf.

[10] Olivia Conti, 'Political Remix Video as a Vernacular Discourse,' in *The Routledge Companion to Remix Studies*, ed. Eduardo Navas, Owen Gallagher and xtine burrough (New York: Routledge, 2015), 332–343.

[11] Nicholas Mirzoeff, *How to See the World* (London: Pelican, 2015).

YouTube play a crucial part in the production, distribution and consumption of protest music. Focusing on the specific intersection of digital media and protest music, we seek to demonstrate how, in the format of music videos, activists use mash-up techniques, remixing images and music to reframe media images already in the public domain with the aim to raise awareness of police brutality, communicate solidarity and express resistance to dominant political discourse. By doing so they give new meaning to both images and music and contribute to a reorientation of protest to include online audiovisual outputs by individual producers. Many of the music videos in our data set employ sophisticated methods of combining sound, lyrics, and visual material to make specific rhetorical points or to provoke new interpretations, either by turning the lyrics into a commentary on the images or using specifically chosen images to give new meaning to a well-known song. We also argue that activists tap into pre-existing popular culture notions of an authentic political voice, such as the association of rap music with social protest, a tactic that also has the potential to reach new audiences and build solidarity.

Examining why protestors deploy particular aesthetics and how these are mediated and understood across social media we looked at different forms of creative political expressions as 'communication which have the potential to inspire and mobilize people to action'.[12] Quite soon on in our analysis of data collected via Twitter, it became apparent that we were dealing with a wide array of creative outputs, including photography, digital visual art, comics, poetry and music videos. Looking at the music videos separately, we could discern many different styles and genres of music. This in itself not only tells a story about the richness of the creative output, but also illustrates that the Gezi Park movement was made up of people of diverse backgrounds, ages, cultures, and tastes. The crowds, which consisted of diverse, even conflicting identities, united against what they called the 'authoritarian rule'[13] and mobilized around 'concerns for detrimental urban policies and for the environment'.[14] During the protests, nationalists, Kurds, Kemalists, socialists, feminists, vegan activists, anti-capitalist Muslims, LGBTQI groups, and white-collar workers stood 'shoulder to shoulder

---

[12] Aidan McGarry et al., 'Beyond the Iconic Protest Images: The Performance of "Everyday Life" on Social Media during Gezi Park', *Social Movement Studies* 18, no. 3 (2019): 284–304.

[13] Itir Erhart, 'United in Protest: From "Living and Dying with Our Colors" to "Let All the Colours of the World Unite"', *International Journal of the History of Sport* 31, no. 14 (2014): 1728.

[14] Kıvanç Atak, "From Malls to Barricades: Reflections on the Social Origins of Gezi," paper presented at the symposium *Rebellion and Protest from Maribor to Taksim Social Movements in the Balkans*, Graz, Austria, December 12–14, 2013, 19.

against fascism'[15] and resisted together.[16] In light of this, we ask how do music videos operate to mobilize and unite the movement musically and as a multimodal form of online communication? How do the videos amplify the movement's critiques to reach a wider audience? And what does the online music video format offer to activists today?

Music can permeate protest in many different ways.[17] illustrates the function of music performances in the park and in the streets as part of the protest. Building on these insights, this chapter focuses specifically on Gezi Park protest music videos on YouTube. We argue that these videos not only offer opportunities for the music to reach beyond live performances, and thus extend the momentum of the movement, but also perform distinct corrective responses to mainstream media representations. They subvert the dominant message by remixing images and music in new and creative ways. Therefore, availing such music videos on YouTube requires us to look at protest music as part of a mediated commercial-cultural terrain and to elaborate on them as part of a digital space that allows people to participate in protest in different ways.

Online music videos can be sampled in various ways.[18] Our approach involved starting with a data set of 300,000 tweets generated by querying the Twitter API using the key word *Gezi Parkı* (as it would be written in Turkish) from 27 May to the end of June 2013. This was the time period during which *Gezi Parkı* was a regularly trending topic on Twitter and the protests were in full swing. As many as 20% of the tweets contained images and a smaller yet significant number of tweets contained links to content uploaded to YouTube (see Table 12.1). A random sample of 133 videos were harvested for qualitative thematic analysis.

Dissatisfied with the mainstream media coverage of the Gezi Park protests, protestors resorted to live-tweeting of protests as well as live-streaming and sharing YouTube videos. Thereafter, YouTube became a symbolic rallying point for the protestors. Of the 133 videos studied, the majority were pro-Gezi Park protests and anti-government policies and police violence. The YouTube videos shared via Twitter varied from documentaries, TV clips, collages and commentary all relating to the protest. As expected, documentary footage dominated and

---

[15] Erhart, 'United in Protest', 1725.
[16] Yeşım Arat, 'Violence, Resistance, and Gezi Park,' *International Journal of Middle East Studies* 45, no. 4 (2013): 807–9.
[17] Raffaella Bianchi, 'Istanbul Sounding Like Revolution: The Role of Music in the Gezi Park Occupy Movement,' *Popular Music* 37, no. 2 (2018): 212–36.
[18] cf. Lyndon Way, 'YouTube as a Site of Debate through Populist Politics: The Case of a Turkish Protest Pop Video,' *Journal of Multicultural Discourses* 10, no. 2 (2015): 180–96.

**Table 12.1** Data set of tweets and content from the 'Aesthetics of Protest' project

| Type of tweets | Numbers | Percentages |
| --- | --- | --- |
| Total | 243,912 | 100% |
| Images | 51,781 | 21% |
| YouTube videos | 3,903 | 1.6% |

made up 29% of the sample whilst, somewhat surprisingly, the second largest category was music videos, which represented 25% of the sample. The latter stands out as a particularly interesting category and becomes the focus for this chapter. Our analysis of YouTube videos is based on the visual and textual content of videos circulated via Twitter as well as the descriptions and the titles that frame these videos.

In addition to examining the protest message put across in the lyrics of the music videos, we also took into consideration the material qualities and aesthetic forms of each video. In our analysis, hence, we aimed to capture the multimodal aesthetical and formal characteristics of the music videos in order to elaborate on what makes them performative. When dealing with music videos published online, we came across several communicative elements coming in to play. These are namely the musical score, the lyrics, the visual style, the narrative arch, the tone and genre of the video itself. In addition, there is the context of conditions of production and distribution, and importantly for videos on social media, the social dimension. This comes to fore thanks to the audience's responses to the video within the comments field and, as in the case of the sample here, the remediation of the videos to appear in a new context, for example, embedded in a tweet. Our analytic strategies seek to respond to some of these multiple aspects and avoid treating protest music videos as static digital artefacts.[19] In order to offer a more detailed analysis of the YouTube music video as protest communication, we have performed a close reading on three of the videos selected from our sample.

## Music as Protest

Protest music in itself is a broad term and academically a wide field that expands far beyond the scope of this chapter, both historically and geographically. On the

---

[19] Due to space constraints this chapter does not consider the comments field content.

face of it, protest music is a relatively simple concept by which we mean music carrying a political message that is associated with a particular political protest or social movement. In other words, we are interested in deliberate political communication expressed through music. But actually, it is rarely this straightforward. Different cultures have different traditions and histories of protest music. Furthermore, part of the power of music, and the appeal of a particular song, is that it conveys sentiments and ideas through an aesthetics of protest that is layered, semantically unfixed, and playful rather than insistent.

The role of music in relation to social movements has mainly been explored from a musical point of view[20] or through a political typology.[21] Both approaches have primarily focused on lyrics as the main conveyor of protest messages. However, Frith and Way investigated how musical sounds could also convey political meaning.[22] Musical sound has 'a particularly powerful affective role in communication' because of its, 'very fluid affordances, which are highly adaptable in multimodal texts'.[23] In other words, it is important not to reduce protest music to the contents of a song's lyrics. It is important to approach music as multimodal to be able to appreciate its function and effectiveness when understood as part of a movement's communication. In this chapter, we seek to expand the focus on music (sound and lyrics) to also include the visual aspects of activist produced music videos.

## YouTube and Protest Communication

YouTube plays a significant role as a platform for protest communication. In terms of grassroots campaigners' use of the platform, YouTube has mainly been discussed in terms of its potential for citizen journalism in relation to political conflict and activism.[24] Live-streaming has become an important tool enabling activists to

---

[20] John Street, *Rebel Rock: The Politics of Popular Music* (Oxford: Blackwell, 1986); Lynskey, '33 Revolutions per Minute'; Lyndon C. S. Way, 'Protest Music, Populism, Politics and Authenticity: The Limits and Potential of Popular Music's Articulation of Subversive Politics', *Journal of Language and Politics* 15, no. 4 (20 October 2016): 422–45.
[21] Mark Mattern, *Acting in Concert: Music, Community, and Political Action* (New Brunswick: Rutgers University Press, 1998).
[22] Simon Frith, *Performing Rites: On the Value of Popular Music* (Cambridge, MA: Harvard University Press, 1996); Way, 'Protest Music, Populism, Politics and Authenticity'.
[23] Simon McKerrell and Lyndon C.S. Way, 'Understanding Music as Multimodal Discourse,' in *Music as Multimodal Discourse: Semiotics, Power and Protest*, ed. Lyndon C.S. Way and Simon McKerrell (London: Bloomsbury Academic, 2017), 15.
[24] Thomas Poell and Erik Borra, 'Twitter, YouTube, and Flickr as Platforms of Alternative Journalism: The Social Media Account of the 2010 Toronto G20 Protests,' *Journalism* 13, no. 6 (2012): 695–713.

'evidence' the concerns they have (based on witnessing) and to report directly from rallies or protests as events are unfolding.[25] Yet, groups and individual activists also use YouTube to upload more technically and aesthetically proficient and crafted campaign videos, vlogs, and montages.[26] Other researchers of YouTube activism have mainly focused on the comments field as a textual and discursive space,[27] noting that the platform 'extend[s] the discursive opportunities' of other activist spheres, importantly 'facilitating debate between otherwise disparate publics'.[28] In their analysis of comments posted in relation to the politically explicit punk band Pussy Riots' music videos on YouTube, Weij and Berkers found that 'for YouTube audiences, political music is first and foremost a vehicle to discuss politics on levels beyond what is actually raised in the music'.[29] Arguably, this tells us that the function of music, and the music video specifically, is broadening and evolving with new media.

Limited research is available on the use of music videos, the otherwise dominating popular culture format on YouTube, as part of protest communication. Railton and Watson highlight how music videos are complex media texts in their own right with carefully crafted images and dramatizations.[30] They demonstrate how even a minute visual cue as the singer mouthing the lyrics signify meaning through visual codes that can be studied in terms of how these acts can lead to different political interpretations and readings. Railton and Watson's concern is purely the professionally produced music video, but today we also need to consider the music video as a media form open to digital remixing and amateur production – a tool online activists creatively put into productive use. Citizen or amateur creativity is widespread in fan communities. There are not necessarily any clearly delimiting lines between such playful fan praxis and more dedicated political applications. In both cases, Internet platforms such as YouTube are important for the mediation and remediation of both industry-produced music videos and user-generated productions.

---

[25] Michele Martini, 'On the User's Side: YouTube and Distant Witnessing in the Age of Technology-Enhanced Mediability', *Convergence* 24, no. 1 (1 February 2018): 33–49.
[26] Kjerstin Thorson, Brian Ekdale, Porismita Borah and Kang Namkoong, 'YouTube and Proposition 8: A Case Study in Video Activism', *Information, Communication & Society* 13, no. 3 (2010): 325–49.
[27] Frank Weij and Pauwke Berkers, 'The Politics of Musical Activism: Western YouTube Reception of Pussy Riot's Punk Performances', 25, no. 2 (2019): 287–306.
[28] Julie Uldam and Tina Askanius, 'Online Civic Cultures: Debating Climate Change Activism on YouTube', *International Journal of Communication* 7 (2013): 1200.
[29] Weij and Berkers, 'The Politics of Musical Activism', 14.
[30] Diane Railton and Paul Watson, *Music Video and the Politics of Representation* (Edinburgh: Edinburgh University Press, 2011).

Both Bianchi and Way note the importance of the Internet for the distribution of music during the Gezi Park protest.[31] Turkish political music operates within a 'tightly controlled mediascape' dominated by the ruling AKP (Justice and Development Party) ideology[32]. Noriko Manabe argues that even internationally, the music industry is clearly discouraging protest songs[33]. Therefore, the Internet and platforms such as YouTube become important for 'alternative musical voices'[34] and may be employed as 'a "subaltern tactic"'[35] to reverse an asymmetry of power'.[36]

We should also note that uploading Gezi Park videos on YouTube was largely un-coordinated. Yet, the videos served to foster a sense of collective identity, solidarity and participation. For example, documentary footage from the protest features heavily, creating a link between the viewer and offline events and, as we will go on to discuss, the videos invite a viewer position of solidarity and identification with the çapulcu identity: a term that translates into 'marauder' and was first used by the government as a derogatory term to defame the protestors, but through its reappropriation by the movement the repressive meaning of the term was reversed and created a political community.[37] Some videos more directly encourage viewers to participate or connect by promoting the different Gezi Park protest hashtags such as #occupyGezi etc. Such mobilization on social media as an alternative to collective action is what Bennett and Segerberg call 'connective action'.[38] But what were people connecting to? In the case of music videos this question becomes quite complex. It may be that individuals' personal ideas connect with those of the protest movement[39], but equally in the case of a pop song or hip-hop video, for example, the aesthetics of the video or the recognizable composition of the music may be what primarily resonates with an individual in the way a catchy pop tune may hold the listeners' attention. The algorithmic structure of YouTube adds another layer of complexity

---

[31] Bianchi, 'Istanbul Sounding Like Revolution'; Way, 'Protest Music, Populism, Politics and Authenticity'.
[32] Way, 'Protest Music, Populism, Politics and Authenticity', 426.
[33] Kutschke and Street, 'Responses to Peter Manuel's "World Music and Activism Since the End of History [Sic]"'.
[34] Way, 'Protest Music, Populism, Politics and Authenticity'.
[35] Michel de Certeau, *The Practice of Everyday Life* (Berkeley: University of California Press, 1984).
[36] Dan Mercea and Helton Levy, 'The Activist Chroniclers of Occupy Gezi: Counterposing Visibility to Injustice', in *The Aesthetics of Global Protest: Visual Culture and Communication*, ed. Aidan McGarry et al. (Amsterdam University Press, 2019), 233–46.
[37] McGarry et al., 'Beyond the Iconic Protest Images'.
[38] Bennett and Segerberg, 'The Logic of Connective Action'.
[39] Simon Lindgren, *Digital Media & Society* (Los Angeles: SAGE, 2017).

to this as users navigate content in ways that are determined by the platform's algorithm. If you have been watching Turkish rap videos, further rap videos relating to the Gezi Park protests may be recommended to you, based on a combination of data about the musical style and aggregated user choices.[40]

## Music and Gezi Protest

On the one hand, research on the relationship between popular music and the Gezi Park protest includes the work by Parkinson and Way, both looking at Turkish indie rock as a politically oppositional voice in popular culture, coinciding with the Gezi Park movement by resisting rampant consumerism and value conservatism[41]. Bianchi's research, on the other hand, explores the music performed at the location during the occupation of the park and how the image of making music also features in the visual representation of Gezi Park protest, such as the iconic image of the man with a guitar facing the riot police[42]. The centrality of music making in the protest context is also exemplified by the music videos we have studied. Several videos visually represent people interacting around music, signalling its social dimension and function as collective action. Thus, as Bianchi states, 'music became political activism'[43]. In the first month of protest, 'about 30 new songs were specifically composed'[44], but perhaps more importantly it is to a large extent through music that the protest energy has lived on beyond the couple of weeks of actual occupation through continuous subsequent engagement online and across other performance venues and cultural fora. In this way, the YouTube music videos discussed in this chapter are part of the protest continuum across the digital realm and the streets. Looking at our sample of music videos, we find typical features of online participatory popular culture, employed as activist efforts. These include different types of audio-visual remixes (often referred to as mash-ups) and digital bricolage combining moving image, text, graphics, music

---

[40] Massimo Airoldi, Davide Beraldo and Alessandro Gandini, 'Follow the Algorithm: An Exploratory Investigation of Music on YouTube', *Poetics* 57 (2016): 1–13.
[41] Tom Parkinson, '"Indiestanbul": Counter-Hegemonic Music and Third Republicanism in Turkey', *Popular Music* 37, no. 1 (2018): 40–62; Way, 'Protest Music, Populism, Politics and Authenticity'.
[42] Bianchi, 'Istanbul Sounding Like Revolution'.
[43] Ibid., 212.
[44] Ibid., 213.

and sometimes spoken word. In the section that follows we seek to explore some of these aesthetics and practices that contribute to the efficiency of the music videos as protest communication and explore some of the defining features of the Gezi Park protest musical output online.

## Hybrid Sounds, Hybrid Forms: Unity in Diversity

One of the main themes of Gezi Park protest was unity in diversity. A most unexpected alliance was formed for example between the rival fans of Beşiktaş, Fenerbahce, and Galatasaray – 'The Big Three' of the Turkish Football League. During the protests, fans got together and formed 'Istanbul United', symbolized by a new hybrid flag that combined the colours and the logos of all three teams. Such hybridity is also evident in the music videos we analysed. There were hybrid sounds borrowing from folk, rock, pop, rap and jazz. Lyrics of old songs were often adapted to speak to Gezi themes and videos created by combining multiple short video clips or still images from both broadcast media and citizen footage collected from social media. Footage of police violence, usage of water cannon and gas, people's involvement in the protests, and collective resistance was edited either to illustrate and dramatize a performed piece of music or was simply published with an added musical soundtrack. There is also linguistic hybridity: to appeal to international audiences, some songs are multilingual (English-Turkish) or have English subtitles and several have text superimposed on the images, for example, displaying lyrics or the #direngeziparki hashtag onscreen. By combining sounds, forms, images and languages the protestors tried to present protest as something creative and artistic.

Visual mash-ups are one of the most commonly used creative strategy in the music videos. The most basic form of mash-up videos that we found are those that consist of a visually intact newscast package, reporting on the protest, with the original voiceover simply replaced with music. These videos still cast the documentary images in new light as the anchorage provided by the reporter is removed and images set to music are much more open to interpretation. Shared across different social networking sites and online platforms, they also provide cultural material for political commentary. The appropriation of mainstream (anti-Gezi) reporting performs a 'reading against the grain', suggesting that the same images can be interpreted differently. This is a significant strategy whereby activist use aesthetics to perform a critique of state ideology.

However, there are also some more sophisticated or skilful remixes, where an assortment of found footage (moving image) is carefully synced to the beat of the music. Typically, in these activist-produced videos the lyrics work to provide commentary to mainly documentary images. In one of the most viral videos from the protests, *Everyday I'm Çapulling*, a techno beat instrumental piece of music is used to convey the energy and atmosphere of the protests. By skilful editing of footage of protestors in the street, bodies are made to look like they move in sync with the music, conveying a gleeful portrayal of the protests as a dance party, or at least as something dynamic that you want to be part of. This video also, perhaps inadvertently, foregrounds the performativity of protest through the recasting of bodies in movement to music. The video is both playful and serious, and hence achieves a sense of legitimacy by adding authentic sound recordings of chants from the protests mixed with the techno music. In a way, this video is exemplary of the merging of popular culture and protest reporting that the Gezi Park protest music videos establish as a mode of online activism. It illustrates how the online DIY popular culture praxis of manipulating found footage in adept, often witty ways, to be eye-catching and fun to share, is used strategically in protest communication.

Several videos in the sample employ the strategy of 'recycling' a well-known and already popular song adding newly written Gezi specific lyrics to it. An example of this is the video by the internationally known Bogaziçi Jazz Choir. During the protests, a choir member rewrote the lyrics of one of their most popular songs 'Entarisi ala benziyor' (Her dress is a beautiful red),[45] otherwise a folk song popular across the Balkans, to convey a protest message and a call to mobilize:

Are you a *çapulcu vay vay* (well, well)
Are you an activist *vay vay* (well, well)

The gas mask like red
Pepper spray is like honey
My TOMA[46] is spraying at me

There will be a solution – people have risen
They are on barricades on the way to Taksim

---

[45] The choral arrangement is by Muammer Sun.
[46] A TOMA (Toplumsal Olaylara Müdahale Aracı, or Intervention Vehicle against Social Incidents) is an armoured water cannon designed for riot control manufactured by a Turkish company.

Gas masks come in many different styles
I'm marching for Taksim
Don't hang about,
Come for your rights

Gas masks come in many different styles
Gezi Park is as old as you
Come banging pans and pots[47]
With forks and spoons[48]

The video is shot by a member of the crowd that gathered around the choir members. It is lit up using mobile phones operating as torch lights as the choir were rehearsing the newly written lyrics, and posted on YouTube the next day. Despite being immersed in the political discourse and events of the protest, this video is clearly also about showcasing the group as musicians. It is a spontaneous street performance, channelling the 'Gezi spirit' symbolized by spontaneous collective singing. This instils some of the atmosphere from the protest on the ground into the online communication. The video is also an invitation to participate in protest (e.g. 'don't hang about come for your rights', 'come banging pans and pots') and protesting is depicted as social and fun (they can't help laughing at the new lyrics while singing) yet absurd (the TOMA spraying at its own people). A sense of hope dominates the video and it clearly seeks to unite around the Gezi activist identity of the *çapulcu*, which is a strongly emerging theme in the music videos. There are two main rhetorical mechanisms at play here: first the re-signification of the term '*çapulcu*', giving it the new meaning of 'social activist' (as in the lyrics above where the two meanings are intertwined in the opening lines) and second a unifying of the movement around the *çapulcu* identification. The playful and rebellious remixes of songs, sounds, genres, as well as of clips and images hint at the characteristics of the *çapulcu*: all-embracing, witty and glocal. Extending the idea of the glocal, in the next section we will take a closer look at an example of *çapulcu* rap.

---

[47] Refers to the protest where people violently hit kitchenware with spoons in support of Gezi around 9 pm every evening.
[48] '*Çapulcu musun vay vay. Eylemci misin vay vay. Gaz maskesi ala benziyor. Biber gazı bala benziyor. Benim tomam bana sıkıyor. Bulunur bi çare halk ayaktadır. Taksim yolunda barikattadır. Çapulcu musun vay vay. Eyleci misin vay vay. Gaz maskesi biçim biçim. Yürüyorum taksim için. Üşenme gel hakkın için. Bulunur bir çare halk ayaktadır. Taksim yolunda barikattadır. Çapulcu musun vay vay. Eylemci misin vay. Gaz maskesi çeşit çeşit. Gezi Parkı senle yaşıt. Vur tencere çatal kaşık. Bulunur bir çare halk ayaktadır. Taksim yolunda barikattadrı*'

## *Çapulcu* Rap

We were particularly drawn to the rap videos in our sample of music videos relating to the Gezi Park protest because of the way they exemplified an attempt to link the 'local' protest in Istanbul to wider international social justice movements. By using the genre of rap music, the activists not only stylistically link their music to socially conscious music that preceded them, but also take on the characteristics of the rebel performer telling it like it is, strongly associated with the genre. Taking a closer look at the example of the *Ayakta Kal çArşı* (Stand strong çArşı) video, posted by RAAD,[49] we will discuss how the rap video calls out the injustices caused by the government's and media's treatment of the Gezi activists, how it aims to mobilize protestors and authenticate the *çapulcu* identity by linking it to the well-known Turkish football supporter group çArşı.[50]

Rap is broadly seen as giving voice to a disadvantaged, disenfranchised, and racialized group in American society – poor black urban youth – and thus has rebellion and resistance to oppression at its core. Despite the fact that many contemporary forms of hip-hop, both the commercial and sub-cultural scenes, are not primarily produced or consumed as radical expressions of politics or activism, the sounds, styles and composition of rap music have resonated with groups involved with political struggle around the world[51] (Kahf 2012; Kellerer 2017; Tarifa 2012). Music journalist Andy Morgan, who has written about the role of music in the Arab uprisings, portrays how rapper El Général helped spark the uprising in Tunisia by posting his videos challenging the regime on Facebook[52]. As a commercially successful American popular culture export, rap culture has a global market and is accessible to huge audiences via online distribution. It is also highly adaptable to local tastes as illustrated by highly successful domestic artists rapping in their own language. Its bricolage or 'sampling' tradition means that it lends itself to playful remixes bringing in

---

[49] Also known as the Gezi Park March.
[50] An Istanbul-based football supporter group, founded in 1982 on leftist, anarchist, anti-establishment principles by small shop owners in the Beşiktaş's çArşı district.
[51] Usama Kahf, 'Arabic Hip-hop: Claims of Authenticity and Identity of a New Genre,' in *That's the Joint!: The Hip-hop Studies Reader*, 2nd ed., ed. Murrey Forman and Mark Anthony Neal (Abingdon: Routledge, 2012), 359–85; Katja Kellerer, '"Mweya weToyitoyi – The Spirit of Protest": Re-inventing Toyi-toyi in Zimbabwean Hip Hop,' *Social Dynamics* 43, no. 2 (2017): 199–214; Ariana Tarifa, 'Hip Hop as Empowerment: Voices in El Alto, Bolivia,' *International Journal of Qualitative Studies in Education* 25, no. 4 (2012): 397–415.
[52] Andy Morgan, 'THE SOUNDTRACK TO THE ARAB REVOLUTIONS – From Fear to Fury', *Andy Morgan Writes* (blog), 2011, https://www.andymorganwrites.com/soundtrack-to-the-arab-revolutions-from-fear-to-fury/.

local and traditional music styles or borrowing highly recognizable cords and lines from a well-known song, which is essentially what the *Everyday I'm Çapulling* video does by channelling rapper Rick Ross's 2006 song 'Everyday I'm Hustlin".

The tradition of Turkish rap dates back to Germany and the Turkish minority, those so-called Turkish guest workers.[53] Nonetheless, Turkish rappers are also active in other countries thanks to the Internet operating as an important tool for the Turkish-speaking hip-hop community.[54] Solomon discusses insidious Turkish hip-hop culture and presents the example of two rap groups – R.A.K. Sobataj and Tuzak, who explore and promote Islamic and conservative values. But Islam is not the only theme among rappers in Turkey.[55] For instance, the group called Tahribad-ı İsyan, one of the groups that were active during the Gezi Park protests, uses rap to resist the restructuring of Istanbul neighbourhoods.[56]

The political merit of rap music in itself is not something we seek to settle in this chapter.[57] However, what is clear is that the marketing strategy of rap to achieve 'authenticity' through a 'telling it like it is' rhetoric and image pairs with political communication.[58] It produces, what Kane calls, 'moral capital' as a form of emotional authenticity lending valuable rhetorical 'ethos' to the music as protest communication.[59] In the case of the video posted by RAAD, performing the song *Ayakta Kal çArşı* (Stand strong çArşı), the 'moral capital' is compounded by the association with the football supporter group çArşı, one of the key actors during the protests with an established public image of being the guardians of

---

[53] Caroline Diessel, 'Bridging East and West on the "Orient Express": Oriental Hip-hop in the Turkish Diaspora of Berlin,' *Journal of Popular Music Studies* 13, no. 1 (2001): 165–87; Ayhan Kaya, 'Aesthetics of Diaspora: Contemporary Minstrels in Turkish Berlin,' *Journal of Ethnic and Migration Studies* 28, no. 1 (2002): 43–62.

[54] Thomas Solomon, '"Living Underground Is Tough": Authenticity and Locality in the Hip-hop Community in Istanbul, Turkey,' *Popular Music* 24, no. 1 (2005): 1–20.

[55] Thomas Solomon, 'Hardcore Muslims: Islamic Themes in Turkish Rap in Diaspora and in the Homeland,' *Yearbook for Traditional Music* 38 (2006): 59–78.

[56] Büşra, 'Tahribad-ı isyan Gezizekalılar', YouTube video, 00:05:36, 13 August 2015, https://www.youtube.com/watch?v=FB253Dz4XGU. Further noteworthy examples of Turkish rap videos referencing the Gezi Park protest on YouTube include: *Şanışer & Alef High #direngezi*, https://www.youtube.com/watch?v=DOMAE-MTXBk; Fuat Ergin's *Karar Bizim* (in collaboration with Işıl Eğrikavuk and Jozef E. Amado), Fuat Ergin, 'Fuat Ergin | Karar Bizim', YouTube video, 00:03:52, 9 June 2013, https://www.youtube.com/watch?time_continue=19&v=Mxcw4gxNf2U, and *OZBİ – Asi (Gezi Park Şarkısı)*, youtupec youtu, 'OZBİ - Asi (Gezi Park Şarkısı) Bu Klip Çok Konuşulur', YouTube video, 00:04:08, 21 July 2013, https://www.youtube.com/watch?v=3jFpsKhfdMQ.

[57] See Geoffrey Baker, 'Preachers, Gangsters, Pranksters: MC Solaar and Hip-hop as Overt and Covert Revolt,' *Journal of Popular Culture* 44, no. 2 (2011): 233–55.

[58] Katina R. Stapleton, 'From the Margins to Mainstream: The Political Power of Hip-hop,' *Media, Culture & Society* 20, no. 2 (1998): 219–34.

[59] Kane in Street, *Music and Politics*.

justice and a vocal voice against anything unfair[60]. Their choice of the genre, therefore, also strikes a cord with çArşı's rebellious image. The group's logo contains the anarchist 'A', and their motto is 'çArşı is against everything'. With their creative and witty banners, they have announced being against many things including fascism, animal rights abuses, capitalism, nuclear plants, domestic violence, child pornography and climate change. The group was one of the first to join the Gezi Park protests (see Figure 12.1) and the witty humour and antagonism its members brought to Gezi helped generate public support[61]. The connection between the supporter group and the protest movement is manifested in the rap video when the performers speaking as çArşı members not only celebrate the *çapulcu* but fully take on the identity:

I'm just a '*ÇAPULCU*'
I know who I am[62]

**Figure 12.1** A çArşı supporters' banner in Gezi Park with the slogan 'Taksim is ours. çArşı is ours. The street is ours'. licensed under the creative commons Attribution-Share Alike 2.0 Generic license.

---

[60] Hakan Övünç Ongur and Tevfik Orkun Develi, 'Bir Alt Kültür Olarak Türkiye'de Rock Müzik ve Toplumsal Muhalefet İlişkisi,' *VII. Uluslararası Sosyoloji Kongresi* (02–05 Ekim Muğla, 2013), 155–80.
[61] Erhart, 'United in Protest'.
[62] '*Ben sadece bir çapulcuyum. Ne olduğumu biliyorum*'.

This video brings together amateur footage from the protests in the streets, interspersed with close ups of Bora Gramm performing his rap, energetically expressed to camera, with genre-characteristic body language. Bora Gramm is depicted in multifarious ways: recording in a studio setting, establishing him as a professional musician; street rapping whilst marching with the crowd; rapping outdoors in the night using a shaky handheld camera to give the impression of a spontaneous performer, and as such an integral part of the protest with his make-do approach to performance of protest. In this sense, the video also connects to a core characteristic of rap videos where artists often perform in an urban 'street' environment. The video makes a case for the right to protest and offers strong criticism of the media and the police. This relates to the point made by Özge Özdüzen that within video activism, activists' bodies either depicted or indirectly represented through the movements of the handheld camera function as a source of protest narrative[63].

Images and text are juxtaposed to draw attention to the gap between what should be the case in terms of democratic justice and the freedom of expression, on the one hand, and the political reality of the situation in Turkey, on the other. The video starts with a quotation from the constitution of the Republic of Turkey noting Article 34, which says that 'everyone has the right to hold meetings, demonstrations without prior permission unarmed and peacefully'. Then follows a set of dictionary entries presented in a stylistically formal way, using typewriter lettering for key words such as *direniş* (resistance), *dayanişma* (solidarity), *adalet* (justice), *polis* (police) and *medya* (media). The media entry is accompanied the image of a penguin, one of the symbols of the protests that mocks the Turkish mainstream media's refusal to report on the events (CNN Türk broadcasted a documentary about penguins whilst protest events were unfolding in Istanbul and reported on by CNN International). The image of 'penguin media' draws heavily on irony as a rhetorical tool, and this indirect argumentative reasoning is used throughout the video: for instance, the police is seen destroying tents, removing banners and attacking the protestors which is juxtaposed with the dictionary entry for *polis* (police), which mentions the police force's duty to protect the citizens. The paradox of the 'universally' accepted dictionary definitions in contrast with what unfolds in the protest footage dramatizes the video. Similarly, the quote about the right to protest is set in contrast to images

---

[63] Özge Özdüzen, 'Bearing Witness to Authoritarianism and Commoning through Video Activism and Political Film-Making after the Gezi Protests', in *The Aesthetics of Global Protest*, 191–210.

of protestors suffering violence and others helping those exposed to tear gas. For this strategy to be effective, we argue, the 'moral capital' of the sender, as discussed earlier, is imperative, and thus the 'rapper-protestor' position is what makes the ironic delivery ring true.

In the song rapper Bora Gramm addresses those who have been taken in custody during the protests urging them to 'stay strong'. It opens with a section sung in English:

> You gotta stand on ya feet
> If y'all need equality
> Stand on ya feet
> This is 'Anonymous'
> 'Red' and all these
> Other colours around it

Hereby, the group is calling for citizens to mobilize, to stand up for what they believe in, and thereafter connects the Gezi Park struggle to the Internet-based activists of 'Anonymous' and places themselves at the heart of contemporary protest movements. Then the performer begins rapping in Turkish about the 'Istanbul United' spirit at Gezi, and how it has eradicated longstanding football fan antagonism declaring that the rivals Fenerbahçe and Galatasaray are no longer enemies with the following lines: 'See, we are not enemies anymore – Galatasaray Fenerbahçe and Beşiktaş are everywhere', and declaring that what unites them is their stance 'against this system' [the AKP government]. Later in the song the theme of standing united against a common opponent is further emphasized in the lines 'a day comes when there are jackals all around – merging is the only solution', and 'when it is time to defy, hold my arm – we are one although our colours are different'. The main chorus is sung in the style of a melodic chant:

> Go on Gezi Park!
> Resist Gezi Park!
> Merge!
> Stay strong!
> Go on Gezi Park!
> Resist Gezi Park![64]

The video shifts from Turkish to English and the narrative continues to talk about togetherness and brotherhood, drawing on the notion of a shared football

---

[64] 'Hadi gezi parkı / Diren gezi parkı / Tek yürek ooo'.

fan identity, extending it to also apply to the protest movement. In some lines the political expression is more explicit: the performer advocates anti-consumption, anti-individualism – very much in the çArşı sprit he calls to 'say goodbye to buyin' anything you wanna have – Y'd betta share cuz we share this life'. He paints a picture of the Gezi protest as a leaderless movement that anyone can join: 'You should realize that a single hand can't make a noise – there are no commanders in us – this is a public resistance!' and describes çArşı as a group that is against all that is unfair, if need be, even against itself.[65] However, the lyrics also narrate street bravado and toughness, typical of 'gansta rap': 'they all swore to die for their hood' and 'we are fair and tough in any hood', thus making it universally recognizable as a rap text, appealing to audiences that are into the music genre, as an expression of urban youth culture, but not necessarily attuned with Turkish politics. For example, utilizing the image of 'the hood', which is a hallmark trope of the genre, makes it familiar to listeners and widens its appeal. Social media is absolutely key to the global spread of a socially conscious hip-hop as an idiom of opposition that many different social movements have appropriated and engendered, but as we have demonstrated in this chapter, its aesthetics could equally be a resource for musical political communication.

## Concluding Remarks

The Gezi protest yielded a wide range of musical expression across a diverse range of genres. The way it mediated and remediated recordings and remixes of music and visual content on YouTube served to amplify the protest voice, mobilized through energy and emotion, and both consolidate and make accessible to wider publics the *çapulcu* identity. Online platforms and social media are not only used to create audiences, but enable a wider participation. Digitally 'creative citizens' as well as activist performers contribute to movements and generate political commentary by producing music videos, ranging from visual collages of found footage set to music to recorded live performances and sharing these on social media. Thus, the proliferation of music online constitutes an additional dimension to how the 'local' protest in Istanbul has gained support

---

[65] Here, he is referring to an actual incident in 2008 when the spokesperson for the group announced that çArşı will put an end to all its actions. The unconfirmed reason was unrest within the group. A banner was also held by which the group members announced that çArşı was now against itself.

around the world and resonated with wide ranging and diverse publics. The online output, we suggest, is a continuum of the protests that extends beyond the occupation of the Gezi Park area. Music videos, both original recordings and remixes, could be a vital part of a movement's larger ecology of communication, expressions and connections.

As demonstrated in this chapter, looking at the YouTube videos, music is often used to dramatize images, and to convey emotions. Editing practices are one tool through which vernacular voices express dissent, for example, by combining music, text and images in ways that reveal and challenge dominant framings of the protest movement, but also other strategies such as producing new lyrics to already popular songs were used. Furthermore, we found a particularly vital output in the rap videos. The remix ethos of rap music combined with its energy, and subaltern rebellious perspective, encapsulate the musical aesthetics of protest. Online music videos are a form of digital activism that sustains social and political consciousness affectively both during and beyond the protest event and as we have sought to demonstrate here are utilized to resist symbolic domination.

# Bibliography

Airoldi, Massimo, Davide Beraldo and Alessandro Gandini. 'Follow the Algorithm: An Exploratory Investigation of Music on YouTube.' *Poetics* 57 (2016): 1–13.

Arat, Yeşım. 'Violence, Resistance, and Gezi Park.' *International Journal of Middle East Studies* 45, no. 4 (2013): 807–9.

Askanius, Tina. 'Online Video Activism and Political Mash-up Genres.' *JOMEC Journalism, Media and Cultural Studies* 4 (2013): http://portal.research.lu.se/ws/files/4197460/4180639.pdf.

Atak, Kıvanç. 'From Malls to Barricades: Reflections on the Social Origins of Gezi,' paper presented at the symposium Rebellion and Protest from Maribor to Taksim Social Movements in the Balkans, Graz, Austria, 12–14 December 2013.

Baker, Geoffrey. 'Preachers, Gangsters, Pranksters: MC Solaar and Hip-hop as Overt and Covert Revolt.' *Journal of Popular Culture* 44, no. 2 (2011): 233–55.

Bennett, Lance and Alexandra Segerberg. 'The Logic of Connective Action.' *Information, Communication & Society* 15, no. 5 (2012): 739–68.

Bianchi, Raffaella. 2018. 'Istanbul Sounding Like Revolution: The Role of Music in the Gezi Park Occupy Movement.' *Popular Music* 37, no. 2 (2018): 212–36.

Certeau, Michel de. *The Practice of Everyday Life*. Berkeley: University of California Press, 1984.

Conti, Olivia. 'Political Remix Video as a Vernacular Discourse.' In *The Routledge Companion to Remix Studies*, edited by Eduardo Navas, Owen Gallagher and xtine burrough, 332–43. New York: Routledge, 2015.

Diessel, Caroline. 2001. 'Bridging East and West on the "Orient Express": Oriental Hip-hop in the Turkish Diaspora of Berlin.' *Journal of Popular Music Studies* 13, no. 1 (2001): 165–87.

Edwards, Bob and John McCarthy. 'Resources and Social Movement Mobilization.' In *The Blackwell Companion to Social Movements*, edited by David Snow, Sarah Soule and Hanspeter Kriesi, 116–52. Oxford; Blackwell, 2004.

Erhart, Itir. 'United in Protest: From "Living and Dying with Our Colors" to "Let All the Colours of the World Unite".' *International Journal of the History of Sport* 31, no. 14 (2014): 1724–38.

Frith, Simon. *Performing Rites: On the Value of Popular Music*. Cambridge, MA: Harvard University Press, 1996.

Kahf, Usama. 'Arabic Hip-Hop: Claims of Authenticity and Identity of a New Genre.' In *That's the Joint!: The Hip-hop Studies Reader*, 2nd ed., edited by Murrey Forman and Mark Anthony Neal, 359–85. Abingdon: Routledge, 2012.

Kaya, Ayhan. 'Aesthetics of Diaspora: Contemporary Minstrels in Turkish Berlin.' *Journal of Ethnic and Migration Studies* 28, no. 1 (2002): 43–62.

Kellerer, Katja. '"Mweya weToyitoyi – The Spirit of Protest": Re-inventing Toyi-toyi in Zimbabwean Hip Hop.' *Social Dynamics* 43, no. 2 (2017): 199–214.

Kutschke, Beate, Noriko Manabe and John Street. 'Responses to Peter Manuel's "World Music and Activism since the End of History [sic]".' *Music and Politics* 11, no. 1 (2017): https://quod.lib.umich.edu/m/mp/9460447.0011.102/--responses-to-peter-manuels-world-music-and-activism-since?rgn=main;view=fulltext.

Lindgren, Simon. *Digital Media & Society*. Los Angeles: SAGE, 2017.

Lynskey, Dorian. *33 Revolutions per Minute: A History of Protest Songs*. London: Faber, 2010.

Manuel, Peter. 'World Music and Activism Since the End of History.' *Music and Politics* 11, no. 1 (2017): https://quod.lib.umich.edu/m/mp/9460447.0011.101/--world-music-and-activism-since-the-end-of-history-sic?rgn=main;view=fulltext.

Martini, Michele. 'On the User's Side: YouTube and Distant Witnessing in the Age of Technology-Enhanced Mediability.' *Convergence* 24, no. 1 (2018): 33–49.

Mattern, Mark. *Acting in Concert: Music, Community, and Political Action*. New Brunswick: Rutgers University Press, 1998.

McGarry, Aidan, Olu Jenzen, Hande Eslen-Ziya, Itir Erhart and Umut Korkut. 'Beyond the Iconic Protest Images: The Performance of "Everyday Life" on Social Media During Gezi Park.' *Social Movement Studies* 18, no. 3 (2019): 184–204.

McKerrell, Simon and Lyndon C.S. Way. 'Understanding Music as Multimodal Discourse.' In *Music as Multimodal Discourse: Semiotics, Power and Protest*, edited by Lyndon C.S. Way and Simon McKerrell, 1–20. London: Bloomsbury Academic, 2017.

Mercea, Dan and Helton Levy. 'The Activist Chroniclers of Occupy Gezi: Counterposing Visibility to Injustice'. In *The Aesthetics of Global Protest: Visual Culture and Communication*, edited by Aidan McGarry, Itir Erhart, Hande Eslen-Ziya, Olu Jenzen, and Umut Korkut, 233–46. Amsterdam University Press, 2019..

Mirzoeff, Nicholas. *How to See the World*. London: Pelican, 2015.

Morgan, Andy. 'The Soundtrack to the Arab Revolutions – From Fear to Fury' (2011), at https://www.andymorganwrites.com/soundtrack-to-the-arab-revolutions-from-fear-to-fury/.

Övünç Ongur, Hakan and Tevfik Orkun Develi. 'Bir Alt Kültür Olarak Türkiye'de Rock Müzik ve Toplumsal Muhalefet İlişkisi', *VII. Uluslararası Sosyoloji Kongresi*. 02–05 Ekim Muğla, 155–80, 2013.

Parkinson, Tom. '"Indiestanbul": Counter-hegemonic Music and Third Republicanism in Turkey.' *Popular Music* 37, no. 1 (2018): 40–62.

Poell, Thomas and Erik Borra. 'Twitter, YouTube, and Flickr as Platforms of Alternative Journalism: The Social Media Account of the 2010 Toronto G20 Protests.' *Journalism* 13, no. 6 (2012): 695–713.

Railton, Diane and Paul Watson. *Music Video and the Politics of Representation*. Edinburgh: Edinburgh University Press, 2011.

Solomon, Thomas. '"Living Underground Is Tough": Authenticity and Locality in the Hip-Hop Community in Istanbul, Turkey.' *Popular Music* 24, no. 1 (2005): 1–20.

Solomon, Thomas. 'Hardcore Muslims: Islamic Themes in Turkish Rap in Diaspora and in the Homeland.' *Yearbook for Traditional Music* 38 (2006): 59–78.

Stapleton, Katina R. 'From the Margins to Mainstream: The Political Power of Hip-Hop.' *Media, Culture & Society* 20, no. 2 (1998): 219–34.

Street, John. *Rebel Rock: The Politics of Popular Music*. Oxford: Blackwell, 1986.

Street, John. *Music and Politics*. Cambridge: Polity, 2012.

Tarifa, Ariana. 'Hip Hop as Empowerment: Voices in El Alto, Bolivia.' *International Journal of Qualitative Studies in Education* 25, no. 4 (2012): 397–415.

Taylor, Verta and Nella Van dyke. '"Get up, Stand up": Tactical Repertoires of Social Movements.' In *The Blackwell Companion to Social Movements*, edited by David Snow, Sarah Soule and Hanspeter Kriesi, 262–93. Oxford; Blackwell, 2014.

Thorson, Kjerstin, Brian Ekdale, Porismita Borah and Kang Namkoong. 'YouTube and Proposition 8: A Case Study in Video Activism.' *Information, Communication & Society* 13, no. 3 (2010): 325–49.

Uldam, Julie and Tina Askanius. 'Online Civic Cultures: Debating Climate Change Activism on YouTube.' *International Journal of Communication* 7 (2013): 1185–1204.

Way, Lyndon. 'YouTube as a Site of Debate through Populist Politics: The Case of a Turkish Protest Pop Video.' *Journal of Multicultural Discourses* 10, no. 2 (2015): 180–96.

Way, Lyndon. 'Protest Music, Populism, Politics and Authenticity: The Limits and Potential of Popular Music's Articulation of Subversive Politics.' *Journal of Language and Politics* 15, no. 4 (2016): 422–45.

Weij, Frank and Pauwke Berkers. 'The Politics of Musical Activism: Western YouTube Reception of Pussy Riot's Punk Performances.' *Convergence: The International Journal of Research into New Media Technologies* 25, no.2 (2019): 287–306.

# List of Contributors

**Juan Bermúdez** is a Mexican ethnomusicologist. He studied music (marimba) at the University of Sciences and Arts of Chiapas, as well ethnomusicology at the University of Music and Performing Arts in Graz. Bermúdez received his PhD in ethnomusicology from the University of Vienna with a thesis about the musicking of the smartphone application TikTok. He has worked as a research assistant at the Institute of Ethnomusicology, University of Music and Performing Arts, Graz, and later as a university assistant and uni:docs fellow at the Department of Musicology, University of Vienna. Currently, he is visiting scholar at the Department of Arts and Musicology, Autonomous University of Barcelona. His current work focuses on music and dance practices in digital media and multimedia contexts.

**Jay David Bolter** is the Wesley Chair of New Media and co-Director of the Augmented Environments Lab at the Georgia Institute of Technology. He is the author of *Remediation* (1999), with Richard Grusin; and *Windows and Mirrors* (2003), with Diane Gromala. Bolter is working with colleagues Blair MacIntyre and Maria Engberg to create AR and VR experiences for cultural heritage, entertainment and expression. Together they have recently published *Reality Media: Augmented and Virtual Reality* (2021).

**Christine Boone** is Associate Professor of Music at the University of North Carolina Asheville. Since receiving her Ph.D. in Music Theory from the University of Texas at Austin, Christine has established herself as one of the foremost scholars on mashups, and her work on this subject has been published in several national and international forums. Christine, a soprano, is an active performer in both choral ensembles and solo work. She has also put her musical knowledge to work on National Public Radio's classical music game show, "Piano Puzzler." For more on Christine's work with mashups, see http://christineboone.wix.com/mashademia.

**Brian Drawert** is a researcher at the University of North Carolina Asheville. His research is focused on computational science, specifically using computer and mathematical models to understand complex biological systems. He received his Ph.D. in Computer Science from University of California Santa Barbara in 2013, with an emphasis on Computational Science and Engineering, a M.S. in Physics from DePaul University in 2007, and B.S. in Computer Science from the Illinois Institute of Technology in 2001. Prior to his academic career, he was a software industry professional and entrepreneur, working at five different startup companies.

**Júlia Durand** is a musicology PhD candidate at the NOVA University of Lisbon, Portugal. She is a member of the Center of Sociology and Musical Aesthetics (CESEM). In addition to several papers on music and audiovisuals presented at international conferences such as *Music and the Moving Image*, her research has been published as chapters in edited volumes and in the journals *Music, Sound and the Moving Image and Revista Portuguesa de Musicologia*. Her PhD is funded with an FCT grant (SFRH/BD/132254/2017) and it focuses on the production and use of library music in online media.

**Itır Erhart** is an Associate Professor in the Department of Media and Communication Systems, Istanbul Bilgi University. She is the author of the book *What Am I?* and several articles on gender, sports, human rights, social movements and media, including 'United in Protest: From "Living and Dying with Our Colors" to "Let All the Colors of the World Unite"' and 'Ladies of Besiktas: A Dismantling of Male Hegemony at Inönü Stadium'. She is also a social entrepreneur and an Ashoka fellow.

**Hande Eslen-Ziya** is an Associate Professor of Sociology at the University of Stavanger. She has a gender specialization from Central European University, in Budapest, Hungary. Her research has been published in *Social Movement Studies, European Journal of Women's Studies, Culture, Health and Sexuality, Leadership, Men and Masculinities and Social Politics*. Eslen-Ziya has also authored a book that investigates how men construct their identities throughout their developmental trajectories: *The Social Construction and Developmental Trajectories of Masculinities* (2017).

**Joana Freitas** is a PhD candidate in Musicology at the School of Social Sciences and Humanities of the NOVA University of Lisbon with a FCT PhD Scholarship (SFRH/BD/139120/2018). She completed her Master's degree with a dissertation titled '"The Music is the Only Thing you Don't Have to Mod": The Musical Composition in Modification Files for Videogames' and is an integrated researcher of the Centre for the Study of the Sociology and Aesthetics of Music (CESEM). She is also a member of the Research Clusters in Music and Cyberculture (CysMus) and Gender and Music (NEGEM), integrated in the Group of Critical Theory and Communication (GTCC). Her main areas of interest are video game music, film music, audiovisual media, interactivity, digital culture and cybercommunities, gender and sexuality. Joana is co-editor of this book's companion volume, *YouTube and Music: Online Culture and Everyday Life* (2023).

**Aidan McGarry** is a Reader in International Politics at the Institute for Diplomacy and International Governance at Loughborough University, London. His research focuses on social movements, protest, political voice, and marginalized communities (www.aidanmcgarry.com). He is the author of four books, including *Who Speaks for Roma?* (2010) and *Romaphobia: The Last Acceptable Racism in Europe* (2017). He was Principal Investigator of an Arts and Humanities Research Council (AHRC)-funded project 'Aesthetics of Protest: Visual Culture and Communication in Turkey' (www.aestheticsofprotest.com) from 2016 to 2018. In 2018-2019 he is a EURIAS/Marie Curie Fellow at the Netherlands Institute for Advanced Study in Amsterdam, where he is writing a book on political voice.

**Dr Michael N. Goddard**, is Reader in Film and Screen Media at Goldsmiths, University of London. He has published widely on international cinema and audiovisual culture as well as cultural and media theory. He is also a media theorist, especially in the fields of media ecologies and media archaeology, as well as in digital media. In media archaeology, his most significant contribution is the monograph, *Guerrilla Networks* (2018), the culmination of his media archaeological research to date, which was published by Amsterdam University Press. His previous book, *Impossible Cartographies* (2013) was on the cinema of Raúl Ruiz. He has also been doing research on the fringes of popular music focusing on groups such as The Fall, Throbbing Gristle and Laibach, which has culminated in two edited books on noise, *Reverberations* (2012) and *Resonances* (2013). He is currently working on a book on the British post-industrial group Coil, and a new research project on genealogies of immersive media and virtuality.

**Derya Güçdemir** holds an MA Degree in Cultural Studies and Media from Hacettepe University, Ankara Turkey with a thesis entitled 'Algorithmic Culture and Data Ethics'. Derya is interested in digital inequalities and the social implications of algorithms and data and is currently a Program Officer at Re:Coded, working towards providing youth with the skills and mindset to thrive in the digital economy.

**Dr Olu Jenzen** is a Reader in Media Studies at the University of Brighton, UK and the Director of the Research Centre for Transforming Sexuality and Gender. Her research ranges over different themes in digital media cultural studies and gender and sexuality, with a particular interest in LGBTQ+ digital activism. She is the co-editor of *The Aesthetics of Global Protest* (2020) and the special issue 'Global Feminist and Queer Visual Activism' (2022) for the *Journal of Cultural Analysis and Social Change*.

**Umut Korkut** is Professor in International Politics at Glasgow School for Business and Society at Glasgow Caledonian University. Prof. Korkut has expertise in how political discourse makes audiences and has recently studied visual imagery and audience making. Prof. Korkut is the Lead for the EU AMIF (Asylum and Migrant Integration Fund)-funded project 'VOLPOWER: Enhancing Community Building and Social Integration through Dialogue and Collaboration amongst Young Europeans and Third Country Nationals', which assesses youth volunteering in sports, arts, and culture in view of social integration. He is also the Primary Investigator for the Horizon 2020-funded RESPOND and DEMOS projects on migration governance and populism.

**Lisa Perrott** is Senior Lecturer at the University of Waikato. Her interests include documentary, animation and transmedia, with an emphasis on the relations between audio and visual media, popular music and music video. Lisa is co-editor, with Holly Rogers and Carol Vernallis, of this Bloomsbury book series *New Approaches to Sound, Music and Media*, and the edited collection *Transmedia Directors: Artistry, Industry and New Audiovisual Aesthetics* (2019). She is also co-editor, with Ana Cristina Mendes, of the Routledge book *David Bowie and Transmedia Stardom* (2019). Lisa is author of the books *David Bowie and the Art of Music Video* (2023) and *David Bowie and the Transformation of Music Video (1984–2016 and Beyond)* (2024).

**João Francisco Porfírio** is a PhD student in Musicology at NOVA FCSH and an FCT PhD Grant holder (SFRH/BD/136264/2018). He completed his Master's degree in Musical Arts at the same institution with the dissertation 'Sounds Like Home' – *The Domestic Soundscapes in the Construction of Daily Life and as Object of Composition*. At CESEM, he is a member of the Critical Theory and Communication Group where he develops research on subjects related to ambient music and the soundscapes of domestic everyday life. João is co-editor of this book's companion volume, *YouTube and Music: Online Culture and Everyday Life* (2023).

**Holly Rogers** is Professor of Music and Director of Research at Goldsmiths, University of London, where she runs the MA Music (Audiovisual Cultures). She is author of *Sounding the Gallery: Video and the Rise of Art-Music* (2013), *Re/Sounding Spaces* (2024) and co-author of *Studying Twentieth-Century Music in the West* (2022). She has edited several books on audiovisual culture, including *Music and Sound in Documentary Film* (2014), *The Music and Sound of Experimental Film* (2017), *Transmedia Directors: Artistry, Industry and New Audiovisual Aesthetics* (2019), *Cybermedia* (2021) and *YouTube and Music: Online Culture and Everyday Life* (2023). Holly is also a founding editor for this Bloomsbury book series and the Goldsmiths journal "Sonic Scope: New Approaches to Audiovisual Culture".

**Henrik Smith-Sivertsen** is a senior researcher at the Royal Danish Library, responsible for the Danish popular music archives. He did his PhD on popular music translation and cover theory and has primarily worked with European popular music history from a wide range of perspectives, including value, technology, the music industry and musical versioning practices. His publications include studies of the Anglophone pop revolution in the early 1960s, music industry history, music radio history and the digital music revolution. Since 2012 he has specialized in digital archives and has conducted several collecting and research projects on digital music heritage.

**Edward Katrak Spencer** is Lecturer I in Music at Magdalen College, University of Oxford, and a Postdoctoral Research Fellow at the University of Birmingham, where he works on the AHRC project 'Music and the Internet: Towards a Digital Sociology of Music' led by Christopher Haworth. His present research investigates popular music's entanglements with internet subcultures, populist politics and conspiratorial sentiments. He is also currently a Postdoctoral Research Associate on the AHRC project 'Everything is Connected: Conspiracy Theories in the Age of the Internet' led by Peter Knight at the University of Manchester.

**Dr. Scott B. Spencer** is an Assistant Professor of Musicology at the University of Southern California's Thornton School of Music. His research explores the intersections of oral tradition and digital culture. He has published in the journals *Explorations in Media Ecology*, the *Journal of the Society for American Music* and a variety of edited volumes. He also edited the book *The Ballad Collectors of North America* (2011). In addition to teaching, Spencer runs the Sound in Sacred Spaces working group – sponsored by USC's Levan Institute for the Humanities and UCLA's Stavros Niarchos Foundation Center for the Study of Hellenic Culture.

**Jonas Wolf** is a PhD candidate in musicology at the International Graduate Centre for the Study of Culture (GCSC) at Justus Liebig University in Giessen, Germany. His work focuses on issues of digitality, intermediality and performativity with a special emphasis on contemporary audiovisual aesthetics and music theatre. He has contributed articles to several journals such as *Die Tonkunst, On_Culture and Seiltanz*. Currently, he is writing his doctoral thesis on vernacular musical aesthetics on YouTube.

# Index

2Cellos 19
'2 Girls, 1 Cup' 75
"7 Years, The Honest Version" (video by Edmondson) 103–4
'7 Years and Lukas Graham' 97
*7 Years of Lukas Graham* (documentary) 93
'7 Years' (song by Lukas Graham) 24, 93–4, 97–110
   cover versions 102–8
   music tutorial 106–7
   numbers of uploads 108
   original version(s) 98–101
   promotional tour 100–1
   versions 94, 97–110
$crim (Scott Arceneaux Jr.) 173–5
$uicideboy$ 172–5

Aasman, Susan 109–10
aca-fan 23, 244, 244n6, 264
acapellas 16, 40–2, 44, 101, 253
*Adaptation and Natural Selection* (Williams) 227
Adorno, Theodor 38
advertisement/advertising methods 156–7
'Aesthetics of Protest' project 268
affective labour 73, 76, 77–83, 89; *see also* free labour; reaction videos
affordances 3, 6, 9, 16, 76, 83, 113, 132, 169, 173, 210
   Born on 11
   musical sound 272
   protest music 268–9
   spreadability 3
African Americans 24, 76, 82–3, 86, 87, 90; *see also* Harlem Shake (meme/video); hip hop
   Harlem Shake (dance) 61
   racial conflicts 82
   reactors (*see* reaction videos)
   soul music 243
   twerking 13–14

The All-American Rejects 87
Allocca, Kevin 147
'All the Small Things' 87
alternative musical voices 274
Amazon Music 147
*Americana* (album) 86–7
Anderson, Chris 8
'Any Dream Will Do' (Webber) 12
Apple Music 22, 147
Archibold, Race 39–40
aria 12
Artemiev, Edward 115
Arthurs, Jane 156–7
Artificial Intelligence (AI) 26, 35–49; *see also* automated mashups
artistic integrity 263–5; *see also* authorship
Arts and Humanities Research Council (AHRC) 268
Ashley, Rick 14, 17
Atlasito 11
Audio Blocks 209
Audio Library 211
Audio Network 210
audiovisual remediation 8, 10–20; *see also* remediation
Auslander, Philip 193
authorship 27–8, 29, 66, 67, 152, 240
   artistic integrity 263–5
   collaborative 249, 250, 251–2, 258, 264
   de-centring 131–2
   dispersed 249, 252–3
   distribution 132, 134
   Jenkins' alternative model 250
   re-authorship 249, 252, 253–60, 263
   sole 252, 264
automated mashups 35–49
   Magic iPod 38–40, 43
   Rave DJ 42–9
   YouTube DJ 40–2
*Ayakta Kal çArşı* (Stand strong cArşı) 279, 280–1

Bailey, Madilyn 17, 19
bait-and-switch trolling 14, 52, 61; *see also* trolling
bass drop memes; *see also* memes
　bottle-flip 53, 64–7
　Harlem Shake meme 52, 59–62
　mic drop 52–3, 62–4
BBC 103, 104, 118
Beach Boys 42, 43
'Beat It' (Jackson) 11
*The Beatles: Get Back* 247
bebop (jazz genre) 224
bedroom music culture 7
behaviour-driven memes 54, 55, 64; *see also* memes
behind-the-scenes footage 10
Benjamin, Walter 85
Bennett, W. Lance 274
Berkers, Pauwke 273
Bernstein, Jonathan 82
Bertha (professional videographer) 207–8
'The Best Troll Songs' 213
Bianchi, Raffaella 274, 275
Bieber, Justin 192
*Big Brother* 74
BillyYouSoCrazy 87–8
Black, Alex 208
Black Lives Matter (#BlackLivesMatter) 82, 192
Blink-182 87
'Blink-182 Reacts to Kids Reacting to Blink-182' 87
Bocelli, Andrea 127
Bolter, Jay 9, 10, 21, 26, 77
'Boris Johnson's Mashup Years – No Confidence Vote Remix' 12
Born, Georgina 11, 63
bottle-flip bass drop memes 53, 64–7; *see also* bass drop memes
Bourdieu, Pierre 59
Bowie, David 23, 243–65
　handclapping 256, 256n40
Boym, Svetlana 179
'BRAAAM' sound 152
bricolage 261, 275–6, 279–80
brostep 56, 62; *see also* dubstep
Brown, James 41
Bruns, Axel 5, 94, 116–17, 189, 228

BTS 129
Buhler, James B 148, 150
Bull, Michael 190
Burgess, Adam 57–8
Burgess, Jean 23, 126, 147
Busch, Fie Karlskov 101–2
Bush, George 65
Bush, Kate 21–2

'California Gurls' (Perry) 45
'Call Your Girlfriend' (Robyn) 16, 20, 24
cancellation of the future 85
Candea, Matei 56
*Candid Camera* 74, 88
'Cardigan' (Swift) 129
*Carmen* (Bizet) 198
'Carmen by Carmen' 198
'Caroline No' (Beach Boys) 42, 43–4
Carr, Nicholas 123
Cavalli-Sforza, L. L. 226–7
Cayari, Christopher 16n50, 18
Cenciarelli, Carlo 12
censorship 26, 89, 120
'Centipede' (Knife Party) 62–4
Cepeda, Maria Elena 82
Chambers, Paul 224
*A Chance to Cut Is a Chance to Cure* (Matmos) 124
Charli XCX 21
chillwave 8, 177
Chion, Michel 115–16
circle of fifths 224
Cities and Memory project 135–7
citizen journalism 126, 131
Clark, Robin 243
Clarke, Candy 261
classic rock 76, 82, 83, 91; *see also* reaction videos; rock
Cloud rap; *see* SoundCloud Rap
Colebrook, Claire 165
collaborations 3, 5, 15, 17, 23, 27, 58, 66, 161, 180, 244, 246, 251–4, 258, 264; *see also* cross-platform musicking; produsage; sonic elongation
　compositional 123–7, 132–7
　as experiments 198–9
　fan 251
　innovative forms 114

moving image media 114
online culture 116
sound art 132–7
collaborative authorship 249, 250, 251–2, 258, 264; *see also* authorship
Coltrane, John
  bebop 224
  *Giant Steps* (Coltrane) 51, 223–40
  improvised solos 226
  theoretic compositional style 224
*Coltrane on Coltrane* 224
Columbia Records 195
*Com&Com* 168
community(ies) 5, 6, 14, 15, 63, 120–6; *see also* epic music; Gezi Park protests in Turkey; sonic elongation; YouTube
  cancel culture-hungry 22–3
  conspiratorial 68
  creation 24–5
  cross-platform discussion 136
  fan/fan creators/editors 245–65, 273
  informal archival practices 110
  local 122
  niche 173, 180, 248–9
  political 274
  protest-oriented 27
  sense 26, 91, 250
  sound art 132–7
competitive imitation 52, 61; *see also* Harlem Shake (meme/video)
Constandinides, Costas 16–17
*The Consuming Flame: Open Exercises in Group Form* (Matmos) 124
*Contemporary Sound Art* 117–18
Content ID 29, 62, 209–10, 219
Cook, Braxton 234
Cook, Nicholas 205–6
Coppa, Francesca 14
copyright 27, 28–9, 75, 77, 91, 104n42, 203, 209, 211–12, 216, 239, 246
*Corbin*; *see* Spooky Black
*Coronavirus Etude For Piano and Disinfecting Wipe* (DePaoli) 130
corporate classicism 151
covers/cover songs/versions 3, 16–19
  '7 Years' (song by Lukas Graham) 102–8
Covid-19 Collection of BBC 118

COVID-19 pandemic 53, 64–7, 117–39; *see also* bass drop memes; sonic elongation; trolling
*Cracked Actor* 244
Craig, David 74
Crawford, Garry 154
Creative Commons 30, 204, 206, 211, 219
creative forums 190; *see also* YouTube
*Creator Culture* (Cunningham and Craig) 74
cross-cultural mediation 76, 86
cross-platform musicking 28, 187–99; *see also* Instagram; TikTok; YouTube
  collaborations are experiments 198–9
  interrelationships 192–3
  media swirl 195, 199
  meta-musical persona 194
  musical persona 193–4
  recontextualization 196–7
  transmedia movements 193
cultural fetishization 61
Cunningham, Stuart 74
Curtis, Caleb 229–33, 234, 235, 238, 239
Cyrus, Miley 13
Czach, Liz 207

D'Amelio, Charlie 193
Daniel, Drew 124–6, 132
Danish Web Archive 97
*Dark Souls III* 157
Darrell, Johnny 97
Daub, Adrian 152
*David Bowie: Five Years* 244, 246–7
*David Bowie is The Man Who Fell To Earth* (Nacho's documentary) 261–3
Davis, Miles 224
Dawkins, Richard 52, 53–4, 55, 227
de-centring authorship 131–2; *see also* authorship
DeNora, Tia 190
DePaoli, Jeff 130
Derrida, Jacques 177, 178n29
Derulo, Jason 195
DeVito, Chris 224
*Die Entführung aus dem Serai* (Mozart) 198
Digital Audio Workstations 6
Digital Song Sales chart 129
Dijck, Jose van 4
DiNucci, Darcy 3, 114

dispersed authorship 249, 252–3; *see also* authorship
distributed authorship 132, 134; *see also* authorship
DIY (Do-It-Yourself) 5, 7
 cultural resistance 7
DJ Cummerbund 36
DJ Earworm 11, 46
DJ Mighty Mike 46
DJ Place Boing 45
Dj Pyromania 10–11
'Don't Lie to Me' (Lena) 195, 197–8
Doritos 21
double reading 12, 15–16
*Dragon Ball* 158
drumstep 62
dubstep 62–3, 234–5
Durkheim 56, 57, 58–9
Dylan, Bob 15
'Dynamite' (BTS) 129

ear rape audio distortion meme 67
echo-jams 8–9; *see also* remediation
EDM; *see* electronic dance music
*Elder Scrolls* 150, 157
electronic dance music (EDM) 58, 60, 234
*The Elephant Man* 260
El General 279
elongated sounds 115–16; *see also* sonic elongation
*Encanto* 196
epic (as a word/term) 145–6
epic music 26, 145–61
 advertising methods 156–7
 background 146–9
 contemporary media 149–54
 films 152–3
 gender 152–3, 153n20, 160
 masculine signifiers 152–3
 paywalled music tracks 149
 reiteration 160–1
 searching 155–6
 tags 160
 video games 146, 147, 149–52, 154–5, 157, 158
 visual designs 159–60
Epic Music World 156, 157, 158
Epidemic Sound 208, 209, 210, 216

Erato 16
Ermes, Yoca 126
*Eternal Home* (Marcloid) 181
ethnomusicology 223, 228
European Song Contest (ESC) 94–5
*Everyday I'm Çapulling* 280
'Everyday I'm Hustlin'' (Ross) 280

Facebook 13, 58, 64, 67, 68, 78, 98–9, 104, 120, 136, 188, 203, 205, 208, 215, 217, 229, 233, 237, 238, 279
fan-creators/editors 248–50; *see also* authorship; Nacho/Nacho's fan-made video
fannish vids (fanvids) 3, 12, 15, 28, 29, 30, 106, 108, 109; *see also* '7 Years' (song by Lukas Graham)
Feldman, Marcus 226–7
Ferraro, James 178
*Field Whispers (Into The Crystal Palace)* (Marcloid) 180
'50 Heartbreaking Movie Moments/ SUPERCUT' 14
films 152–3; *see also* epic music
Fire-Toolz (Marcloid) 180–1
first-person shooter (FPS) 62
First Viennese School 54
Fisher, Mark 85, 178n29
flaming 52; *see also* trolling
Flanagan, Tommy 224, 225–6, 235–6
flashmob 28
flickers of authenticity 260, 260n45
*Flow* 82
*Folklore* (Swift) 129
*Forbes* 208
Forchhammer, Lukas Graham 93, 109; *see also* '7 Years' (song by Lukas Graham)
Forest, Emmelie de 94
Fortnite 62
Fowkes, Stuart 136
Franklin, Aretha 41
'#FREE_Constanze' 198
free labour 73, 78–79; *see also* affective labour
free-to-use track 29
free use of copyrighted songs 29
*Friends* 86

Frisch, Michael B. 239
Frith, Simon 272
'Funky Drummer' (Brown) 41, 42

Gabalier, Andreas 197
Gabney, Elizabeth 119
*Game of Thrones* 75
'Gangnam Style' (PSY) 60
'Gas, Gas, Gas' meme 68
Gaunt, Kyra D. 13-14
gender 152-3, 153n20, 160; *see also* epic music
Generative Adversarial Network (GAN) 36-8
  Generator and Discriminator 37-8
  machine learning algorithms 37-8
Gersh, Geoff 136
Gezi Park protests in Turkey 27, 267-85
  authoritarian rule 269-70
  *çapulcu* 274, 278, 279-84
  hybrid sounds and forms 276-8
  mainstream media coverage 270
  rap music 279-84
'Giant Step (Dubstep Remix)' (Wong) 234-5
'Giant Steps Bee Gees' (Reijngoud) 234
*Giant Steps* (Coltrane) 51, 223-40
'Giant Steps in C (Live)' 229-33, 234, 235, 238
'Giant Steps/Work' (Ostaszewski) 235
Gillespie, Dizzy 224
'Gives you Hell' (The All-American Rejects) 87-8
'God meme' 53
Google 29, 97, 109-10, 135, 188
Google Trends 118
Gossolt, Marcus 168
Gove, Michael 12
Gramm, Bora 282, 283
'Great Meme War' 52, 62-64
Green, Joshua 126
'Green, Green Grass of Home' (Darrell) 97
Grusin, Richard 9-10, 21, 26, 77
Gudgeon, Oli 117-18
Guetta, David 17

hackability 4, 15, 23, 131
handclapping 256, 256n40

'Happy' (Williams) 191
Harlem Shake (dance) 61
Harlem Shake (meme/video) 13, 52, 59-62
Harris, Calvin 28-9
*Harry Potter* 150
Hart, Corey 21
Hartley, John 206
hauntology 177-8
Hedinger, Johannes 168
Hegarty, Paul 133
'Hello (From the Inside)' (Mann) 131
Hentoff, Nat 225
Herbsman, Hafer, Weber & Frisch, LLP 239
Hesmondhalgh, David 205-6
'Hexatonic Cycle with a Calm Stanley' (Shlomowitz) 130
hip hop 6, 76
  artists using quotation 8
  Cloud rap 171-2
  contemporary forms 279
  DJs 41
  global spread 284
  hypermediacy 10
  jazz musicians 226
  racial representations 87
  reaction videos 87, 88, 90, 91
  '7 Years' (song by Lukas Graham) 106
  Turkish culture 280
Hollywood films; *see* films
hooking 52, 61, 68; *see also* 'Gas, Gas, Gas' meme; Harlem Shake meme; trolling
Hoppen, Mara 102
Howard, Dani 130
Huang, Andrew Thomas 3
humour 104, 130, 146
  Bowie's subversive 256, 258
  MLG montage parody 63
  perverse 65-6
  reaction videos 86-8
  trolling 52
Huvet, Chloe 152
hypermediacy 9, 10, 12, 15, 23, 25, 77, 173
hypnagogic pop 8, 177

'"I Am" Oldschool HipHop Beat' 41
Icons8 210
'Imagine a Jump' (DJ Mighty Mike) 46

'Imagine' (Lennon) 46
imitation 6, 25, 28; *see also* memes; trolling
   competitive 52, 61
   Dawkins's perspective 53–4
   imitation-as-invention 53, 64–7
   by sign 52–3, 62–4
   Tardean 55–8
imitation-as-invention 53, 64–7
imitation-as-opposition 56, 63–4
immediacy 9, 10, 25
'Impressions' (Coltrane) 231, 235
*Inception* 152
Incompetech 212
'Industry Baby' (Lil Nas X) 11
Instagram 1, 21, 25, 28, 79, 114, 188, 191, 193–4, 197, 198; *see also* cross-platform musicking
   influencers 204
   memes 134
   reels and stories 114
   visual self-representations 169
instrumentals 39, 40–1, 42, 44, 46, 48
intellectual property 28, 75, 89, 203, 207, 239; *see also* copyright
interpellation 66
interrelationships 9, 171, 183, 187–8, 192–3, 199; *see also* cross-platform musicking
*Interstellar* 152
intertextuality of form 7–8, 67
ironic distance 165–6
ironic expression 165–6
'Ironies of Web 2.0' (Young) 240
Iron Maiden 19
irony; *see also* post-ironic approaches
   aesthetic modes 168
   ambiguous and undirected 167
   defining 165
   as a form of (post-) authenticity 167
   Internet-mediated communication 166–7
   Kierkegaard's thematization 167
Islam 280
Istanbul United 276, 283

Jackson, Michael 11
Jackson, Peter 247
Jameson, Fredric 85, 166, 179
Jan, Steven 54
Janz, Tobias 167
Japanese television quiz shows 75
Jawsh 685 195
JayveeTV 89
The Jayy Show 80
jazz 223–40; *see also Giant Steps* (Coltrane)
   riffing 239–40
jazz sessions 224
Jenkins, Henry 2–3, 15, 26, 61, 147, 205, 249–50, 261
'Jerusalema' (Master KG and Nomcebo) 191
Jinjer 88
Johannsen, Rene Sascha 93, 100
'John I'm Only Dancing' (Bowie) 253–8
Jones, Ellis 7
Jones, Tom 97
*Journal of Memetics* 55
'Jump' (Van Halen) 46

Kassabian, Anahid 150, 190
Ke$ha 45
Kierkegaard, Soren 167
*Kill Bill* 15
King Vader 66–7
Kirchhof, Matt 46
Koc, Alison 179
Konstantinou, Lee 167
Korsgaard, Mathias 8, 11–12
Kramer, Jonathan D. 7
kudos trolling 52, 62; *see also* trolling

Lange, Patricia 190
*Laws of Imitation* (Tarde) 55
Lawson, Johnnie 118, 122
'Laxed (Siren Beat)' (Jawsh 685) 195; *see also* 'Savage Love (Laxed – Siren Beat)' (Jawsh 685 and Derulo)
Lehman, Frank 153
Lena 193, 195, 197
Lennon, John 46
Leubner, Ben 224
library music 203–20
   blogs and social media pages 210–11
   business-to-business model 207
   demand 211

licensing/licences 203, 204–5, 206–8, 209, 211, 212, 214, 216, 218–19
  multiple transformations 205
  playlists 210
  royalty-free libraries 207, 208, 212
license/licensing 203
  Creative Commons 30, 204, 206, 211, 219
  free 136, 138
  library music 203, 204–5, 206–8, 209, 211, 212, 214, 216, 218–19
#LIEBELEBEN Dance Challenge 197
'LIEBELEBEN' (Gabalier) 197
'Life on Mars?' (Bowie) 259–60
Liikkanen, Lassi 96
Lil Nas X 1, 11, 25, 27
'Live From the Upside Down – The Doritos Music Fest '86' 21
live-streaming 272–3
logic of lulz 65
Lopatin, Daniel 178
Lovink, Geert 73
*Low* (album by Bowie) 261–2
Luisa 196–7
Lukas Graham (band) 24, 93; see also '7 Years' (song by Lukas Graham)
*Lukas Graham – Blue Album* 99
Lyotard, Jean-Francois 6

machine learning algorithms 37–8
MacLeod, Kevin 211, 212–15
Magic iPod 38–40, 43
  tracks/songs 38–9
Major League Gaming 62
Maker Studios 60–1; see also Harlem Shake (meme/video)
Manabe, Noriko 274
Mancini, Henry 230
Mandiberg, Michael 3, 4, 126
Mangaoang, Aine 26
Mann, Chris 131
Manning, Peter 58
Manovich, Lev 4, 126
*The Man Who Fell to Earth* 261–2
Marcloid, Angel 180–2
Marsden, Paul 55, 56, 57
Marshall, Wayne 62
Martin, Dean 97

mashups 3, 10–12; see also memes
  automated 35–49
  concept 35–6
  creators 38
  critiques 38
  genre clash 35–6
  playback tempos 41–2
  satire 12
*Mass Effect* 158
'Master of Puppets' (Metallica) 22
Matmos 124
Mauss, Marcel 58
maximization of minimalism 153
Maynard, Conor 102–4
McLuhan, Marshall 9
media objects 169–70
media swirl 2, 195, 199
memes 3, 51–68, 192
  bass drop 52–3, 59–67
  behaviour-driven 54, 55, 64
  bottle-flip bass drop 53, 64–7
  concept 226–7
  as cultural curation 240
  digital life and human interface 228
  examples 53
  *Giant Steps* (Coltrane) 229–39
  Harlem Shake meme 13, 52, 59–62
  mentalist-driven 54, 55
  mic drop bass drop 52–3, 62–4
  monopoly 62
  multimodality 228
  publications 226–7
  synecdochic character 54
memetic; see memes
mentalist-driven memes 54, 55; see also memes
Mera, Miguel 206
Metallica 22
meta-musical persona 194
Metzer, David 7
mic drop bass drop 52–3
microgenres 177
Middleton, Richard 97
milking 67
Miller, George 60
Miller, Vincent 57–8
Milner, Ryan M. 228
'Mimetics and Folkloristics' (Oring) 227

'Mindblowing SIX song country mashups' (Sir Mashalot) 10
Minecraft 212, 213
MLG montage parodies 62–3
MONTERO (Call Me By Your Name) 2–3, 25
*Moonage Daydream* 245, 263
Moore, Allan 59
Moore, Sarah 57–8
Moores, J. R. 86
moral capital 280, 283
Morgan, Andy 279
Morgan, Mary 55, 63
Morgen, Brett 245, 263
moving-image media 5
multimedia borrowings 8
Muriel, Daniel 154
Murphy, John 14
musical intertextuality 6
Musical.ly app 193
musical persona 193–4
musical practices 187–9
musical vernaculars 27
musical versioning practices 95–7
*Music For Cohabiters* project 130
muting 53, 63–4, 68; *see also* 'Centipede' (Knife Party); 'Great Meme War'; 'Remove Kebab' memeMyspace.com 109–10

Nacho/Nacho's fan-made video 243–65
    artistic integrity 263–5
    *David Bowie is The Man Who Fell To Earth* 261–3
    'John I'm Only Dancing' (Bowie) 253–8
    'Life on Mars?' (Bowie) 259–60
    playlists 245
    'Right' (Bowie) 244, 246–7
    YouTube channel 243, 245
Nanai, Joshua; *see* Jawsh 685
*Naruhodu* 75
*Nashville* 16
National Independent Venue Association 127
*Nature Research Journal* 119
Nauman, Bruce 74
Neely, Adam 234

neologism 53
Netflix 21, 22, 198
networked sonic elongation; *see* sonic elongation
'Never Gonna Give You Up' (Ashley) 14
*The New York Times* 120–1
Nextdoor 122
Next Up 5
*Nier* 158
Nintendo Entertainment System (NES) 233
Nirvana 24
NoCopyrightSounds 211
Nolan, Christopher 152
nostalgia 83–6; *see also* reaction videos; vaporwave
    self-reflective musical approaches to 177–80
'Now Watch This Drive' meme 65

Ockelford, Adam 54
The Offspring 86–7
'1 Corona Boi' 64–7
'Only Teardrops' (Forest) 94
Ooijen, Erik van 171–2
open-access database 122
Opernloft team 198
orchestral-electronic hybrid sounds 160
*Orchestral Music Mix* 157
O'Reilly, Tim 4, 114
original recording 95, 96
Oring, Elliott 227
Ostaszewski, Ian 235
Ozduzen, Ozge 282

Palfrey, John 123
para-adaptation 17–20, 23–4
Park, Lawrence 107–8
parodies 3, 7, 12–13, 24, 25, 62–3, 79, 87, 103–6, 131, 146, 161, 165, 190, 230, 238
participation gap 26
participatory culture 52, 61, 93, 147, 205, 206, 249
Partnership Programme 5
Paul, Rand 64
Pazaratz, Mike 46–7, 48
Peck, Navarro 227, 228–9

Pegg, Nicholas 247
penguin media 282
permission laws 28
Perry, Katy 45, 237
Pew Research Centre 121
Phillips, Whitney 65–6
phonography 132–3; *see also* sonic
 elongation
PinkMetalHead 80, 82–3
'Pink Panther Theme' (Mancini) 230
'Pisces' (Jinjer) 88
The Pitchmap software 230
playback tempos 41–2
Plonges, Sebastian 168, 169
political remix videos 268
political trolling 52, 53, 62–4; *see also*
 trolling
pop punk 76, 83, 86–7; *see also* punk;
 reaction videos
popular culture 12–14
Porfirio, João Francisco 120
portable devices 190–1
post-ironic approaches
 literature and visual arts 167–8
 media objects 169–70
 selectivity 169
 self-expression/representation 169–84
 SoundCloud rap 171–7
 vaporwave 177–80, 183
 vernacular qualities 169
*THE POWER OF EPIC MUSIC* 157
PremiumBeat 210
'Pretty Fly (for a White Guy)' (The
 Offspring) 86, 87
Pride Month 197
produsage 5, 94, 116, 125, 136–7, 206; *see
 also* collaborations
professionally generated content (PGC) 4
promotional tour 100–1
protest music 27, 267–83
 concept 272
 lyrics 272
 musical sounds 272
 political communication 272
 rap 275, 278, 279–284
 YouTube 272–5
protest-oriented communities 27
*Psychologie Économique* (Tarde) 61

punk 7, 76, 83, 89, 91, 273
 participation 82
 pop 76, 83, 86–7
 as white 82
*The Punk Rock MBA* 87
Pussy Riots 273

'Quarantine Supercut' 125–7, 131–2
Queen 24
*The Quietus* 86
Quintilian, Marcus Fabius 165
quiz shows 75
quotation-heavy music 7–8

RAAD 279, 280–1
Railton, Diane 273
R.A.K. Sobataj 280
rally call 268
R and B 90, 91
rap 41
 AI 44–5
 emo 172
 gansta 284
 Gezi Park protests 275, 278, 279–84
 global market 279
 local tastes 279–80
 political struggle 279
 racialized group 279
 sad 172
 social protest and 269
 SoundCloud 27, 171–6
rappers/rap artists 106, 172, 175, 279–84
Rathsack, Kai 158
Rave DJ 42–9
'React' channel 74, 83
reaction videos 3, 24, 73–91
 diversity among reactors 76
 humour/laughter 86–8
 nostalgia 83–6
 organized 74
 shock/surprise 88–9
 theoretical approach 77–83
 transmedia history 74–5
'Ready for the Weekend' (Harris) 28–9
reality television formats 74–5
re-authorship 249, 252, 253–60, 263; *see
 also* authorship
Reckwitz, Andreas 166

record industry
  digital threat 28
  material uploads 8
  unauthorized use of copyrighted material 28
redactive creativity 206, 213; see also library music
redactive revisualization 11
Reddit 60, 63, 178
Reels (Instagram) 191–2, 197; see also Instagram
reference original 97
reference original concept 97
Reijngoud, Ilja 234
remediation 3, 5, 9–20; see also memes
  collision of media 9
  concept 9
  mashups (see mashups)
  mimicry 9
  modes 79
  process 9, 25
remixability 4, 7, 8; see also remediation
Remote Control Productions (RCP) 151–2
'Remove Kebab' meme 68
reproduction technology 95
retromania 6–10, 85, 132
reviralization 24
Reyland, Nicholas 151
Reynolds, Simon 6, 8–9, 178n29
Rickrolling 14, 52; see also bait-and-switch trolling
'Ride of the Valkyries' (Wagner) 42, 43–4
'Right' (Bowie) 244, 246–7
right to protest 282–3
Rihanna 235
'Ring Them Bells' (Dylan) 15
Ritter, Tyson 87
r/montageparodies 62–3
'Roar' (Perry) 237
Robbins, Joel 58
Robyn 16
rock 76, 88
  alternative forms 83
  classic 76, 82, 83, 91
  coded as white 24, 82, 83
  punk (see punk)
  Turkish indie 275
rock ideology 95

Rock, Mick 253–60; see also Nacho/Nacho's fan-made video
Roeg, Nicolas 261–2
Rogers, Jim 28
Rogers, Holly xiii
Role Playing Games (RPG) 150
Ronson, Mick 256
Roscoe, Jane 260
Rosen, Jay 5, 116
Ross, Rick 280
Roth, David Lee 46
Ruby Da Cherry 173–5
'Running Up That Hill (A Deal With God)' (Bush) 21–2

Sadoff, Ronald H. 151, 160
Salovaara, Antti 96
'Salut Salong "Wettstreit zu viert"/Competitive Foursome' 18–19
'Savage Love' (Derulo) 195
'Savage Love (Laxed – Siren Beat)' (Jawsh 685 and Derulo) 195
Scarlett, Liz 22–3
Schafer, R. Murray 133
'Scheming Weasel' (MacLeod) 213, 214
Scherzinger, Martin 206
Schmoyer, Tim 209
Schneider, Stefan 46
Science Magazine 119
Segerberg, Alexandra 274
seismic noise reduction 119
self-expression/representation 169–84; see also post-ironic approaches
The Selfish Gene (Dawkins) 52, 227
Shifman, Limor 54, 64, 68, 228
shitposting 52, 64–7; see also trolling
'The Shitposting of Jazz to Come' 229, 233
Shlomowitz, Matthew 130
Shmailyuk, Tatiana 88
shock/surprise 88–9, 174; see also reaction videos
short music videos 191
Shorts (YouTube) 191–2; see also YouTube
shredding 53, 66–7, 68; see also '1 Corona Boi'
Sia 17
Sidemen 2, 9, 30
sign, imitation by 52–3, 62–4
Silent Cities Project 122

Silvestri, Alan 151
Sing! by Smule 107
Sir Mashalot 10
skrubs 62
Slavik, Nathan 176
Smith, Brad 233–4
'Sneaky Snitch' (MacLeod) 213, 214
'Snow is Falling' (Stevens) 12
social contagion 55
sociality 58, 77, 81, 91
*Social Media Entertainment* (Cunningham and Craig) 74
sole authorship 252, 264
'Someone that I used to Know' (Gotye) 18
sonic elongation 115–17
    concept 115–16
    COVID-19 pandemic 117–23
    overview 117
    poles 116
    process 116
    remediation 116–17, 132–9
    sounds of quarantine 123–7
#SOSFEST 127
*The Sound and Memory* 122
SoundCloud Rap 27, 171–6
    audiovisual aesthetic 172
    ideological products 175
    lo-fi sound production 171, 172
    rappers/rap artists 172
soundscape video 117–18
*Spectres de Marx* (Derrida) 177
Spencer-Shapiro, Zev 229
*Spooky Black* 175–7
Spotify 20, 22, 42, 99, 147, 158
spreadability 2–3
*Stalker* (Artemiev) 115
*Star Wars* 158
*Station to Station* (Bowie) 262
'Stay Home' (Howard) 130
#StayHomeSounds 135
Steele, Catherine 61
Stevens, Shakin' 12
Stockmusic.net 210
*Stranger Things* 21–2
Stylebreeder 36
suicidal ideation/thoughts 172–3
SUNN ST. CLAIRE 17
*Sunshine* (Murphy) 14

SUPERCUT 14
'Surface Pressure' (Luisa's dance performance) 196–7
Swift, Taylor 129
Swunk, Jasper 236–7
synchresis 115–16

Tahribad-ı İsyan 280
tangible cultural artifacts 25, 26
Tanner, Grafton 84–5
Tarantino, Quentin 15
Tarde, Gabriel 52, 55–9, 61, 63–4, 67
target trolling 52; *see also* trolling
Tarkovsky, Andrey 115
Tavenner, Matt 66, 67
Taylor, Art 224
tempos; *see* playback tempos
Terranova, Tiziana 78
Thieves (Facebook user) 67
thiscatdoesnotexist.com 36, 37
*Tiger King 2* 198
*Tiger King 2 The TikTopera* 198
TikTok 79, 187, 188, 193–9; *see also* cross-platform musicking
    cancel culture-hungry communities 22–3
    #CreatorsForDiversity campaign 198
    'Tik Tok and California Gurls are the same song?' (DJ Place Boing) 45
    #TikTokDanceChallangeMozartEdition 199
'Tik Tok' (Ke$ha) 45
'Titanium' 17, 19, 20
Toews, David 57
'Total Eclipse of the Heart Literal Video Version' 11
Trainer, Adam 178
transmedial franchise 148
transmediality 15, 67
transmedia movements 193
trolling 25, 166–7, 213; *see also* memes
    (anti)social repertoires 52–3, 59–67, 68
    bait-and-switch 14, 52, 61
    as cultural logic 52
    flaming 52
    hooking 52, 61–2, 68
    kudos 52, 62
    musical memes (*see* memes)

muting 53, 63–4, 68
political 52, 53, 62–4
shitposting 52, 64–7
shredding 53, 66–7, 68
Tardean analysis 52
target 52
'Trooper Overture, The' (2Cellos) 19
Truax, Barry 133, 135
Trueblood, Serena 23
Trump, Donald J. 12, 62–4, 84, 85
'Trybals' channel 74
Tsing, Anna 58
Tuzak 280
twerking 13–14
Twitter 1, 14, 25, 29, 63, 67, 98, 101, 103, 114, 124, 134, 136, 171, 268, 269, 270–1
TwoSetViolin 194

*Ultimate Care II* (Matmos) 124
*Urban Dictionary* 145
user-copied content (UCC) 4, 24, 30
user-generated content (UGC) 4, 5, 23, 29, 30, 52, 73, 77, 79, 126, 132

Vaidhyanathan, Siva 28
@valerisssh 192
Vandross, Luther 243, 247
Van Halen 46
vaporwave 7, 8, 10, 177–80, 183
Vernallis, Carol 2, 5, 11, 160, 161, 195
vidding 14–16
video activism 268, 282
Video Creators 209
video games 146, 147, 149–52, 154–5, 157, 158; *see also* epic music
Video ID 29
video loops 74, 147
videoludification 154
videos 10, 146–7; *see also* epic music; memes; YouTube
'Viral Counterpoint of the Corona Virus Spike Protein' 130
vlogs 10, 17, 125, 180, 203, 208, 217, 273

Wagner, Richard 42
waipu' box 75
Warner Music Japan 100

Watson, Chris 119
Watson, Paul 273
wave of silence 118–19
Way, Lyndon C. S. 272, 274, 275
web-based platforms for automated mashups 38–49
  Magic iPod 38–40, 43
  Rave DJ 42–9
  YouTube DJ 40–2
Webber, Andrew Lloyd 12
Wehrs, William 153
Weij, Frank 273
Whyton, Tony 226
Wikstrom, Peter 171–2
'Wild is the Wind' (Bowie) 263
Wilke, Thomas 170
William, John 150, 151
Williams, George C. 227
Williams, John 151
Williams, Pharrell 191
*Wipe Cycle* video installation 74
'Without You' *(Spooky Black)* 176
witness documentation 268
Wixon, Steve 227
Wong, Diane 234–5
'Work' (Rihanna) 235
World Soundscape Project 133
Wright, Benjamin 151–2

Yabanci Muzikler 10–11
*You Can't Stump The Trump* 62
'(You Make Me Feel like a) Natural Woman' 41
Young, Damon R. 240
*Young Americans* (Bowie) 244
YouTube 146–7; *see also* cross-platform musicking
  'Broadcast Yourself' 3, 4
  content 4
  creative forums 190
  educational opportunities 5
  epic music (*see* epic music)
  filters 29
  generative qualities 23
  library music (*see* library music)
  long tail 8
  mashups (*see* mashups)
  pandemic musicking 127–31

participatory nature 3
platform vernacular 180
playback feature 41n11
regeneration of music 3
regulation and control mechanisms 29
as a tangible cultural artifact 26
as a universal resource 26
as a video-sharing site 4

YouTube DJ 40–2
   playback tempo 41–2
YouTube Music 147, 190
Yukihiro Tada 100

Zimmer, Hans 152–4
Zittrain, Jonathan 23
Zynaptiq 230

www.ingramcontent.com/pod-product-compliance
Lightning Source LLC
Chambersburg PA
CBHW070015010526
44117CB00011B/1583